D1748944

Energy Pricing Models

Energy Pricing Models

Recent Advances, Methods, and Tools

Edited by

Marcel Prokopczuk

palgrave
macmillan

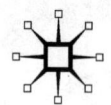

ENERGY PRICING MODELS
Copyright © Marcel Prokopczuk, 2014.

All rights reserved.

First published in 2014 by
PALGRAVE MACMILLAN®
in the United States—a division of St. Martins Press LLC,
175 Fifth Avenue, New York, NY 10010.

Where this book is distributed in the UK, Europe and the rest of the world, this is by Palgrave Macmillan, a division of Macmillan Publishers Limited, registered in England, company number 785998, of Houndmills, Basingstoke, Hampshire RG21 6XS.

Palgrave Macmillan is the global academic imprint of the above companies and has companies and representatives throughout the world.

Palgrave® and Macmillan® are registered trademarks in the United States, the United Kingdom, Europe and other countries.

ISBN: 978–1–137–37734–0

Library of Congress Cataloging-in-Publication Data

    Energy pricing models : recent advances, methods, and tools / edited by Marcel Prokopczuk.
      pages cm.
    Includes bibliographical references and index.
    ISBN 978–1–137–37734–0 (hardcover :alk. paper)
     1. Energy industries–Prices. 2. Stochastic models. I. Prokopczuk, Marcel, editor.
HD9502.A2E54944 2014
333.79—dc23   2014022207

A catalogue record of the book is available from the British Library.

Design by Newgen Knowledge Works (P) Ltd., Chennai, India.

First edition: December 2014

10 9 8 7 6 5 4 3 2 1

Contents

List of Figures		vii
List of Tables		xi
Preface		xiii
List of Contributors		xv
1	Efficient Pricing of Energy Derivatives *Anders B. Trolle*	1
2	A Supply and Demand Based Energy Pricing Model *Takashi Kanamura*	21
3	Joint Dynamics of American and European Oil Prices *Gamze Celik, Karl Frauendorfer, and Florentina Paraschiv*	43
4	Energy Spread Modeling Using Copulas *Sjur Westgaard*	97
5	Modeling and Estimating Electricity Futures: A Non-Gaussian Market Model Approach *Enzo Fanone*	115
6	Hourly Resolution Forward Curves for Power: Statistical Modeling Meets Market Fundamentals *Michael Coulon, Christian Jacobsson, and Jonas Ströjby*	147
7	Modeling Price Spikes in Electricity Markets—The Impact of Load, Weather, and Capacity *Rangga Handika, Chi Truong, Stefan Trück, and Rafal Weron*	195

8 Indifference Pricing of Weather Futures Based
   on Electricity Futures
   Fred Espen Benth, Stephen Ebbeler, and Rüdiger Kiesel   223

Index   269

Figures

1.1	Impact of σ_S, α, γ, and ρ_{12} on volatility term structure	11
1.2	Impact of σ_v on implied volatility smiles	12
1.3	Impact of ρ_{13} on implied volatility smiles	13
1.4	Impact of ρ_{23} on implied volatility smiles	14
1.5	Impact of κ on implied volatility smiles	15
2.1	Equilibrium energy prices	24
3.1	Brent and WTI daily crude oil prices from 03/01/2000 to 31/08/2012	49
3.2	Absolute price delta (WTI-Brent) in $/bbl	55
3.3	WTI discount to Brent compared with weekly Cushing crude stocks	56
3.4	Brent and WTI daily prices, log returns and QQ-plots	60
3.5	Autocorrelation function of the squared residuals	60
3.6	CU.S.UM tests for MGARCH models	71
3.7	Comparison of MGARCH models: conditional variances and covariances	72
3.8	Conditional variance and correlation for Brent and WTI from the diagonal BEKK model	73
3.9	Rolling ADF for Brent and WTI log prices—full sample	77
3.10	Rolling ADF for Brent and WTI log prices—subsample	85
4.1	The price ($/gallon) of NYMEX front-month futures of oil	104
4.2	The the returns (log of price changes) of NYMEX front-month futures of oil	106
4.3	The distribution of daily returns (log of price changes) of NYMEX front-month futures of oil	107
4.4	The density function of a Clayton copula with $\alpha = 3.4471$	109
4.5	Simulation results for the Clayton copula with $\alpha = 3.4471$	110
5.1	Seasonality and fitted normal density	119

5.2	Smoothing forward curve. Example of the smoothing procedure for EEX futures	121
5.3	Autocorrelation of prices	122
5.4	Principal component analysis. Results of the PCA on Brent futures price returns	126
5.5	Principal component analysis. Principal component analysis (PCA) for the TTF futures contracts	127
5.6	Principal component analysis. PCA for EEX monthly and quarterly futures contracts	135
5.7	Independent component analysis. ICs of EEX monthly futures returns	136
5.8	Fitted normal and NIG density	137
5.9	Empirical and fitted volatilities.	139
5.10	Cross-sectional analysis of simulations	141
6.1	Changing fuel mix in the German power market	151
6.2	Historical EEX hourly spot prices and peak to offpeak price spread	152
6.3	Sample supply and demand curves from EEX for hour 13, 2013/03/04	156
6.4	The transformation to the price curve using Equation (1)	158
6.5	(a) Supply curves, (b) demand curves, and (c) price curves, from seven consecutive days	158
6.6	(a) Supply curves, (b) demand curves, and (c) price curves, from six representative hours during one day	159
6.7	(a) National demand vs. market clearing volume; (b) National demand vs "inelastic" demand	160
6.8	A histogram view of the stack on hour 13, 03/04/2013	160
6.9	The relationship between volume offered at -3000 and total production from renewables	161
6.10	One year of stack data from EEX and the corresponding fit using a Gaussian mixture model	162
6.11	Illustration of converting an MDN model fit to a price curve fit	163
6.12	Weekly patterns output from the MDN model	164
6.13	An illustration of the periodic (x, y) clock	167
6.14	Analysis of the (transformed) inelastic demand process in EEX	168
6.15	Results from fitting the wind model	170
6.16	Results from fitting the solar model	171
6.17	Illustration of fit to forward quotes	181
6.18	Numerical tests of the approximation	190

7.1	Half-hourly electricity price (AUD/MWh) for the QLD market	206
7.2	Scatter plot for the relationship between the log transformation of observed price spikes and the explanatory variables' market load for the QLD market	208
8.1	Daily average temperature and the estimated deterministic, seasonal function Λ^{temp}	248
8.2	Calculated CAT prices for May and June	257
8.3	Calculated CAT prices for July and August	258
8.4	Calculated CAT prices for September	259
8.5	Sensitivity analysis of the risk aversion coefficient γ	261
8.6	Sensitivity analysis of the MPR coefficient θ	263
8.7	Sensitivity analysis of the correlation ρ	263

Tables

2.1	EKF time update equations	35
2.2	EKF measurement update equations	35
2.3	Parameter estimates using natural gas futures prices	36
2.4	Parameter estimates using WTI crude oil futures prices	37
2.5	Parameter estimates using heating oil futures prices	38
3.1	Ljung–Box Q-statistics (p-values) for daily returns and daily squared returns	61
3.2	VAR optimal lag length selection for Brent and WTI	65
3.3	VAR(7) estimation results and diagnostic tests for Brent and WTI	67
3.4	VAR(7) – CCC estimates	68
3.5	VAR(7) – diagonal BEKK estimates	68
3.6	Diagnostic tests for the CCC and diagonal BEKK model	69
3.7	Unit root test for log prices and its first differences	76
3.8	Johansen cointegration test results	79
3.9	ECM regression results	81
3.10	Granger causality test results	83
3.11	Unit root test for log prices and its first differences on the subsample	84
3.12	Johansen cointegration test results for the subsample	86
3.13	Granger causality test results for the subsample	87
4.1	Descriptive statistics of returns (log of price changes) of NYMEX front-month futures of heating oil and crude oil	108
5.1	Estimated mean-reversion parameters	134
5.2	Estimated GH parameters	138
5.3	Empirical and fitted correlation matrix for EEX monthly futures	138
5.4	Empirical and fitted correlation matrix for EEX quarterly futures	140
5.5	Empirical and fitted correlation matrix for EEX yearly futures	140

7.1	Descriptive statistics of half-hourly electricity prices for NSW, QLD, SA, VIC	207
7.2	Sample size (number of observations) details for each state	209
7.3	Estimation results for Heckman selection method for the log transformation of spot electricity prices.	210
7.4	Optimal Box-Cox parameter estimates for each state based on maximum likelihood estimation	212
7.5	Estimation results for Heckman selection method for the Box-Cox transformation	213
7.6	Estimation results using OLS for the entire sample of electricity spot prices	214
7.7	Estimation results using OLS for the subsample of price spikes	215
7.8	MAE, MAPE, and log likelihood of the estimated models	217
8.1	Parameter estimation for the seasonal temperature function Λ^{temp} with the corresponding p-values in parentheses	247
8.2	Parameter estimation for the autoregression coefficients a_1, a_2, a_3	249
8.3	Parameter estimation of the variance function $\eta^2(t)$ with the corresponding p-values	250
8.4	Results of the parameter estimation of the seasonal function for arithmetic and geometric spot price model	251
8.5	Results of the parameter estimation for the mean reversion and volatility of the spot price model	251
8.6	Results of the correlation analysis for the winter period	254
8.7	Results of the correlation analysis for the summer period	255

Preface

Over the last decades, energy markets have undergone extensive transformations. Energy, be it in the form of oil, gas, or electricity, can now be traded in similar ways as financial assets. This development has improved competition and market efficiency. However, it has also increased the complexity of pricing and risk management in energy markets. In this book, leading international experts in energy market modeling present some of their most recent research.

In *Chapter 1*, Anders Trolle discusses efficient pricing and hedging of energy derivatives. His model is based on the Heath-Jarrow-Morton (HJM) framework but is extended for stochastic volatility. The presence of unspanned stochastic volatility is explicitly taken into account. The author discusses the pricing of options and also how jumps can be added to the model.

In *Chapter 2*, Takashi Kanamura presents a stochastic energy price model that explicitly considers the characteristics of supply and demand in energy markets. He shows that several reduced-form modeling approaches are based on his model setup. Finally, the author demonstrates that logarithmic transformation, which is frequently employed in reduced-form energy pricing models, is not justified empirically for several energy markets.

Chapter 3, by Gamze Celik, Karl Frauendorfer, and Florentina Paraschiv, examines the dynamic relationship between two major international oil benchmarks, West Texas Intermediate (WTI) and Brent. The authors provide background information on crude oil markets, including the factors driving oil prices and the historical events that affected these prices. Using multivariate GARCH models and cointegration analysis, they study the empirical features of the two markets. They find that although the WTI market seems to be the leading benchmark for oil prices, the two markets are unified in the long run. In the short run, however, regional developments are important.

In *Chapter 4*, Sjur Westgaard discusses the modeling of energy spreads, that is, spark spreads, dark spreads, and crack spreads, using copulas. After outlining the basic theory behind this approach, information on calibration and simulation techniques are provided. In an application to the crack spread, the author discusses in detail how to obtain value-at-risk estimates by using the presented methodology.

Chapter 5 by Enzo Fanone focuses on the pricing of electricity futures. After discussing the key features of electricity prices, he presents a Levy market model for electricity prices. The author demonstrates how the model can be empirically implemented by employing an independent component analysis (ICA).

In *Chapter 6*, Michael Coulon, Christian Jacobsson, and Jonas Ströjby also focus on modeling electricity prices. They present a flexible stack-based approach that explicitly incorporates a range of market fundamentals while remaining analytically tractable. They apply their methodology to the German electricity market and analyze the performance of their model. Special attention is paid to the rapidly growing capacity provided by renewable sources, that is, wind and solar.

Chapter 7 by Rangga Handika, Chi Truong, Stefan Trück, and Rafal Weron examines the impact of load, weather, and capacity constraints on the occurrence and magnitude of price spikes in electricity markets. The authors apply the Heckman two-stage estimation procedure and apply their methodology to four regional electricity markets in Australia. It is found that for these markets, load, relative air temperature, and reserve margins are significant variables for the occurrence of price spikes, while electricity loads and relative air temperature are significant variables to impact on the magnitude of a price spike.

In *Chapter 8*, Fred Espen Benth, Stephan Ebbeler, and Rüdiger Kiesel present a model for pricing temperature futures based on the indifference pricing approach and electricity futures. After discussing the theoretical background, they apply their framework to some real world data in order to demonstrate the empirical performance of the model. Furthermore, the authors conduct an in-depth analysis of the pricing model with respect to risk aversion and the market price of risk.

MARCEL PROKOPCZUK
Hannover, Germany
November 1, 2014

Contributors

Fred Espen Benth is a professor of mathematical finance at the University of Oslo. His research interests focus on energy and weather markets, in particular, modeling and pricing. He has more than 80 publications in scientific journals and has coauthored two monographs. He enjoys close collaboration with the energy industry through various courses.

Gamze Celik graduated from the University of St. Gallen with a master of arts degree in banking and finance. She is currently working in the Credit Risk Portfolio Management Division at the Cantonal Bank of Zurich.

Michael Coulon is a lecturer in finance at the University of Sussex, UK, having joined here from Princeton University in 2013. His research and teaching activities center on quantitative finance and its application to energy and other commodity markets. He has developed and published various commodity price models and derivative pricing techniques, especially for wholesale electricity markets and environmental markets, and has collaborated with a variety of practitioners from the energy industry as well as other academics. Michael holds a PhD in mathematics from the University of Oxford.

Stephan Ebbeler holds a PhD from the University of Duisburg-Essen. Previously, he graduated with a diploma in mathematical economics from the University of Ulm as well as with a masters degree in mathematical sciences from the State University of New York at Binghamton. Stephan's research focuses on modeling energy prices and weather derivatives.

Enzo Fanone is head of portfolio and risk management at Energetic Source SPA of Renova Group. He gained professional experience holding responsibilities of managing gas and power trading portfolio, pricing, and risk management of commodity derivatives and optimization methods for valuing real assets. Enzo holds a BSc in economic science from University of Cassino, an MSc in quantitative methods for finance from University of Verona and a PhD in mathematical finance from the University of Trieste.

He regularly participates as a speaker in professional and academic conferences.

Karl Frauendorfer is professor for operations research at the University of St. Gallen. He heads the Institute for Operations Research and Computational Finance ior/cf-HSG. His research focuses on stochastic optimization and on design and implementation of management models in the energy and financial sector.

Rangga Handika is a lecturer at the Faculty of Economics, Universitas Indonesia. He holds a PhD from Georg-August-Universität Göttingen, Germany. Rangga's research interests focus on financial risk management, including the field of energy and commodity markets. He teaches accounting and finance courses at undergraduate and postgraduate levels. He also serves as an consultant in various institutions.

Christian Jacobsson is a senior quant analyst at Alpiq, Switzerland, since 2009, and an analyst for European energy markets since 2001. He began his career at EON Sweden as lead developer of models for the Nordic market, then moved to EON Düsseldorf as head of software developments for Pricing, and then in 2008 to Advanced Energy Trading in Munich before moving to Alpiq. While his main focus is short-term modeling and analysis of the European power markets, he also works on forward curves, hydro and thermal asset optimization, and modeling of wind and solar parks for optimal dispatch. Christian holds a PhD in particle physics.

Takashi Kanamura is currently an associate professor at Kyoto University. He holds a PhD from Hitotsubashi Unversity, Tokyo, and has worked for more than 10 years at J-POWER, one of the largest Japanese utility companies. His research interests cover commodity finance, energy finance, financial economics, asset pricing, real options, risk management, electricity markets, weather derivatives, and carbon markets.

Rüdiger Kiesel heads the chair for Energy Trading and Financial Services at the University Duisburg-Essen. He is a visiting professor at the Center for Mathematics for Applications, Oslo University. His main research areas are risk management for power utility companies, design, and analysis of Emission Trading Schemes, valuation and hedging of derivatives (interest rate, credit and energy-related), methods of risk transfer, and structuring of risk(securitization).

Florentina Paraschiv is an assistant professor at the Institute for Operations Research and Computational Finance, University of St. Gallen (ior/cf-HSG). Her research interests include econometrics of electricity, oil, and gas markets, quantification of risk in the electricity business, optimization of power production, and renewable energy.

Jonas Ströjby is a senior risk manager at Nordea Bank in Copenhagen since 2012. Prior to that he worked as a risk manager at Alpiq, Switzerland, with a primary focus on developing and maintaining the quant library for power trading. Jonas holds a PhD in mathematical statistics from Lund University, Sweden.

Anders B. Trolle is an assistant professor at Ecole Polytechnique Fédérale de Lausanne and holds a junior chair at the Swiss Finance Institute. He received his PhD in Finance from Copenhagen Business School. Prior to that, he was a fixed income analyst at Danske Bank. In addition to energy and commodity derivatives, he has worked on interest rate derivatives, interbank risk, and liquidity risk, and his research has appeared in leading academic finance journals.

Chi Truong is a research fellow at the Department of Applied Finance and Actuarial Studies, Macquarie University. He received a PhD on real options and water economics at the University of Sydney. His research interests focus on financial econometrics and optimal investment including systemic risk, operational risk, economics of climate change adaptation, and water economics.

Stefan Trück is a professor of finance and codirector of the Centre for Financial Risk at Macquarie University. Previously, he has held positions at Queensland University of Technology and University of Karlsruhe in Germany where he received a PhD in business engineering. Stefan's research interests focus on risk management and financial econometrics including the fields of credit risk, systemic risk, energy markets, emissions trading, climate change economics, and international financial markets.

Rafal Weron is professor of economics at Wroclaw University of Technology (WUT, Poland). His research focuses on developing risk management and forecasting tools for the energy industry and computational statistics as applied to finance and insurance. With a PhD in applied mathematics and a habilitation in economics, he is periodically engaged as a consultant to energy (Tauron Polska Energia, Vattenfall) and financial (Bank BPH, Bank Millennium, BRE Bank) companies. He is the (co)author of five books and over 100 publications in academic and professional journals. He teaches graduate-level courses on energy and financial markets at Wroclaw University of Technology and NTNU (Trondheim, Norway).

Sjur Westgaard holds an MSc and a PhD in industrial economics from the Norwegian University of Science and Technology and an MSc in finance from the Norwegian School of Business and Economics. He has worked as an investment portfolio manager for an insurance company, a project manager for a consultant company, and as a credit analyst for an international bank. He is now a professor at the Norwegian University of Science and Technology, Department of Industrial Economics and Technology Management and an adjunct professor at the Norwegian University of Life Sciences–Center for Commodity Market Analysis. His teaching involves corporate finance, derivatives and real options, empirical finance and financial risk management. His main research interests include risk modeling of commodity markets, in particular energy markets. Currently he is a project manager for two energy research projects.

1

Efficient Pricing of Energy Derivatives

Anders B. Trolle

1 Introduction

In order to price, hedge, and risk-manage energy derivatives, it is critical to understand the dynamics of volatility in energy markets. Even a cursory look at the data shows that volatility is stochastic. For instance, over the past decade, the volatility implied from at-the-money (ATM) options on the front-month crude oil futures contract has varied between 13 percent (at the end of 2013) and 110 percent (at the end of 2008).[1] It is less obvious as to what extent volatility risk can be hedged by trading in the commodities themselves or, more generally, their associated futures, forward or swap contracts. In a comprehensive analysis of crude oil data, Trolle and Schwartz (2009) show that a significant component of volatility implied from options on futures contracts cannot be hedged by trading in the futures contracts themselves. In other words, a significant component of volatility is *"unspanned"* by the term structure of futures prices. It appears that unspanned stochastic volatility (USV) is also an important feature of other energy commodities.

In this chapter, I present a tractable framework, first developed in Trolle and Schwartz (2009), for pricing energy derivatives in the presence of USV. The model has several attractive features: First, it ensures a perfect fit to the initial futures term structure. Second, it has a fast and accurate Fourier-based pricing formula for European-style options on futures contracts, enabling efficient calibration to liquid plain-vanilla exchange-traded derivatives. Third, by specifying shocks to the futures term structure judiciously, the evolution of the futures curve can be described in terms of a low-dimensional affine state vector. This makes the model ideally suited for pricing complex energy derivatives and real options by simulation, where early exercise features can be handled using the least squares Monte Carlo (LSM) approach of Longstaff and Schwartz (2001); see, for example, Schwartz and Trolle (2010) for a real option application of the model.

Another source of market incompleteness is discontinuous moves in spot prices. For instance, Askari and Krichene (2008) and Larsson and Nossman (2011) find that jumps—in addition to stochastic volatility— is an important characteristic of crude oil prices. At the end of the chapter, I outline an extension of the framework that takes jumps in spot prices into account. The extended model retains the key attributes of the basic USV model.

Throughout the chapter, I focus on the risk-neutral dynamics of the model and efficient pricing of derivatives. Through a change of measure, one can obtain the actual/physical dynamics of the model, which would be relevant for risk-management applications. The change of measure also provides information on risk premia associated with volatility risk. I refer to Trolle and Schwartz (2009) for more discussion of these issues and to Trolle and Schwartz (2010) for an in-depth analysis of volatility risk premia in energy markets.

The model is based on the HJM framework of Heath et al. (1992). Other papers that rely on the HJM framework for modeling commodity derivatives include Cortazar and Schwartz (1994), Miltersen and Schwartz (1998), Crosby (2008), and Andersen (2010). Crosby (2008) considers jumps, while Andersen (2010) considers stochastic volatility.

An alternative approach to modeling commodity derivatives relies on specifying the (typically affine) dynamics of a limited set of state variables and deriving futures prices endogenously. Examples of this approach include Gibson and Schwartz (1990), Schwartz (1997), Schwartz and Smith (2000), and Casassus and Collin-Dufresne (2005). One drawback of this modeling approach is that it is very difficult to generate USV, because volatility is almost invariably completely spanned by the futures term structure.[2] In contrast, in the HJM modeling approach, USV arises naturally.

The chapter is structured as follows: Section 2 lays out notation and explains different modeling approaches. Section 3 considers a basic HJM model. Section 4 extends the model with USV. Section 5 describes the pricing of options on futures contracts. Section 6 shows the effect of model parameters on volatilities implied from options on futures contracts. Section 7 extends the model with jumps in spot prices. Section 8 concludes the chapter.

2 Preliminaries

Throughout the chapter, I work under the risk-neutral measure. Furthermore, I assume that interest rates are deterministic, which is fairly innocuous when pricing energy derivatives with short and intermediate maturities.[3] Let $S(t)$ denote the time-t spot price of the commodity and let $F(t, T)$ denote the time-t price of a futures contract maturing at time T. In commodity markets, the relation between spot and futures prices is determined by the cost of carry, which reflects interest rates, storage costs, as well as convenience yields associated with holding the physical commodity instead of a contract for future delivery of the same commodity. In the case of a constant continuously compounded cost of carry rate, δ, the relation between spot and futures prices is simply

$$F(t, T) = S(t)e^{\delta(T-t)}. \qquad (1)$$

In the absence of arbitrage opportunities, futures prices are martingales under the risk-neutral measure (see, e.g., Duffie [2001]) from which it follows that $\frac{1}{dt} E_t \left[\frac{dS(t)}{S(t)} \right] = \delta$. More generally, I let the cost of carry vary stochastically, reflecting stochastic variation in convenience yields. Let $\delta(t)$ denote the time-t instantaneous spot cost of carry rate. Furthermore, let $y(t, T)$ denote the time-t instantaneous forward cost of carry rate at time T, defined such that futures prices are given by

$$F(t, T) = S(t) \exp \left\{ \int_t^T y(t, u) du \right\}. \qquad (2)$$

In the limit as $T \to t$, $y(t, t) = \delta(t)$.[4] It follows that the term structure of forward cost of carry rates can be inferred from the term structure of futures prices.

One strand of the commodity derivatives literature specifies the dynamics of $S(t)$ and $\delta(t)$ and derives futures prices endogenously. Another strand takes futures prices as given and specifies the dynamics of the entire futures curve, which is equivalent to specifying the dynamics of $S(t)$ and the entire forward cost of carry curve. This is the approach taken in this chapter.

3 A Basic HJM Model

I start with a basic HJM model where $S(t)$ and $y(t, T)$ have the following dynamics:

$$\frac{dS(t)}{S(t)} = \delta(t)dt + \sigma_S dW_1(t), \tag{3}$$

$$dy(t,T) = \mu_y(t,T)dt + \sigma_y(t,T)dW_2(t), \tag{4}$$

where $W_1(t)$ and $W_2(t)$ denote Wiener processes under the risk-neutral measure with correlation ρ.

For convenience, introduce the process

$$Y(t,T) = \int_t^T y(t,u)du, \tag{5}$$

the dynamics of which are given by

$$dY(t,T) = \left(-\delta(t) + \int_t^T \mu_y(t,u)du\right)dt$$

$$+ \int_t^T \sigma_y(t,u)du\, dW_2(t). \tag{6}$$

Then, from Equation (2), $F(t,T)$ is given by

$$F(t,T) = S(t)e^{Y(t,T)} \tag{7}$$

with the following dynamics:

$$\frac{dF(t,T)}{F(t,T)} = \left(\int_t^T \mu_y(t,u)du + \frac{1}{2}\left(\int_t^T \sigma_y(t,u)du\right)^2\right.$$

$$\left. + \rho\sigma_S \int_t^T \sigma_y(t,u)du\right)dt + \sigma_S dW_1(t)$$

$$+ \int_t^T \sigma_y(t,u)du\, dW_2(t). \tag{8}$$

Setting the drift in Equation (8) to zero (futures prices are martingales under the risk-neutral measure) and differentiating w.r.t. T yields

$$\mu_y(t,T) = -\sigma_y(t,T)\left(\rho\sigma_S + \int_t^T \sigma_y(t,u)du\right). \tag{9}$$

This condition on the drift of $y(t,T)$ is similar to the famous HJM drift conditions in term structure modeling. It has the important implication that the drift cannot be specified exogenously but is determined by the diffusion term, $\sigma_y(t, T)$. This is in contrast to traditional models of commodity derivatives, where both the drift and diffusion terms of $\delta(t)$ can be specified independently of each other.

The particular model depends on the choice of $\sigma_y(t, T)$. Throughout the chapter, I consider the following time-homogeneous specification

$$\sigma_y(t, T) = \alpha e^{-\gamma(T-t)}. \tag{10}$$

This choice has two advantages: First, it implies that long-term forward cost of carry rates are less volatile than short-term forward cost of carry rates, which seems intuitive. Second, the evolution of the futures curve can be described in terms of a low-dimensional affine state vector, as I now show. From Equation (9), it follows that the drift $\mu_y(t, T)$ is given by

$$\mu_y(t, T) = -e^{-\gamma(T-t)}\left(\rho\alpha\sigma_S + \frac{\alpha^2}{\gamma}\right) + \frac{\alpha^2}{\gamma}e^{-2\gamma(T-t)}. \tag{11}$$

Integrating Equation (4) and using the fact that $e^{-\gamma(T-u)} = e^{-\gamma(T-t)}e^{-\gamma(t-u)}$, one obtains

$$y(t, T) = y(0, T) + e^{-\gamma(T-t)}x(t) + \frac{\alpha^2}{2\gamma^2}e^{-2\gamma T}\left(e^{2\gamma t} - 1\right), \tag{12}$$

where

$$x(t) = -\int_0^t \left(\rho\alpha\sigma_S + \frac{\alpha^2}{\gamma}\right)e^{-\gamma(t-u)}du + \int_0^t \alpha e^{-\gamma(t-u)}dW_2(u). \tag{13}$$

It follows that $x(t)$ has the mean-reverting dynamics

$$dx(t) = \gamma(\theta - x(t))dt + \alpha dW_2(t), \quad x(0) = 0, \tag{14}$$

where $\theta = -\left(\rho\alpha\sigma_S/\gamma + \alpha^2/\gamma^2\right)$. Finally, from Equation (2) and using the fact that $\frac{F(0,T)}{F(0,t)} = \exp\left\{\int_t^T y(0, u)du\right\}$, futures prices are given by

$$F(t, T) = S(t)\frac{F(0, T)}{F(0, t)}\exp\left\{B(T - t)x(t) + A(t, T)\right\}, \tag{15}$$

where

$$B(T - t) = \frac{1}{\gamma}\left(1 - e^{-\gamma(T-t)}\right) \tag{16}$$

$$A(t, T) = \frac{\alpha^2}{4\gamma^3} \left(1 - e^{2\gamma t}\right) \left(e^{-2\gamma T} - e^{-2\gamma t}\right). \tag{17}$$

This model is the HJM equivalent of the two-factor Gibson and Schwartz (1990) model, in which the dynamics of $S(t)$ are given by Equation (3) and $\delta(t)$ (or, alternatively, the convenience yield) follows a mean-reverting Gaussian process. To see the equivalence, note that $\delta(t)$ is obtained by setting $T = t$ in Equation (12). It is straightforward to show that the dynamics of $\delta(t)$ are given by

$$d\delta(t) = \gamma(\theta_\delta(t) - \delta(t))dt + \alpha dW_2(t), \quad x(0) = 0, \tag{18}$$

with

$$\theta_\delta(t) = \frac{1}{\gamma} \frac{dy(0,t)}{dt} + y(0,t) - \frac{\rho \alpha \sigma_S}{\gamma} - \frac{\alpha^2}{2\gamma^2} \left(1 - e^{-2\gamma t}\right). \tag{19}$$

Therefore, the present model implies dynamics of $S(t)$ and $\delta(t)$ that are similar to Gibson and Schwartz (1990), with the exception that the mean-reversion level is time-dependent, due to the model matching the initial futures curve.

4 Stochastic Volatility

The basic HJM model has constant volatility and is not suited for the pricing of options and other nonlinear derivatives. I now extend the framework with stochastic volatility. The resulting model is equivalent to the SV1 model in Trolle and Schwartz (2009). $S(t)$ and $y(t, T)$ have the following dynamics:

$$\frac{dS(t)}{S(t)} = \delta(t)dt + \sigma_S \sqrt{v(t)} dW_1(t) \tag{20}$$

$$dy(t, T) = \mu_y(t, T)dt + \sigma_y(t, T) \sqrt{v(t)} dW_2(t) \tag{21}$$

$$dv(t) = \kappa(\theta - v(t))dt + \sigma_v \sqrt{v(t)} dW_3(t), \tag{22}$$

where $W_1(t)$, $W_2(t)$, and $W_3(t)$, denote correlated Wiener processes under the risk-neutral measure, with ρ_{12}, ρ_{13}, and ρ_{23} denoting pairwise correlations. This is the most general correlation structure that preserves the tractability of the model.

The model features unspanned stochastic volatility. The dynamics of futures prices are given by

$$\frac{dF(t,T)}{F(t,T)} = \sqrt{v(t)}\left(\sigma_S dW_1(t) + \int_t^T \sigma_y(t,u)du\, dW_2(t)\right). \tag{23}$$

Volatility of futures prices depends on $v(t)$, but since futures prices are only exposed to $W_1(t)$ and $W_2(t)$, while $v(t)$ is only exposed to $W_3(t)$, it is immediately clear that volatility risk cannot be completely hedged by trading in futures (or spot) contracts. To the extent that $W_1(t)$ and $W_2(t)$ are correlated with $W_3(t)$ (i.e., ρ_{13} and/or ρ_{23} are nonzero), volatility contains a spanned component, and volatility risk is partly hedgeable. If these correlations are both zero, volatility risk is completely unhedgeable.

By going through the same steps as in Section 3, one can derive the condition on $\mu_y(t,T)$ that must hold to ensure absence of arbitrage opportunities. This condition is given by (see also Trolle and Schwartz [2009]):

$$\mu_y(t,T) = -v(t)\sigma_y(t,T)\left(\rho_{12}\sigma_S + \int_t^T \sigma_y(t,u)du\right). \tag{24}$$

To model the dynamic of the futures curve in terms of a low-dimensional affine state vector, I again assume that $\sigma_y(t,T)$ is given by Equation (10). In this case, $y(t,T)$ is given by

$$y(t,T) = y(0,T) + \alpha e^{-\gamma(T-t)}x(t) + \alpha e^{-2\gamma(T-t)}\phi(t), \tag{25}$$

where

$$x(t) = -\int_0^t \left(\rho_{12}\sigma_S + \frac{\alpha}{\gamma}\right)e^{-\gamma(t-u)}v(u)du$$

$$+ \int_0^t e^{-\gamma(t-u)}\sqrt{v(u)}dW_2(u) \tag{26}$$

$$\phi(t) = \int_0^t \frac{\alpha}{\gamma}e^{-2\gamma(t-u)}v(u)du, \tag{27}$$

with the following dynamics:

$$dx(t) = \left(-\gamma x(t) - \left(\frac{\alpha}{\gamma} + \rho_{12}\sigma_S\right)v(t)\right)dt$$

$$+ \sqrt{v(t)}dW_2(t), \quad x(0) = 0 \tag{28}$$

$$d\phi(t) = \left(-2\gamma\phi(t) + \frac{\alpha}{\gamma}v(t)\right)dt, \quad \phi(0) = 0. \tag{29}$$

Consequently, futures prices are given by

$$F(t, T) = S(t)\frac{F(0, T)}{F(0, t)}\exp\{B(T-t)x(t) + C(T-t)\phi(t)\}, \tag{30}$$

where

$$B(T-t) = \frac{\alpha}{\gamma}\left(1 - e^{-\gamma(T-t)}\right), \tag{31}$$

$$C(T-t) = \frac{\alpha}{2\gamma}\left(1 - e^{-2\gamma(T-t)}\right). \tag{32}$$

Obtaining the expression for $\delta(t)$ from Equation (25), the dynamics of the log spot price, $s(t) \equiv \log(S(t))$, are given by

$$ds(t) = \left(y(0,t) + \alpha(x(t) + \phi(t)) - \frac{1}{2}\sigma_S^2 v(t)\right)dt$$

$$+ \sigma_S\sqrt{v(t)}dW_1(t). \tag{33}$$

It follows that futures prices are exponentially affine in $s(t)$, $x(t)$, and $\phi(t)$, which, along with $v(t)$, jointly constitute an affine state vector. Note that $\phi(t)$ is an "auxiliary," locally deterministic, state variable that captures the path information of $v(t)$. By augmenting the state vector with this variable, the model becomes Markovian.

Trolle and Schwartz (2009) consider extensions of the framework with multiple volatility factors. Those models are able to capture the empirical observation that some shocks to volatility are transitory, while others are more persistent.

5 Option Pricing

The pricing of European options on futures contracts is highly tractable. I continue with the case in which $\sigma_y(t, T)$ is given by Equation (10). For most exchange-traded products, options expire slightly before the expiry of the underlying futures contract.[5] Let $\mathcal{C}(t, T_0, T_1, K)$ denote the time-t price of a European call option expiring at time T_0 with strike K on a futures contract expiring at time T_1. Such an option can be priced quasi-analytically within the framework of this chapter. First, the dynamics of the log futures price, $f(t, T_1) \equiv \log(F(t, T_1))$, are given by

EFFICIENT PRICING OF ENERGY DERIVATIVES 9

$$df(t, T_1) = -\frac{1}{2}\left(\sigma_S^2 + B(T_1 - t)^2 + 2\rho_{12}\sigma_S B(T_1 - t)\right) v(t) dt$$

$$+ \sqrt{v(t)}\left(\sigma_S dW_1(t) + B(T_1 - t) dW_2(t)\right). \tag{34}$$

Next, using standard arguments, one can show that the characteristic function of $f(T_0, T_1)$ defined as

$$\psi(u, t, T_0, T_1) \equiv E_t\left[e^{iuf(T_0, T_1)}\right], \quad i = \sqrt{-1} \tag{35}$$

has the exponentially affine solution

$$\psi(u, t, T_0, T_1) = e^{M(T_0 - t) + N(T_0 - t) v(t) + iuf(t, T_1)}, \tag{36}$$

where $M(\tau)$ and $N(\tau)$ solve the following system of ordinary differential equations (ODEs)

$$\frac{dM(\tau)}{d\tau} = N(\tau)\kappa\theta \tag{37}$$

$$\frac{dN(\tau)}{d\tau} = N(\tau)\left(-\kappa + iu\sigma_v(\rho_{13}\sigma_S + \rho_{23}B(T_1 - T_0 + \tau))\right)$$

$$+ \frac{1}{2}N(\tau)^2 \sigma_v^2 - \frac{1}{2}(u^2 + iu)\bigl(\sigma_S^2 + B(T_1 - T_0 + \tau)^2$$

$$+ 2\rho_{12}\sigma_S B(T_1 - T_0 + \tau)\bigr) \tag{38}$$

subject to the boundary conditions $M(0) = 0$ and $N(0) = 0$.

Finally, following Carr and Madan (1999), one can show that the Fourier transform of the modified call price

$$\widehat{C}(t, T_0, T_1, K) = e^{\varphi \log(K)} C(t, T_0, T_1, K)$$

can be expressed in terms of the characteristic function of $f(T_0, T_1)$.[6] Consequently, the modified call price (and from that the original call price) can be obtained by applying the Fourier inversion theorem. In particular, $C(t, T_0, T_1, K)$ is given by

$$C(t, T_0, T_1, K) = P(t, T_0)\frac{e^{-\varphi \log(K)}}{\pi}$$

$$\times \int_0^\infty \mathrm{Re}\left[\frac{e^{-iu\log(K)}\psi(u - (\varphi + 1)i, t, T_0, T_1)}{\varphi^2 + \varphi - u^2 + i(2\varphi + 1)u}\right] du,$$

where $P(t, T_0)$ denotes the time-t price of a zero-coupon bond maturing at time T_0.

The pricing approach here differs from the one in Trolle and Schwartz (2009) and has two advantages: First, it permits the use of the computationally efficient fast Fourier transform algorithm. Second, it only requires the evaluation of one integral (as opposed to two integrals).

Note that most exchange-traded options are American, whereas our pricing formula is for European options.[7] With a large number of options, calibration in real time is only feasible in the case of European options, necessitating a conversion of American prices to European prices prior to calibration. Trolle and Schwartz (2009) outline one approach for doing this, and show that it introduces minimal biases, at least for short-to-medium-term options that are at or out of the money.

6 Interpreting Model Parameters

Trolle and Schwartz (2009) conduct an extensive empirical analysis of the model using a panel data set of New York Mercantile Exchange (NYMEX) crude oil derivatives from January 1990 to May 2006 (4,082 business days). Each business day in the sample, they observe a volatility surface implied from options on crude oil futures contracts. Maturities are up to one year, and moneyness—defined as the option strike divided by the price of the underlying futures contract—is between 0.78 and 1.22. Given that the data set contains both cross-sections and time-series information, Trolle and Schwartz (2009) are able to estimate both the risk-neutral dynamics (from the cross-sections) and physical dynamics (from the time series) of the model.[8] Here, I focus on the risk-neutral dynamics, for which they obtain the following parameter values: $\kappa = 1.0125$, $\theta = 0.9877$,[9] $\sigma_v = 2.8051$, $\sigma_S = 0.2289$, $\alpha = 0.1373$, $\gamma = 0.7796$, $\rho_{12} = -0.8797$, $\rho_{31} = -0.0912$, and $\rho_{32} = -0.1128$. Note that ρ_{31} and ρ_{32} are relatively close to zero, implying that volatility is predominantly unspanned by the futures contracts.

Parameters σ_S, α, γ, and ρ_{12} impact the term structure of volatility. Panel A in Figure 1.1 shows the impact on the term structure of instantaneous futures volatility, while Panel B shows the impact on the term structure of implied volatility. The time-t instantaneous volatility of a futures contract with maturity $T - t$ is given by

$$\sigma_F(t, T) = \sqrt{v(t)}\sqrt{\sigma_S^2 + B(T-t)^2 + 2\rho_{12}\sigma_S B(T-t)}. \qquad (39)$$

For the baseline set of parameters, where ρ_{12} is large and negative, the volatility term structure is downward-sloping. This is sometimes referred

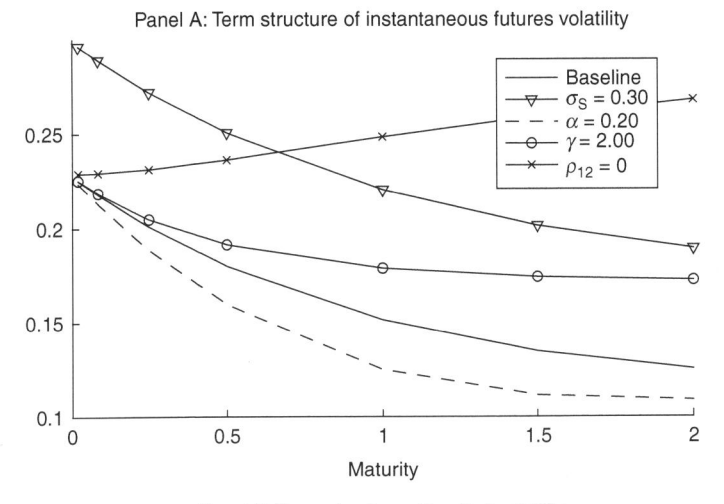

EFFICIENT PRICING OF ENERGY DERIVATIVES 11

Panel A: Term structure of instantaneous futures volatility

Panel B: Term structure of implied volatility

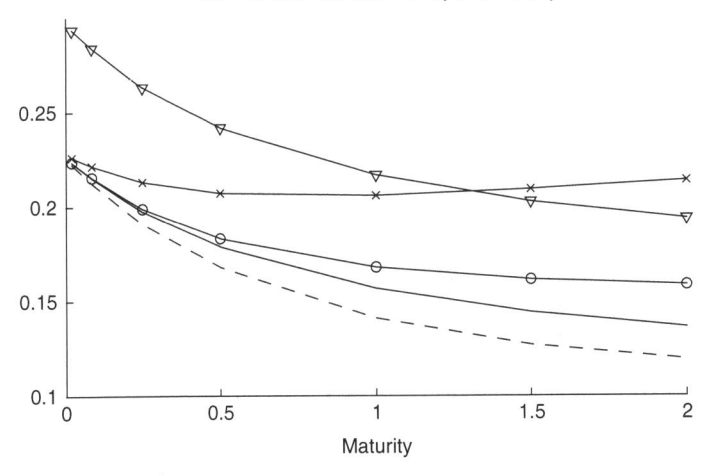

Figure 1.1 Impact of σ_S, α, γ, and ρ_{12} on volatility term structure.
This figure shows how σ_S, α, γ, and ρ_{12} impact the volatility term structure. Panel A shows the impact on the term structure of instantaneous futures volatility. Panel B shows the impact on the term structure of implied volatility. Baseline parameters of the model are those obtained by Trolle and Schwartz (2009) ($\sigma_S = 0.2289$, $\alpha = 0.1373$, $\gamma = 0.7796$, and $\rho_{12} = -0.8797$) and $v(t) = \theta$.

to as the "Samuelson effect" (see Samuelson [1965]). Increasing σ_S causes an almost parallel upward shift in the volatility term structure. Changing α affects the slope of the volatility term structure; in combination with ρ_{12} being large and negative, increasing α makes the volatility term structure more downward-sloping. A futures contract with an infinite maturity has an instantaneous volatility of $\sqrt{v(t)}\sqrt{\sigma_S^2 + \frac{\alpha^2}{\gamma^2} + \frac{2\rho_{12}\sigma_S\alpha}{\gamma}}$, and γ affects how fast the term structure approaches this level; increasing γ increases the speed of convergence. Finally, increasing ρ_{12} increases the slope of the volatility term structure, and for $\rho_{12} = 0$ the term structure is upward-sloping instead of downward-sloping.

The volatility smiles implied from options on futures contracts reflect the risk-neutral distributions of log futures returns. Figures 1.2–1.5 show how parameters σ_v, ρ_{13}, ρ_{23}, and κ impact the implied volatility smiles at

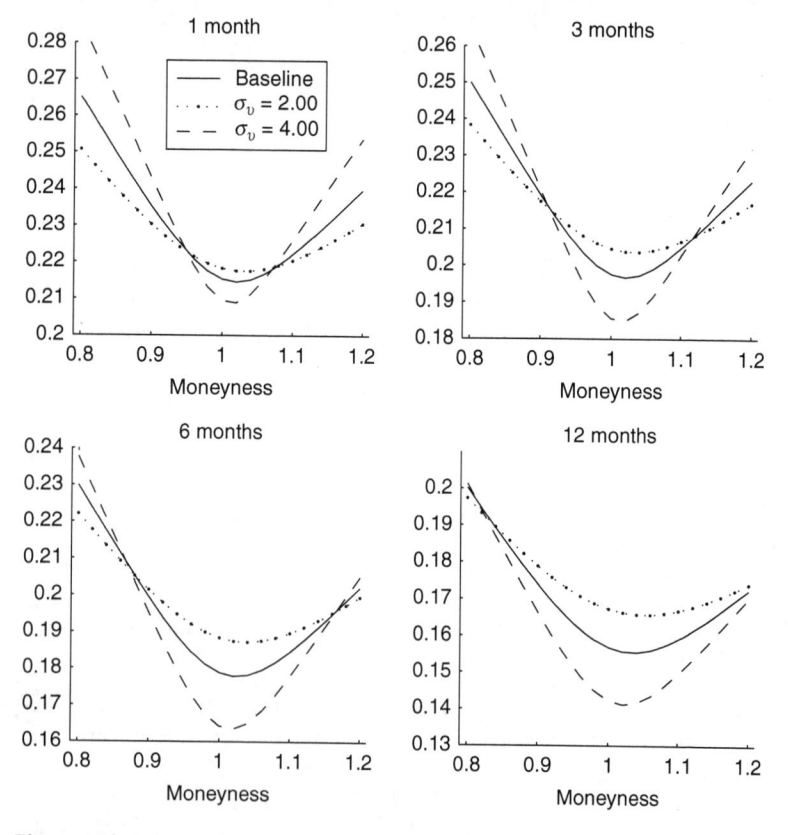

Figure 1.2 Impact of σ_v on implied volatility smiles.
This figure shows how σ_v impacts the implied volatility smiles at option maturities of 1, 3, 6, and 12 months. Baseline parameters of the model are those obtained by Trolle and Schwartz (2009) ($\sigma_v = 2.8051$) and $v(t) = \theta$. Moneyness is defined as an option strike divided by the price of the underlying futures contract.

maturities of 1, 3, 6, and 12 months. At the baseline parameters, there are pronounced volatility smiles at all horizons. This is due to the high value of σ_v, which induces significant excess kurtosis in the distribution of log returns. Also, the volatility smiles are skewed to the left at all horizons. This is due to the negative correlation between futures returns and innovations to volatility (caused by the negative values of ρ_{13} and ρ_{23}), which induces negative skewness in the distribution of log returns. Figure 1.2 shows how the curvature of the implied volatility smiles are impacted by σ_v. Figures 1.3 and 1.4 show how the skewness of the implied volatility smiles is impacted by ρ_{13} and ρ_{23}. ρ_{13} has an impact at all maturities,

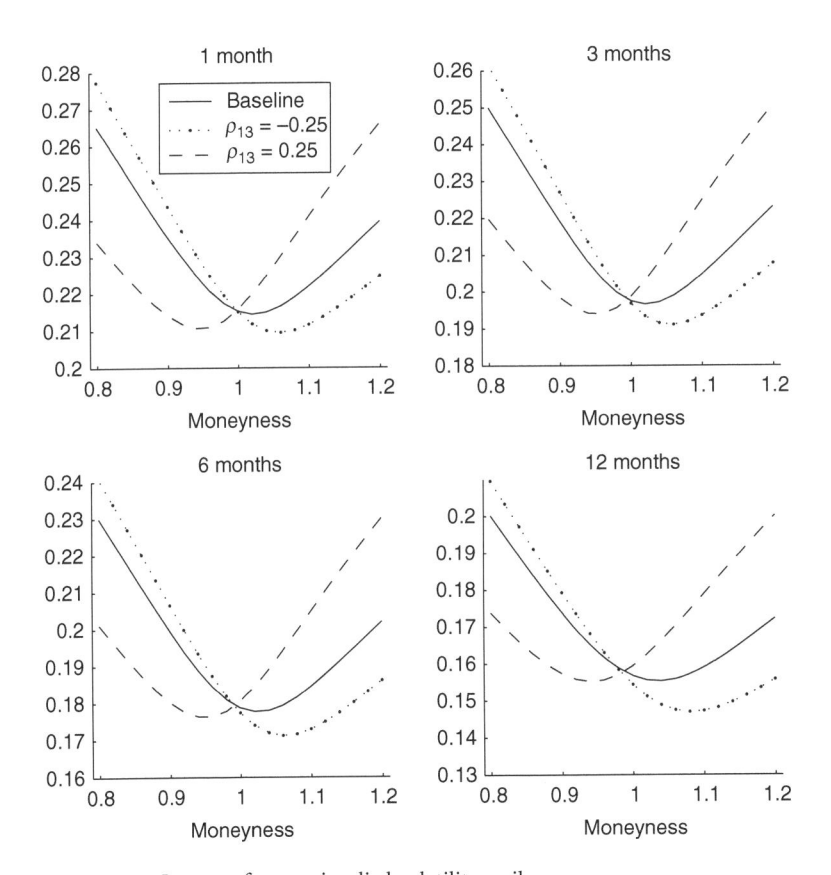

Figure 1.3 Impact of ρ_{13} on implied volatility smiles.
This figure shows how ρ_{13} impacts the implied volatility smiles at option maturities of 1, 3, 6, and 12 months. Baseline parameters of the model are those obtained by Trolle and Schwartz (2009) ($\rho_{13} = -0.0912$) and $v(t) = \theta$. Moneyness is defined as an option strike divided by the price of the underlying futures contract.

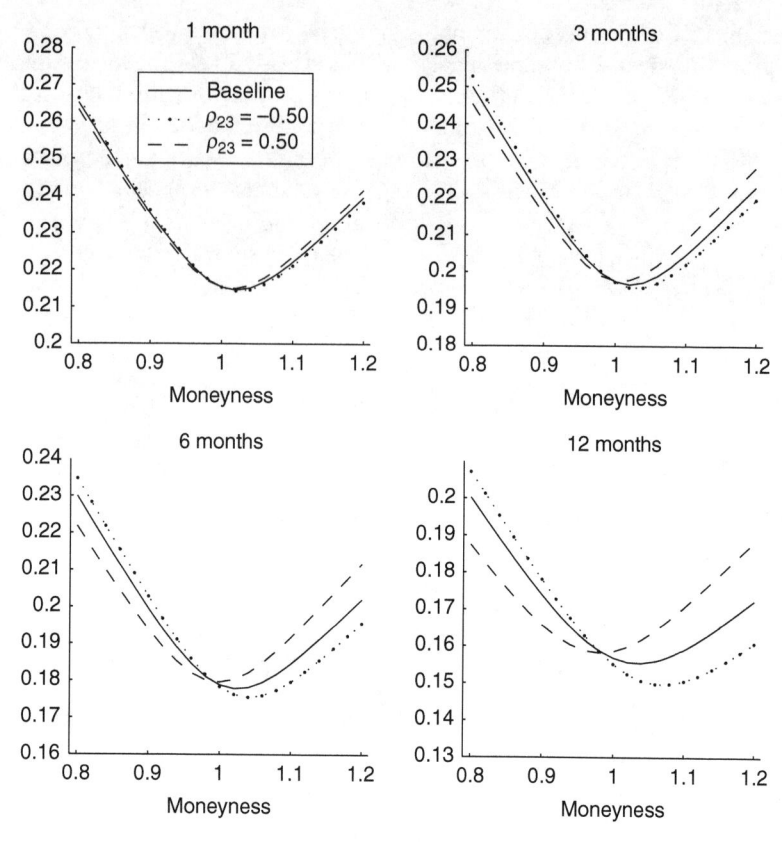

Figure 1.4 Impact of ρ_{23} on implied volatility smiles.
This figure shows how ρ_{23} impacts the implied volatility smiles at option maturities of 1, 3, 6, and 12 months. Baseline parameters of the model are those obtained by Trolle and Schwartz (2009) ($\rho_{23} = -0.1128$) and $v(t) = \theta$. Moneyness is defined as an option strike divided by the price of the underlying futures contract.

while the impact of ρ_{23} increases with maturity. Finally, Figure 1.5 shows how the implied volatility smiles are affected by κ. It is well known that in a stochastic volatility framework, the implied volatility smiles flatten out as the option maturity goes to zero or infinity. The maturity at which implied volatility smiles are most pronounced depends on the degree of mean-reversion in volatility; see Das and Sundaram (1999) for an analysis of the term structure of conditional moments in stochastic volatility models. Figure 1.5 shows that increasing κ makes longer-term smiles less pronounced.

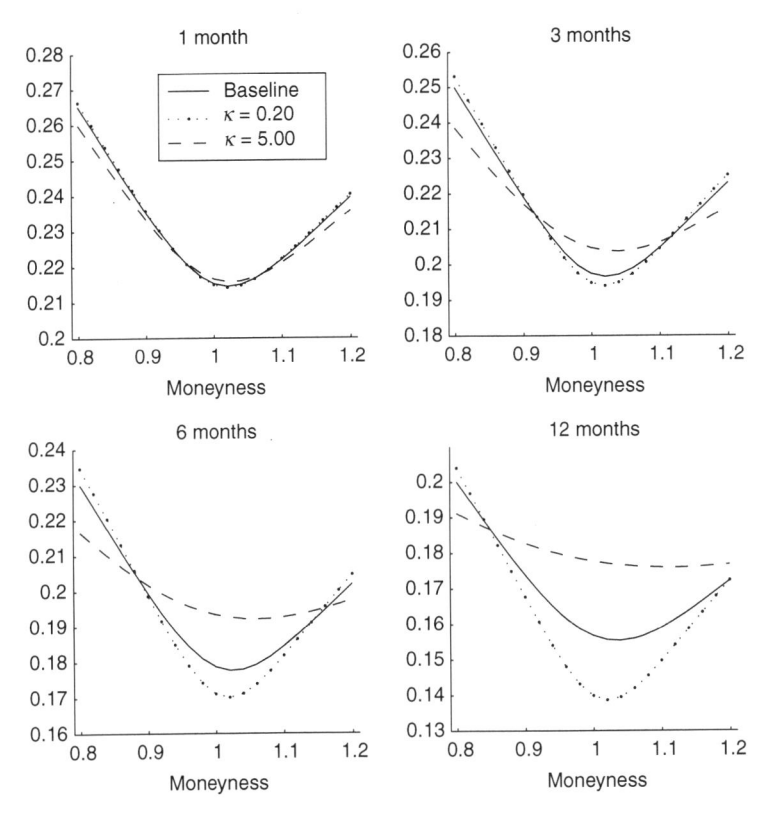

Figure 1.5 Impact of κ on implied volatility smiles.
This figure shows how κ impacts the implied volatility smiles at option maturities of 1, 3, 6, and 12 months. Baseline parameters of the model are those obtained by Trolle and Schwartz (2009) ($\kappa = 1.0125$) and $v(t) = \theta$. Moneyness is defined as an option strike divided by the price of the underlying futures contract.

7 Jumps

Several papers have documented jumps in energy prices; see, for example, Askari and Krichene (2008) and Larsson and Nossman (2011) for the crude oil market. In this section, I outline an extension of the framework that takes jumps in spot prices into account. I replace Equation (20) by

$$\frac{dS(t)}{S(t-)} = \delta(t)dt + \sigma_S\sqrt{v(t)}dW_1(t) + \left(e^z - 1\right)dq(t) - \overline{\mu}\lambda dt, \qquad (40)$$

where $q(t)$ is a Poisson jump counter (assumed independent from the Wiener processes) with instantaneous intensity λ.[10] Conditional on a jump occurring, z is the size of the jump in the log spot price and has the distribution

$$z \sim N(\mu_z, \sigma_z^2). \tag{41}$$

$\overline{\mu}$ is the expected percentage jump in the spot price and is given by

$$\overline{\mu} = E[e^z - 1] = e^{\mu_z + \frac{1}{2}\sigma_z^2} - 1. \tag{42}$$

In this extended model, the dynamics of futures prices are given by

$$\frac{dF(t, T)}{F(t-, T)} = \sqrt{v(t)} \left(\sigma_S dW_1(t) + \int_t^T \sigma_y(t, u) du dW_2(t) \right)$$
$$+ (e^z - 1) dq(t) - \overline{\mu} \lambda dt. \tag{43}$$

There are now two sources of market incompleteness: the USV component and the jump component.

With $\sigma_y(t, T)$ given by Equation (10), it is still the case that futures prices are exponentially affine in the three state variables $s(t)$, $x(t)$, and $\phi(t)$, which, along with $v(t)$, jointly constitute an affine state vector. Only now, the dynamics of $s(t)$ are given by

$$ds(t) = \left(y(0, t) - \overline{\mu}\lambda + \alpha(x(t) + \phi(t)) - \frac{1}{2}\sigma_S^2 v(t) \right) dt$$
$$+ \sigma_S \sqrt{v(t)} dW_1(t) + z dq(t). \tag{44}$$

Option pricing proceeds as in Section 5; only now, Equation (37) needs to be replaced by

$$\frac{dM(\tau)}{d\tau} = N(\tau)\kappa\theta + \left(e^{iu\mu_z - \frac{1}{2}u^2\sigma_z^2} - 1 - iu\overline{\mu} \right) \lambda. \tag{45}$$

When fitting the model to an implied volatility surface, the effect of the jump component is most pronounced at short option maturities. In particular, a negative mean jump size, μ_z, will add negative skewness to the implied volatility smiles. For typical parameter values, the effect of the jump component decays fairly rapidly as option maturity increases; see, for example, the discussion in Gatheral (2006) in the context of equity index options.

Many extensions that preserve the tractability of the model are possible. The jump intensity could be made an affine function of variance, $\lambda(t) = \lambda_0 + \lambda_v v(t)$. This captures the fact that jumps are more likely to occur when the market is more volatile. Also, following Duffie et al. (2000) for equity options, the variance process could be extended with (positive) jumps, possibly correlated with jumps in spot prices. Larsson and Nossman (2011) show that this is an important characteristic of the time series of crude oil prices.

8 Conclusion

In this chapter, I presented a tractable framework, first developed in Trolle and Schwartz (2009), for pricing energy derivatives in the presence of USV. Among the model features are (i) a perfect fit to the initial futures term structure, (ii) a fast and accurate Fourier-based pricing formula for European-style options on futures contracts, enabling efficient calibration to liquid plain-vanilla exchange-traded derivatives, and (iii) the evolution of the futures curve being described in terms of a low-dimensional affine state vector, making the model ideally suited for pricing complex energy derivatives and real options by simulation, where early exercise features can be handled using the LSM approach of Longstaff and Schwartz (2001). I also consider an extension of the framework that takes jumps in spot prices into account.

Notes

1. Throughout the chapter, implied volatilities are obtained using the Black (1976) model.
2. Following Collin-Dufresne and Goldstein (2002), one could derive parameter restrictions such that volatility is unspanned, but such restrictions are highly nonlinear and severely impact model flexibility.
3. In these cases, the pricing error that arises from not explicitly modeling stochastic interest rates is negligible, since the volatility of interest rates is typically orders of magnitudes smaller than the volatility of futures returns, and the correlation between interest rates and futures returns tends to be relatively low.
4. Because of the assumption that interest rates are deterministic, I do not distinguish between forward and future cost of carry; see Miltersen and Schwartz (1998).
5. For instance, in the case of crude oil, regular options expire three business days prior to the expiration of the underlying futures contract.
6. The control parameter φ must be chosen to ensure that the modified option price is square integrable, which is a sufficient condition for its Fourier transform to exist.
7. In some cases, such as crude oil, European options trade side by side with American options. In these cases, American options tend to be the most liquid.

8. The latter requires a specification of the change of measure from risk-neutral to physical.
9. Note that in the model, $\sigma_S, \alpha, \kappa\theta$, and σ_v are not simultaneously identified; see, e.g., the discussion of invariant affine transformations in Dai and Singleton (2000). Trolle and Schwartz (2009) normalize $\kappa\theta$ to one.
10. The $S(t)$-process is right-continuous. The value of S right before a jump at time t is the left limit $S(t-) = \lim_{u \uparrow t} S(u)$.

References

Andersen, L. (2010). Markov models for commodity futures: Theory and practice. *Quantitative Finance*, 10:831–854.

Askari, H. and Krichene, N. (2008). Oil price dynamics (2002–2006). *Energy Economics*, 30:2134–2153.

Black, F. (1976). The pricing of commodity contracts. *Journal of Financial Economics*, 3:167–179.

Carr, P. and Madan, D. (1999). Option valuation using the fast fourier transform. *Journal of Computational Finance*, 2:61–73.

Casassus, J. and Collin-Dufresne, P. (2005). Stochastic convenience yield implied from commodity futures and interest rates. *Journal of Finance*, 60:2283–2331.

Collin-Dufresne, P. and Goldstein, R. (2002). Do bonds span the fixed income markets? Theory and evidence for unspanned stochastic volatility. *Journal of Finance*, 57:1685–1730.

Cortazar, G. and Schwartz, E. S. (1994). The valuation of commodity contingent claims. *Journal of Derivatives*, 1:27–39.

Crosby, J. (2008). A multi-factor jump-diffusion model for commodities. *Quantitative Finance*, 8:181–200.

Dai, Q. and Singleton, K. (2000). Specification analysis of affine term structure models. *Journal of Finance*, 55:1943–1978.

Das, S. R. and Sundaram, R. K. (1999). Of smiles and smirks: A term structure perspective. *Journal of Financial and Quantitative Analysis*, 34:211–239.

Duffie, D. (2001). *Dynamic Asset Pricing Theory*. Princeton University Press, Princeton, NJ.

Duffie, D., Pan, J., and Singleton, K. (2000). Transform analysis and asset pricing for affine jump-diffusions. *Econometrica*, 68:1343–1376.

Gatheral, J. (2006). *The Volatility Surface*. Wiley, New York.

Gibson, R. and Schwartz, E. S. (1990). Stochastic convenience yield and the pricing of oil contingent claims. *Journal of Finance*, 45:959–976.

Heath, D., Jarrow, R., and Morton, A. (1992). Bond pricing and the term structure of interest rates: A new methodology for contingent claims valuation. *Econometrica*, 60:77–105.

Larsson, K. and Nossman, M. (2011). Jumps and stochastic volatility in oil prices: Time series evidence. *Energy Economics*, 33:504–514.

Longstaff, F. and Schwartz, E. (2001). Valuing american options by simulation: A simple least-square approach. *Review of Financial Studies*, 14:113–147.

Miltersen, K. and Schwartz, E. S. (1998). Pricing of options on commodity futures with stochastic term structures of convenience yields and interest rates. *Journal of Financial and Quantitative Analysis*, 33:33–59.

Samuelson, P. A. (1965). Proof that properly anticipated prices fluctuate randomly. *Industrial Management Review*, 6:41–49.

Schwartz, E. S. (1997). The stochastic behavior of commodity prices: Implications for valuation and hedging. *Journal of Finance*, 52:923–973.

Schwartz, E. S. and Smith, J. E. (2000). Short-term variations and long-term dynamics of commodity prices. *Management Science*, 46:893–911.

Schwartz, E. S. and Trolle, A. B. (2010). Pricing expropriation risk in natural resource contracts – a real options approach. Working paper, William Hogan and Federico Sturzenegger, eds., *Populism and Natural Resources*. MIT Press, Cambridge, Massachusetts.

Trolle, A. B. and Schwartz, E. S. (2009). Unspanned stochastic volatility and the pricing of commodity derivatives. *Review of Financial Studies*, 22:4423–4461.

Trolle, A. B. and Schwartz, E. S. (2010). Variance risk premia in energy markets. *Journal of Derivatives*, 17:15–32.

2
A Supply and Demand Based Energy Pricing Model

Takashi Kanamura[1]

1 Introduction

The deregulation of world energy markets and the transition to spot energy contracts from long-term energy contracts has caused increasing volatilities in energy prices, since these are now strongly affected by supply and demand. Market participants, such as energy producers, traders, and consumers cannot avoid such risks. As a simple example for the influence of volatility, consider a thermal power plant procuring natural gas for power generation from the spot market in the United States. Since natural gas prices in the United States are volatile due to the supply and demand in the market, the risk management team in charge of natural gas procurement at this plant has to monitor the volatility risk as accurately as possible using an appropriate energy price model since the spark spread, that is, the difference between the electricity and the natural gas price, may be squeezed by the volatilities and thus directly affecting the profitability of the plant. As a consequence, energy price models have been introduced in the energy industry in order to manage such risks.

Several energy market price models have been developed based on price models for financial markets. However, these models have been directly applied to energy pricing without any consideration or adjustment for the characteristics of energy markets. The continuous time models used in stock markets, such as the Heston model introduced by Heston (1993) and the constant elasticity of variance (CEV) model proposed by Cox (1975) and extended by Emanuel and MacBeth (1982), have been directly used for pricing in energy markets (see, e.g., Eydeland and Wolyniec [2003]). Similarly, the discrete time price return and volatility models such as the ARCH, GARCH, and ARCH-M models of Engle (1982), Bollerslev (1986), and Engle et al. (1987) have been employed for energy markets by Duffie et al. (1999), Pindyck (2004), and Deaves and Krinsky (1992), respectively. Of course, to some extent, energy markets may employ the same pricing models as financial markets. However, the characteristics of energy prices are not necessarily the same as the characteristics of financial asset prices. For instance, the inverse leverage effect, that is, the observation that volatility increases in prices, often appears in energy markets. In contrast, stock markets usually exhibit a leverage effect, that is, a negative relationship between volatility and prices.

Energy price models have often been developed as reduced-form asset pricing models. Gibson and Schwartz (1990) propose a two-factor model for crude oil in which the logarithm of the spot price follows a Brownian motion and the convenience yield follows a mean reverting process. Brennan (1991) also models commodity spot prices and convenience yields using separate stochastic processes with a constant correlation. Schwartz (1997) compares one-, two-, and three-factor models in which the logarithm of the spot price follows a simple stochastic process to describe commodity prices. Another relevant paper in this class is Kolos and Ronn (2008), in which energy forward price returns exhibit a volatility-in-mean effect. While these models work relatively well to describe energy prices, the supply and demand relationship of energy products, which is considered the main driver of energy prices by energy market participants, is not explicitly structured in such energy price models. Thus, their economic insights are limited.

This chapter reviews a supply- and demand-based energy pricing (SDEP) model that can accurately capture the characteristics of volatility in energy prices using the supply-demand relationship based on Kanamura (2009) and Kanamura and Ōhashi (2007b). More precisely, we assume an upward-sloping, convex, and fixed supply curve and a stochastically moving inelastic demand curve, in order to characterize the equilibrium price. This model is referred to as the "SDEP model." One reasonable choice for the supply curve may be an exponential function. However, the question is how well a supply curve can be approximated by the exponential function. To investigate the goodness of the exponential approximation, Kanamura (2009) analyzes the volatility of energy prices in the supply-demand based model. Following the results from this work, we employ an inverse Box–Cox transformation function, which includes an exponential function as a special case, to represent the supply curve for an energy product. By using an inverse Box–Cox transformation supply curve and a simple stochastic process for demand, we derive the equilibrium price process for the energy product. It can be shown that the inverse Box–Cox transformation supply curve yields an inverse leverage effect, that is, a positive correlation between energy prices and volatilities. The SDEP model is also used to show that the (G)ARCH-M model has its foundations in the supply-demand relationship. We further show that the SDEP model relates to the Schwartz (1997) two-factor model when the supply curve is represented by an exponential function. In this setting, the log-transformed energy price model can be regarded as a special case of the SDEP model in which the supply curve is approximated by an exponential function, that is, the price is given by the exponential transformation of the demand stochastic process. Therefore, we call the SDEP model "an extended Schwartz model."

The most important parameter in the SDEP model is the Box–Cox transformation parameter of the supply curve. If this parameter is set to zero, the supply curve is represented by an exponential function, which implies that the standard price model such as the model of Schwartz (1997) should work well to model energy prices. If the Box–Cox transformation parameter is not zero, however, the exponential function is not a good approximation for the supply curve, and the energy price model can be improved by incorporating the inverse Box–Cox transformation supply function, which is more general and has a larger curvature than the exponential function. By using the extended Kalman filter (EKF) method, we empirically estimate the SDEP model for natural gas, WTI (West Texas Intermediate) crude oil, and heating oil futures prices traded at the New York Mercantile Exchange (NYMEX). The results show that for all three energy markets, the Box–Cox transformation parameter of the supply curves is non-zero and significantly negative. This suggests that the extended Schwartz model with an inverse Box–Cox transformation supply curve has the potential to improve the performance of the energy price model.

2 Model

2.1 A Supply- and Demand-Based Energy Pricing Model

Demand and prices for natural gas in the United States are generally considered to be positively related (see, e.g., Kanamura, 2009). This observation gives us a motivation to incorporate the supply-demand relationship for energy directly into an energy spot price model. In order to set up the model, we employ a simplified relationship between the demand and price for energy.

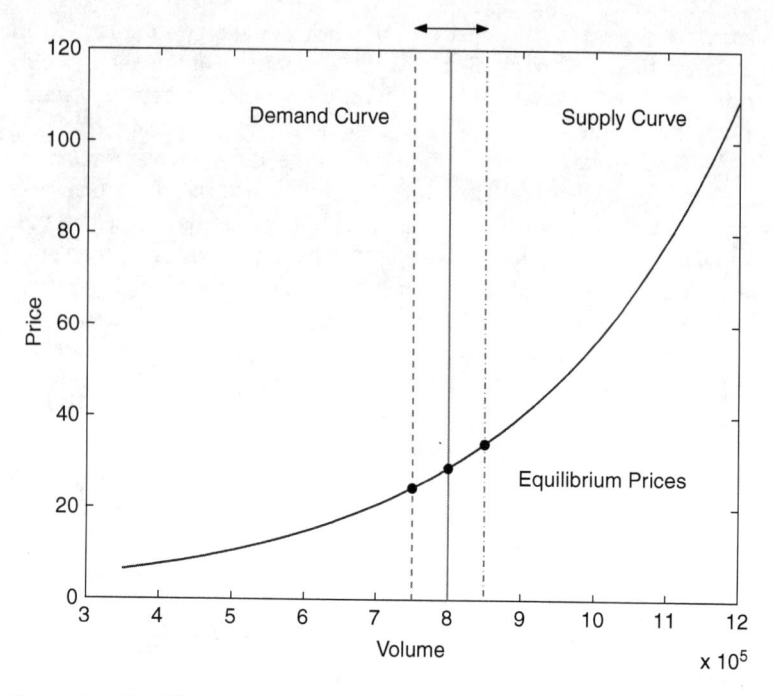

Figure 2.1 Equilibrium energy prices.

As illustrated in Figure 2.1, we assume that equilibrium prices are determined by a fixed increasing supply curve and a stochastically fluctuating vertical demand curve. The assumption of a fixed supply curve comes from the fact that both the number and constitution of energy production facilities are almost constant in the short term. The assumption of a vertical demand curve arises from the demand inelasticity to prices in the short run, that is, energy use seems to be independent of price changes in the short run if it is more or less irrelevant to the seasonality of demand. In this sense, the model can be considered as a first-order approximation. This idea has been already applied to spot price models for electricity, such as in Barlow (2002) and Kanamura and Ōhashi (2007a). It should be noted that, as can be seen from Figure 2.1, that the model is able to generate a large rate of price changes with respect to demand, as demand (i.e., price) increases, assuming that the supply curve is dramatically upward–sloping.

Based on the above idea, we formulate an energy price model. We denote the fixed supply curve for energy by $P_t = g(S_t)$, which is a second-order differentiable, monotone, and increasing convex function with respect to supply S_t. In a related discussion on the supply curve, Pirrong and Jermakyan (2008) suggest a convex supply stack for the PJM market. Given the assumption of demand inelasticity for energy, equilibrium energy prices are determined by the supply curve, replacing the supply S_t by the demand D_t. Here, we model the stochastic process for energy demand by assuming

$$dD_t = \mu_D dt + \sigma_D dw_t. \tag{1}$$

Proposition 1 *Suppose that equilibrium prices for energy are given by a function of demand as $P_t = g(D_t)$, where the demand stochastic process is generated by Equation (1). Then, a supply and demand based energy pricing (SDEP) model can be expressed as follows:*

$$\frac{dP_t}{P_t} = \mu_t dt + \sigma_t dw_t, \tag{2}$$

$$\sigma_t = \frac{g'(D_t)}{g(D_t)} \sigma_D, \tag{3}$$

$$\mu_t = \left(\frac{\mu_D}{\sigma_D} + \frac{1}{2}\frac{g''(D_t)}{g'(D_t)}\sigma_D\right)\sigma_t. \tag{4}$$

Proof We apply Itô's Lemma to $P_t = g(D_t)$ by using Equation (1).

Equation (3) shows that the energy price volatility, σ_t, is proportional to the ratio of the first derivative of $g(D)$ to the level of the supply curve function $g(D)$, which causes time-varying volatility driven by the demand shocks as long as $\frac{g'(D)}{g(D)}$ does not become a constant. Moreover, the drift term of the SDEP model in Equation (4) changes with the volatility in energy prices, which leads to the existence of a volatility-in-mean effect. In addition, since the supply curve, g, is a second-order differentiable, monotonic, and increasing convex function, $\frac{g''(D)}{g'(D)} \geq 0$ holds in Equation (4). This implies that volatility in energy prices positively affects the drift term in Equation (4), when μ_D is greater than or equal to 0. Summarizing, this simple model for energy prices based on the supply-demand relationship can produce two significant characteristics for the volatility. First, the SDEP model exhibits a time-varying property, since the volatility of the price returns depends on demand. Second, there exists a volatility-in-mean effect in the energy price dynamics because the drift term is a function of volatility. In an effort to deepen the discussion on the volatility, Section 2.2 explicitly specifies the supply curve function that reflects energy markets appropriately.

2.2 One-factor SDEP Model

In order to examine the characteristics of the SDEP model in detail, we create a one-factor SDEP model that is tractable and whose solution exists by employing an explicit supply function that reflects an energy market observation. To identify the supply curve for energy in detail, we need to estimate it. While consumption demand for natural gas may exhibit seasonality, storage of natural gas can be used to mitigate seasonality. Hence, the total demand for energy expressed by the sum of consumption and storage demands for energy will be less seasonal than the consumption demand. Therefore, as a first-order approximation, we aggregate the data across seasons and years.

The exponential function may be a reasonable choice for the second-order differentiable, monotonic, and increasing convex function assumed in Proposition 1. This is because, as is seen in commodity asset pricing models, the log transformations of prices follow a simple stochastic process such as a Brownian motion and a mean reverting process: prices are obtained from the exponential transformation of a simple stochastic process. However, as shown in Kanamura (2009), fitting the exponential curve to the data, one can observe that the rate of change of prices with respect to the demand seems to be much larger than that of the exponential function.

For this reason, we employ the inverse Box–Cox transformation as the supply curve that does not only have the exponential function built in but also exhibits larger gradients of the supply curve than the exponential function (see, Kanamura, 2009). However, there exists a problem on the asymptote for the supply function. In order to avoid this problem, we propose the following supply curve assuming the existence of a constant $c\tau$ close to and less than the asymptote $-\frac{c}{a}$ where we introduce the inverse Box–Cox supply curve until the supply limit $c\tau$ in the natural gas market and more than $c\tau$ use the exponential supply curve whose first and second derivatives are the same as the first and second derivatives of the inverse Box–Cox supply curve at $c\tau$, respectively:[2]

$$P_t = \begin{cases} \left(1 + a\frac{S_t}{c}\right)^{\frac{1}{a}} & (S_t \leq c\tau) \\ \frac{(1+a\tau)^{\frac{1}{a}}}{1-a}\left[\exp\left(\frac{1-a}{1+a\tau}\left(\frac{S_t}{c} - \tau\right)\right) - a\right] & (S_t \geq c\tau), \end{cases} \quad (5)$$

where a is assumed to be less than or equal to 0. The intuition of this supply curve is that the smaller is a, the more convex is the supply curve. If a in Equation (5) is zero, it collapses to the exponential function, which corresponds to an exponential transformations of a simple stochastic process as in commodity price models such as Schwartz (1997). If a is less than 0, it has larger slope changes than the exponential function.[3]

For simplicity, we assume that demand for energy can be described by a one-factor process:

$$dD_t = \mu_D dt + \sigma_D dw_t. \tag{6}$$

Supposing the inelasticity of demand to prices, energy prices are given as the inverse Box–Cox transformation of demand. Applying Itô's Lemma to Equations (5) and (6) and then replacing the drift term for $S_t \geq c\tau$ by that for $S_t \leq c\tau$ in order to guarantee the existence of the solution, we have the one-factor SDEP model that is tractable given by Equations (7)–(9):

$$\frac{dP_t}{P_t} = \mu_t dt + \sigma_t dw_t, \tag{7}$$

$$\sigma_t = \begin{cases} \sigma P_t^{-a} & P_t \leq (1+a\tau)^{\frac{1}{a}} \\ \sigma \frac{1-a}{1+a\tau}\left(1 + \frac{a}{P_t}\frac{(1+a\tau)^{\frac{1}{a}}}{1-a}\right) & P_t \geq (1+a\tau)^{\frac{1}{a}}, \end{cases} \tag{8}$$

$$\mu_t = k_1 \sigma_t + k_2 \sigma_t^2, \tag{9}$$

where $\sigma = \dfrac{\sigma_D}{c}$, $k_1 = \dfrac{\mu_D}{\sigma_D}$, and $k_2 = \dfrac{1-a}{2}$.

The first intuition of the model lies in the volatility term in Equation (8). It implies an inverse leverage effect because σ_t increases in P_t for negative a, that is, for $a < 0$, σ_t is monotonically increasing with respect to P_t and bounded.[4] The second intuition lies in the drift term. It represents the volatility-in-mean effect because μ_t is a function of σ_t. We investigate the characteristics of the volatility in the one-factor SDEP model. According to Equation (8),[5] the volatility is proportional to the price to the power of the negative Box–Cox transformation parameter.[6] Since the Box–Cox transformation parameter stands for the curvature of the supply curve, the magnitude of the volatility changes with the curvature. If the curvature of the inverse Box–Cox transformation is larger than the curvature of the exponential function, that is, a is negative, the price has a positive impact on volatility. If a is zero, implying the exponential function, the price does not affect volatility at all. It means that if the supply curve becomes steeper than the exponential function, the volatility increases with prices, which is often observed in energy markets and referred to as the "inverse leverage effect."

The fact that the drift term of the price returns is driven by volatility, implying that the SDEP model implies a volatility–in–mean effect as in (G)ARCH-M models. The next section sheds light on the relationship between both models.

2.3 (G)ARCH-M Models for Energy Prices

Many previous works on energy price return models employ (G)ARCH models to capture the heteroskedasticity of the volatility in energy prices due to the statistica08l good fit to energy market data. This section tries to find an economic motivation behind the selection of a (G)ARCH-M model for energy prices by employing the SDEP model.

To investigate the relationship between the SDEP model and (G)ARCH models, we represent the SDEP model in discrete time. Equations (7) and (9) are restated as follows:

$$r_t = \mu_t + \sigma_t \varepsilon_t, \quad \mu_t = \mu_1 \sigma_t + \mu_2 \sigma_t^2, \tag{10}$$

where $r_t = \log(P_{t+1}) - \log(P_t)$, $\mu_1 = \frac{\mu_D}{\sigma_D}$, and $\mu_2 = -\frac{a}{2}$. Using Equations (5) and (8),[7] σ_t^2 becomes a function of energy demand:

$$\sigma_t^2 = \frac{\sigma_D^2}{(c + aD_t)^2}. \tag{11}$$

Moreover, we assume that the demand follows an AR(1) model:[8]

$$D_t = (1 - \lambda_D) D_{t-1} + \mu_D + \sigma_D \varepsilon_t. \tag{12}$$

Suppose that energy price returns are represented by the one-factor SDEP model. Then, the discrete time SDEP model is expressed as follows:

$$r_t = \mu_t + \sigma_t \varepsilon_t, \quad \mu_t = \mu_1 \sigma_t + \mu_2 \sigma_t^2, \tag{13}$$

$$\eta_t = \sigma_t \varepsilon_t, \tag{14}$$

$$\sigma_t^2 = \frac{\sigma_D^2}{c^2} \left(1 + \sum_{k=1}^{\infty} (-1)^k (k+1) \left(\frac{a}{c}\right)^k \left(M_t + \sum_{i=1}^{t} k_i \varepsilon_{t+1-i}\right)^k \right), \tag{15}$$

where $M_t = (1 - \lambda_D)^t D_0 + \frac{\mu_D}{\lambda_D}\{1 - (1 - \lambda_D)^t\}$, $k_i = \sigma_D (1 - \lambda_D)^{i-1}$. Suppose, in addition, that the squares of the past demand shocks only dominate the volatility, as in Equation (15). Then, the SDEP model collapses to a ARCH(t)-M model:

$$\sigma_t^2 \approx \frac{\sigma_D^2}{c^2} \sum_{i=1}^{t} \left(A_{i,0} + A_{i,2} \eta_{t-i}^2 \right), \tag{16}$$

where $A_{i,k} = \sum_{l=k}^{\infty} (-1)^l (l+1) \left(\frac{a}{c}\right)^l a_{l-k,i,l} b_{i,k},$ (17)

$a_{j,i,n} = {}_nC_j M_t^j k_i^{n-j} (j \neq n), \quad a_{j,i,n} = \frac{1}{t} M_t^n (j = n),$ and

$b_{i,k} = \left(\frac{c + aM_{t+1-i}}{\sigma_D}\right)^k.$

The proofs for Equations (13)–(17) are provided in the Appendix of Kanamura (2009).

We now investigate the influence of the supply curve shape, that is, the Box–Cox transformation parameter, a, on the volatility. If the Box–Cox transformation parameter is zero, implying that the supply curve is exponential, the volatility is σ_D^2/c^2 and thus constant. This can be seen by inserting $a = 0$ into Equation (15). More importantly for energy markets, we analyze the influence of a more upward-sloping supply curve than the exponential function on the volatility, that is, the case $a < 0$. We then obtain the following property for $A_{i,k}$: $A_{i,k}$ is positive for all i and k. The proof is offered in Appendix of Kanamura (2009). Hence, if a is negative, then the volatility in Equation (16) always increases with past demand shocks, because it includes the squares of the past demand shocks with positive coefficients. In addition, a negative value of a guarantees the non-negativeness of σ_t^2 in Equation (16).

It is well known that ARCH(∞) collapses to GARCH(1,1). Recalling that the model accommodates the volatility-in-mean effect as in Equation (13), an existing GARCH(1,1)-M model for energy prices creates the foundations for the supply-demand relationship.

2.4 An Extended Schwartz Model for Energy Prices

We now examine the relationship between the supply and demand based energy pricing model and existing models by following the ideas laid out in Kanamura and Ōhashi (2007b). To describe the movement of energy prices in a relatively short period, we assume that the supply curve is stable while the demand fluctuates stochastically. Equilibrium prices of energy commodities are determined by the intersection of supply and demand curves.

More precisely, we formulate the supply curve as a monotonically increasing, twice differentiable convex function g with respect to supply S_t as

$$P_t = g(S_t). \tag{18}$$

We assume that the demand D_t is inelastic to the price and is represented by the following equations

$$D_t = \sum_{i=1}^{n} D_t^i, \tag{19}$$

$$dD_t^i = \mu_D^i(D_t^i)dt + \sigma_D^i dz_t^i, \tag{20}$$

$$E_t[dz_t^i dz_t^j] = \rho_{ij}dt, \tag{21}$$

where $\mu_D^i(D_t^i)$ is a linear function of D_t^i at most and both σ_D^i and ρ_{ij} are constant. The equilibrium price P_t equates supply and demand, and thus is given by $P_t = g(D_t)$. Using Itô's lemma, we obtain the following price return process:

$$\frac{dP_t}{P_t} = \frac{1}{g}\left(\frac{\partial g}{\partial t} + \frac{\partial g}{\partial D}\mu_D + \frac{1}{2}\frac{\partial^2 g}{\partial D^2}\sigma_D^2\right)dt + \frac{1}{g}\frac{\partial g}{\partial D}\sigma_D dz_t, \tag{22}$$

$$\mu_D = \sum_{i=1}^{n} \mu_D^i(D_t^i), \quad \sigma_D^2 = \sum_{i,j=1}^{n} \rho_{ij}\sigma_D^i\sigma_D^j, \quad dz_t = \frac{1}{\sigma_D}\sum_{i=1}^{n} \sigma_D^i dz_t^i.$$

Note that the shape of the supply curve affects the characteristics of the equilibrium price return process, such as the volatility $\frac{1}{g}\frac{\partial g}{\partial D}\sigma_D$. In the following, we examine this simple supply-demand based model. To facilitate the analysis, following Kanamura (2009), a candidate for the supply curve has the following parametric form:

$$P_t = \left(1 + a\frac{S_t}{c}\right)^{\frac{1}{a}} \quad (a < 0) \tag{23}$$

$$= \exp\left(\frac{S_t}{c}\right) \quad (a = 0), \tag{24}$$

where the scale parameter $c > 0$. That is, the supply curve is given by the inverse Box–Cox transformation, which coincides with the exponential function when the Box–Cox transformation parameter $a = 0$. One can show that if $a < 0$, this inverse Box–Cox transformation supply curve has a larger curvature than the exponential curve. The characteristics are in accordance with energy price–supply relations. Indeed, Kanamura (2009) shows that for the US natural gas market, the inverse Box–Cox transformation supply curve with $a < 0$ fits better than the exponential supply curve. Therefore, the inverse Box–Cox transformation supply curve with the strictly negative parameter $a < 0$ is preferred to the exponential supply curve.

One drawback of the formulation in Equation (23) comes from its mathematical intractability. That is, the inverse Box–Cox transformation has a asymptote above a certain supply level. In order to avoid this problem and similar as before, we reformulate the supply curve as follows. Take $c\tau$ to be greater than the observed supply levels and less than the asymptote. For the negative Box–Cox transformation parameter $a < 0$, we redefine the supply function for S_t less than or greater than $c\tau$ as

$$P_t = \left(1 + a\frac{S_t}{c}\right)^{\frac{1}{a}} \quad (S_t \leq c\tau) \tag{25}$$

$$= \frac{(1+a\tau)^{\frac{1}{a}}}{1-a}\left[\exp\left(\frac{1-a}{1+a\tau}\left(\frac{S_t}{c}-\tau\right)\right) - a\right] \quad (S_t \geq c\tau), \tag{26}$$

where the level, the first derivative, and the second derivative with respect to S for Equation (25) at $c\tau$ are the same as those for Equation (26) at $c\tau$. By construction, $P_t \equiv P(t, S) \in C^2([0, \infty) \times R)$, and hence we can apply Itô's Lemma to this redefined supply curve. We represent the total energy demand D_t as the sum of the two demands C_t and ξ_t following normal and mean reverting processes, respectively. That is,

$$D_t = C_t + \xi_t, \tag{27}$$

$$dC_t = \mu_C dt + \sigma_C dv_t, \tag{28}$$

$$d\xi_t = \kappa(\beta - \xi_t)dt + \sigma_\xi du_t, \tag{29}$$

where $E_t[dv_t du_t] = \rho dt$ and $\mu_C, \sigma_C, \kappa, \beta$, and σ_ξ are constants.

We now have a characterization of the equilibrium price process.[9]

Proposition 2 *Suppose that the supply curve is given by Equations (24) – (26), and , and the demand is given by Equations (27)–(29). Define the new variable $\delta_t = \frac{\kappa}{c}\xi_t$. Then, the equilibrium price for energy satisfies the following equations:*

$$\frac{dP_t}{P_t} = (\mu(\sigma_t) - \delta_t)\frac{\sigma_t}{\sigma}dt + \sigma_t dz_t, \tag{30}$$

$$d\delta_t = \kappa(\alpha - \delta_t)dt + \sigma_\delta du_t, \tag{31}$$

$$\sigma_t = \begin{cases} \sigma P_t^{-a} & (P_t \leq (1+a\tau)^{\frac{1}{a}}) \\ \sigma \frac{1-a}{1+a\tau}\left(1 + \frac{a}{P_t}\frac{(1+a\tau)^{\frac{1}{a}}}{1-a}\right) & (P_t \geq (1+a\tau)^{\frac{1}{a}}), \end{cases} \tag{32}$$

$$E_t[dz_t du_t] = \gamma\, dt, \tag{33}$$

$$\mu(\sigma_t) = \frac{1-a}{2}\sigma\sigma_t + \mu, \tag{34}$$

where $\alpha = \frac{\kappa\beta}{c}$, $\sigma_\delta = \frac{\kappa\sigma_\xi}{c}$, $\sigma = \frac{1}{c\kappa}\sqrt{(\kappa\sigma_C)^2 + (c\sigma_\delta)^2 + 2c\kappa\rho\sigma_C\sigma_\delta}$, $\mu = \frac{\mu_C}{c} + \alpha$, $dz_t = \frac{1}{\sigma}(\frac{\sigma_C}{c}dv_t + \frac{\sigma_\delta}{\kappa}du_t)$, and $\gamma = \frac{\rho\frac{\sigma_C}{c} + \frac{\sigma_\delta}{\kappa}}{\sigma}$. Especially for $a < 0$, σ_t is bounded. Moreover, there exists the solution P_t for Equations (30)–(34).

The transformation of $\delta_t = \frac{\kappa}{c}\xi_t$ implies that the decrease in the storage demand gives rise to the decrease in the convenience yield because both the scale parameter c and the mean reversion parameter κ are positive. Thus, the convenience yield is low when the storage is high, that is, the storage demand is low. This is consistent with the theory of storage as in, for example, Richter and Sorensen (2002). Note that if $a = 0$ in Proposition 2, then the supply curve becomes exponential. Both the drift and volatility terms become constant such that $\mu(\sigma_t) = \frac{1}{2}\sigma^2 + \mu$ and $\sigma_t = \sigma$, respectively, and Equations (30)–(34) collapse to

$$\frac{dP_t}{P_t} = (\mu + \frac{1}{2}\sigma^2 - \delta_t)dt + \sigma\, dz_t, \tag{35}$$

$$d\delta_t = \kappa(\alpha - \delta_t)dt + \sigma_\delta du_t, \tag{36}$$

$$E_t[dz_t du_t] = \gamma\, dt, \tag{37}$$

where $\alpha = \frac{\kappa\beta}{c}$, $\sigma_\delta = \frac{\kappa\sigma_\xi}{c}$, $\sigma = \frac{1}{c\kappa}\sqrt{(\kappa\sigma_C)^2 + (c\sigma_\delta)^2 + 2c\kappa\rho\sigma_C\sigma_\delta}$, $\mu = \frac{\mu_C + \alpha}{c}$, $dz_t = \frac{1}{\sigma}(\frac{\sigma_C}{c}dv_t + \frac{\sigma_\delta}{\kappa}du_t)$, and $\gamma = \frac{\rho\frac{\sigma_C}{c} + \frac{\sigma_\delta}{\kappa}}{\sigma}$. This is the two–factor model of Schwartz (1997). Thus, we call the model in Proposition 2 "An extended Schwartz model."

3 Empirical Analysis of Energy Prices

In Schwartz's (1997) two-factor model, which is obtained by taking $a = 0$ in Equations (30)–(34), the relationship between forward price F and spot price P under the risk neutral probability is given by

$$F(P, \delta, t, T) = P\exp(\Upsilon(t, T) - \Omega(t, T)\delta), \tag{38}$$

where the coefficients $\Upsilon(t, T)$ and $\Omega(t, T)$ are defined by

$$\Upsilon(t, T) = \left(r - \hat{\alpha} + \frac{\sigma_\delta^2}{2\kappa^2} - \frac{\gamma \sigma \sigma_\delta}{\kappa}\right)(T - t) + \frac{1}{4}\sigma_\delta^2 \frac{1 - e^{-2\kappa(T-t)}}{\kappa^3}$$
$$+ \left(\hat{\alpha}\kappa + \gamma \sigma \sigma_\delta - \frac{\sigma_\delta^2}{\kappa}\right) \frac{1 - e^{-\kappa(T-t)}}{\kappa^2}, \tag{39}$$

$$\Omega(t, T) = \frac{1}{\kappa}(1 - e^{-\kappa(T-t)}), \tag{40}$$

with $\hat{\alpha} = \alpha - (\lambda/\kappa)$. Schwartz (1997) applies the Kalman filter method to estimate the model, where both unobservable spot price and convenience yield processes satisfy the time update equations and the measurement update equation. To estimate the extended Schwartz model and test the null hypothesis that the Box–Cox transformation parameter $a = 0$, we employ the extended Kalman filter (EKF) method for the unobserved spot price and the convenience yield processes in Equations (30) and (31) while using the futures-spot relationship of Schwartz (1997) in Equation (38).

Note that whether we accept or reject the standard Schwartz two–factor model depends on the estimate of a: If a is significantly different from zero and negative, then the price model associated with the exponential function is unlikely to be a good approximation, and thus the standard Schwartz two–factor model is rejected. In this case, the extended Schwartz model with the inverse Box–Cox transformation supply curve, which has strictly a larger curvature than the exponential one, is likely to better describe the movement of energy prices. In the following, we empirically investigate the model by using energy futures prices from NYMEX.

3.1 Data

We use closing prices of the futures of natural gas, WTI crude oil, and heating oil quoted at NYMEX. Each futures contract includes six different delivery months ranging from one to six. The data are obtained from Bloomberg. In total, we employ 249 observations covering the period from April 3, 2000, to March 30, 2001.

3.2 Parameter Estimation

To simplify the calculation, we transform the spot price P_t into a new variable x_t such that $x_t = \frac{1}{a\sigma} P_t^a$.[10]

$$dx_t = \frac{1}{\sigma}(\mu - \delta_t)dt + dz_t \qquad (41)$$

To estimate the extended Schwartz model by using the NYMEX energy futures prices, the nonlinearity of x_t should be treated appropriately. We thus apply the EKF.[11] The EKF consists of time and measurement update equations. We discretize the continuous model for x in Equation (41) into the following linear equation:

$$x_t = x_{t-1} - \frac{1}{\sigma}\Delta t \delta_{t-1} + \frac{\mu}{\sigma}\Delta t + \epsilon_{t-1} \equiv f_1(x_{t-1}, \delta_{t-1}, \epsilon_{t-1}). \qquad (42)$$

Similarly, δ in Equation (31) is given by

$$\delta_t = (1 - \kappa \Delta t)\delta_{t-1} + \kappa \alpha \Delta t + \sigma_\delta \eta_{t-1} \equiv f_2(x_{t-1}, \delta_{t-1}, \eta_{t-1}). \qquad (43)$$

These equations represent the linear time update equations in the EKF system. The measurement update equation is obtained from the futures–spot price relationship. We define the log of F_t as the new variable y_t (i.e., $y_t = \ln F_t$), and discretize Equation (38) as follows:

$$y_t = \frac{1}{a}\log(a\sigma x_t) - \Omega(t, T)\delta_t + \Upsilon(t, T) + \xi_t \equiv h_1(x_t, \delta_t, \xi_t) \qquad (44)$$

which represents the nonlinear measurement update equation in the EKF system.

Following Welch and Bishop (2004), time and measurement update equations are expressed by using the matrices

$$\begin{pmatrix} x_t \\ \delta_t \end{pmatrix} = \begin{pmatrix} \tilde{x}_t \\ \tilde{\delta}_t \end{pmatrix} + A_t \begin{pmatrix} x_{t-1} - \hat{x}_{t-1} \\ \delta_{t-1} - \hat{\delta}_{t-1} \end{pmatrix} + W_t \begin{pmatrix} \epsilon_{t-1} \\ \eta_{t-1} \end{pmatrix}, \qquad (45)$$

$$y_t \approx h_1(\tilde{x}_t, \tilde{\delta}_t, 0) + B_t \begin{pmatrix} x_t - \tilde{x}_t \\ \delta_t - \tilde{\delta}_t \end{pmatrix} + V_t \xi_t, \qquad (46)$$

where $\tilde{x}_t = f_1(\hat{x}_{t-1}, \hat{\delta}_{t-1}, 0)$, $\tilde{\delta}_t = f_2(\hat{x}_{t-1}, \hat{\delta}_{t-1}, 0)$,

$$A_t = \begin{pmatrix} 1 & -\frac{1}{\sigma}\Delta t \\ 0 & 1 - \kappa \Delta t \end{pmatrix},$$

$$W_t = \begin{pmatrix} 1 & 0 \\ 0 & \sigma_\delta \end{pmatrix}, B_t = \begin{pmatrix} \frac{1}{a\tilde{x}_t} & -\frac{1}{\kappa}(1 - e^{-\kappa(T-t)}) \end{pmatrix},$$

Table 2.1 EKF time update equations

$\hat{x}_t^- = f_1(\hat{x}_{t-1}, \hat{\delta}_{t-1}, 0)$	(47)
$\hat{\delta}_t^- = f_2(\hat{x}_{t-1}, \hat{\delta}_{t-1}, 0)$	(48)
$\Phi_t^- = A_t \Phi_{t-1} A_t^T + W_t Q_{t-1} W_t^T$	(49)

Table 2.2 EKF measurement update equations

$K_t = \Phi_t^- B_t^T (B_t \Phi_t^- B_t^T + V_t R_t V_t^T)^{-1}$	(50)
$\hat{x}_t = \hat{x}_t^- + K_t(y_t - h_1(\hat{x}_t^-, \hat{\delta}_t^-, 0))$	(51)
$\hat{\delta}_t = \hat{\delta}_t^- + K_t(y_t - h_1(\hat{x}_t^-, \hat{\delta}_t^-, 0))$	(52)
$\Phi_t = (I - K_t B_t) \Phi_t^-$	(53)

$$V_t = 1, Q_t = \begin{pmatrix} \Delta t & \gamma \Delta t \\ \gamma \Delta t & \Delta t \end{pmatrix}, \text{ and } R_t = \text{diag}[m_1, m_2, m_3, m_4, m_5, m_6]$$

Tables 2.1 and 2.2 show the complete set of the EKF equations which include time and measurement update equations so as to calculate the a priori estimate error covariance matrix (Φ_t^-) and the a posteriori estimate error covariance matrix (Φ_t), respectively.

Note that we define the a priori estimation error and the covariance by $e_t^- \equiv \begin{pmatrix} x_t - \hat{x}_t^- \\ \delta_t - \hat{\delta}_t^- \end{pmatrix}$ and $\Phi_t^- \equiv E[e_t^- e_t^{-T}]$, and that we also define the a posteriori estimate error and the covariance by $e_t \equiv \begin{pmatrix} x_t - \hat{x}_t \\ \delta_t - \hat{\delta}_t \end{pmatrix}$ and $\Phi_t \equiv E[e_t e_t^T]$, where K_t is the Kalman gain. Using the recursive updates of time and measurement update equations provided in Tables 2.1 and 2.2, measurement errors ($\tilde{e}_{y_t}$) and the covariance matrices (Σ_t) are given by

$$\tilde{e}_{y_t} = y_t - h_1(\hat{x}_t^-, \hat{\delta}_t^-, 0), \tag{54}$$

$$\Sigma_t = B_t \Phi_t^- B_t^T + V_t R_t V_t^T. \tag{55}$$

Using the measurement errors and the covariance matrices, the parameters (Θ) in Equations (30) and (31) are estimated by the maximum

Table 2.3 Parameter estimates using natural gas futures prices

Parameter	a	σ	μ	κ	α	σ_δ	γ
Estimate	−1.23	0.21	0.00	1.53	−1.30	2.95	0.52
Standard error	0.08	0.04	0.49	0.46	0.21	1.27	0.26

Parameter	λ	m_1	m_2	m_3	m_4	m_5	m_6
Estimate	−3.94	0.0002	0.0014	0.0027	0.0010	0.0001	0.0017
Standard error	0.70	0.0008	0.0002	0.0012	0.0003	0.0017	0.0002
Loglikelihood	3.71×10^3						
AIC	-7.40×10^3						
SIC	-7.42×10^3						

likelihood method:

$$\hat{\Theta} = \arg\min_{\Theta} \sum_{t=1}^{N} \ln|\Sigma_t| + \sum_{t=1}^{N} \tilde{e}_{y_t} \Sigma_t^{-1} \tilde{e}_{y_t}^T, \qquad (56)$$

where $\Theta = (a, \sigma, \mu, \kappa, \alpha, \sigma_\delta, \gamma, \lambda, m_1, m_2, m_3, m_4, m_5, m_6)$.

We examine the natural gas market first and estimate the model parameters for natural gas futures daily prices at NYMEX by using the EKF–based maximum-likelihood estimation (MLE). The results are presented in Table 2.3. They demonstrate that the estimated Box–Cox transformation parameter a is negative (−1.23) and statistically significant with a standard error of 0.08. This implies that the supply curve of natural gas has much larger curvature than the exponential function would allow. It also implies that the extended Schwartz model with a non-exponential inverse Box–Cox transformation supply function fits better than the standard (i.e., exponential) Schwartz model. In addition, the correlation coefficient γ is statistically significant and positive. This implies that the correlation between convenience yield and price, that is, volatility is positive. This result supports the theory of storage (e.g., Telser, 1958) which states that the convenience yield can be interpreted as timing option.

Similarly, we estimate the model parameters for WTI crude oil and heating oil futures daily prices of the NYMEX. The results are given in Tables 2.4 and 2.5, respectively. The estimated Box–Cox transformation parameters (a) for WTI crude oil and heating oil are again statistically significant and negative (−1.00 and −0.77). Thus, for both energy markets, the extended Schwartz model associated with a non-exponential inverse Box–Cox transformation supply function is likely to

Table 2.4 Parameter estimates using WTI crude oil futures prices

Parameter	a	σ	μ	κ	α	σ_δ	γ
Estimate	−1.00	0.04	0.20	2.64	−0.54	1.38	0.67
Standard error	0.00	0.00	0.00	0.00	0.00	0.00	0.00

Parameter	λ	m_1	m_2	m_3	m_4	m_5	m_6
Estimate	−2.18	0.000230	0.000010	0.000010	0.000010	0.000010	0.000010
Standard error	0.00	0.000001	0.000006	0.000004	0.000028	0.000000	0.000010
Loglikelihood	6.39×10^3						
AIC	-1.27×10^4						
SIC	-1.28×10^4						

Table 2.5 Parameter estimates using heating oil futures prices

Parameter	a	σ	μ	κ	α	σ_δ	γ
Estimate	−0.77	0.04	0.17	0.07	−1.24	1.27	0.37
Standard error	0.00	0.00	0.05	0.02	0.03	0.02	0.01

Parameter	λ	m_1	m_2	m_3	m_4	m_5	m_6
Estimate	−0.42	0.00071	0.00000	0.00003	0.00000	0.00027	0.00180
Standard error	0.02	0.00012	0.00001	0.00001	0.00001	0.00003	0.00017
Loglikelihood	4.83×10^3						
AIC	-9.64×10^3						
SIC	-9.66×10^3						

fit the data better than the standard (i.e., exponential) Schwartz two-factor model.

4 Conclusion

This chapter reviewed an energy pricing model based on Kanamura (2009) and Kanamura and Ōhashi (2007b), in which energy prices are determined by supply and demand and which is referred to as "a supply- and demand-based energy pricing (SDEP) model." We showed that the supply curve shape in the SDEP model determines the characteristics of the volatility in energy prices, which is in a sharp contrast to reduced–type energy price models. It was demonstrated that the inverse Box–Cox transformation supply curve reflecting energy markets causes an inverse leverage effect, that is, positive correlation between energy prices and volatility. The SDEP model was also used to show that an existing (G)ARCH–M model has its foundations in the supply-demand relationship for energy products. We showed that the SDEP model nests Schwartz (1997)'s two-factor model as a special case, for which the supply curve is given by an exponential function.

Using futures prices of natural gas, WTI crude oil, and heating oil traded at NYMEX, we estimated the extended Schwartz model and tested whether the exponential supply curve is consistent with the data. The results rejected the null hypothesis that the supply functions are exponential for all three markets, and thus showed that all three energy commodity prices require the price model to include supply curves that have a larger curvature than the exponential function. Thus, the extended Schwartz model associated with a non-exponential inverse Box–Cox transformation supply function is likely to fit the data better than the standard Schwartz two-factor model that corresponds to a special example of the extended Schwartz model with an exponential supply function.

Notes

1. Views expressed in this chapter are those of the author. All remaining errors are mine. The author thanks Toshiki Honda, Ryozo Miura, Izumi Nagayama, Nobuhiro Nakamura, Marcel Prokopczuk, and in particular Kazuhiko Ōhashi for their helpful comments.
2. We assume that $c\tau$ is an extremely high supply level that is not reached in reality.
3. Otherwise, that is, if a is positive, there does not exist the problem of this asymptote. Thus, in the whole supply region, $P_t = (1 + a\frac{S_t}{c})^{\frac{1}{a}}$ holds.

4. Recall the expression of σ_t and $1 + a\tau > 0$, then σ_t is monotonically increasing with respect to P_t and bounded such as $\sigma_t \leq \lim_{P_t \to \infty} \sigma_t = \sigma \frac{1-a}{1+a\tau}$.
5. We examine σ_t for $P_t \leq (1 + a\tau)^{\frac{1}{a}}$, because the price level in reality is almost included in this region. However, σ_t for $P_t \geq (1 + a\tau)^{\frac{1}{a}}$ also represents the inverse leverage effect, as we will later explain.
6. The one–factor SDEP model is partly categorized as a constant elasticity of variance (CEV) model because the volatility term is expressed as $\sigma_t = \sigma P_t^{-a}$. The remarkable point is that the CEV model parameter a has an economic interpretation such that a represents the curvature of the supply curve.
7. We focus on the price region $P_t \leq (1 + a\tau)^{1/a}$ for the supply curve and σ_t, because the price in reality is almost included in this region.
8. Since energy is often used for heating or cooling, it is well known that demand for energy is related to temperature. Recalling that temperature is often modeled using an Ornstein–Uhlenbeck (OU) process, we employ the following process for demand:

$$dD_t = (\mu_D - \lambda_D D_t)dt + \sigma_D dw_t. \tag{57}$$

We obtain the AR(1) model by transforming the continuous time model for the demand as in Equation (57) to the discrete equivalent. Note that the mean reversion of the demand restricts the coefficient to $0 \leq 1 - \lambda_D \leq 1$ in general.
9. The proof is in the Appendix of Kanamura and Ōhashi (2007b).
10. The empirical studies assume that $P_t \leq (1 + a\tau)^{\frac{1}{a}}$ holds for the data.
11. See, for example, Welch and Bishop (2004).

References

Barlow, M. T. (2002). A diffusion model for electricity prices. *Mathematical Finance*, 12(4):287–298.

Bollerslev, T. (1986). Generalized autoregressive conditional heteroskedasticity. *Journal of Econometrics*, 31(4):307–327.

Brennan, M. J. (1991). The price of convenience and the valuation of commodity contingent claims. In Lund, D. and Oksendal, B., editors, *Stochastic Models and Option Models*, volume 3, chapter 3, pages 127–150. North Holland, Amsterdam.

Cox, J. (1975). Notes on option pricing I: Constant elasticity of variance diffusions. Technical report, Stanford University (reprinted in *Journal of Portfolio Management*, 1996, 22: 15–17).

Deaves, R. and Krinsky, I. (1992). Risk premiums and efficiency in the market for crude oil futures. *The Energy Journal*, 13(2):93–117.

Duffie, D., Gray, S., and Hoang, P. (1999). Volatility in energy prices. In Kaminski, V., editor, *Managing Energy Price Risk*, volume 2, chapter 3, pages 273–289. Risk Publications, London.

Emanuel, D. and MacBeth, J. (1982). Further results on the constant elasticity of variance call option pricing model. *Journal of Financial and Quantitative Analysis*, 17(4):533–554.

Engle, R. (1982). Autoregressive conditional heteroscedasticity with estimates of the variance of united kingdom inflation. *Econometrica*, 50(4):987–1007.

Engle, R., Lilien, D., and Robins, R. (1987). Estimating time varying risk premia in the term structure: The Arch-M model. *Econometrica*, 55(2):391–407.

Eydeland, A. and Wolyniec, K. (2003). *Energy and Power Risk Management: New Developments in Modeling, Pricing, and Hedging*. John Wiley & Sons, Inc., Hoboken, NJ.

Gibson, R. and Schwartz, E. (1990). Stochastic convenience yield and the pricing of oil contingent claims. *Journal of Finance*, 45(4):959–976.

Heston, S. (1993). A closed-form solution for options with stochastic volatility with applications to bond and currency options. *The Review of Financial Studies*, 6(2):327–343.

Kanamura, T. (2009). A supply and demand based volatility model for energy prices. *Energy Economics*, 31(5):736–747.

Kanamura, T. and Ōhashi, K. (2007a). A structural model for electricity prices with spikes: Measurement of spike risk and optimal policies for hydropower plant operation. *Energy Economics*, 29(5):1010–1032.

Kanamura, T. and Ōhashi, K. (2007b). A supply and demand based energy price model: An extension of Schwartz model. in *Proceedings of the 15th Nippon Finance Association Annual Meeting*, 344–353.

Kolos, S. P. and Ronn, E. I. (2008). Estimating the commodity market price of risk for energy prices. *Energy Economics*, 30(2):621–641.

Pindyck, R. S. (2004). Volatility in natural gas and oil markets. Technical report, Massachusetts Institute of Technology.

Pirrong, C. and Jermakyan, M. (2008). The price of power: The valuation of power and weather derivatives. *Journal of Banking and Finance*, 32(12):2520–2529.

Richter, M. and Sørensen, C. (2002). Stochastic volatility and seasonality in commodity futures and options: The case of soybeans. Technical report, Copenhagen Business School.

Schwartz, E. S. (1997). The stochastic behaviour of commodity prices: Implication for valuation and hedging. *Journal of Finance*, 52(4):923–973.

Telser, L. G. (1958). Futures trading and the storage of cotton and wheat. *Journal of Political Economy*, 66(3):233–255.

Welch, G. and Bishop, G. (2004). An introduction to the Kalman filter. Technical report, University of North Carolina at Chapel Hill.

3

Joint Dynamics of American and European Oil Prices

Gamze Celik, Karl Frauendorfer, and Florentina Paraschiv

1 Introduction

1.1 Motivation and Objectives

Since 2002, the oil market has experienced a sustained increase in price, in response to the fast growth in economic activity. This surge in oil prices has been accompanied by high volatility—oil prices have steadily risen from a minimum of $17/bbl in 2001 to $145/bbl in July 2008, and then dramatically dropped to $40/bbl during the financial crisis of 2008 and recovered again to a level of $100/bbl in 2012. This price behavior indicates that the oil market is characterized by high vulnerability to shocks and significant uncertainties regarding future oil price developments. According to Fan and Xu, 2011, the oil market has undergone significant changes since 2000 and can be characterized by the following two features: First, petroleum has become a global commodity, with world oil markets gradually unifying into a global market. Second, oil markets are becoming more and more related to the macroeconomic and financial markets, known as the financial attribute of petroleum. Given the important role of crude oil in the world economy, it is important to understand the stochastic process underlying the prices.

In this chapter, we address the dynamics of daily oil prices and returns during the period from January 3, 2000, to August 31, 2012. The dynamics of the two crude oil markets are of interest, namely West Texas Intermediate (WTI) and Brent. These international oil benchmarks are reference crudes for the American and European market, respectively.

Due to its relatively higher quality, WTI was more likely to trade at a premium to Brent in the past. However, in early 2011, WTI began to sell at a large discount to Brent and it continued to widen during the year, mainly due to transportation bottlenecks near Cushing, Oklahoma, the trading hub for WTI. The current WTI discount is wider than previous ones and seems to persist. Due to this recent dislocation of WTI, doubts have been cast on the benchmark status of this crude oil.

Based on the above specifications, the aim of this chapter is twofold: First, we will employ generalized autoregressive conditional heteroscedasticity (GARCH) models, with multivariate extensions, to capture the volatility characteristics and co-movements of the two crude oil markets. Second, we shall investigate their long- and short-term relationship in more detail in the context of the cointegration analysis and vector error correction models (VECM).

There has been a growing theoretical and empirical literature devoted to the study of oil. We try to contribute to this growing research by introducing a new set of data. This additional data are of importance to understand if the strong historical relationship between these benchmarks still exists or if the prices in these different geographical markets have been decoupled. Moreover, this study solely focuses on a detailed analysis of American and European oil markets without taking into account other benchmarks with their own geographical characteristics.

The structure of this chapter is as follows. In Subsection 1.2 we discuss the existing literature related to oil markets. In Section 2 we discuss market fundamentals and show the various structural breaks that have marked oil prices over time. In Section 3 we show a descriptive analysis of the data. In Sections 4 and 5 we discuss the results of the empirical part of our study, based on a multivariate GARCH analysis and cointegration. Finally, Section 6 concludes the chapter.

1.2 Literature Overview

There has been a growing theoretical and empirical literature devoted to the study of oil markets. In this section, we will give a summary of recent and major studies dealing with modeling of oil price volatility using GARCH models and the globalization–regionalization hypothesis of crude oil markets.

Modeling Oil Price Volatility Using GARCH Models

There exist a large number of empirical studies that have investigated different issues of oil price volatility and examined various aspects of the characteristics of these markets. Overall, the empirical findings suggest that time series of crude oil prices contain unit roots. Oil returns have excess kurtosis, are negatively skewed, follow a fat tail distribution and are characterized by volatility clustering, asymmetry and mean reversion, and thus show similar characteristics to other financial time series (Bina and Vo, 2007; Mohammadi and Su, 2010; Gileva, 2010; Salisu and Fasanya, 2012). In addition, oil price dynamics are characterized by high volatility, high intensity jumps, and strong upward drift (Askari and Krichene, 2008).

The GARCH model and its various variants are one of the most widely used specifications in the empirical literature on modeling oil price volatility (Hou and Suardi, 2012). According to Hou and Suardi (2012), the use of such models is mainly focused on the evaluation of their forecasting performance (Day and Lewis, 1993; Morana, 2001; Fong and See, 2002; Sadorsky, 2006; Agnolucci, 2009; Cheong, 2009; Kang et al., 2009; Vo, 2009; Mohammadi and Su, 2010; Wei et al., 2010; Hou and Suardi, 2012) and their application to value-at-risk (VaR) estimations (Cabedo and Moya, 2003; Sadeghi and Shavvalpour, 2006; Aloui and Mabrouk, 2010). In the multivariate framework, GARCH models account for volatility spillover effects between markets, and the calculation of optimal portfolio weights and hedge ratios (Haigh and Holt, 2002; Lanza et al., 2006; Jalali-Naini and Kazemi-Manesh, 2006; Chang et al., 2009, 2010, 2011; Jin et al., 2012).

Kang et al. (2009) conclude that the CGARCH and FIGARCH models are more appropriate for modeling and forecasting persistence in the volatility of crude oil prices compared to simple GARCH and IGARCH models. More recently, Hou and Suardi (2012) show that the out-of-sample volatility forecast of the nonparametric GARCH model yields better performance compared to an extensive class of parametric GARCH models. Salisu and Fasanya (2013) analyze daily WTI and Brent returns from 1986 to 2012 and model their volatility process by estimating GARCH(1,1), GARCH-M(1,1), TGARCH(1,1) and EGARCH(1,1) with structural breaks. They detect two structural changes in 1990 and 2008, which correspond to the Iraq–Kuwait conflict and the global financial crisis, respectively. Gileva (2010) and Salisu and Fasanya (2012) conclude that the asymmetric GARCH models appear superior to the symmetric ones in dealing with oil price volatility.

There are also many empirical studies devoted to the volatility of crude spot, forward and futures returns in the multivariate framework. Lanza et al. (2006) apply multivariate conditional volatility models and find that dynamic conditional correlations can vary dramatically. Chang et al. (2009) estimate four multivariate volatility models, namely CCC, DCC, VARMA-GARCH, and VARMA-AGARCH, for the spot, forward, and futures returns of Brent, WTI, and Dubai for the time period 1991–2008 and examine volatility spillovers to aid risk diversification in crude oil markets. They find volatility spillovers and asymmetric effects on the conditional variances for most pairs of series. Jin et al. (2012) employ a VAR-BEKK model to investigate crude oil markets' integration using daily data from 2005 to 2011 for WTI, Dubai and Brent futures contracts. They find evidence that Brent and Dubai are highly responsive to market shocks, whereas WTI shows the least responsiveness of the three benchmarks. This finding creates questions about its predominance as a benchmark crude oil.

As also stated by Salisu and Fasanya (2012), modeling oil price volatility is more and more gaining prominence in the literature. There are different dimensions emerging to provide useful insights into the appropriate framework for dealing with oil price volatility. This study contributes to this growing research by introducing basic volatility models in the multivariate setting in order to capture the dynamics in oil prices.

1.2.1 Globalization versus Regionalization of Crude Oil Markets
The statistical relationship among different crude oil prices and the question of a unified world oil market has been examined by different empirical studies.

Bentzen (2007) analyzes the crude oil prices of Brent, OPEC, and WTI during 1988–2004. He finds bi-directional causality among these crude oil prices and rejects the regionalization hypothesis, while simultaneously casting doubt on the benchmark role of Brent and WTI. Using a copula approach, Reboredo (2011) finds evidence that the crude oil markets of WTI, Brent, Dubai, and Maya are linked with the same intensity during bull and bear markets, and thus are unified between 1997 and 2010. Almadi and Zhang (2011) find a cointegration relationship between WTI, Brent, Dubai, and Oman during 1990–2010 and also support the globalization hypothesis of world oil markets. Hammoudeh et al. (2008) analyze four oil benchmark prices, namely WTI, Brent, Dubai, and Maya, over the period 1990–2006. They find a long-run equilibrium relationship between these different benchmarks but identify an asymmetric adjustment process in long-run equilibrium. Moreover, they cast some doubts on the leadership and benchmark position of WTI. The changing status of the WTI benchmark over time is also investigated by Kao and Wan (2012). They conclude that the rising inventories in Cushing significantly deteriorate WTI's benchmark role.

Milonas and Henker (2001) find evidence that the two oil markets, Brent and WTI, during 1985–1991 are not fully integrated. Fattouh (2010) applies a two-regime threshold autoregressive process to the crude oil price differentials between seven types of crude oil, using weekly data from 1997 to 2008. There is strong evidence of threshold effects in the adjustment process to the long-run equilibrium. His findings suggest that crude oil prices are linked, but not necessarily integrated in every time period. The changing benchmark role of WTI is also reinforced by Fattouh (2010). Liao et al. (2012) examine the price differentials between WTI, Brent, and Dubai by applying the quantile unit root test for the period 1997–2011. They suggest that these markets are still generally cointegrated so that globalization still exists in the world oil market from the co-movement of these three benchmark prices, although each of them has deviated due to regionalization. Regarding the benchmark role of WTI, doubts about its benchmark status are expressed by Bentzen (2007), Hammoudeh et al. (2008), Kaufmann and Ullman (2009), and Kao and Wan (2012).

Overall, there seems to be a general consensus of empirical findings, which supports the hypothesis of globalization, that is, unified world crude oil markets. However, recent studies question the benchmark role of WTI. Based on the existing literature about co-movements of world oil markets, we will adopt the approach of globalization–regionalization solely on the American and European markets. Cointegration analysis will be used for this purpose. We will investigate the long-term historical relationship as well as the continued divergence between Brent and WTI after 2010.

2 Fundamentals of Crude Oil

The market value of a specific grade of crude oil depends essentially on two quality features, namely its viscosity (thickness or density) and its sulfur content. Density is usually measured by API[1] degrees, whereby crude oil with high API has a low density, referred to as light crude. Crude oil is classified as sweet and sour on the basis of its sulfur content. Crude oil is considered sour (sweet) when oil has a total sulfur level greater (lower) than 0.5%. In general, heavy oils tend to be sour and light oils tend to be sweet (Fattouh, 2010; Geman, 2005).

Because of the high diversity of crude oils, the industry has been able to concentrate on a limited number of reference qualities, so that buyers and sellers usually price the crude at a discount or a premium to particular benchmarks, both for physical and derivatives trading (Fattouh, 2010; Geman, 2005). We will focus on the following two major benchmarks in the world of international trading today:

- West Texas Intermediate (WTI), delivery point Cushing, Oklahoma, gravity 39.6 API, 0.24% sulfur content, traded at the New York Mercantile Exchange (NYMEX).
- Brent blend, the reference crude oil for the North Sea, gravity 38.06 API, 0.37% sulfur content, traded at ICE Futures Europe.

These two benchmarks are used as references in their respective areas (Geman, 2005). WTI is a benchmark reflective of supply and demand issues in the American Midwest, while Brent is a European benchmark reflective of specific European issues with slightly higher exposure to regions such as Africa and the Middle East (Jenkins, 2012).

Both are light sweet crude oils but WTI is generally sweeter and lighter than its European counterpart. Because of the different quality characteristics and marine and pipeline transportations cost, WTI historically (2000–2010) carries about ± $5/bbl average premium over Brent (EIA, 2012b). An increase in the premium can occur when crude oil was in short supply in the Midwest, where most WTI is refined (EIA, 2011).

2.1 History of Crude Oil Prices

The international oil market has undergone significant changes since 2000 and has been characterized by steep rise and high volatility. There are two increasingly clear characteristics (Fan and Xu, 2011):

- The globalization trend of petroleum markets has been strengthening. Petroleum has become a global commodity, driven by booming international trade and the information technology revolution, so that world oil markets have been gradually unifying into a global market.
- Oil markets are becoming increasingly related to macroeconomic and financial markets, exhibiting a financial attribute. Oil prices are no longer fully subject to the impact of the supply and demand relationship but are increasingly interconnected with other financial markets. Much of the oil trade has been conducted through financial markets, participating in oil deals not for use but for profit-making. These activities in turn exacerbate the market's volatility.

The time series of WTI and Brent daily prices (in $/bbl) from 2000 to 2012 are shown in Figure 3.1.[2] According to Fan and Xu (2011) the oil market mechanism has undergone two significant adjustments since 2000, corresponding to two structural breaks in March 2004 and June 2008. The first breakpoint was mainly caused first by strong oil demand resulting from the rapid growth of the world economy, and second by the large amounts of speculative funds pouring into the futures market since 2003. The second breakpoint was caused by the outbreak of the financial crisis and forced the oil market to undergo a major readjustment (Fan and Xu, 2011). Moreover, WTI and Brent crude oil prices closely tracked each other prior to 2010, with WTI generally having a slight premium

JOINT DYNAMICS OF OIL PRICES   49

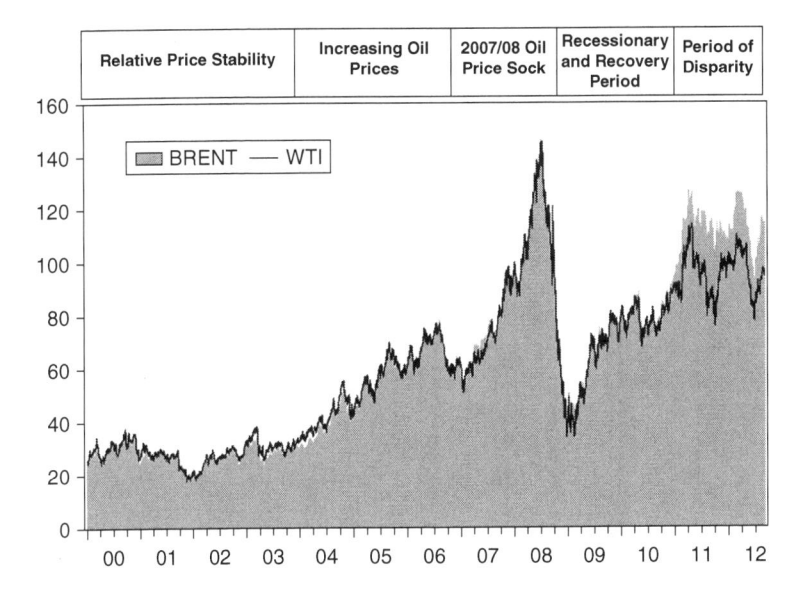

Figure 3.1 Brent and WTI daily crude oil prices from 03/01/2000 to 31/08/2012.

over Brent. In late 2010 and into 2011, prices began consistently to diverge.

In order to analyze the main drivers of the price movements of WTI and Brent, we split the whole sample period from 2000 to 2012 into five sub-periods according to Izzard et al. (2010): a period of relative price stability (2000–2003), a period of increasing oil prices (2004–2006), the 2007/2008 oil price shock period, the subsequent recessionary and recovery period (2009–2010), and lastly, the period of disparity between WTI and Brent crude oil prices (2011–2012).

The next section deals with each of the subperiods in detail and reviews the drivers and events that influenced oil prices during each subperiod. This analysis is mainly conducted from the perspective of the American market, that is, WTI prices. If not mentioned explicitly, price indications in the following sections refer to WTI prices, which are close to Brent prices until 2010 and therefore also valid for the European oil market.

2.1.1 Period of Relative Price Stability (2000–2003)
Between January 2000 and December 2003, there was a period of relative price stability in the oil market. WTI and Brent prices varied only around $5 above or below $30/bbl. OPEC's considerable spare production capacity is one way to explain this period's stability, as it helped to stabilize oil prices into a range that was acceptable for most cartel members (Izzard et al.,

2010). The invasion of Iraq was one of the main events occurring in this period. Moreover, after the September 11, 2001, attacks, there was slow economic growth, lower oil demand, and falling prices.

The implications of the repeal of the US Glass-Steagall Act in 1999 for world oil prices would not become evident until 2004 (Izzard et al., 2010).[3] This issue will be discussed in more detail further below.

2.1.2 Period of Increasing Oil Prices (2004–2006)

Starting in 2004, the price of WTI, which averaged only $34/bbl in January 2004, rose steadily. In August and September 2005, hurricane Katrina and Rita caused severe damage to offshore oil and natural gas rigs, pipelines and onshore oil refineries in the Gulf of Mexico (Izzard et al., 2010). Oil prices briefly increased up to $70/bbl at the end of August 2005 and then fell back to $60/bbl at the end of October 2005. During the Israel–Lebanon war of July 2006, oil prices reached on average $74/bbl. In December 2006 oil prices averaged $62/bbl and then fell briefly below $55/bbl in January 2007 because of the mild winter. After each peak, oil prices seemed to retreat temporarily then returned to higher peaks (Askari and Krichene, 2008).

In the opinion of the OECD/IEA (2008), the surge in oil prices since the end of 2003, and especially since the beginning of 2007, can legitimately be described as an "oil shock," albeit a slow-motion one. The run-up in oil prices in the mid-2000s was mainly caused by the sharp rise in oil demand from China and other Asian developing nations, due to their continuing strong economic growth (OECD/IEA, 2008; Izzard et al., 2010). China's GDP growth rates, as an example, averaged 10 percent per year between 2000 and 2008. Starting in 2004, this high demand from Asia attracted financial investors to the oil market, because oil was seen as underpriced. This can be called the "financialization" of oil markets, which will be discussed in more detail in the next section.

In summary, it can be said that oil price dynamics during 2002–2006 were characterized by high volatility, implying big uncertainties regarding future price developments, strong upward drift and high intensity jumps, indicating that oil markets were vulnerable to shocks. The price developments were concomitant with underlying fundamentals of the oil markets and the world economy, namely pressure on oil prices resulting from rigid crude oil supply and expanding world demand for crude oil (Askari and Krichene, 2008).

2.1.3 Period of 2007/2008 Oil Price Shocks (2007–2008)

This period can be described as the most volatile period in the history of oil prices, as the volatility was characterized by sharp increases in price, followed by equally sharp declines (Izzard et al., 2010). After January 2007, the price resumed its upward path and reached an intra-day peak of over $145/bbl in July 2008, which is an all-time record.

Hamilton (2009a,b) has reviewed a number of theories regarding the causes of high oil prices in summer 2008. He mentions three key features (Hamilton, 2009b): the low price elasticity of demand, the strong growth in demand from China, the Middle East, and other newly industrialized economies, and the failure of global production to increase. Taken together this means that this price run-up was caused by strong demand confronting stagnating world production (Hamilton, 2009a). According to the OECD/IEA (2008), the upward pressure on price had been magnified by geopolitical factors, including civil strife in Nigeria and worries over Iran's nuclear program. The decline in the value of the US dollar also played a role in the oil spike of 2007/2008, so that oil prices have been bid up partly to hedge against the fall in the value of the US dollar (OECD/IEA, 2008). In July 2008, at the time of oil price peak, the US dollar had fallen to a value of only 0.63 Euros (Izzard et al., 2010). All these factors explain the initial strong pressure on prices that may have triggered commodity speculation in the first place (Hamilton, 2009b).

The oil price increases and declines of 2007/2008 may be magnified and influenced by the growing financial investment in the oil futures market. As discussed in Medlock and Jaffe (2009), the proportion of noncommercial[4] trading increased sharply beginning in 2003, and accelerated through 2008. The share of noncommercial players averaged approximately 20 percent of contracts in the oil futures markets in the early 2000s. In 2008, however, this dramatically increased to more than 55 percent of trading activity, which coincided with the peak in crude oil prices (see Figure 3.1). The effect of this growing "financialization" of the oil market, which is likely to have contributed to increased oil price fluctuations, is most pronounced in the period of 2007–2008 (Izzard et al., 2010).

There have been many studies, examining the relationship between oil prices and speculation. Cifarelli and Paladino (2010), Kaufmann and Ullman (2009), and Kaufmann (2011), for example, show that speculation has played a significant role in the surge of oil prices. According to Sauer (2012), "these prices were completely artificially effectuated by futures trading on an unimagined and unprecedented scale by financial institutions which had been liberated from all meaningful consequences of restraints by the removal of the Glass-Steagall Act in 1999." However, in the opinion of the OECD/IEA (2008), the role of speculation, and the emergence of oil as an "asset class" for investors, remain unclear due to lack of information on the real financial flows into the oil market. Also Fattouh et al. (2012) do not find evidence of an important role of speculation in driving the price of oil after 2003. The International Monetary Fund (IMF) shares this view and states in the World Economic

Outlook from September 2011 that recent research does not provide strong evidence of obvious destabilizing effects of the commodity market "financialization"(IMF, 2011).

Fattouh (2010) has reviewed the main theoretical and empirical evidence on the relationship between speculative flows and oil prices. His findings are that there is no analysis of broader aspects related to speculation, so that there is no consensus on this issue. On the one hand, the current commodity boom is explained by fundamentals such as strong demand, low inventory and spare capacity, and adverse supply shocks. On that view, financial investors cannot systematically drive oil prices. Others are of the opinion that the oil market has been distorted by substantial and volatile passive investments that caused a bubble in oil prices (Fattouh, 2010).

In mid-September 2008 prices had fallen back substantially to around $100/bbl. This sudden drop in oil prices, in the absence of any obvious major shift in demand or supply, lends support to the argument that financial investors may have amplified the impact (OECD/IEA, 2008).

2.1.4 Recessionary and Recovery Period (2009–2010)

Collapses in US housing prices, the failure of many financial institutions under the weight of bad debt and a dramatic decline in the stock and commodity market are main characteristics of the 2008–2009 global recession.[5] The recession caused a reduction in oil demand in many sectors including transportation, manufacturing and construction (Izzard et al., 2010). While the world oil demand was 86.2 Mb/d in 2008, it dropped by 1.3 Mb/d to 84.9 Mb/d in 2009 (OECD/IEA, 2010). The OECD countries accounted for the most pronounced oil demand declines. In addition, oil demand growth in key emerging economies, such as China and the Middle East, slowed considerably (OECD/IEA, 2010).

The oil price collapse in late 2008 and early 2009 was mainly due to this weak oil demand caused by the recession. In July 2008, the daily oil price peaked at $145/bbl. By late December 2008, however, the price declined to a low of only $35/bbl.

In October 2009, the IMF stated in the World Economic Outlook that the global recession appeared to be ending but announced that the recovery would be weak by historical standards, with continued credit constraints and slow employment growth (IMF, 2009). According to Izzard et al. (2010), there are four main measures that have caused world crude oil prices to recover:

- In Fall 2008, OPEC announced 4.2 Mb/d of production cuts, which were the largest cuts in the history of the organization, to respond to falling oil prices and weak oil demand.

- Moreover, an oil price target of $70 to $80/bbl for a barrel of crude oil was announced. At that target price, the budgets of most OPEC member countries would be balanced.

As the global economy recovered, there was an increase in world oil. IMF estimated the global economic growth at 3.0% in 2010 because of recent stimulus measures (IMF, 2009). The crude oil price averaged $85/bbl in April 2010, mainly due to the abovementioned factors. This is more than double the low price of December 2008 and the prices remained in the range of $70 and $85/bbl until the end of 2010. OPEC's high spare capacity since 2009 possibly had a stabilizing effect on oil prices, signaling that there was enough oil to deal with possible supply disruptions (Izzard et al., 2010), such as the BP *Deepwater Horizon* oil spill that followed the explosion of offshore oil-drilling platform in the Gulf of Mexico in April 2010 caused short-term supply disruptions in the US Gulf (Jin et al., 2012).

2.1.5 Period of Disparity (2011–2012)

In 2011, the crude oil markets sustained high price levels. Brent averaged $111/bbl and marked the first time the global benchmark averaged more than $100/bbl for a year. The average price of WTI in 2011 was $95/bbl, up $15/bbl from 2010, reflecting a discount to the Brent crude oil price, despite representing a higher quality. Historically, the differential between the prices of Brent and WTI, referred to as the Brent–WTI spread, ranged from about ± $5/bbl. However, in early 2011 different factors caused the price of WTI to decline vs. Brent, increasing the spread from around $4/bbl in early 2011 to $24/bbl on average in September 2011 (EIA, 2012a,b).

The price increases in 2011 marked the highest crude oil prices since 2008 and reflected tightness in the global crude oil market beginning in 2010 (EIA, 2012a). According to EIA (2012a), key factors affecting crude oil prices in 2011 included:

- *Arab Spring:* The Arab Spring and the civil war in Libya affected oil markets during the first half of 2011. In late February, when protests in Libya intensified, prices quickly escalated. The market coped with the loss of 1.5 Mb/d of exports from Libya. This is the reason the price of Brent increased by $15/bbl from mid-February to the beginning of March. This sudden supply loss challenged the ability of the OECD producers, with low spare production capacity, to provide incremental supplies to an already tight market.
- *Demand:* Growing demand for petroleum products in emerging markets, particularly China and the Middle East, also led to increasing crude oil prices in 2011. Even with declining OECD country

demand in 2011, overall global demand rose by 1.2% (1.1 Mb/d), just as the market was coping with the loss of Libyan exports.
- *Transportation Bottlenecks:* In the first half of 2011, WTI could not match Brent's price strength and became dislocated from the global crude oil market. The main reasons were transportation bottleneck issues in the US Midwest, the main market for WTI, to the refineries on the Gulf Coast. In September 2011, the premium of Brent to WTI reached a record average level of $24/bbl. Between October and December the premium fell, ending the year with $10/bbl, most likely as a result of signs that transportation constraints out of the US Midwest were easing. However, the price spread did not narrow in 2012 and increased to an average of about $19/bbl in August 2012, still wide by historical standards.

These recent price developments give us reason to further investigate the relationship between these two major benchmarks and analyze the price spread in more detail. In Subsection 2.2 we will also give a short-term outlook for crude oil prices.

2.2 The Brent–WTI spread

Prices of various crude oils may evolve independently for a period of time but their movements are unlikely to deviate very widely (Fattouh, 2010). After all, crude oil prices are linked through the cost-of-carry relationship, so that any deviation from this relationship would be restored through arbitrage. These dynamics especially hold for crude oils of similar quality and with liquid futures market such as the Brent-WTI relationship (Fattouh, 2010). More specifically, Brent and WTI are linked by the following relationship (Alizadeh and Nomikos, 2004):

$$P_{BR,t} + C_{BR} + D = P_{WTI,t} \qquad (1)$$

P_{BR} and P_{WTI} are the prices of dated Brent (BR) and WTI at time t, C_{BR} represents the carrying costs that are necessary to transport the physical Brent against WTI futures and include insurance, losses, custom duty costs, and the pipeline tariff. D is the quality discount, which is usually 0.30 cents. If the WTI-Brent price differential, after having adjusted for carrying costs, is greater than zero, refiners in the United States would increase their imports of Brent and those crude oils priced off Brent.[6] This transatlantic arbitrage window would remain open until the price relationship in the Equation (1) is attained, which would happen quite speedily because of the highly liquid futures market in Brent and WTI

(Alizadeh and Nomikos, 2004; Fattouh, 2010). Arbitrage opportunities may arise due to the existence of regional supply and demand imbalances, regulatory changes or market distortions created by participants with large positions and seasonal shortages (Alizadeh and Nomikos, 2004; Milonas and Henker, 2001).

Since early 2011, however, high inventory levels at Cushing, Oklahoma, the trading hub for WTI, have been a symptom of transportation constraints that have resulted in WTI trading at a discount relative to Brent (EIA, 2012d). In September 2011, the premium of Brent to WTI reached a monthly average high of about $24/bbl, making about 30 percent of the price of WTI. In August 2012, the price difference fell back to around $19/bbl, making about 20 percent of the price of WTI. In the past, for example in May 2007 and February 2009 (see Figure 3.2), similar price differences have occurred for brief periods. However, the current widening of the WTI price discount to Brent[7] is unusual in its scope and duration (EIA, 2011).

The WTI discount to Brent is attributed to logistics' constraints at Cushing, caused by a historic change in US crude supply sources (Fielden, 2012a). Increased crude oil production from US tight oil plays, particularly from the Williston Basin in North Dakota, and the startup of the TransCanada Cushing Extension (Keystone Phase 2) pipeline in February 2011, which allowed greater volumes of Canadian crude oil to be moved into Cushing, resulted in high crude surpluses. Crude oil inventories in

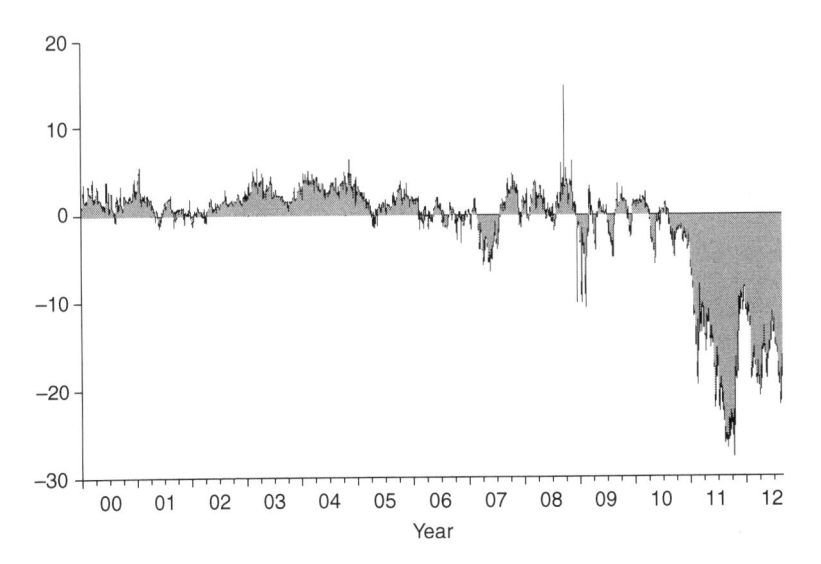

Figure 3.2 Absolute price delta (WTI-Brent) in $/bbl.

Cushing began to rise because there were few pipelines currently available to move this new volume of crude, which exceeded the Midwest refining capacity, from Cushing to the large refining complexes on the US Gulf Coast (EIA, 2012b; Fielden, 2012a). This surplus exerted downward pressure on WTI prices while Gulf Coast refiners, unable to source lower-priced domestic crude, were paying higher Brent-related prices for imports (Fielden, 2012a). The price effects of such logistical bottlenecks are widespread, given the major role of WTI in the pricing of US domestic crude, imported oil into the US and global financial markets (Fattouh, 2011).

Looking at weekly data, Figure 3.3 shows the Brent minus WTI spread (dashed line, left axis) and the growing stockpile at Cushing (solid line, right axis) since July 2010. The Brent-WTI differential started to rise a few months before the TransCanada pipeline was completed, from an average $3/bbl in December 2010 to an average $14/bbl in February 2011 (EIA, 2012b). In September 2011, the WTI discount reached a high of about $24/bbl on average. To relieve a stockpile of crude at Cushing, the reversal of the 150'000-barrel-per-day (bbl/d) Seaway pipeline between Cushing and the Gulf Coast was announced in December 2011, which contributed to a decline in the Brent-WTI spread to an average of $9/bbl in December 2011. The WTI discount rose back to $18/bbl by March 2012, as it became clear that the Seaway reversal would be insufficient to clear the bottleneck between Cushing and the US Gulf Coast (EIA, 2012b). Since then,

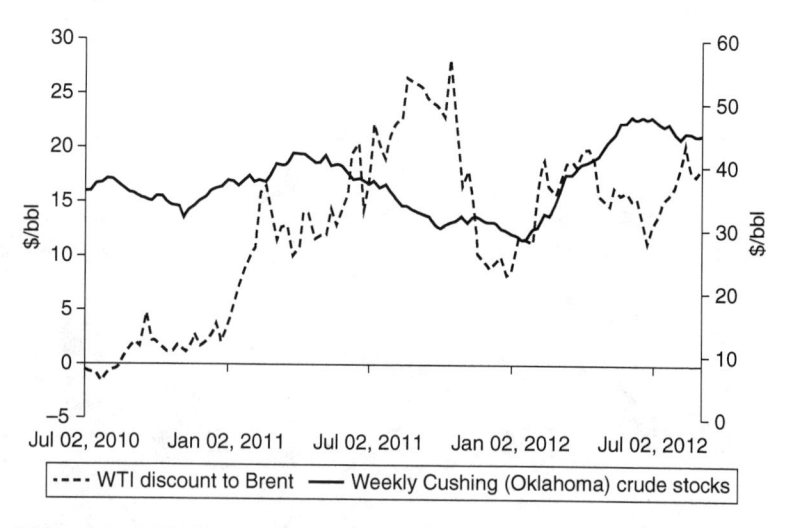

Figure 3.3 WTI discount to Brent compared with weekly Cushing crude stocks. Data source for weekly Cushing crude stocks: EIA.

the weekly average Brent-WTI spread has ranged from $14/bbl to $18/bbl. This means that from early 2011 up to August 2012, the WTI discount to Brent did not fall below $10/bbl, except for this brief period in December 2011, and Cushing inventories reached record levels between January and July 2012. According to OPEC's monthly oil market report of November 2012, this behavior was a result of differing pressures affecting the two benchmarks (OPEC, 2012):

- Brent: Escalating Middle East tensions and the physical shortage of Brent crude in the North Sea because of an overall decline in production in the region, seasonal maintenance, and persistent problems at the Buzzard oil field are main factors affecting Brent.
- WTI: Besides growing US shale oil production, which has pushed US oil output to an estimated 9.7 Mb/d in 2012, its highest level in over 24 years, planned and unplanned outages of a number of US refineries also negatively affected WTI.

In the absence of sufficient outlets to US coastal refining markets, WTI is currently disconnected from world markets, so that international events have far more impact on Brent than they do on WTI, causing the two crude oil benchmarks to trade further apart when Brent prices rise (Fielden, 2012b). All the same, the Brent-WTI spread is expected to drop to about $9/bbl by the end of 2013 according to EIA, as a number of factors will contribute to easing the supply glut at Cushing-US. As new Cushing–U.S. Gulf Coast pipelines are built and existing pipelines expanded, crude supply and demand in Cushing should be balanced, while supplying the Gulf Coast with additional crude. The Seaway pipeline was expected to expand its capacity from 150,000 bbl/d to 400,000 bbl/d by early 2013 and then to 850,000 bbl/d by mid-2014. In late 2013, TransCanada's Gulf Coast Pipeline project is expected to add between 700,000 and 830,000 bbl/d of capacity from Cushing to the Gulf Coast (EIA, 2012b).

The Brent-WTI spread, although expected to narrow, is likely to persist, due to ongoing constraints in infrastructure combined with rising crude production from US shale fields. On the other hand, the strengthening of Brent, driven by a continued decline in the mature North Sea fields, combined with growing Asian demand for North Sea grades as well as Brent-like crudes from West Africa, will support a continuation of the Brent premium over WTI (OPEC, 2012). On the other hand, Brent has been in steady backwardation since the beginning of 2011, boosting investors' returns, gaining roll yield by holding Brent contracts and rolling them over. This makes the European oil benchmark superior to its US counterpart, which has been in contango since 2008 (Hosp, 2012). It remains to be seen whether there will be a reversal to historical trends and whether the recent period was just a parenthesis (Chevillon and Rifflart, 2009).

2.3 The Role of WTI and Brent as Global Benchmarks

The answer to the question "What is the price of oil?" used to be easy: whatever was the cost of WTI or Brent. Both benchmarks provided a good proxy for global prices. As the world produces hundreds of different crude streams, this simplification proved to be good enough. However, this is no longer the case. The boom in North American oil production on the back of the shale and oil sands revolution, coupled with a lack of pipeline capacity, has created a series of regional gluts that are distorting the price of oil. Government, companies and investors rely on benchmarks for planning purposes and the wrong benchmark could lead to poor investments. This is why the distortions are important (Blas, 2012).

Because of the frequent dislocations of WTI from other major benchmarks, the usefulness of the WTI benchmark in pricing crude oil has been increasingly debated in the world oil market (Kao and Wan, 2012). This behavior in price differentials is not an indication that the WTI market is not reflecting fundamentals. On the contrary, price movements are efficient reflections of the local supply and demand conditions in Cushing. However, when local conditions become dominant, the WTI price can no longer reflect the supply and demand balance in the United States or in the world. Thus, WTI no longer acts as a useful international benchmark for pricing crude oil for the rest of the world (Fattouh, 2011). According to Kao and Wan (2012), the ability of WTI in reflecting market conditions decreased sharply and WTI's efficiency in processing information has been surpassed by Brent's since the second half of 2004. Thus, they give evidence that WTI had lost its place as a pricing center for years and support the opinion prevailing in markets that WTI benchmark has broken down. This weakening in WTI's status as a global benchmark led some oil-consuming and oil-producing companies to shift to other benchmarks. In the opinion of Hammoudeh et al. (2008), however, the broken benchmark phenomenon for WTI is transitory and can occur sporadically, particularly if the pipeline logistics are solved. On the other side, production volumes for the Brent basket are declining, leading to concerns regarding its own robustness as a benchmark (Dunn and Holloway, 2012).

3 Descriptive Analysis

The empirical analysis is based on 3,305 daily observations from the generic light sweet crude oil futures based on the WTI traded at the

NYMEX (ticker CL1) and Brent traded on ICE Futures Europe (ticker C01). The data are sampled from January 3, 2000, to August 31, 2012, and are obtained from Bloomberg. The daily closing prices of the first-nearby-month futures contracts have been used for this purpose.

This section analyzes the daily returns for Brent and WTI. Crude oil price returns (r_t) are computed on a continuous compounding basis by taking the logarithm of the ratio of two consecutive days' closing prices. The Brent and WTI sample returns display similar statistical properties. The sample means of the two return series are quite small in comparison to the standard deviations. Oil price returns display a very high volatility as the 2.247 percent and 2.455 percent daily standard deviation for Brent and WTI, respectively are turned into 35.662 percent and 38.977 percent annual volatility with 252 trading days, whereas the volatility for returns on the WTI crude oil price is slightly higher than for Brent. Both series display negative skewness statistics, with slightly higher value for the Brent return series, signifying that the series has a longer tail to the left (extreme losses) than to the right (extreme gains). The excess kurtosis, which shows the peakedness of the two distributions, is 2.928 and 4.362 for Brent and WTI, respectively. It indicates a leptokurtic distribution, which is a consequence of both a majority of observations peaking around the mean and a few extremely large returns (positive and negative) creating fatter tails than the normal distribution. The Jarque-Bera test statistics of crude oil returns in each market are statistically significant, thereby suggesting that the distributions of these returns are not normal, as also evidenced by a high excess kurtosis and negative skewness.

As shown in Figure 3.1, Brent and WTI oil prices move in the same pattern, implying high contemporaneous correlation. However, the pattern they follow is rather uneven. Oil prices have experienced one major crisis during our sample period, which is the financial crisis in 2008. This event is clearly visible in the effect on prices and returns. Moreover, the recent price boom stretching from 2002 up to the end of 2008 is another interesting feature of the data. Figure 3.4 presents the plot of Brent and WTI crude oil returns and the quantile-to-quantile plots (QQ-plot) for both return series against the quantiles of a normal distribution. As we can see from the time series plots of Brent and WTI crude oil returns, there is a strong evidence of volatility clustering in the returns series (McNeil et al., 2005).

The intensity of clustering increased during the financial turmoil around 2008, so volatility is clearly not constant. The QQ-plots for the return series against the Gaussian distribution confirm the fat tails and nonnormality of the return series. As shown in Figure 3.5, the ACF of the squared returns are all positive and highly significant, revealing high positive autocorrelation. This is explained by the fact that large (small) returns

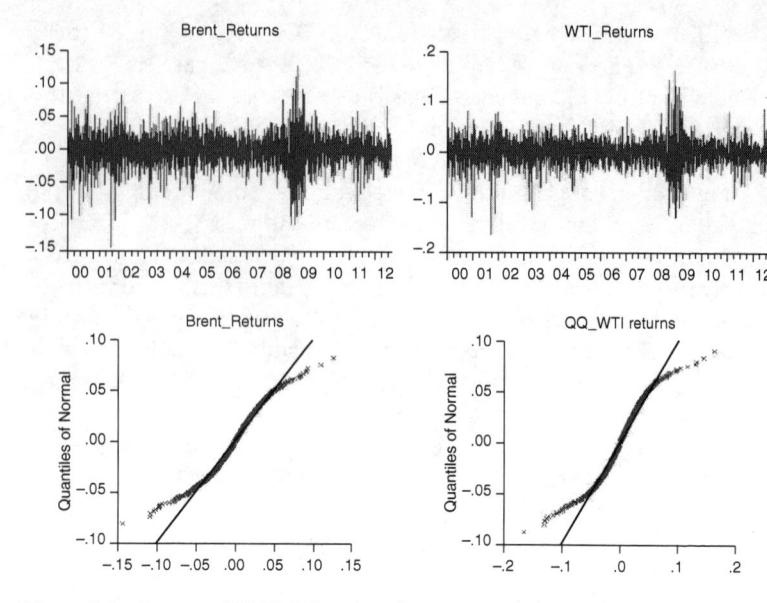

Figure 3.4 Brent and WTI daily prices, log returns and QQ-plots.

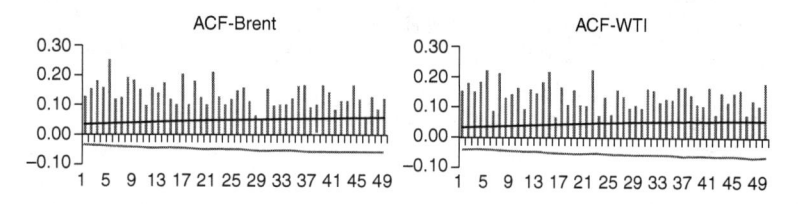

Figure 3.5 Autocorrelation function of the squared residuals.

tend to be followed by large (small) returns (Hafner, 2011) and reflect the volatility clustering pattern. The *p*-values of the Ljung-Box *Q*-statistics for serial correlation for the returns and squared returns are reported for lags 1–5, 10, and 15 in Table 3.1. The *Q*-statistic is often used as a test of whether the series is white noise, with the null hypothesis that there is no autocorrelation up to order k (EViews 7, 2010a). For Brent returns, the null hypothesis of no serial correlation can be rejected at the 1 percent significance level up to all lags considered. For lag 1 of the WTI series, we cannot reject the null of no autocorrelation. However, for higher lags up to lag 4, the null can be rejected at the 5 percent significance level and up to lag 15 at the 1 percent significance level. Squared returns of both series reject the null of no serial correlation at all significance levels for all lags considered.

Table 3.1 Ljung–Box Q-statistics (p-values) for daily returns and daily squared returns

	Returns		Squared Returns	
Lag	Brent	WTI	Brent	WTI
Q(1)	0.003	0.170	0.000	0.000
Q(2)	0.010	0.023	0.000	0.000
Q(3)	0.007	0.023	0.000	0.000
Q(4)	0.004	0.021	0.000	0.000
Q(5)	0.000	0.002	0.000	0.000
Q(10)	0.000	0.004	0.000	0.000
Q(15)	0.000	0.006	0.000	0.000

One of the most prominent tools that has emerged for characterizing changing variances is the GARCH model and its various extensions, as conventional time series and econometric models operate under an assumption of constant variance (Bollerslev, 1986; Engle and Bollerslev, 1986). Since such GARCH-class models address the phenomenon of volatility clustering, they are very appealing approaches for the analysis of high-frequent time series (Oberndorfer, 2009). In Section 4, we will introduce this class of conditional volatility models and model the volatility process of the Brent and WTI return series in the bivariate setting. Furthermore, above findings give us a motivation for more rigorous testing of cointegration and the possibility of establishing error correction models.

4 Multivariate GARCH Processes

The purpose of this section is to estimate multivariate conditional volatility models, namely the constant conditional correlation (CCC) model and the BEKK model of Baba, Engle, Kroner, and Kraft, for the return series of Brent and WTI. These models capture the dynamics of variance and covariance over time (Chevallier, 2012; Silvennoinen and Terasvirta, 2009). Our main interest here is to identify cross-innovations and volatility spillover effects between American and European markets and to investigate the persistence of shocks over time.

The main difficulty encountered with MGARCH models is to find an appropriate system that describes the dynamics of the conditional covariance matrices parsimoniously while maintaining flexibility, since the number of parameters in an MGARCH model often increases rapidly with the dimensions of the model. Another aspect that has to be taken into account in the specification is imposing positive definiteness of the conditional covariance matrices (Chevallier, 2012; Silvennoinen and Terasvirta, 2009).

4.1 Theoretical Background

We consider N time-series of return innovations $\{X_{i,t}, i = 1, ..., N\}$ and stack these innovations into a vector X_t, with $\sigma_{ii,t} = \text{var}\left(X_{i,t}|\mathfrak{F}_{t-1}\right)$ and $\sigma_{ij,t} = \text{cov}\left(X_{i,t}, X_{j,t}|\mathfrak{F}_{t-1}\right) = \Sigma_t$, where $\mathfrak{F}_{t-1}$ denotes the history of the process up to time $t-1$ and Σ_t is the conditional variance-covariance matrix of all the time series (Chevallier, 2012).

The stochastic vector process (X_t) with dimension $N \times 1$ is said to be a MGARCH process, if it is strictly stationary and satisfies equations of the form (McNeil et al., 2005):

$$X_t = \sum_t^{\frac{1}{2}} Z_t, \tag{2}$$

where Z_t is an i.i.d. vector error process and $\Sigma_t^{\frac{1}{2}}$ is the Cholesky factor of a positive-definite matrix $\sum_t$ which is measurable with respect to the history of the process up to time $t-1$.

The conditional covariance matrix Σ_t in a MGARCH model is equivalent to the squared volatility σ_t^2 in a univariate GARCH model. We can write $\Sigma_t = D_t P_t D_t$, where $D_t = diag\left(\sigma_{t,1}, ..., \sigma_{t,N}\right)$ is a diagonal matrix known as the volatility matrix and P_t is the conditional correlation matrix. When building MGARCH models it is important to specify the dependence of Σ_t (or of D_t and P_t) on the past in such a way that the Σ_t always remains symmetric and positive definite (McNeil et al., 2005).

What remains to be specified is the matrix process $\sum_t$. While in the BEKK model the conditional covariance matrix is modeled directly, the CCC model is built on the idea of modeling the conditional variances and correlations, instead of directly modeling of the conditional covariance matrix (Silvennoinen and Terasvirta, 2009). As a next step, these two models are explained.

4.1.1 The CCC model of Bollerslev (1990)

The first model we are going to present is a relatively parsimonious model where the conditional correlation matrix P_t is assumed to be constant for all t. The process X_t is a $CCC - GARCH(p, q)$ process if the conditional covariance matrix is of the form $\sum_t = D_t P_c D_t$, where

(i) P_c is a constant, positive-definite correlation matrix; and

(ii) D_t is a diagonal volatility matrix with elements $\sigma_{t,k}$ satisfying

$$\sigma_{t,k}^2 = \omega_{k0} + \sum_{i=1}^{pk} \alpha_{ki} X_{t-i,k}^2 + \sum_{j=1}^{qk} \beta_{kj} \sigma_{t-j,k}^2, \qquad k = 1,...,N \quad (3)$$

where $\omega_{k0} > 0, \alpha_{ki} \geq 0, \beta_{kj} \geq 0$ (McNeil et al., 2005).

The CCC-GARCH model defined earlier is well defined in the sense that Σ_t is almost surely positive definite for all t, since all the N conditional variances are assumed to be positive and P_c is assumed to be positive definite. Moreover, this model is covariance stationary if and only if $\Sigma_{i=1}^{pk} \alpha_{ki} + \Sigma_{j=1}^{qk} \beta_{kj} < 1$ for $k = 1,...,N$ (Hafner, 2011; McNeil et al., 2005).

As can be seen from the above specification, the individual conditional variances can be defined by univariate GARCH models, so that the CCC–GARCH model represents a simple way of combining univariate GARCH processes (McNeil et al., 2005).

A criticism of the model is the assumption that the conditional correlations are constant in this model, which is unrealistic and too restrictive. It is often observed in financial time series that correlations between series increase in turbulent periods (Bauwens et al., 2006; Hafner, 2011; McNeil et al., 2005). An extension of the CCC model is the dynamic conditional correlation (DCC) model introduced by Engle (2002), which allows for time-varying conditional correlations. However, we leave this modeling approach for further research.

4.1.2 The BEKK model of Baba, Engle, Kroner, and Kraft (Engle and Kroner, 1995)

The process X_t is a BEKK process if the conditional covariance matrix Σ_t satisfies (Chevallier, 2012; McNeil et al., 2005):

$$\Sigma_t = CC' + \sum_{i=1}^{pk} A'_{ki} X_{t-i} X'_{t-i} A_{ki} + \sum_{j=1}^{qk} B'_{kj} \Sigma_{t-j} B_{kj}, \qquad k = 1,...,N \quad (4)$$

where A_{ki}, B_{kj}, and C are $N \times N$ matrices, and C the lower triangular to ensure the positive definiteness of Σ_t, provided that CC' is positive definite. k is an integer, defining the generality of the model.

The BEKK model is covariance stationary if and only if the eigenvalues $\Sigma_{i=1}^{pk} A_{ki} \otimes A_{ki} + \Sigma_{j=1}^{qk} B_{kj} \otimes B_{kj}$ are less than one in modulus, where $\otimes$ denotes the Kronecker product of two matrices (Silvennoinen and Terasvirta, 2009).

The advantage of this model is that its construction ensures the positive definiteness of Σ_t without the need for further conditions (McNeil et al., 2005). However, the estimation procedure involves heavy computations because of several matrix inversions. The number of parameters is quite large, given by $(p+q)KN^2 + \frac{N(N+1)}{2}$ in the full BEKK model (Silvennoinen and Terasvirta, 2009). To reduce this number and, as a consequence, to reduce the generality, a diagonal BEKK model can be imposed, where A_i and B_j are diagonal matrices (Bauwens et al., 2006). The number of parameters in the diagonal model is given by $(p+q)KN + \frac{N(N+1)}{2}$ (Silvennoinen and Terasvirta, 2009). With $N=2, K=p=q=1$, this results in 11 parameters in the full BEKK model but (only) seven parameters in the diagonal one. The diagonal BEKK model is covariance stationary if $A_{ii}^2 + B_{jj}^2 < 1$.

4.2 Model Setup

The specification of the mean equation is important, since the conditional mean parameters enter the conditional variance specification through the residuals, although the GARCH parameters do not affect the conditional mean (Bauwens et al., 2006). Given the stationarity of the return series, we can use the bivariate vector autoregressive (VAR) model to estimate the conditional mean equations for Brent and WTI returns. The residuals are then used to estimate the multivariate conditional volatility models.

The VAR model has been chosen because it is easy to estimate and works well in many of the financial and econometric applications (Chevallier, 2012; McNeil et al., 2005). The VAR(p) model is given by the following equation (Tsay, 2010):

$$r_t = c + A_1 r_{t-1} + \cdots + A_p r_{t-p} + \epsilon_t, \tag{5}$$

where in our case r_t is a 2×1 vector of returns for Brent and WTI, A_i are 2×2 coefficient matrices for $i = 1, ..., p$ and ϵ_t is a two-dimensional vector of innovations with mean zero and time-invariant positive definite covariance matrix Σ.

The optimal lag length for the unrestricted VAR has been selected by using the AIC, BIC and Hannan-Quinn (HQ) information criteria by allowing a maximal lag number of 8. The results are presented in Table 3.2.

While the AIC and HQ show an optimal lag order of 7, the BIC selects a lag length of 1. Since a lag length of 1 would be insufficient in order to model the dynamics of Brent and WTI return series, we estimate a

Table 3.2 VAR optimal lag length selection for Brent and WTI

Lag	0	1	2	3	4	5	6	7	8
AIC	−10.5566	−10.5717	−10.5763	−10.5808	−10.5810	−10.5817	−10.5844	**−10.5914**	−10.5904
BIC	−10.5529	**−10.5606**	−10.5578	−10.5549	−10.5477	−10.5410	−10.5363	−10.5359	−10.5275
HQ	−10.5553	−10.5677	−10.5697	−10.5715	−10.5691	−10.5672	−10.5672	**−10.5716**	−10.5679

Note: Bold marked numbers indicate lag order selected by the criterion.

VAR(7) model. The estimated parameters and the robust standard errors are reported in Table 3.3, together with the diagnostic tests.

From the results of the VAR(7) model, we can conclude that each return series is negatively impacted by its own lags and positively influenced by lags from the other series, if there is any significance. We can infer that there is positive dependence structure between these two markets, with the Brent lag returns having a slightly higher impact on the WTI series than vice-versa. Moreover, the negative influence of the Brent lag on its own series is slightly higher than the impact of the WTI lag returns on its own series.

The results of the diagnostic tests reveal that there is no autocorrelation left in the residuals. This means that the VAR(7) model is able to remove the serial correlation present in the residuals of Brent and WTI. However, there is significant autocorrelation in the two series of squared residuals. Therefore, we will apply MGARCH models for further analysis. This will be done by fitting a MGARCH model to the residuals of the VAR(7) model for the Brent and WTI variables, assuming multivariate t innovations.

4.3 Empirical Results

This section presents the estimation results of the VAR(7)-CCC and VAR(7)-diagonal BEKK models.[8] The results for the VAR(7)-CCC model are summarized in Table 3.4.

All parameters of this model are significant at the 1 percent level and the positive definiteness of the covariance matrix Σ_t is provided, since the conditional correlation matrix P_t is positive definite. Moreover, the model satisfies the condition for covariance-stationarity.

The CCC model also detects the high degree of persistence present in the return series. The very high correlation value of 0.902 indicates high interaction between these two markets. The sum of the ARCH and GARCH parameters is very close to 1, so that we cannot reject an infinite unconditional variance with certainty. The reason for this behavior is the fat tails present in the data, also indicated by the high kurtosis value. A diagnostic test for this model will be discussed in Section 4.4, when we compare it to the diagonal BEKK model.

The assumption of constant conditional correlation is not realistic, so we have also implemented the diagonal BEKK model. The estimates of the diagonal BEKK model, together with the conditional variance and covariance equations, are given in Table 3.5. The estimated parameters of the diagonal BEKK model are all significant at the 1 percent level. As we have seen already, the conditional variances are functions of their own lags and lagged shocks and the conditional covariances depend on

Table 3.3 VAR(7) estimation results and diagnostic tests for Brent and WTI

	Estimation Results			Diagnostic tests	
	BRENT_RET	WTI_RET		BRENT_RET	WTI_RET
C	0.000502 (0.00039)	0.000396 (0.00043)			
BRENT_RET(−1)	−0.126557*** (0.03254)	0.026080 (0.03559)			
BRENT_RET(−2)	−0.00933 (0.03282)	0.078890** (0.03590)			
BRENT_RET(−3)	0.027465 (0.03289)	0.123345*** (0.03597)			
BRENT_RET(−4)	−0.0231 (0.03297)	0.007610 (0.03606)	Log(L)	7858.781	7563.302
BRENT_RET(−5)	−0.04323 (0.03291)	0.001577 (0.03599)	Q(10)	0.881	0.871
			Q(15)	0.420	0.683
			Q(20)	0.479	0.624
BRENT_RET(−6)	0.000449 (0.03283)	0.067584* (0.03591)	Q2(10)	0.000	0.000
			Q2(15)	0.000	0.000
BRENT_RET(−7)	−0.090586*** (0.03252)	−0.0116 (0.03557)	Q2(20)	0.000	0.000
			AIC	−4.758	−4.579
WTI_RET(−1)	0.080891*** (0.02978)	−0.04758 (0.03257)	BIC	−4.730	−4.551
WTI_RET(−2)	−0.00144 (0.02994)	−0.100444*** (0.03274)	JB	1083.157	2123.166
WTI_RET(−3)	0.001051 (0.03005)	−0.074592** (0.03287)			
WTI_RET(−4)	0.058318* (0.03011)	0.015156 (0.03294)			
WTI_RET(−5)	−0.00486 (0.03004)	−0.0484 (0.03285)			
WTI_RET(−6)	−0.0026 (0.02993)	−0.081223** (0.03274)			
WTI_RET(−7)	0.080156*** (0.02974)	−0.0086 (0.03253)			

Note: Log(L) is the logarithm maximum likelihood function value. Q() and Q2() are the p-values of the Ljung–Box Q-statistics of the corresponding order computed on the standardized residuals and squared standardized residuals, respectively. ***, **, * denote significance at the 1%, 5% and 10% level, respectively. Standard errors are in parentheses.

Table 3.4 VAR(7) – CCC estimates

Parameter	Estimate
GARCH parameters	
ω_{Brent}	0.000*** (0.000)
ω_{WTI}	0.000*** (0.000)
α_{Brent}	0.052*** (0.008)
α_{WTI}	0.049*** (0.008)
β_{Brent}	0.936*** (0.008)
β_{WTI}	0.936*** (0.009)
$\alpha_{Brent} + \beta_{Brent}$	0.988
$\alpha_{WTI} + \beta_{WTI}$	0.985
Correlation parameters	
$\rho_{Brent,WTI}$	0.902*** (0.004)

Note: *** indicates significance at the 1% level. Standard errors are in parentheses.

Table 3.5 VAR(7) – diagonal BEKK estimates

Parameter	Estimate
GARCH parameters	
C_{Brent}	0.000*** (0.000)
C_{WTI}	0.000*** (0.000)
A_{Brent}	0.282*** (0.014)
A_{WTI}	0.294*** (0.014)
B_{Brent}	0.945*** (0.005)
B_{WTI}	0.938*** (0.005)
Covariance parameters	
$C_{Brent,WTI}$	0.000*** (0.000)
Conditional variance and covariance equations	
$GARCH1 = 0.000 + 0.079 * RESID1(-1)^2 + 0.893 * GARCH1(-1)$	
$GARCH2 = 0.000 + 0.087 * RESID2(-1)^2 + 0.879 * GARCH2(-1)$	
$COV1\_2 = 0.000 + 0.083 * RESID1(-1) * RESID2(-1) + 0.886 * COV1\_2(-1)$	

Note: *** indicates significance at the 1% level. Standard errors are in parentheses.

the lagged covariances and lagged cross-products of the shocks. Looking at the conditional variances, the ARCH parameters are slightly higher, and the GARCH parameters slightly lower compared to the CCC model for both time series. This means that there is a higher contribution of lagged innovations and a lower contribution of lagged variances. The conditional covariance equation indicates that the lagged cross-products of the shocks increase the covariance between the Brent and WTI series by 8.3 percent and the past covariance has a weight of 88.6 percent. The sum of the ARCH and GARCH effects from the estimates of the conditional variances and covariances is close to one (Brent = 0.972;

WTI = 0.966), giving covariance stationarity but with high volatility persistence.

Overall, these results regarding the CCC and diagonal BEKK model applied on Brent and WTI return series are in line with the findings of Chang et al. (2011). The performance of this model will be assessed in Section 4.4.

4.4 Model Comparison

We compare the two applied MGARCH models, namely the CCC and the diagonal BEKK model, to each other. These models differ in the way the conditional covariance matrix is estimated, whereby the CCC assumes constant conditional correlations.

Table 3.6 summarizes the results of the diagnostic tests. The VAR(7) – diagonal BEKK model is clearly preferred to the VAR(7) – CCC model, since it is able to remove more of the autocorrelation present in the squared standardized residuals.[9] For the Brent series, the null hypothesis of no serial correlation cannot be rejected for the considered lags at any significance level. However, for the WTI series very little autocorrelation can be removed in the squared residuals but still slightly more than with the VAR(7) – CCC model. Moreover, the diagonal BEKK model is able to

Table 3.6 Diagnostic tests for the CCC and diagonal BEKK model

Diagnostics	VAR(7)–CCC		VAR(7)–diag BEKK	
	Brent	WTI	Brent	WTI
Q(10)	0.977	0.082	0.926	0.207
Q(15)	0.986	0.194	0.980	0.266
Q(20)	0.952	0.140	0.957	0.262
Q2(10)	0.000	0.000	0.705	0.006
Q2(15)	0.000	0.000	0.798	0.004
Q2(20)	0.000	0.000	0.805	0.012
Log(L)	18617.62		18726.91	
AIC	−11.2876		−11.3539	
BIC	−11.2691		−11.3354	
ν	3.727*** (0.209)		4.122*** (0.240)	

Note: ν is the degree of freedom for the Student's t distribution. Log(L) is the logarithm maximum likelihood function value. Q() and Q2() are the p-values of the Ljung-Box Q-statistics of the corresponding order computed on the standardized residuals and squared standardized residuals, respectively. *** indicates significance at the 1% level.

remove more of the autocorrelation present in the standardized residuals than the CCC model. The log likelihood value and the AIC and BIC information criteria confirm the outperformance of the VAR(7)-diagonal BEKK model.

Because of the autocorrelations still present in the squared residuals, we have further investigated the stability of the two MGARCH models by following a similar approach to Kramer and Ploberger (1992) and Chevallier (2012). The cumulated sums (CUSUM) and the squares of the cumulated sums have been plotted to test for the presence of structural changes in the components of the MGARCH models (see Figure 3.6). The CUSUM plots show a downward trend, while the squares of the CUSUM exhibit an upward trend. The Brent series displays two major jumps: one in 2008, at the time of the financial crisis, and the other one in 2011, when the decoupling of the Brent and WTI series began. Overall, the fluctuation processes stay within reasonable bounds, so that the two MGARCH models can be seen as stable.

Additionally, the likelihood ratio test[10] has been applied to support our finding that the diagonal BEKK is preferred to the CCC model. The likelihood ratio statistic yields a value of 218.58 (p-value: 0.000) and reveals that the CCC model is rejected at any significance level in favor of the unrestricted diagonal BEKK model. This means that there is insufficient statistical evidence in support of the CCC model. The diagonal BEKK adequately explains the variability in the return series when compared to the more restricted CCC model. Figure 3.7 depicts the estimated conditional variances and the conditional covariances from the two MGARCH models. The CCC and diagonal BEKK conditional variances and covariances between the two time series show an almost perfect match, with the diagonal BEKK generating higher estimates during the volatile periods. This means that the diagonal BEKK gives a higher weight to new information than the CCC model. The diagonal BEKK model is clearly preferred to the CCC model. This result is not surprising, since the assumption of a constant conditional correlation is too restrictive, as discussed already.

The conditional variance and correlation for Brent and WTI returns obtained from the preferred diagonal BEKK model with Student t innovations are shown in Figure 3.8. The phenomenon of volatility clustering is clearly evident in both return series. Moreover, the conditional variance estimate of WTI is much higher compared to Brent, throughout almost the whole sample period. This means that WTI is more responsive to market shocks than Brent, which enforces its position as a leading benchmark for crude oil pricing. According to Jin et al. (2012) and Kaufmann (2011), the volatility spikes are mainly caused by an increase in fundamental uncertainty and speculative behavior in crude oil futures markets.

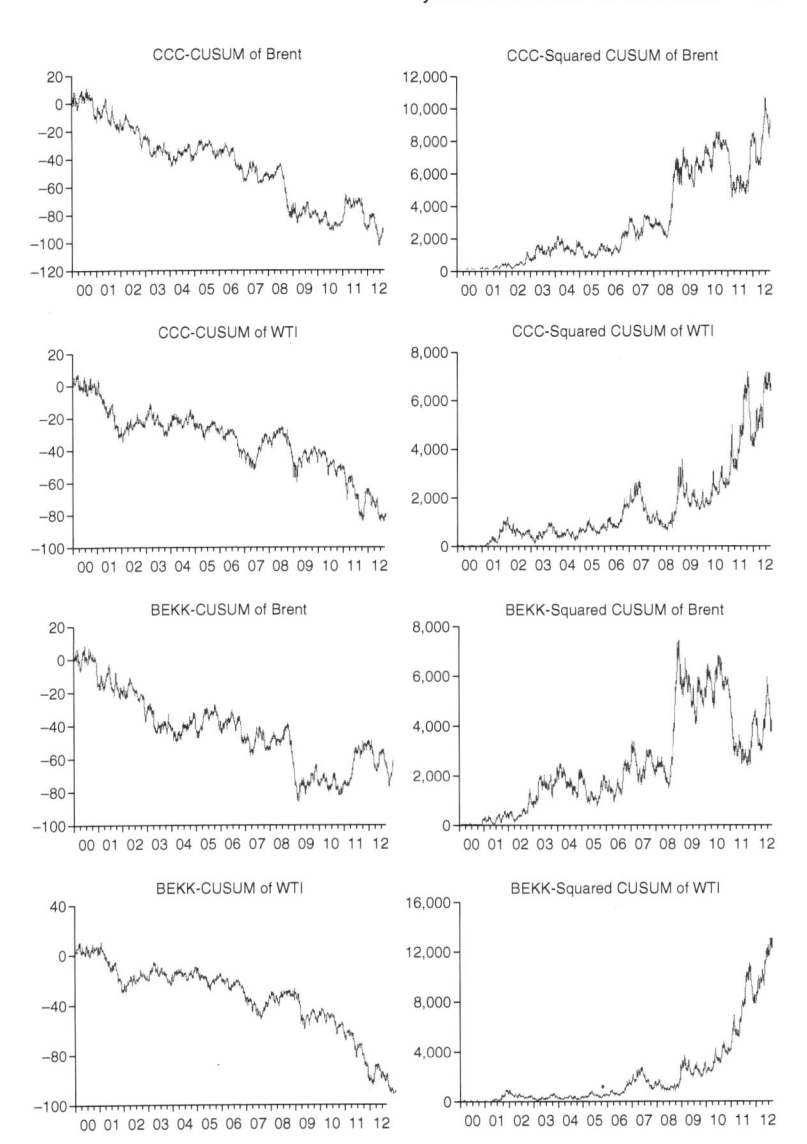

Figure 3.6 CU.S.UM tests for MGARCH models.

The conditional correlation between the benchmarks is rather high, with somewhat severe variations. However, the increased volatility correspondingly causes the disconnections between markets, and thus downward spikes occur in the conditional correlation between WTI and Brent (Jin et al., 2012).

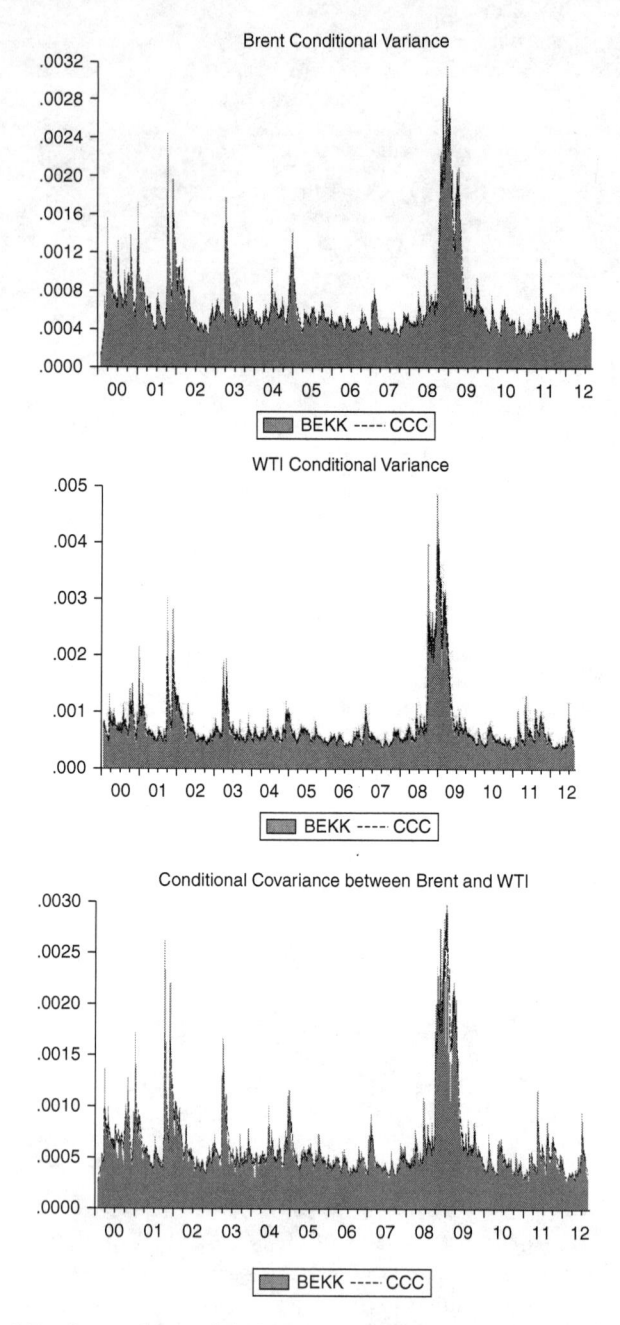

Figure 3.7 Comparison of MGARCH models: conditional variances and covariances.

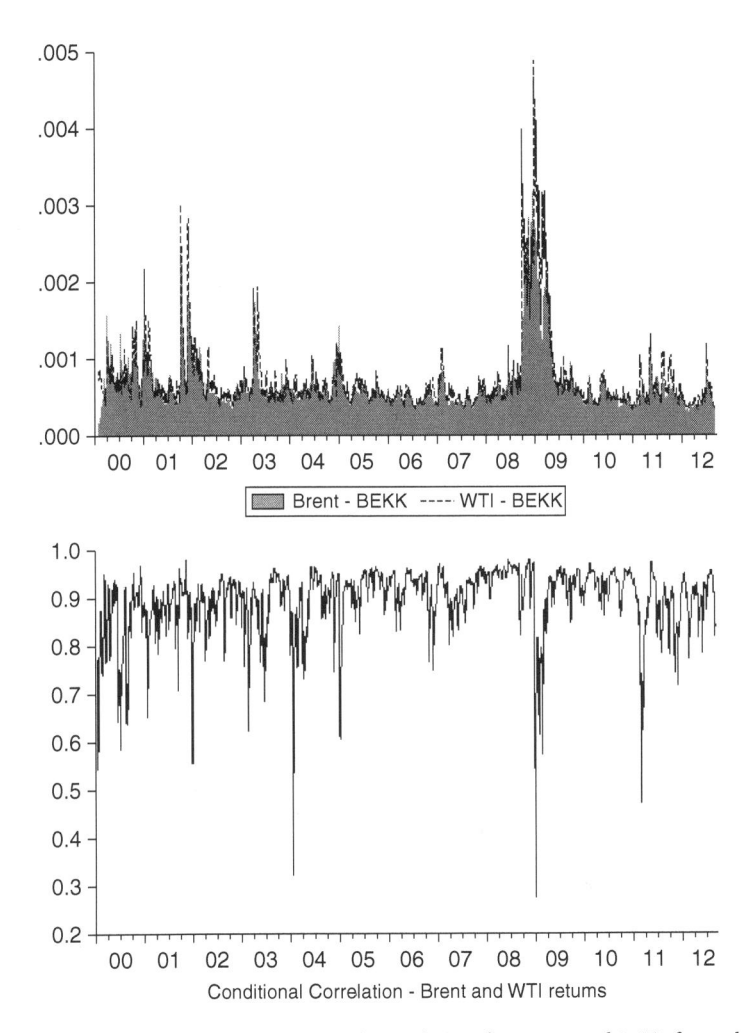

Figure 3.8 Conditional variance and correlation for Brent and WTI from the diagonal BEKK model.

4.5 Intermediate Summary

Multivariate volatility models allow us to capture the joint dynamics between the Brent and WTI return series. The VAR(7) model, which has been used to model the mean equation, reveals a bivariate relationship between the Brent and WTI series. Since the squared residuals exhibited autocorrelation, the residuals of the VAR(7) model have been used to compute the CCC and the diagonal BEKK models. The estimation results indicate high linear dependence between the variables and high volatility persistence in these markets, with tendency to explode in the CCC model. WTI is more sensitive to news than Brent, supporting the benchmark role of WTI. The diagonal BEKK is clearly preferred to the CCC model.

4.6 Limitations and Further Research

Jin et al. (2012) propose to use volatility impulse response functions (VIRF) to quantify the size and persistence of connections between different markets. They use VIRF for two historical shocks, namely the 2008 financial crisis and the BP *Deepwater Horizon* oil spill. They apply it to WTI, Dubai, and Brent futures contracts using daily data from 2005 to 2011. This methodology can be applied to our sample period by using additional historical shocks and incorporating asymmetric effects in the conditional volatility to understand the volatility dynamics of crude oil prices. Based on the approach of Narayan and Narayan (2007), the above analysis can be applied to subsamples with a time horizon of one or two years in order to detect the changing behavior of oil prices over short periods of time and check the robustness of these results. In particular, the recent period of disparity between these two benchmarks can be analyzed in more detail, in order to investigate the changing roles of these markets as international benchmarks.

5 Cointegration Analysis

5.1 Introduction

Many time series are nonstationary but "move together" over time. This means that there exist some influences on the series, that is, market forces, which imply that in the long run the two series are linked by some relationship. A cointegration relationship can also be described as a long-term or equilibrium phenomenon, since in the short run it is possible that cointegrating variables may deviate from their relationship, but in the long run, their association will return (Brooks, 2008). If two series are cointegrated and have stationary cointegrated regression residuals, than the spread (or linear forms of it) is also stationary, which suggests that the spread will not deviate without bounds and will revert to equilibrium (Fattouh, 2010; Westgaard et al., 2011). This means, if spreads are mean-reverting, asset prices are tied together in the long run by a common stochastic trend (Alexander, 1999).

In this section, we investigate the co-movement analysis of similar-quality crude oil prices from different regions of the world. If such a co-movement can be identified, the oil market is said to be "unified" or "globalized" (Gülen, 1997, 1999; Weiner, 1991). If the opposite is true, the oil market is identified to be "regionalized," in which oil prices move independently of each other in response to local market conditions and regional shocks (Fattouh, 2010). According to Gülen (1997, 1999), regionalized markets give rise to arbitrage opportunities and may render the market inefficient, if arbitrage fails to bring prices in different markets together.

For our purpose, the null hypothesis of regionalization, equivalent to the technical null hypothesis of no cointegration, is tested against the alternative of globalization for the American and European markets. This means, if the null hypothesis of no cointegration can be rejected, these two markets are unified and WTI and Brent price series move together over time. The analysis will be done based on the full sample and a subsample, ranging from August 2010 to August 2012, in order to investigate the recent decoupling of these two oil markets. We will use Johansen (1995) cointegration approach to test whether these two crude oil prices are cointegrated. The vector error correction model (VECM) will be applied to further detect short- and long-term relationships and identify the direction of causal relationships together with the Granger causality test.

Cointegration refers not to co-movements in returns, but to co-movements in asset prices (Alexander, 1999). Here, we will use the logarithm of prices to test the existence of cointegration between the two series. As a preliminary step, we analyze if the price series are nonstationary processes, an essential precondition to apply cointegration.

5.2 Unit Root Tests

The augmented Dickey-Fuller (ADF) test and the Phillipps-Perron (PP) test are used to test the log price series and its first differences in each market under the null hypothesis of a unit root, that is, nonstationarity against the alternative hypothesis of stationarity.

Given the equation: $u_t = \rho u_{t-1} + \epsilon_t$, where ϵ_t is i.i.d. $(0, \omega^2)$, a time series u_t is said to be stationary if $|\rho| < 1$, and nonstationary otherwise. With t going to infinity, $|\rho| < 1$ ensures that the variance of u_t converges to a limiting value rather than increasing without limit. Because of the finite variance, a stationary process can never drift too far from its mean. This is the well-known mean-reversion property of stationary series (Alexander, 1999). Most economic time series are nonstationary, that is, $|\rho| \geq 1$. However, the most common form of non-stationarity is a unit root, when $\rho = 1$. In such a case, u_t is said to have a unit root, which is

Table 3.7 Unit root test for log prices and its first differences

		Log level			First difference in log level		
		BIC	ADF	PP	BIC	ADF	PP
Brent							
Intercept	1	−1.070	−1.053	0	−60.541***	−60.525***	
Trend & intercept	1	−2.614	−2.687				
WTI							
Intercept	0	−1.491	−1.402	0	−58.836***	−59.005***	
Trend & intercept	0	−2.910	−2.742				

Note: *** indicates rejection at the 1% significance level.

equivalent to be integrated of order one, that is, $I(1)$, since differencing the series once would render it stationary. The best known example of a unit root nonstationary time series is the random-walk model (Gülen, 1997; Tsay, 2010). Depending on the time series properties, different methodologies exist to analyze the dependency structure of stochastic processes. While for stationary time series a VAR model should be applied, cointegration analysis and VECM should be implemented for nonstationary processes, since the VAR assumes mean-reverting properties of the series under study.

The results of the unit-root tests are summarized in Table 3.7. Both tests allow for a drift and time trend in the regression equation. This is why the results are presented once with including only an intercept and once with an intercept and a trend. For the first differences only an intercept has been included in the regression equation. The lag length for the ADF test equation is selected according to the Bayesian information criterion (BIC), also known as the Schwarz information criterion (SIC). The results reveal that the log of crude oil price series is non-stationary in levels, that is, has a unit root, showing no sign for mean reversion. For the differenced log series, both tests strongly reject the null hypothesis of a unit root, which implies that the log returns are stationary. A stationary first difference series means that the price series are integrated in order 1, and hence are $I(1)$.

To get a better understanding of the nonstationarity property of our time series, the ADF unit root test has been computed on a rolling window of 200 days to get a sort of yearly ADF. The test has been performed without adding a constant or a trend variable in the test equation. Figure 3.9 shows the rolling ADF for Brent (left plot) and WTI (right plot). The rolling ADF confirms that the nonstationary properties of both price series are maintained throughout the entire period, although it touches the 5 percent critical value for a brief period in 2008, at the time of the financial crisis. Cointegration analysis is therefore an appropriate tool in order to investigate the long-run equilibrium relationship between the price series.

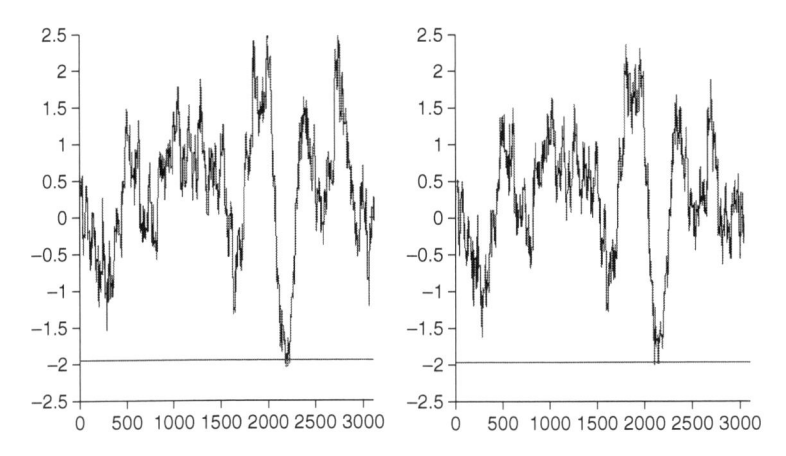

Figure 3.9 Rolling ADF for Brent and WTI log prices—full sample.

5.3 Johansen Cointegration Test

The Johansen (1991, 1995) test for cointegration is a maximum likelihood estimation procedure, allowing testing for multiple cointegrating relations among variables. Since the details of this procedure are very complex, we focus on fundamental aspects in our analysis.[11]

Johansen's cointegration analysis is based on the following vector autoregressive (VAR) model of order p (EViews 7, 2010b):

$$y_t = A_1 y_{t-1} + \cdots + A_p y_{t-p} + B x_t + \epsilon_t, \quad (t = 1, ..., T) \tag{6}$$

where y_t is a k-vector of non-stationary I(1) variables, x_t is a d-vector of deterministic variables and ϵ_t is a vector of innovations. This model can be rewritten in first differences:

$$\Delta y_t = \Pi y_{t-1} + \sum_{i=1}^{p-1} \Gamma_i \Delta y_{t-i} + B x_t + \epsilon_t, \tag{7}$$

where

$$\Pi = \sum_{i=1}^{p} A_i - I, \quad \Gamma_i = -\sum_{j=i+1}^{p} A_j. \tag{8}$$

Π captures information about long-run relationships between the variables in the system (Gülen, 1997). According to Westgaard et al. (2011) the rank of the Π matrix determines how many linear relations between the y are stationary and hence how many cointegrated relationships exist. The rank of a matrix is equal to the number of its characteristic roots, that is, eigenvalues (denoted by λ_i), that are different from zero (Brooks, 2008). The Johansen cointegration approach is therefore a test of the rank of the Π matrix with the rank number representing the number of cointegrated vectors (Westgaard et al., 2011). With respect to the rank of the Π matrix, we can distinguish following cases (EViews 7, 2010b; Gülen, 1997):

- If $rank(\Pi) = k$: Π is full rank and all variables in y_t are stationary.
- If $rank(\Pi) = 0$: the model corresponds to a VAR in first differences.
- If $0 < rank(\Pi) = r < k$: there exist $k \times r$ matrices α and β such that $\Pi = \alpha\beta'$. r is the number of cointegrating relations (the cointegrating rank), β is the matrix of cointegrating vectors which render $\beta' y_t$ stationary, even though y_t is non-stationary and α is a matrix of adjustment parameters in the VECM.[12]

The cointegration rank r can be found by using the trace (λ_{trace}) and maximum eigenvalue (λ_{max}) test statistics:

$$\lambda_{trace}(r) = -T \sum_{i=r+1}^{k} \log(1 - \hat{\lambda}_i),$$

$$\lambda_{max}(r) = -T \log(1 - \hat{\lambda}_{r+1}),$$

where T is the sample size and $\hat{\lambda}_i$ is the estimated value for the i-th eigenvalue from the Π matrix. The trace statistic is a joint test where the null is that the number of cointegrating vectors is less or equal to r against an unspecified or general alternative that there are more than r (Brooks, 2008). In the case of two variables (i.e., Brent and WTI in our case), the trace statistic tests the null of zero cointegrated vectors against the alternative of one cointegrated vector (Westgaard et al., 2011). The maximum eigenvalue test computes separate tests on each eigenvalue, with the null hypothesis that the number of cointegrating vectors is r against an alternative of $r + 1$ (Brooks, 2008).

Table 3.8 displays the results of the Johansen test. The BIC criterion is utilized to determine the optimal lag length, which yields 2 for Brent and WTI. Moreover, the model has been estimated by a default test specification in EViews 7, assuming trends to be stochastic in the series, which is sensible to assume for macroeconomic and financial data (EViews 7, 2010b). The trace test and the maximum eigenvalue test reveal that there is a strong long-run relationship between the Brent and WTI price series,

Table 3.8 Johansen cointegration test results

			Unrestricted Cointegration Rank Test (Trace and Maximum Eigenvalue)			
Hypothesized No. of CE(s)	Eigenvalue	Trace Statistic	Trace: 0.05 Critical Value	Max-Eigen Statistic	Max-Eigen: 0.05 Critical Value	Prob.**
None *	0.008872	30.52463	15.49471	29.42762	14.26460	0.0001
At most 1	0.000332	1.097010	3.841466	1.097010	3.841466	0.2949

Trace test indicates 1 cointegrating eqn(s) at the 0.05 level
Max-eigenvalue test indicates 1 cointegrating eqn(s) at the 0.05 level
* denotes rejection of the hypothesis at the 0.05 level
**MacKinnon-Haug-Michelis p-values

since we can reject the null hypothesis that $r = 0$ but cannot reject the null hypothesis that $r \leq 1$ under the 1 percent significance level. This means that there exists one cointegration vector. Even if there are short-term external shocks causing some deviations, the two price series are tied together in the long run. In a next step, we investigate the short and long-run dynamics using the VECM.

5.4 The Vector Error Correction Model

If a set of variables are cointegrated, then there exists a valid error-correction representation of the data that describes the short-run dynamics consistently with the long-run cointegrating relationship (Engle and Granger, 1987; Verbeek, 2004). The presence of a long-run relationship has also implications for the short-run behavior of the I(1) variables as there has to be some mechanism driving the variables to their long-run equilibrium relationship (Verbeek, 2004). Apart from distinguishing between short- and long-term relationships between the variables, the VECM can detect the direction of causality.

The VECM for the Brent (y_t) and WTI (x_t) series takes the following form (Kang and Yoon, 2012):

$$\Delta y_t = \beta_{y,0} + \gamma_y ec_{t-1} + \sum_{i=1}^{2} \beta_{yx,i} \Delta x_{t-i} + \sum_{i=1}^{2} \beta_{yy,i} \Delta y_{t-i} + \epsilon_{y,t},$$

$$\Delta x_t = \beta_{x,0} + \gamma_x ec_{t-1} + \sum_{i=1}^{2} \beta_{xx,i} \Delta x_{t-i} + \sum_{i=1}^{2} \beta_{xy,i} \Delta y_{t-i} + \epsilon_{x,t},$$

where Δy_t and Δx_t represent the first differences of the variables, that is, the log returns, which are I(0). The error correction term ec_{t-1} stands for the cointegration term since the deviation from the long-run equilibrium is corrected gradually through a series of partial short-run adjustments (EViews 7, 2010b). The error correction coefficients γ_y and γ_x describe the speed of adjustment back to the long-run equilibrium and measure the proportion of the equilibrium error in the last period being corrected for γ_y and γ_x, respectively. While a value close to -1 implies a fast speed of adjustment, a value close to 0 suggests a slow speed back to equilibrium, that is, leading to a more frequent decoupling of the two price series (Engle and Granger, 1987; Westgaard et al., 2011). At least one of these variables has to be nonzero since at least one of the variables has to adjust to deviations from the long-run equilibrium (Verbeek, 2004). The returns have been regressed on

Table 3.9 ECM regression results

Δy_t (Brent)	$\beta_{y,0}$	γ_y	$\beta_{yx,1}$	$\beta_{yx,2}$	$\beta_{yy,1}$	$\beta_{yy,2}$
	0.001	0.003	0.077***	−0.008	−0.124***	−0.006
	(0.000)	(0.006)	(0.030)	(0.030)	(0.033)	(0.032)
Δx_t (WTI)	$\beta_{x,0}$	γ_x	$\beta_{xx,1}$	$\beta_{xx,2}$	$\beta_{xy,1}$	$\beta_{xy,2}$
	0.000	0.022***	−0.025	−0.079**	0.005	0.053
	(0.000)	(0.007)	(0.033)	(0.032)	(0.036)	(0.035)

Note: ** and *** indicate significance at the 5% and 1% levels. The values in brackets are the standard errors.

their own lagged values, to detect the degree of mean-reverting behavior from both series, and the lagged value of the other oil price returns, to explain the causality relationship between the two crude oil markets (Kang and Yoon, 2012).

Table 3.9 summarizes the estimation results of the VECM model.[13] The coefficient of the error correction term is significant only in the case of WTI: 2.2 percent of the disequilibria at $t-1$ is adjusted in the WTI price changes in the next period. This means when the two crude oil benchmarks deviate from their long-run cointegration relationship in the previous period, WTI is more likely to adjust than Brent. However, the low value of the error correction term indicates a slow adjustment of a price differential to the long-term equilibrium. Nevertheless, this results show that the American and European oil markets are integrated in the long run, albeit shocks tend to persist over long time periods before reverting back to equilibrium.

The results reveal also a strong short-term relationship between Brent and WTI, captured by the statistically significant transmission coefficient $\beta_{yx,1}$. WTI returns have an impact on Brent returns but not vice versa, since the other transmission coefficients are not statistically significant in our model. This signals that shocks are transferred from one oil market to the other in the short run, but only in one direction, that is, there exists a unidirectional relationship. From the estimated results of the VECM, it seems that WTI slightly leads Brent. However, this is a result of the low lag number selected for our model. Increasing the number of lagged variables included in our model gives evidence of a bivariate causality relation (results are available upon request). Besides, the significance of coefficients for the own lagged values of each variable ($\beta_{yy,1}$, $\beta_{xx,2}$) indicates to the mean-reverting property present in the return series.

5.5 Granger Causality Test

The existence of cointegration indeed rules out the possibility of spurious correlation but does not specify the direction of the causal relationships (Kang and Yoon, 2012). Even if the regression of the error correction models identifies dependence of two variables it does not imply causation (Westgaard et al., 2011). The Granger causality test can be applied in order to test for the direction of influence between two series and its further findings will help to confirm the results from the VECM. In the case of bilateral causality, we test for Granger causality by estimating and testing the following bivariate VAR(p) model (Granger, 1969):

$$Y_t = \mu_1 + \sum_{i=1}^{p} \alpha_{1,i} X_{t-i} + \sum_{i=1}^{p} \beta_{1,i} Y_{t-i} + \epsilon_{1,t},$$

$$X_t = \mu_2 + \sum_{i=1}^{p} \alpha_{2,i} Y_{t-i} + \sum_{i=1}^{p} \beta_{2,i} X_{t-i} + \epsilon_{2,t},$$

where $\epsilon_{1,t}$ and $\epsilon_{2,t}$ are taken to be two uncorrelated white-noise series. Four different cases can be distinguished from the two equations. If the null hypothesis $H_0 = \Sigma_{i=1}^{p} \alpha_{1,i}$ is rejected X is said to Granger cause Y. If this is the case and not vice versa, there exists unidirectional causality from X to Y, so that the lags of X are significant in the equation for Y. Conversely, if the null hypothesis $H_0 = \Sigma_{i=1}^{p} \alpha_{2,i}$ is rejected, Y is said to Granger cause X. If both sets of lags are significant, there exists a bilateral causality or feedback relationship. If neither set of lags is statistically significant in the equation for the other variable, X and Y are said to be independent. The causality direction is decided using an F-test of joint significance. It should be noted, that the word "causality" in this context means only a correlation between the current value of one variable and the past values of others and does not mean that movements of one variable cause movements of another (Brooks, 2008; Granger, 1969; Tudor and Anghel, 2012; Westgaard et al., 2011).

As Granger causality test results are very sensitive to the specification of the lag length, we implement a lag-length test with 20 days as the maximum lag length for both variables (Tudor and Anghel, 2012). According to Thornton and Batten (1984) the Akaike's final prediction error (FPE) criterion performs well relative to other existing tests. This is why we will use this selection criterion to define the optimal lag-length. The results are summarized in Table 3.10. The optimal lag length according the FPE criterion is 17. Moreover, we reject the hypotheses that "WTI does not Granger cause Brent" and "Brent does not Granger cause WTI." Therefore, we find

Table 3.10 Granger causality test results

Null Hypothesis	Obs	F-Statistics	Prob.
WTI does not Granger Cause BRENT	3,288	2.04769	0.0068
BRENT does not Granger Cause WTI		3.70867	0.0000

strong evidence for bi-directional Granger causality, that is, there is contemporaneous feedback between Brent and WTI crude oil price series at the 1 percent significance level. This means that the lagged information of Brent provides statistically significant information about WTI in the presence of lagged variables of WTI and vice versa.

5.6 Causality and Cointegration Analysis on the Subsample

The above analyses are conducted based on the full sample from January 3, 2000, to August 31, 2012. In order to verify the decoupling in American and European oil prices in the last two years, we will apply the above causality and cointegration analysis on a subsample with 524 observations, ranging from August 31, 2010 to August 31, 2012.

As initial analysis, the price series have again been tested for nonstationarity, that is, $I(1)$. When including an intercept, the ADF and PP unit root tests for Brent and WTI subsamples are rejected at the 10 percent and 5 percent significance levels, which might be because of the small sample size (see Table 3.11). However, with a linear trend and intercept included in the test equation, the test results reveal nonstationarity. In order to strengthen our argumentation for nonstationarity of the log prices, a third unit root test has been computed, namely the KPSS test statistic. This test statistic takes as null hypothesis the stationarity of the time series and nonstationarity as alternative, while the role of the null and alternative hypothesis are reversed for the ADF and PP tests. The KPSS model additionally verifies the nonstationarity of the log prices. Furthermore, all three applied unit root tests prove the stationarity of the first differences at all significance levels, indicating $I(1)$ for our price series. The rolling ADF computed on a rolling window of 60 days, i.e. one quarter, confirms the nonstationarity of the log prices in the subsample (see Figure 3.10). Although the sample crosses the 5 percent critical value for a brief period towards the end of 2012, the log prices stay nonstationary for the great part of the sample period. After having shown that the log price series are nonstationary and integrated of order 1, we can continue with our cointegration analysis, that is, with the Johansen cointegration test and the Granger causality test.

Table 3.11 Unit root test for log prices and its first differences on the subsample

			Log level				First difference in log level		
		BIC	ADF[1]	PP[1]	KPSS[2]	BIC	ADF[1]	PP[1]	KPSS[2]
Brent_sub	intercept	0	−2.811*	−2.802*	1.179***	0	−24.372***	−24.399***	0.259
Brent_sub	trend & intercept	0	−2.520	−2.460	0.464***				
WTI_sub	intercept	0	−2.978**	−2.965**	0.506**	0	−23.559***	−23.565***	0.136
WTI_sub	trend & intercept	0	−2.840	−2.824	0.245***				

Note: *, ** and *** indicate rejection at the 10%, 5% and 1% significance levels
[1] Null Hypothesis: unit root process, [2] Null Hypothesis: stationary process

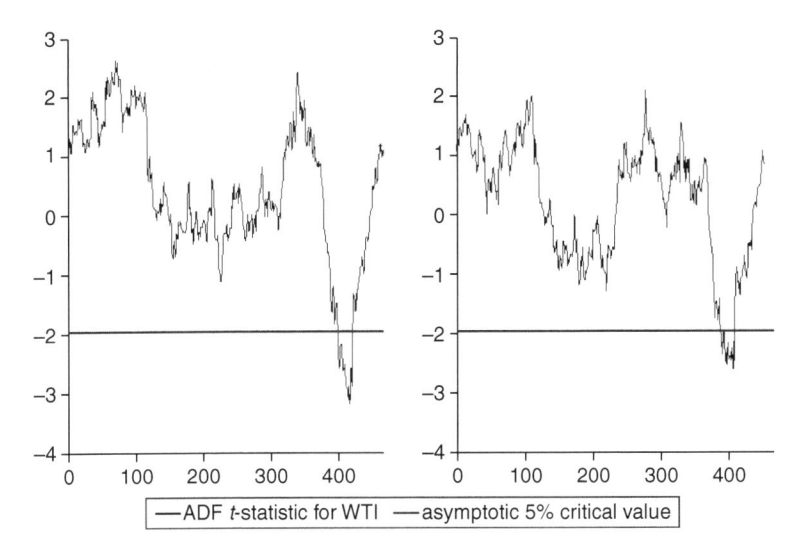

Figure 3.10 Rolling ADF for Brent and WTI log prices—subsample.

5.6.1 Johansen Cointegration Test
The Johansen test indicates no cointegration relationship in the subsample. The test results are summarized in Table 3.12, with the trace and maximum eigenvalue test statistics rejecting the existence of a cointegration relationship at the 5 percent significance level.

5.6.2 Granger Causality Test
To conclude our analysis on the subsample, the Granger causality test has been applied. The null hypotheses that the subsample of WTI "does not Granger cause Brent" and vice versa cannot be rejected at any significance level, resulting in an independent relationship between the American and European oil market in the short run.

5.7 Intermediate Summary

This section has analyzed the co-movement of WTI and Brent price series in the long and short run and has tested the regionalization hypothesis for the American and European oil markets based on the full sample and a sub period. For this purpose, the Johansen cointegration test, VECM, and the Granger causality test have been applied.

We find evidence in favor of the existence of a cointegration relationship between these two global benchmarks, indicating that in the long run these two oil markets are unified rather than regionalized.

Table 3.12 Johansen cointegration test results for the subsample

	Unrestricted Cointegration Rank Test (Trace and Maximum Eigenvalue)						
Hypothesized No. of CE(s)	Eigenvalue	Trace Statistic	Trace: 0.05 Critical Value	Prob.**	Max-Eigen Statistic	Max-Eigen: 0.05 Critical Value	Prob.**
None	0.017336	14.60825	15.49471	0.0677	9.146148	14.26460	0.2742
At most 1 *	0.010389	5.462097	3.841466	0.0194	5.462097	3.841466	0.0194

Trace test indicates no cointegration at the 0.05 level
Max-eigenvalue test indicates no cointegration at the 0.05 level
* denotes rejection of the hypothesis at the 0.05 level
**MacKinnon–Haug–Michelis (1999) p-values

Table 3.13 Granger Causality Test results for the subsample

Null Hypothesis	Obs	F-Statistic	Prob.
WTI_SUB does not Granger Cause BRENT_SUB	523	0.48799	0.4851
BRENT_SUB does not Granger Cause WTI_SUB		0.25637	0.6128

The relationship is predominantly bi-directional with a somewhat overwhelming influence of WTI over Brent. The analysis over the full sample reveals significant statistical evidence that the Brent and WTI prices series have shared a common long-run trend. However, this statement does not hold when analyzing the period between 2010 and 2012. The applied causality and cointegration tests strongly reject the cointegration relationship and prove the recent decoupling in Brent and WTI price series. The oil price differential follows a nonstationary process, providing support for the regionalization hypothesis in the subperiod. According to Fattouh (2010), such market dislocations may occur, but do not last long, so that the market eventually finds its equilibrium.

5.8 Limitations and Further Research

The implemented cointegration analysis should be considered under the limitations discussed in this section. According to Gülen (1997) conventional unit root tests (such as ADF, PP, and KPSS) are not appropriate in the case of the oil market, since structural breaks in the time series might cause unit roots tests to lose power, leading to misleading conclusions regarding the existence of unit roots. Perron (1989) showed that the application of unit root test with structural breaks leads more reliable results. Since we cannot reject the existence of structural breaks in our time series, a unit root test that account for structural breaks would be more appropriate.

In mid-February 2013, the price spread between Brent and WTI was at $20/bbl. This indicates that the current widening between these global benchmarks seems to persist. In order to investigate whether this price divergence is only a short-term phenomenon or represents a new pricing paradigm, cointegration analysis should be applied to larger data samples in the future. Moreover, other global benchmarks, such as Dubai/Oman and Tapis representative for the Middle East and Asia-Pacific, respectively, could be incorporated into the analysis to investigate these developments on a global basis.

6 Conclusion

The main objective of this chapter is to examine the dynamics of the American and European oil prices. For this purpose, we have analyzed daily oil prices and returns of two major international oil benchmarks, namely WTI and Brent, ranging from January 3, 2000, to August 31, 2012. There exist a large number of empirical studies that discussed in detail price dynamics in the oil markets. We aim to contribute to this growing research by introducing a new set of data and by carefully discussing structural breaks in the oil markets.

The theoretical part of this chapter has provided background information about the fundamentals of oil. Historical events occurring during this time period have been reviewed by dividing the whole sample period into five different subperiods: a period of relative price stability (2000–2003), a period of increasing oil prices (2004–2006), the 2007–2008 oil price shock period, the subsequent recessionary and recovery period (2009–2010), and lastly, the period of disparity between WTI and Brent crude oil prices (2011–2012).

During the investigated sample period, oil prices have undergone significant variations. In the period from 2002 to 2008, the oil market experienced a sustained increase in price, with a collapse toward the end of 2008, and then recovered again to high levels in recent years. WTI and Brent crude oil prices closely tracked each other prior to 2010, with WTI generally having a slight premium over Brent. However, in early 2011, prices began consistently to diverge, mainly due to transportation constraints at Cushing, the trading hub for WTI. Apart from this, the return series exhibit excess kurtosis (i.e., fat tails) and negative skewness, and are characterized by volatility clustering and time-varying volatility.

The technical part of this chapter investigates the joint dynamics of European and American oil prices. We therefore employed a GARCH analysis in the multivariate framework and cointegration analysis to assess long- and short- term co-movements among the two oil prices.

In the multivariate framework, the CCC and the diagonal BEKK model have been computed by using a VAR(7) specification for the mean equation. The VAR(7) indicates a bivariate relationship between the Brent and WTI series. Moreover, the CCC model reveals a high volatility correlation. This positive relation between the volatilities of Brent and WTI is also confirmed by the diagonal BEKK model. The estimated conditional variances are highly persistent, with a tendency to explode in the CCC model. WTI is more responsive to news than Brent, so that there is no evidence to cast doubt on its benchmark role.

The second part of our empirical section is devoted to cointegration analysis. The Johansen cointegration test finds evidence for the presence of one cointegrating relationship between the oil prices and confirms that there exists a common long-term trend between Brent and WTI. The results of the VECM analysis reveal that the causality relationship is predominantly bi-directional with a somewhat overwhelming influence of WTI over Brent. This findings provide evidence for the globalization hypothesis for the American and European market in the long run. The causality between the price series has been assessed by employing the Granger causality test. We observe that the causality is predominantly bi-directional.

We applied the same econometric techniques to a subsample, ranging from August 31, 2010 to August 31, 2012. Even though these price series have had a strong relationship in the past, the cointegration relationship is strongly rejected in the subsample. We find strong evidence for regionalization, that is, the oil prices move independently of each other in response to regional shocks. Also in the context of Granger causality test, we conclude that there is independence between European and American oil prices. The recent decoupling is wider than previous ones and seems to persist. Further research is required to investigate whether the regionalization of oil markets is only a temporary phenomenon, or it will become the new state of the art in the oil markets.

Notes

1. API stands for American Petroleum Institute. This association, which is based in Washington DC, standardizes the industry's equipment and procedures (Geman, 2005).
2. Figures and tables with no indication of source are based on our own computations and illustrations.
3. Before the repeal of the Glass-Steagall Act (1934) in November 1999, financial institutions were prohibited from investing in risky products such as crude oil and gasoline futures contracts. With its repeal, there was an increasing participation in these risky investments. Many analysts are of the opinion that this new market for crude oil futures significantly impacted crude oil prices (Izzard et al., 2010).
4. Traders on the New York Mercantile Exchange (NYMEX) fall into two basic categories: (1) commercial traders, including producers and consumers, who trade in futures to offset the risk of price moving unfavorably for their ongoing business activities and (2) noncommercial traders, including both speculators and financial institutions, who seek profit on paper positions from short-term price fluctuations. They are trying to diversify their investment portfolio, spread geopolitical risk and maximize investment returns. Both types are

needed for the exchange to function well (Izzard et al., 2010; Medlock and Jaffe, 2009).
5. The news of the bankruptcy of Lehman Brothers in September 2008 can be defined as the outbreak date of the global financial crisis (Jin et al., 2012).
6. The crude oil futures contracts traded on the NYMEX are primarily based on the delivery of WTI crudes. However, Brent in London is also one of the grades acceptable for delivery on the NYMEX. Therefore, the price differential between these two crude oils should never exceed the costs of shipping Brent across the Atlantic (Schofield, 2007; Kao and Wan, 2012).
7. Since Brent is a waterborne crude oil, it does not suffer from pipeline bottlenecks (Fattouh, 2010).
8. There is no possibility to estimate the full BEKK model in EViews 7.
9. The standardized residuals have been generated by the square root of the covariance of each series.
10. The likelihood ratio statistic has been computed with the MATLAB software. The CCC model is taken to be the restricted model, since by definition it is the simplest multivariate correlation model that is nested in the other conditional correlation models (Bollerslev, 1990). The more elaborate diagonal BEKK model is defined as the unrestricted model.
11. Further details can be found in Johansen (1991, 1995); Johansen and Juselius (1990); Hamilton (1994), and Brooks (2008).
12. See Section 5.4.
13. No exogenous variables have been included in the regression equation.

References

Agnolucci, P. (2009). Volatility in Crude Oil Futures: A Comparison of the Predictive Ability of GARCH and Implied Volatility Models. *Energy Economics*, 31(2).

Alexander, C. (1999). Correlation and Cointegration in Energy Markets. http://www.icmacentre.ac.uk/pdf/energy.pdf. Accessed January 21, 2013.

Alizadeh, A. and Nomikos, N. (2004). Cost of Carry, Causality and Arbitrage between Oil Futures and Tanker Freight Markets, Transportation Research Part E. *Logistics and Transportation Review*, 40(4): 297–316.

Almadi, M. and Zhang, B. (2011). Lead–Lag Relationships between World Crude Oil Benchmarks: Evidence from West Texas Intermediate, Brent, Dubai and Oman. *International Research Journal of Finance and Economics*, 80:13–26.

Aloui, C. and Mabrouk, S. (2010). Value-at-Risk Estimations of Energy Commodities via Long-Memory, Asymmetry and Fat-Tailed GARCH Models. *Energy Policy*, 38(5).

Askari, H. and Krichene, N. (2008). Oil Price Dynamics (2002–2006). *Energy Economics*, 30(5).

Bauwens, L., Laurent, S., and Rombouts, J. (2006). Multivariate GARCH Models: A Survey. *Journal of Applied Econometrics*, 21(1).

Bentzen, J. (2007). Does OPEC Influence Crude Oil Prices? Testing for Co-movements and Causality between Regional Crude Oil Prices. *Applied Economics*, 39(11).

Bina, C. and Vo, M. (2007). OPEC in the Epoch of Globalization: An Event Study of Global Oil Prices. *Global Economy Journal*, 7(1).

Blas, J. (2012). Shale has Distorted Oil Benchmarks. www.ft.com. Accessed December 19, 2012.

Bollerslev, T. (1986). Generalized Autoregressive Conditional Heteroskedasticity. *Journal of Econometrics*, 31(3).

Bollerslev, T. (1990). Modelling the Coherence in Short-run Nominal Exchange Rates: A Multivariate Generalized ARCH Model. *The Review of Economics and Statistics*, 72:498–505.

Brooks, C. (2008). *Introductory Econometrics for Finance.* Cambridge University Press, Cambridge, UK, 2nd edition.

Cabedo, J. and Moya, I. (2003). Estimating Oil Price "Value at Risk" using the Historical Simulation Approach. *Energy Economics*, 25(3).

Chang, C.-L., McAleer, M., and Tansuchat, R. (2009). Modeling Conditional Correlations for Risk Diversification in Crude Oil Markets. *The Journal of Energy Markets*, 2(4).

Chang, C.-L., McAleer, M., and Tansuchat, R. (2010). Analyzing and Forecasting Volatility Spillovers, Asymmetries and Hedging in Major Oil Markets. *Energy Economics*, 32(6).

Chang, C.-L., McAleer, M., and Tansuchat, R. (2011). Crude Oil Hedging Strategies using Dynamic Multivariate GARCH. *Energy Economics*, 33(5).

Cheong, C. (2009). Modeling and Forecasting Crude Oil Markets using ARCH-type Models. *Energy Policy*, 37(6).

Chevallier, J. (2012). Time-varying Correlations in Oil, Gas and CO2 Prices: an Application using BEKK, CCC and DCC-MGARCH Models. *Applied Economics*, 44(32):4724–7524.

Chevillon, G. and Rifflart, C. (2009). Physical Market Determinants of the Price of Crude Oil and the Market Premium. *Energy Economics*, 31(4).

Cifarelli, G. and Paladino, G. (2010). Oil Price Dynamics and Speculation: A Multivariate Financial Approach. *Energy Economics*, 32(2).

Day, T. and Lewis, C. (1993). Forecasting Futures Market Volatility. *The Journal of Derivatives*, 1:33–50.

Dunn, S. and Holloway, J. (2012). The Pricing of Crude Oil. Reserve Bank of Australia. Bulletin âĂŞ September Quarter 2012. http://www.rba.gov.au/publications/bulletin/2012/sep/8.html. Accessed December 3, 2012.

EIA (2011). WTI-Brent Crude Oil Price Spread has Reached Unseen Levels. http://www.eia.gov/todayinenergy/detail.cfm?id=290. Accessed November 22, 2012.

EIA (2012a). 2011 Brief: Brent Crude Oil Averages over $100 per Barrel in 2011. http://www.eia.gov/todayinenergy/detail.cfm?id=4550. Accessed November 22, 2012.

EIA (2012b). Brent-WTI Differential to Narrow. http://www.eia.gov/oog/info/twip/twiparch/120912/twipprint.html. Accessed November 22, 2012.

EIA (2012c). Short-Term Energy Outlook. http://www.eia.gov/forecasts/steo/archives/sep12.pdf. Accessed November 18, 2012.

EIA (2012d). Short-Term Energy Outlook Supplement: Brent Crude Oil Spot Price Forecast. http://www.eia.gov/forecasts/steo/special/pdf/2012_sp_02.pdf. Accessed November 18, 2012.

Engle, R. (2002). Dynamic Conditional Correlation: A Simple Class of Multivariate GARCH Models. *Journal of Business and Economic Statistics*, 20:339–350.

Engle, R. and Bollerslev, T. (1986). Modelling the Persistence of Conditional Variances. *Econometric Reviews*, 5(1).

Engle, R. and Granger, C. (1987). Cointegration and Error Correction: Representation, Estimation and Testing. *Econometrica*, 55(2).

Engle, R. and Kroner, K. (1995). Multivariate Simultaneous Generalized ARCH. *Econometric Theory*, 11:122–150.

EViews 7 (2010a). EViews 7 User's Guide I. http://schwert.ssb.rochester.edu/a425/EV71.pdf. Accessed September 5, 2012.

EViews 7 (2010b). EViews 7 User's Guide II. http://schwert.ssb.rochester.edu/a425/EV72.pdf. Accessed September 5, 2012.

Fan, Y. and Xu, J.-H. (2011). What has Driven Oil Prices since 2000? A Structural Change Perspective. *Energy Economics*, 33(6).

Fattouh, B. (2010). The Dynamics of Crude Oil Price Differentials. *Energy Economics*, 32(2).

Fattouh, B. (2011). An Anatomy of the Crude Oil Pricing System. http://www.oxfordenergy.org/2011/02/an-anatomy-of-the-oil-pricing-system/. Accessed December 23, 2012.

Fattouh, B., Kilian, L., and Mahadeva, L. (2012). The Role of Speculation in Oil Markets: What Have We Learned So Far? http://www.oxfordenergy.org. Accessed January 13, 2013.

Fielden, S. (2012a). A Bridge Too Far: When Will the WTI Discount to Brent End? http://www.rbnenergy.com/a-bridge-too-far-when-will-the-wti-discount-to-brent-end. Accessed November 25, 2012.

Fielden, S. (2012b). Place Your Bets on Narrow Brent/WTI Spread for the Super Bowl. http://www.rbnenergy.com/place-your-bets-on-narrow-brentwti-spread-for-the-super-bowl. Accessed November 22, 2012.

Fong, W. and See, K. (2002). A Markov Switching Model of the Conditional Volatility of Crude Oil Futures Prices. *Energy Economics*, 24(1).

Geman, H. (2005). *Commodities and Commodity Derivatives: Modeling and Pricing for Agriculture, Metals and Energy.* Wiley, Chichester.

Gileva, T. (2010). Econometrics of Crude Oil Markets. http://erasmus-mundus.univ-paris1.fr/fichiers_etudiants/1926_dissertation.pdf. Accessed December 23, 2012.

Gülen, S. (1997). Regionalization in the World Crude Oil Market. *The Energy Journal*, 18(2).

Gülen, S. (1999). Regionalization in the World Crude Oil Market: Further Evidence. *The Energy Journal*, 20(1).

Granger, C. (1969). Investigating Causal Relations by Econometric Models and Cross-spectral Methods. *Econometrica*, 37(3).

Hafner, C. (2011). GARCH Modeling. In Meyers, R. A., editor, *Complex Systems in Finance and Econometrics*. Springer Science + Business, New York.

Haigh, M. and Holt, M. (2002). Crack Spread Hedging: Accounting for Time-varying Spillovers in the Energy Futures Markets. *Journal of Applied Econometrics*, 17(3).

Hamilton, J. (1994). *Time Series Analysis*. Princeton University Press, Princeton, NJ.

Hamilton, J. D. (2009a). Causes and Consequences of the Oil Shock of 2007-08. *Brookings Papers on Economic Activity*, 40(1).

Hamilton, J. D. (2009b). Understanding Crude Oil Prices. *The Energy Journal*, 30(2).

Hammoudeh, S., Thompson, M., and Ewing, B. (2008). Threshold Cointegration Analysis of Crude Oil Benchmarks. *The Energy Journal*, 29(4).

Hosp, G. (2012). Preisdifferenz zwischen Erdölsorten—Wo Europa die Vereinigten Staaten hinter sich lädsst. Neue Zürcher Zeitung [NZZ]. http://www.nzz.ch. Accessed January 21, 2012.

Hou, A. and Suardi, S. (2012). A Nonparametric GARCH Model of Crude Oil Price Return Volatility. *Energy Economics*, 34(2).

IMF (2009). World Economic Outlook October 2009: Sustaining the Recovery. www.imf.org. Accessed November 8, 2012.

IMF (2011). World Economic Outlook September 2011: Slowing Growth, Rising Risks. www.imf.org. Accessed November 8, 2012.

Izzard, C., Stringer, K., and Foran, J. (2010). Review of Issues Affecting the Price of Crude Oil. Natural Resources Canada. http://www.nrcan.gc.ca/sites/www.nrcan.gc.ca.energy/files/pdf/eneene/pdf/pcopdp-eng.pdf. Accessed September 2, 2012.

Jalali-Naini, A. R. and Kazemi-Manesh, M. (2006). Price Volatility, Hedging, and Variable Risk Premium in the Crude Oil Market. *OPEC Review*, 30(2).

Jenkins, J. (2012). The Basis of Oil Investing: The WTI-Brent Spread. http://www.investmentu.com/2012/May/wti-brent-spread.html. Accessed November 16, 2012.

Jin, X., Lin, S. X., and Tamvakis, M. (2012). Volatility Transmission and Volatility Impulse Response Functions in Crude Oil Markets. *Energy Economics*, 34(6).

Johansen, S. (1991). Estimation and Hypothesis Testing of Cointegration Vectors in Gaussian Vector Autoregressive Models. *Econometrica*, 59(6).

Johansen, S. (1995). *Likelihood-Based Inference in Cointegrated Vector Autoregressive Models*. Oxford University Press, Oxford.

Johansen, S. and Juselius, K. (1990). Maximum Likelihood Estimation and Inference on Cointegration with Applications to the Demand for Money. *Oxford Bulletin of Economics and Statistics*, 52(2).

Kang, S. and Yoon, S.-M. (2012). Information Transmission between Crude Oil Markets. West East Institute. http://www.westeastinstitute.com/wp-content/uploads/2012/10/ZG12-209-Sang-Hoon-Kang-and-Seong-Min-Yoon.pdf. Accessed January 25, 2013.

Kang, S. H., Kang, S., and Yoon, S. (2009). Forecasting Volatility of Crude Oil Markets. *Energy Economics*, 31(1).

Kao, C.-W. and Wan, J.-Y. (2012). Price Discount, Inventories and the Distortion of WTI Benchmark. *Energy Economics*, 34(1).

Kaufmann, R. K. (2011). The Role of Market Fundamentals and Speculation in Recent Price Changes for Crude Oil. *Energy Policy*, 39(1).

Kaufmann, R. K. and Ullman, B. (2009). Oil Prices, Speculation, and Fundamentals: Interpreting Causal Relations among Spot and Futures Prices. *Energy Economics*, 31(4).

Kramer, W. and Ploberger, W. (1992). The CUSUM Test with OLS Residuals. *Econometrica*, 60(2).

Lanza, A., Manera, M., and McAleer, M. (2006). Modeling Dynamic Conditional Correlations in WTI Oil Forward and Future Returns. *Finance Research Letters*, 3(2).

Liao, H.-C., Huang, H.-C., and Lin, S.-C. (2012). The Story behind the Wider Spread between WTI and Brent: Are Crude Oil Market Globalized or Regionalized? http://eneken.ieej.or.jp/3rd_IAEE_Asia/pdf/paper/018p.pdf. Accessed February 12, 2013.

McNeil, A. J., Frey, R., and Embrechts, P. (2005). *Quantitative Risk Management: Concepts, Techniques and Tools*. Princeton University Press, Princeton, NJ.

Medlock, K. B. and Jaffe, A. M. (2009). Who is in the Oil Futures Market and how has it Changed? http://www.bakerinstitute.org/publications/EF-pub-MedlockJaffeOilFuturesMarket-082609.pdf. Accessed November 8, 2012.

Milonas, N. T. and Henker, T. (2001). Price Spread and Convenience Yield Behaviour in the International Oil Market. *Applied Financial Economics*, 11(1).

Mohammadi, H. and Su, L. (2010). International Evidence on Crude Oil Price Dynamics: Applications of ARIMA-GARCH Models. *Energy Economics*, 32(5).

Morana, C. (2001). A Semiparametric Approach to Short-Term Oil Price Forecasting. *Energy Economics*, 23(3).

Narayan, P. K. and Narayan, S. (2007). Modelling Oil Price Volatility. *Energy Policy*, 35(12).

Oberndorfer, U. (2009). Energy Prices, Volatility, and the Stock Market: Evidence from the Eurozone. *Energy Policy*, 37(12).

OECD/IEA (2008). World Energy Outlook 2008. Technical report, Paris.

OECD/IEA (2010). Oil Market Report–April 2013. Technical report, Paris.

OPEC (2012). Monthly Oil Market Report: November 2012. http://www.opec.org/opec_web/static_files_project/media/downloads/publications/MOMR_November_2012.pdf. Accessed December 8, 2012.

Perron, P. (1989). The Great Crash, the Oil Price Shock, and the Unit Root Hypothesis. *Econometrica*, 57(6).

Reboredo, J. C. (2011). How do Crude Oil Prices Co-move? A Copula Approach. *Energy Economics*, 33(5).

Sadeghi, M. and Shavvalpour, S. (2006). Energy Risk Management and Value at Risk Modeling. *Energy Policy*, 34(18).

Sadorsky, P. (2006). Modeling and Forecasting Petroleum Futures Volatility. *Energy Economics*, 28(4).

Salisu, A. A. and Fasanya, I. O. (2012). Comparative Performance of Volatility Models for Oil Price. *International Journal of Energy Economics and Policy*, 2(3).

Salisu, A. A. and Fasanya, I. O. (2013). Modelling Oil Price Volatility with Structural Breaks. *Energy Policy*.

Sauer, F. N. (2012). How the Few Inflict Inflation on the Many. Fred Sauer Matrix: Deeper Analysis of Economics and Politics. http://www.fredsauermatrix.com/85-How-the-Few-Inflict-Inflation-on-the-Many.html. Accessed November 10, 2012.

Schofield, N. C. (2007). *Commodity Derivatives, Markets and Applications*. Wiley, Chichester.

Silvennoinen, A. and Terasvirta, T. (2009). Multivariate GARCH Models. In T. G. Andersen, R. A. Davis, J.-P. K. and Mikosch, T., editors, *Handbook of Financial Time Series*. Springer, Berlin.

Thornton, D. L. and Batten, D. (1984). Lag Length Selection and Granger Causality. The Federal Reserve Bank of St.Louis: Working Paper. http://research.stlouisfed.org/wp/1984/1984-001.pdf. Accessed January 21, 2013.

Tsay, R. S. (2010). *Analysis of Financial Time Series, 3rd ed.* Wiley, Hoboken, NJ.

Tudor, C. and Anghel, A. (2012). On the Causal Relationship between Oil Prices and Equity Markets. http://www.wseas.us/e-library/conferences/2012/Algarve/EEESD/EEESD-42.pdf. Accessed January 21, 2013.

Verbeek, M. (2004). *A Guide to Modern Econometrics, 2nd Ed.* Wiley, Chichester.

Vo, M. (2009). Regime-switching Stochastic Volatility: Evidence from the Crude Oil Market. *Energy Economics*, 31(5).

Wei, Y., Wang, Y., and Huang, D. (2010). Forecasting Crude Oil Market Volatility: Further Evidence Using GARCH-Class Models. *Energy Economics*, 32(6).

Weiner, R. . (1991). Is the World Oil Market "One Great Pool"? *The Energy Journal*, 12(3):95–107.

Westgaard, S., Estenstad, M., Seim, M., and Frydenberg, S. (2011). Cointegration of ICE Gas Oil and Crude Oil Futures. *Energy Economics*, 33(2).

Data sources

- Bloomberg, accessed on September 2012
- EIA, Cushing, Oklahoma Stocks of Crude Oil and Petroleum Products, retrieved November 30, 2012 from http://www.eia.gov/dnav/pet/pet_stoc_wstk_dcu_ycuok_w.htm

4

Energy Spread Modeling Using Copulas

Sjur Westgaard

1 Introduction: Motivation for Using Copulas in Energy Spread Modeling

Analyzing energy spreads is very important for many market participants. A refinery sells gas oil and other fuel products and uses crude oil as input. The company is therefore exposed to the crack spread (the difference between the gas oil price and the crude oil prices) times the volume produced. A gas (coal) power plant is exposed to the difference between the prices of electricity and natural gas (coal) times the production of electricity. These power plants also need to take into account the carbon price, as they are charged an emission cost depending on the technology and the carbon price traded in the market. In recent years, several important textbooks have appeared covering analysis and discussion of energy modeling (including energy spreads). Some of these include Wengler (2001), Errera and Brown (2002), Ronn (2002), Eydeland and Wolyniec (2003), Geman (2005, 2008), Kaminski (2005a,b, 2012), Burger et al. (2007), Edwards (2010), and James (2008). However, few of these authors discuss the details of modeling energy spreads correctly.

Pricing of multiasset options and risk measurement of positions in two or more energy commodities require proper modeling of the joint distribution of the returns. More generally, the distribution of the returns of an energy commodity portfolio will be a function of the marginal distributions of the individual assets in the portfolio and the dependence structure between those assets. Standard approaches based on the Gaussian distribution assume normally or Student-t-distributed marginals for each energy commodity as well as linear dependencies and symmetric tails. However, in practice we observe various degrees of skewness and excess kurtosis for different energy commodities due to their specific supply and demand conditions. For example, electricity and natural gas can only be stored to a limited extent and hence, if there is a sudden increase in demand when capacity is restricted, it will lead to large upward price jumps. The supply curve in the electricity market is also nonlinear, which leads to a nonlinear relationship between electricity and natural gas prices.

Copulas can capture complex dependence structures, tail behavior, and marginal distributions of different financial assets. A detailed discussion and analysis of copulas applied to financial time series can be found in the major textbooks by McNeil et al. (2006), Alexander (2009), Patten (2009), and Cherubini et al. (2011). However, few of these discuss the application of copulas for modeling energy spreads. In recent years, there have been some academic papers that have appreciated the usage of copula modeling for energy commodities. I will discuss some of these at the end of this chapter together with some proposals for further research. The aim of this chapter is to illustrate how to use copulas in modeling spreads, using the crack spread as an example.

Section 2 gives a brief introduction to energy spreads (crack, spark, and dark spreads). The basics of copula theory are presented in Section 3. Section 4 describes how to calibrate and simulate from a copula with given marginals. Section 5 provides an example where I perform VaR modeling of crack spread positions using the Clayton copula and volatility filtered empirical marginals. Finally, Section 6 concludes and discusses some ideas for further research.

2 Energy Spreads

The most common energy spreads traded are the crack spread (the difference between the prices of fuels and crude oil), the spark spread (the difference between the prices of electricity and natural gas), and the dark spread (the difference between the prices of electricity and coal). The US market is mainly traded on NYMEX (which is part of the CME Group). The European market is traded on Intercontinental Exchange. Different terms, measures, and quotation units are used in the different markets. More details of the contracts can be found in CME Group (2014) and Intercontinental Exchange (2014). More precisely, the spark spread is defined as follows:

$$\text{Spark Spread} = \text{Price of Electricity} - [(\text{Cost of Gas}) * (\text{Heat Rate})]$$
$$= \$/\text{MWh} - [(\$/\text{MMBtu}) * (\text{MMbtu}/\text{MWh})]$$

The spark spread is the theoretical gross margin of a gas-fired power plant from selling a unit of electricity, having bought the gas required to produce this unit of electricity. All other costs, such as operation and maintenance, capital, emission, and other financial costs must be covered from the spark spread. In that sense, a spark spread is an indicator of market conditions, but it is not necessarily an exact measure of profitability for any one specific generator. The heat rate defines how much electricity in MWh we can get out of one unit of natural gas (BTU). Typical heat rates are around 20–60 percent for gas-fired power plants. Less efficient units have higher heat rates, and therefore require more natural gas to produce a MWh of electricity. A combined-cycle unit, which combines a combustion turbine with a combustion turbine, is more efficient than a steam turbine alone.

The dark spread is defined as follows:

$$\text{Dark Spread} = \text{Price of Electricity} - [(\text{Cost of Coal}) * (\text{Heat Rate})]$$
$$= \$/\text{MWh} - [(\$/\$) * (\$/\text{Ton}) * (\text{Ton}/\text{MWh})]$$

The dark spread is the theoretical gross margin of a coal-fired power plant from selling a unit of electricity, having bought the coal required to produce this unit of electricity. Again, all other costs must be covered from the dark spread. Typical heat rates are lower than for gas-fired power plants, usually around 35–40 percent.

Finally, the crack spread is defined as follows:

$$\text{Crack Spread} = [\text{Price of heating oil} * 42 - \text{Price of crude oil}]$$
$$= [(\$/\text{Gallon}) * (\text{Gallon}/\text{Barrel}) - \$/\text{Barrel}]$$

The crack spread is a term used in the oil industry and futures trading for the differential between the price of crude oil and petroleum products extracted from it—that is, the profit margin that an oil refinery can expect to make by "cracking" crude oil. The simplest version of the crack spread focuses just on two products. Heating oil is quoted in gallons and is converted into barrels (similar to crude oil) using a conversion factor of 42 (42 gallons in 1 barrel). It is one made from fractional distillation of petroleum but there are also other fuel products from the distillation process.

Crack spreads appear in many variations. Most refiners wishing to hedge their price exposures have used a crack ratio usually expressed as **X:Y:Z** where **X** represents a number of barrels of crude oil, **Y** represents a number of barrels of gasoline, and **Z** represents a number of barrels of distillate fuel oil subject to the constraint that **X=Y+Z**. This crack ratio is used for hedging purposes by buying **X** barrels of crude oil and selling **Y** barrels of gasoline and **Z** barrels of distillate in the futures market.

The crack spread **X:Y:Z** reflects the spread obtained by trading crude oil, gasoline, and heating oil according to this ratio. Widely used crack spreads are $3:2:1$, $5:3:2$, and $2:1:1$. The $3:2:1$ crack spread is the most popular of these, and widely quoted crack spread benchmarks are the "Gulf Coast $3:2:1$" and the "Chicago $3:2:1$." For simplicity, we focus only on the difference between heating oil (converted into \$/barrel) and crude oil in the following analysis but generalization is certainly possible.

3 Copula Theory and Examples of Copulas

The *joint distribution* of two i.i.d. random variables X_1 and X_2 is the bivariate distribution function that gives the probabilities of both X_1 and X_2 taking certain values at the same time (e.g., think of X_1 and X_2 as daily returns from heating oil and crude oil front-month futures contracts). The joint distribution of two or more asset returns can be found by first specifying the *marginals* or "stand-alone" distributions, and then using a *copula* to represent the association between the returns. Different copulas can be applied to any marginal distribution, and the marginal distributions can be different for each return series. There is a great flexibility using this tool as one can capture cases of skewed and fat-tailed marginal distributions, tail-dependence, asymmetry, and nonlinearity.

Sklar (1959) theorem says that given any joint distribution function $F(x_1, x_2)$, there is a unique copula function $C : [0,1] \times [0,1] \to [0,1]$ such that

$$F(x_1, x_2) = C(F_1(x_1), F_2(x_2)) \tag{1}$$

Conversely, if C is a copula and $F_1(x_1)$ and $F_2(x_2)$ are distribution functions then $F(x_1, x_2)$ defines a bivariate distribution with marginal distributions $F_1(x_1)$ and $F_2(x_2)$.

Differentiating Equation (1) with respect to x_1 and x_2 gives the joint density function $f(x_1, x_2)$ in terms of the marginal density functions $f_1(x_1)$ and $f_2(x_2)$:

$$f(x_1, x_2) = f_1(x_1) f_2(x_2) c(F_1(x_1), F_2(x_2)) \tag{2}$$

When the marginals $F_i(x_i)$ are uniformly distributed, $F(X) \sim U(0,1)$, we can write the *copula density* as $c(u_1, u_2)$ rather than as a function of x_1 and x_2.

Like any joint distribution function, copulas have conditional distributions. A conditional distribution is the distribution of one variable given that the others take some specified fixed values. The only difference between a conditional copula distribution and an ordinary distribution is that the marginals of every copula are uniformly distributed by definition. However, the conditional copula distributions can be quite different for different copulas. To define the conditional copula distribution consider, for simplicity, the bivariate case, that is, $C(u_1, u_2)$ with the following conditional distributions for the copula:

$$C_{1|2}(u_1, u_2) = P(U_1 < u_1 | U_2 = u_2) \tag{3}$$

The conditional distributions are obtained by taking the first derivative of the copula with respect to the variable:

$$C_{1|2}(u_1, u_2) = \frac{\partial C(u_1, u_2)}{\partial C(u_2)} \tag{4}$$

Using the conditional copula functions and the marginal distribution we can, for example, calculate the probability that the return of heating oil is below -2 percent, conditional upon the return of crude oil being zero. We can calculate sets of conditional probabilities according to the tail events we are interested investigating.

Alexander (2009) provides a detailed discussion of the most popular copulas used in finance with excel spreadsheets (bivariate cases). These are:

- Normal or Gaussian copula
- Student-t copula
- Normal mixture copula
- Clayton copula
- Gumbel copula

The Normal copula is the *implicit copula* in a multivariate normal distribution, also called the Gaussian copula. This copula is based on simple correlation as dependence measure and can only capture weak and symmetric tail-dependence. Hence it is somewhat restricted. According to our initial discussion, this is not appropriate for modeling dependencies for energy commodity returns. The Student-t copula can capture stronger tail-dependence but is limited to symmetric dependence (like for the normal copula). The inputs for the Student-t copula are both the correlation coefficient and the degrees of freedom of the t-distribution. The Normal mixture copula is more flexible. It is a mixture of two Normal copulas (in the bivariate case). The parameters in the copula are the correlation coefficient and the probability that governs the mixture of the distributions. Normal mixture copulas are attractive because they can capture complex association patterns but still allow for a very tractable analysis. For instance, the use of a positive correlation in one normal copula and a negative correlation in the other will produce different dependencies between the variables in the four tails of the joint distribution. Two and two tails have to be symmetric, however. To allow for non-symmetric tails, the Clayton copula and the Gumbel copula can be used. These are both part of the large class of what is called Archimedean copulas. The Clayton copula captures lower-tail-dependence and the Gumbel copula captures upper-tail-dependence. In Section 5 of this chapter, we present an application using the Clayton copula. The Clayton copula and the Gumbel copula include only one parameter that governs the one-sided tail-dependence (lower resp. upper). The functional form of these copulas makes calibration simple.

4 Calibration and Simulation from a Copula

Some bivariate copulas (Normal, Student-t, Clayton, and Gumbel) are easy to calibrate as they only depend on one parameter. For these copulas there is a direct link between rank correlations such as Kendall's Tau and the parameters in the copula. Section 5 illustrates a method that first estimates Kendall's Tau from data (volatility-adjusted heating oil and crude oil returns) and then calibrates the dependence parameter of the Clayton copula. For more advanced copulas with more parameters, one needs to apply other techniques, such as maximum likelihood. The principle is to make the copula density as close as possible to the empirical copula density. This is a challenging task, however since the empirical copula density can be "spiky" and small changes in the sample can lead to large changes in the estimated parameters (see Alexander, 2009, for a further discussion on this issue).

When the marginal return distributions are not elliptical and when there are nonlinearities and asymmetric tail behavior, Pearson's linear correlation coefficient is an inaccurate and misleading measure of association between two variables. In this case, we need more general measures of dependence based on ranked data. Rank correlations are nonparametric measures of dependence based on such information. The most common used measures are Spearman's Rho and Kendall's Tau. Kendall's Tau is described later and the measure, which is used in Section 5.

Consider two pairs of observations on continuous random variables X and Y, denoted (x_1, y_1) and (x_2, y_2). E.g. think of X as the returns of heating oil and Y as the returns of crude oil on days 1 and 2. We say that the pairs are concordant if $x_1 - x_2$ has the same sign as $y_1 - y_2$ and disconcordant if $x_1 - x_2$ has the opposite sign as $y_1 - y_2$. That is, the pairs are concordant if $(x_1 - x_2)(y_1 - y_2) > 0$ and disconcordant if

$(x_1 - x_2)(y_1 - y_2) < 0$. Kendall's Tau is calculated by comparing all possible pairs of observations $\{(x_i, y_j), (x_i, y_j)\}$ for $i \neq j$. Ordering does not matter, so the total number of pairs is:

$$\binom{n}{2} = \frac{1}{2}n(n-1) \tag{5}$$

If we count the number of concordant pairs, N_C, and the number of disconcordant pairs, N_D, Kendall's Tau is given by

$$\tau = \frac{N_C - N_D}{\frac{1}{2}n(n-1)} \tag{6}$$

When calibrating copulas it is common to calibrate the marginals first to a parametric distribution or using the empirical distribution and then calibrate the copula. In simulation, it is the other way around: one first simulates uniform distributed variables where the dependence is taken into account and then inverts the uniform distributed variables into a specific parametric distribution or empirical distribution. The benefit of this approach is that many different copulas (capturing different dependency structures) can be applied while preserving the characteristics of the marginal distributions. This two-step procedure is described in the next section when we look at a specific example.

To sum up, the procedure for copula analysis takes four steps:

- First, *visually investigate the empirical facts of the data*. What do the marginal distribution looks like according to the histogram and how does the scatterplot look like? What dependence structure can we see in the data? Is it linear or nonlinear? How does the tail behavior look like (strong or weak)? Is the tail behavior symmetric or asymmetric?
- According to the empirical facts of the data, *choose marginals* (parametric distributions or use the empirical distribution) and a *copula* that fits the data. There are formal procedures (not discussed here) that can be applied to find the "best" copula.
- *Calibrate the parameters* of the copula to the data. For simple one-parametric copulas, there will be a link between the parameter value and rank correlation measures, such as Kendall's Tau.
- After calibration, *simulate* from the copula. This is done by imposing the dependency structure using the copula on uniform distributed variables. Then invert these values using a parametric or empirical marginal distribution.

5 Application: VaR Modeling of Crack Spread Positions Using the Clayton Copula and Volatility Filtered Empirical Marginals

To illustrate how we apply copulas for modeling energy spreads, we consider the front-month futures prices of heating oil and crude oil from NYMEX. These contracts are chosen since they are by far the most liquid. For more details on the contracts, see CME Group (2014). The data are available from Datastream's financial information services. We consider the last 10 years of daily data from April 8, 2004, to April 8, 2014, with 2,517 observations in total.[1] Holidays, weekends, and other days with no trading are deleted from the dataset. Figure 4.1 shows the price data used in the analysis. The figure shows in the upper left panel the price ($/gallon) of the NYMEX front-month futures of heating oil. The lower left panel shows the price ($/barrel) of the NYMEX front-month futures of crude oil. In the lower right panel, prices of heating oil are converted into $/barrel ($/gallon * 42). The upper right panel shows the crack spread (Price of heating oil minus crude oil ($/barrel)).

We see an interesting pattern in these series over the period 2004–2014. Up until the financial crises in 2008, prices of oil were increasing with a

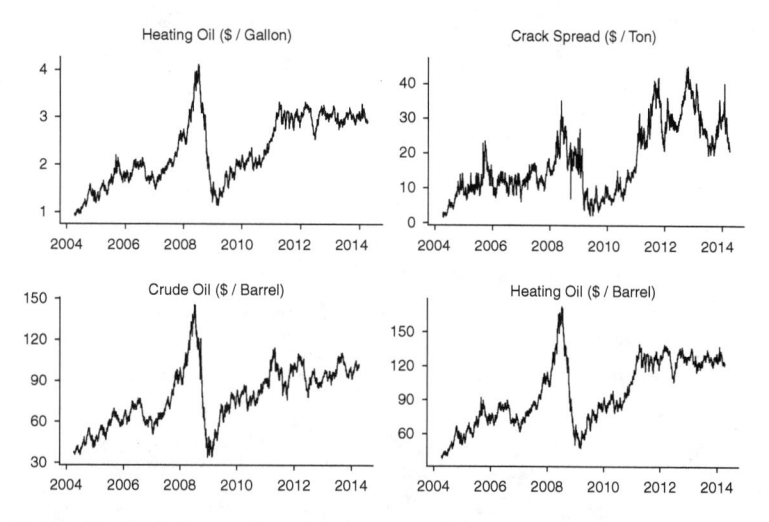

Figure 4.1 This figure shows in the upper left panel the price ($/gallon) of NYMEX front-month futures of heating oil. The lower left panel shows the price ($/barrel) of NYMEX front-month futures of crude oil. In the lower right panel, prices of heating oil is converted into $/barrel ($/gallon * 42). The upper right panel shows the crack spread (Price of heating oil minus crude oil ($/barrel)). All data are on daily basis from the period April 8, 2004, to April 8, 2014. Dates with no trading (holidays and weekends) are deleted from the dataset.

sharp rise the years before 2008. This was a period of rapid economic growth of the world economy, with high demand for oil and refined products. At the peak, the price of crude oil was over 140 $/barrel and the price of heating oil above 4$/gallon. In the year after the financial crises, prices fell dramatically, reaching levels below $40/barrel for crude oil and near 1$/gallon for heating oil. Since then, prices have gone up and have now leveled out at around 100$/barrel and 3$/gallon, respectively. This has followed a slow upswing in the global economy with a moderate increase in demand for oil and fuel products. The crack spread followed the same pattern, but was far more volatile. The crack spread is a product of the interplay of the two commodity prices, each subject to different but related supply and demand balances, and hence the range of values can vary widely. For example, product supply shortages resulting from serious disruptions such as hurricanes or other refinery or pipeline outages can cause large spikes of short duration.

Figure 4.2 shows in the upper left panel the returns (log of price changes of NYMEX front-month futures of heating oil and crude oil. When calculating returns from futures data, there is a so-called roll return in each series on the day of the month when the expiring contract is replaced by a new one. For the period considered, we have removed these returns as they are not realizable and thus meaningless from an economic point of view. It is clear from Figure 4.2 that volatility varies over time (volatility clustering). Since usage of copulas requires independent data, we must account for heteroskedasticity (time-varying volatility) in the data before using a copula on the two series.

One approach would be to apply the well-known method of RiskMetrics, where conditional volatility is a weighted function of previous squared returns and previous estimates of conditional volatility. The exponential-weighted moving average (EWMA) of volatility in the RiskMetrics method weighs previous daily returns by a factor of 0.06 and previous estimates of conditional volatility by 0.94.[2] The conditional volatility is initiated by an estimate of historical standard deviation of returns. The formula is given by

$$\text{EWMA} = \sigma_t = \sqrt{0.06 r_{t-1}^2 + 0.94 \sigma_{t-1}^2} \qquad (7)$$

where σ_t is the conditional volatility and r_t^2 is the squared returns. The EWMA for both series are shown in the lower left panel of Figure 4.2. In general, the conditional volatility of heating oil is lower than that of crude oil. Around the financial crises, daily volatility reached as high as 7 percent (annualized by the number of trading days per year: $7\% * \sqrt{250} = 110.7\%$). The volatility has gone down quite a lot in recent

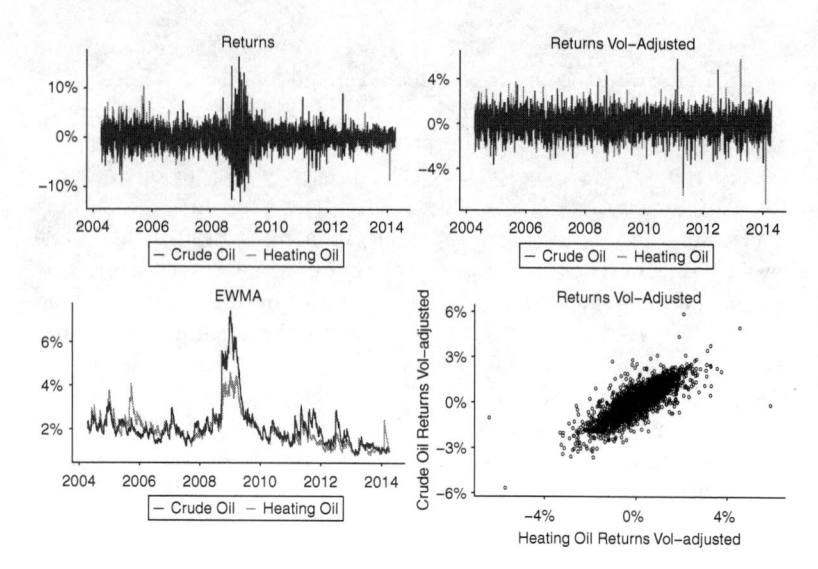

Figure 4.2 This figure shows in the upper left panel the returns (log of price changes of NYMEX front-month futures of heating oil and crude oil. The lower left panel shows the exponential weighted moving average of volatility (EWMA) for heating oil returns and crude oil returns with a weighting parameter of 0.94. In the upper right panel the return series are divided by EWMA and multiplied by 100 (volatility adjusted). A scatter plot of crude oil return (Y-axis) and heating oil return (X-axis) is shown in the lower right panel. All data are on daily basis from the period April 8, 2004, to April 8, 2014. Dates with no trading (holidays and weekends) are deleted from the dataset.

years and is now in the range of 1–2 percent on a daily basis (15.8—31.6 percent annualized). In the upper right panel of Figure 4.2 the return series are divided by EWMA and multiplied by 100. That is, we adjust the series by its volatility such that the data become independent. From the plot, we now have a series looking more like white noise, which can be modeled directly with a copula. A scatter plot of volatility adjusted crude oil returns (Y-axis) and heating oil return (X-axis) is shown in the lower right panel of Figure 4.2. We see somewhat stronger lower tail-dependence (when returns of both series are low) than higher tail-dependence (when both series are high). There is no indication of strong nonlinearity, however, something we would expect if we were dealing with prices of electricity and natural gas. The data indicate that the Clayton copula could be a candidate for modeling this dependence. Using correlation, we would miss the fact that there are different tail dependencies in the data. When modeling risk of spread positions (with measures such as VaR and CVaR) it is crucial that we take this into account.

Figure 4.3 displays the distribution of daily returns (log of price changes) of NYMEX front-month futures of heating oil and crude oil. Table 4.1 displays the descriptive statistics for the series as well as the EWMA for both heating oil and crude oil. It is clear that the energy commodities display the same features that we find in the stock and FX markets. Although the return distribution is rather symmetric, it includes fat tails and which makes the normal distribution inappropriate. Some parametric distributions could be proposed as candidates for the marginals, for example, the Student-t distribution. In this case, though, I would rather calibrate the marginals for heating oil and crude oil using their respective empirical distributions.

The Clayton copula is in the class of Archimedean copulas based on a generator function. It is a simple one-parametric function that can capture lower tail-dependence (unlike, e.g., the Gumbel copula, that captures upper-tail-dependence). The formula for the bivariate Clayton copula is given by

$$c(u_1, u_2) = (\alpha + 1)(u_1^{-\alpha} + u_2^{-\alpha} - 1)^{-2-(\frac{1}{\alpha})} u_1^{-\alpha-1} + u_2^{-\alpha-1} \qquad (8)$$

where u_1 and u_2 are random numbers from a uniform $[0, 1]$ distribution and α is a parameter. The copula has zero upper tail-dependence and positive lower tail-dependence where the level of dependence is governed by the value of α. As $\alpha \to \infty$, the dependence in the lower tail goes to 1.

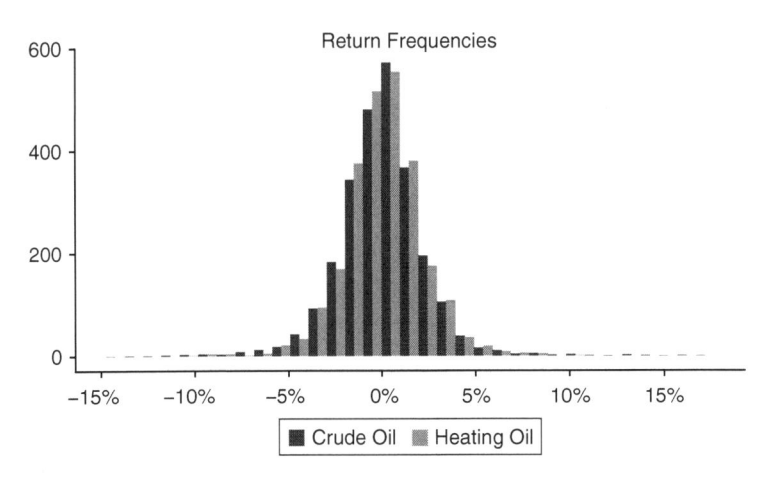

Figure 4.3 The distribution of daily returns (log of price changes) of NYMEX front-month futures of heating oil and crude oil. All data are on daily basis from the period April 8, 2004, to April 8, 2014. Dates with no trading (holidays and weekends) are deleted from the dataset.

Table 4.1 Descriptive statistics of returns (log of price changes) of NYMEX front-month futures of heating oil and crude oil

	Returns		EWMA	
	Heating Oil	Crude Oil	Heating Oil	Crude Oil
Obs	2,517	2,517	2,517	2,517
Mean	0.05%	0.04%	1.96%	2.10%
Median	0.05%	0.11%	1.86%	1.90%
Max	10.40%	16.41%	4.61%	7.43%
Min	−10.20%	−13.07%	0.80%	0.82%
Stdev	2.09%	2.33%	0.73%	1.03%
95% quantile	3.39%	3.44%	3.66%	4.94%
5% quantile	−3.33%	−3.61%	1.01%	1.09%
Skew	−0.01	0.09	1.09	2.59
Kurt	2.13	5.15	1.29	7.68
Correlation		0.80		

Note: All data are on a daily basis from the period 8 April 2004 to 8 April 2014. Dates with no trading (holidays and weekends) are deleted from the dataset. Roll returns (when contracts roll over to a new one) are also deleted. The table displays the number of observations, mean, median, maximum, minimum, standard deviation (daily bases), 95% and 5% quantiles, skewness, excess kurtosis and correlation (between the returns of heating oil and crude oil). We also show similar statistics for the exponential weighting motiving average of volatility (EWMA), using a weighting parameter of 0.94.

In the Clayton copula, the dependence parameter α is given by the following formula where τ is Kendall's Tau given in Equation (6):

$$\alpha = 2\tau(1-\tau)^{-1} \tag{9}$$

Given the data, we estimate Kendall's Tau to be 0.6328 and thus α to be 3.4471.[3] Using this value for α, the density function $c(u_1, u_2)$ of the Clayton copula is exhibited in Figure 4.4. Note the strong lower tail-dependence (when u_1 and u_2 are both low) and the zero dependence in the upper tail (when u_1 and u_2 are both high). u_1 and u_2 are random uniform numbers in the interval [0, 1] on the x- and y-axis.

The conditional value of u_2 given a value of u_1 can also be expressed for the Clayton copula (see Alexander [2009] for derivations):

$$u_2 = C_{2|1}^{-1}(u_2|u_1) = \left(1 + u_1^{-\alpha}\left(v^{-\frac{\alpha}{1+\alpha}} - 1\right)\right)^{-\frac{1}{\alpha}} \tag{10}$$

where u_1, u_2, and v are random numbers from a uniform [0, 1] distribution and α is a parameter. Using this formula ensures that u_1 and u_2 are uniform [0, 1] distributed plus having a Clayton copula-dependence according to a given dependence parameter.

ENERGY SPREAD MODELING 109

Density Function Clayton Copula

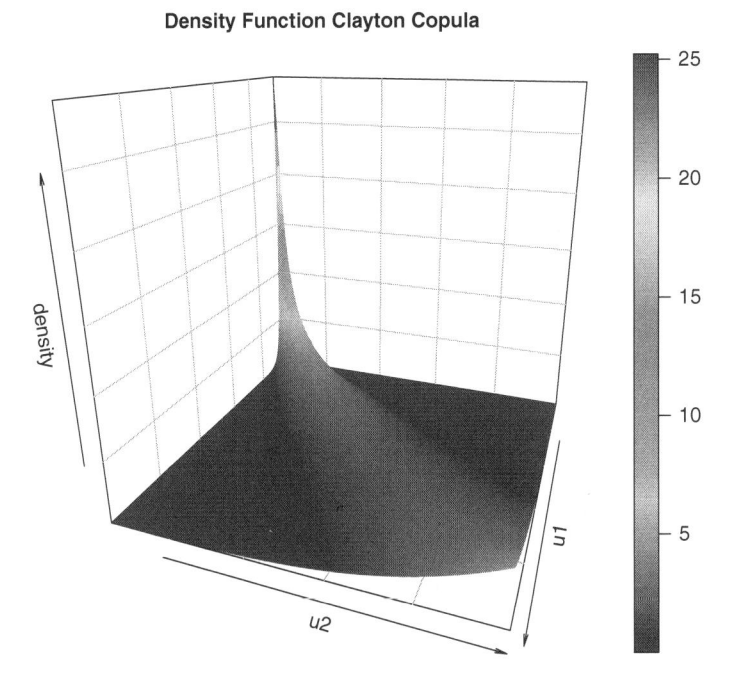

Figure 4.4 The density function of a Clayton copula with $\alpha = 3.4471$ according to the calibration of the data used in Section 5. On the X-axis and Y-axis, we have uniform distributed variables in the range 0 to 1. The Z axis measures the density.

In Figure 4.5 we display the simulation results for the estimated copula. These are obtained as follows:

- First, we start out by drawing a random number from a uniform distribution in the interval [0, 1]. Call this number u_1.
- Then we draw a new random number from a uniform distribution in the interval [0, 1] and call this number v.
- The value of u_2 is now obtained with Equation (10) using the parameter α found in the calibration process.
- u_1 and u_2 are now two uniform [0, 1] distributed variables with a Clayton copula dependence structure (see Figure 4.5, upper left panel).
- The next step is to invert the two uniform [0, 1] distributions into their empirical distributions. We use u_1 and u_2 as probabilities and find the corresponding quantiles from the empirical/historical returns (volatility filtered) distributions of heating oil and crude oil, respectively. These returns series are then de-filtered.

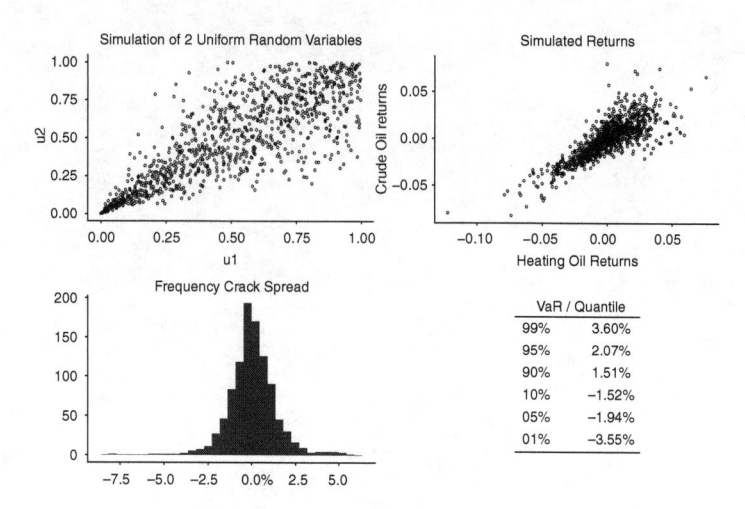

Figure 4.5 Simulation results for the Clayton copula with $\alpha = 3.4471$ and marginals of heating oil and crude oil returns according to their empirical distributions. In the upper left panel, simulation of 2 uniform random variables are displayed with the dependency according to the Clayton copula. In the upper right panel a scatterplot of the heating oil and crude oil returns from the simulation is shown. In the lower panel, the crack spread density is shown (heating oil returns minus crude oil returns) together with empirical quantiles from the simulation.

- The scatterplot in the upper right corner of Figure 4.5 shows realizations of returns for crude oil and heating oil returns. By repeating the simulations, we capture the dependence structure and the marginal distributions that was in the descriptive analysis.
- For each simulation, we can calculate the crack spread in percent and construct a distribution of the crack spread (long one unit of heating oil and short one unit of crude oil). This is shown in the lower left panel of Figure 4.5.
- Having the distribution of crack spreads, we can calculate risk measures such as VaR and CVaR. In Figure 4.5 we show 99, 95, 90, 10, 5, and 1 percent VaR from one simulation. Many simulations need to be performed and the average of the VaR estimates needs to be calculated.

6 Conclusion and Further Research

Pricing of multiasset options and risk measurement of positions in two or more energy commodities requires proper modeling of the joint distribution of returns. We have shown how this can be done for the crack spread (the difference between heating oil and crude oil) using a Clayton copula where we capture the lower tail-dependence and empirical marginals where we capture the stylized facts of the return distributions for the two energy commodities.

This chapter is meant to be a brief survey on how copulas can be applied to energy spread modeling. In the last 5–10 years, many research paths have evolved. Copulas applied to other energy spreads such as the spark and dark spreads are very interesting because of the distinct tail behavior (right tail-dependence) and nonlinearity caused by the supply stack of electricity production. A fruitful starting point for tackling this problem is Benth and Kettler (2010). Another interesting research path is to investigate energy spread derivative pricing with usage of copulas in more detail. Herath and Kumar (2006) provides a starting point for this type of analysis.

Copula modeling can also be used to model energy prices with one market, for example, different oil prices (see Reboredo, 2011) or different electricity area prices (see Ignatieva and Trueck, 2013).

I have only looked at bivariate copula modeling. The extension to multivariate copula modeling is developing (see Emmanouil and Nomikos [2012]) and should be very interesting from both a practical and academic point of view.

An implicit assumption I have made in the preceding analysis is that the dependence between the returns of heating oil and crude oil is constant over time. Put differently, I have represented the dependence with a time-invariant copula. An enhancement for further research would be to apply a dynamic copula approach (see Benth and Kettler, 2010; Cherubini et al., 2011; Lu et al., 2011), allowing for the dependency structure to vary over time. In a similar way one could let also the marginal distributions change over time. Much remains to be examined here, however, on efficient estimation procedures and goodness of fit tests.

Notes

1. The data and the spreadsheet applications are available upon request by contacting the author of this chapter (sjur.westgaard@iot.ntnu.no)
2. An alternative would be to model the volatility as a GARCH process. In sample these methods yield more or less the same results. Out-of-sample forecasting with GARCH and EWMA yields very different results, however, since the former is based on the mean reversion of volatility to an unconditional level, while the latter is based on a random walk for volatility, making the last observation the forecast for the future. Since forecasting is not the topic here, I have applied the simpler method.
3. A VBA for Excel code has been implemented for the Kendallà's Tau calculation.

References

Alexander, C. (2009). *Market Risk Analysis: Value at Risk Models*, volume I,II,III,IV. Wiley, Hoboken, NJ.

Benth, F. E. and Kettler, P. (2010). Dynamic copula models for the spark spread. *Quantitative Finance*, 11(3):407–421.

Burger, M., Graeber, B., and Schindlmayr, G. (2007). *Managing Energy Risk: An Integrated View on Power and Other Energy Markets*. Wiley, Hoboken, NJ.

Cherubini, U., Mulinacci, S., Gobbi, F., and Romagnoli, S. (2011). *Dynamic Copula Methods in Finance*. Wiley, Hoboken, NJ.

CME Group (2014). Futures and Options Trading for Risk Management – CME Group.

Edwards, D. W. (2010). *Energy Trading and Investing: Trading, Risk Management and Structuring Deals in the Energy Markets*. McGraw Hill, New York, NY.

Emmanouil, K. N. and Nomikos, N. (2012). Extreme value theory and mixed canonical vine copulas on modelling energy price risks. Working paper, Cass Business School.

Errera, S. and Brown, S. L. (2002). *Fundamentals of Trading Futures and Options*. PennWell, Tulsa, OK.

Eydeland, A. and Wolyniec, K. (2003). *Energy and Power Risk Management: New Developments in Modeling, Pricing, and Hedging*. Wiley, Hoboken, NJ.

Geman, H. (2005). *Commodities and Commodity Derivatives: Modelling and Pricing of Agriculturals, Metals and Energy*. Wiley, Hoboken, NJ.

Geman, H. (2008). *Risk Management in Commodities Markets: From Shipping to Agriculturals and Energy*. Wiley, Hoboken, NJ.

Herath, H. and Kumar, P. (2006). Non-linear dependence modeling in energy derivatives. Working paper, Department of Accounting, Faculty of Business, Brock University, Ontario, Canada.

Ignatieva, K. and Trueck, S. (2013). Modeling spot price dependence in Australian electricity markets with applications to risk management. Working paper, University of New South Wales, Sydney, Australia.

Intercontinental Exchange (2014). ICE: IntercontinentalExchange, Inc.

James, T. (2008). *Energy Markets: Price Risk Management and Trading*. Wiley, Hoboken, NJ.

Kaminski, V. (2005a). *Energy Modelling: Advances in the Management of Uncertainty*, 2nd ed. Risk Books, London.

Kaminski, V. (2005b). *Managing Energy Price Risk: The New Challanges and Solutions*, 3rd ed. Risk Books, London.

Kaminski, V. (2012). *Energy Markets*. Risk Books, London.

Lu, X. F., Lai, K. K., and Liang, L. (2011). Portfolio value-at-risk estimation in energy futures markets with time-varying copula-GARCH model. *Annuals of Operations Research*, pp. 1–25.

McNeil, A. J., Frey, R., and Embrechts, P. (2006). *Quantitative Risk Management: Concepts, Techniques and Tools*. Princeton University Press, Princeton, NJ.

Patten, A. (2009). *Copula-Based Models for Financial Time Series*. Springer, New York, NY.

Reboredo, J. C. (2011). How do crude oil prices co-move? *Energy Economics*, 33:948–955.
Ronn, E. (2002). *Real Options and Energy Management.* Risk Books, London.
Sklar, A. (1959). *Fonctions de répartition án dimensions et leurs marges.* Publications of l'Institut de Statistique de l'Université de Paris, Paris.
Wengler, J. (2001). *Managing Energy Risk: A Nontechnical Guide to Markets and Trading.* PennWell, Tulsa, OK.

5

Modeling and Estimating Electricity Futures: A Non-Gaussian Market Model Approach

Enzo Fanone

1 Introduction: Review of Electricity Futures Price Models: HJM vs LMM

In the stochastic modeling of electricity markets, there are two main approaches in the literature. The first one starts with a stochastic model for the spot price, and from this derives the futures price dynamics by using no-arbitrage principles. The second one directly models the price dynamics of the complete forward curves and futures contracts traded in commodity markets.

Most of the existing literature focuses on developing models for the spot price. Some examples are Lucia and Schwartz (2002), Benth et al. (2007), and Fanone et al. (2013). The advantage of modeling the forward prices directly in contrast to spot models is that one can work with current forward prices. In addition, since electricity is largely nonstorable, there is no cost-of-carry relationship linking spot and forward prices; this means that electricity forward prices are largely disconnected from current spot prices.

In this chapter, we analyze models of the second group. Also, similar as in fixed-income markets modeling, we can roughly divide the electricity futures models into two groups: HJM (Heath Jarrow Morton model, Heath et al. (1992)) and LMM (Libor Market Model, Brace et al. (1997)) models.

Most of the existing literature focuses on stochastic models of futures contracts based on the HJM approach. Models based on the HJM framework are derived by directly modeling the dynamics of instantaneous forward/futures prices. Bjerksund et al. (2000) were the first to consider the HJM approachs in electricity markets. A discussion of HJM-type models in the context of power futures is given in Koekebakker (2003), Koekebakker and Ollmar (2005), and Fanelli and Musti (2008). Following these authors, a general representation of the instantaneous futures prices in the risk-neutral setting, with a deterministic volatility function proportional to the futures prices level, is given by

$$\frac{df(t,T)}{f(t,T)} = \sum_{k=1}^{p} \Sigma_k(t,T) dB_k(t) \qquad (1)$$

where $f(t, T)$ denotes the futures price at date t for delivery of the commodity at time T, with $t < T$, where $c = 1, \ldots, C$ are the number of different electricity futures contracts and B_k, $k = 1, \ldots, n$ are independent standard Brownian motions. This means that the natural log of the futures price is distributed:

$$\ln f(t,T) \sim \mathcal{N}\bigg(\ln f(0,T)$$

$$-\frac{1}{2} \sum_{k=1}^{p} \int_0^t \Sigma_k(s,T)^2 ds, \sum_{k=1}^{p} \int_0^t \Sigma_k(s,T)^2 ds \bigg) \qquad (2)$$

where $\mathcal{N}(m; v)$ is a normal distribution with mean m and variance v. An important issue in Equation (1) is choosing the volatility structure that represents an input of the model with the initial term structure of the futures prices.

In interest rate theory, these volatility functions can be specified according to different aims: functions yielding Markov spot rates, functions to fit an implied volatility surface (for instance, a model calibrated to caps and swaptions), or functions constructed ad-hoc for fitting loading factors obtained by a principal component analysis (PCA). For example, Bjerksund et al. (2000) propose two different kinds of volatility function, a one- and a three-factor model, respectively, for evaluating and risk management purposes. Koekebakker (2003) and Koekebakker and Ollmar (2005) propose an exponentially decaying volatility function, consistent with Lucia and Schwartz (2002) spot price model that captures the Samuelson effect.[1] Finally, Fanelli and Musti (2008) have proposed a HJM two-regime model for Italian electricity swap prices, assuming that the forward price dynamics are characterized by two different kinds of movements: in normal stable periods they fluctuate around some long-run average, and in turbulent periods they experience jumps and short-lived spikes.[2]

Unlike stochastic models based on the HJM approach, forward models based on the LIBOR model proposed for fixed income markets were not highly regarded in the academic literature on electricity pricing. As far as we know, there are only four studies which apply market models to electricity markets: Benth and Koekebakker (2005), Kiesel et al. (2009), Boerger (2008), and Andresen et al. (2012).

Benth and Koekebakker (2005) provide a mathematical framework to model the swap curve using NordPool data. They use several volatility functions for one-factor models. In particular, they show that seasonality is an important feature of volatility in the futures market. Therefore, they introduce a seasonality function in the volatility specifications by modeling it as a truncated Fourier series. Kiesel et al. (2009) propose a two-factor (log-normal) model for electricity futures to fit the market implied volatilities of the European energy exchange (EEX) futures options.

Few attempts have been made to describe the electricity forward and futures dynamics directly based on Lévy processes. Boerger (2008) considers an extension of the Kiesel et al. (2009) model, a two-factor normal inverse Gaussian (NIG) process for electricity futures prices, and calibrates the model using Fourier option pricing formulas. This can be done since the characteristic function of the log-price, described by a two factor Lévy process, is known analytically. Andresen et al. (2012) present a discrete random-field model for forward prices driven by the multivariate NIG distribution and fit the model to forward prices from NordPool using a Markov chain Monte Carlo algorithm.

In this chapter, we analyze stochastic models based on the LMM idea to describe the price dynamics of forward and futures contracts traded in electricity markets.

2 Key Features of Electricity Futures Prices

Due to the special features of electricity, most notably its nonstorability, the modeling of electricity futures prices is far from trivial. For many applications such as risk management it is, however, essential to be able to properly describe the complex price behavior. Therefore, a detailed analysis of historical data are necessary to accurately build up a model that permits us to capture the characteristics of the dynamics of electricity prices.

Electricity futures contracts have the distinctive feature that they provide a constant volume of power over a period rather than the whole volume at maturity, paying the fixed futures prices. According to the nature of the contracts, they represent an exchange of fixed for floating electricity price. For this reason, futures/forward contracts are also called *swap contracts*.

There are different kinds of futures contracts. For example, at the EEX futures contracts are traded with weekly, monthly, quarterly, and yearly delivery period. For example, 1*MW* baseload *Feb09* is a monthly futures contract that gives the holder the obligation to buy 1MWh of energy for each hour of February, paying the futures price in Euros/MWh. The seller provides the buyer with the amount of energy of 1MW × 24h × 28. In addition to these contracts, called baseload, there are peak-load contracts that have a daily delivery from 8 a.m. to 8 p.m., Monday–Friday.

Another characteristic that can be observed on the futures market is the fact that the very volatile short-lived price movements (spikes) observed in the spot market are not transferred to the futures market or, at least not directly. Lower futures price volatility is explained by the fact that short-term changes in supply and/or demand for electricity have large and immediate effects on spot prices, but have a much smaller effect on futures prices. Futures prices depend on the average spot price during the delivery period, dampening the price movements of the spot. As a result, futures prices are far less sensitive to the arrival of (generally short-lived) shocks to the system. Futures prices will not be significantly influenced when these shocks occur before the start of the delivery period, unless they are expected to persist and influence spot prices during the delivery period.

Stochastic processes driving the forward/futures price dynamics proposed in the extant literature are designed to model several stylized facts. The first is the so-called Samuelson effect, i.e., the fact that local volatility of a short-term forward contract is greater than the local volatility of a long-term contract, and in particular that an exponential decay is observed as the time to maturity of the contract grows. This maturity effect is consistent with the notion that with the expiration date coming closer and closer, more information about market conditions at that date becomes available, which leads to an increase in volatility The second stylized fact is that this volatility does not go to zero, but rather to a fixed value, called long-term volatility, due to long-term uncertainty factors like technological innovation and structural modifications to commodity prices. Moreover, futures/forward prices also demonstrate the following features: time-series and cross-section seasonality, overlapping of delivery periods, mean-reversion and heavy tails of the return distribution of forward prices.

Time-series and cross-sectional seasonal periodic behavior is expected due to weather conditions. For example, the EEX futures average prices are significantly higher during the winter (first and fourth quarter). This

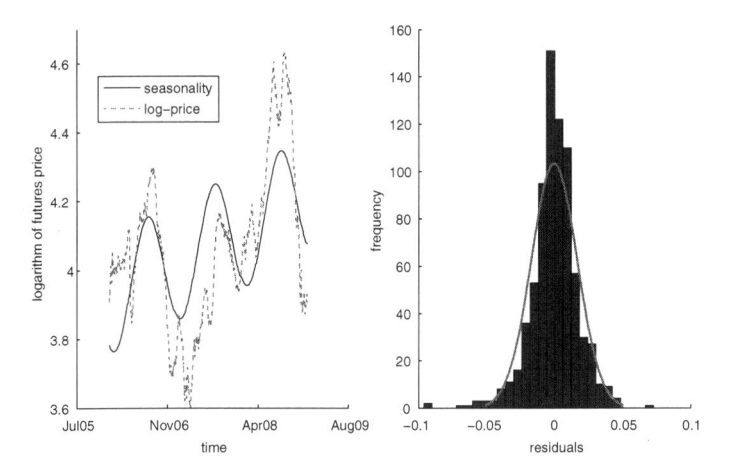

Figure 5.1 Seasonality and fitted normal density. Estimated seasonalities (left graph) and histograms (right graph) of the fifth month ahead futures residuals (are prices after trend, seasonal and AR(1) component have been removed, dashed line in the left graph).

pattern is observed for both monthly and quarterly futures price levels as well as log-returns. This periodic behavior can be called cross-sectional seasonality.

Figure 5.1 displays the time-series seasonality and shows that can it be identified by a parametric periodical function:

$$s_c(t) = \beta_0 + \beta_1 t + \beta_2 \cos\left(2\pi(t - \beta_3)/250\right) \qquad (3)$$

The parameters in Equation (3) can be estimated by using a least squares approach for each futures contract. For example, we plot on the left side of the Figure 5.1 the fitted result for the fifth month ahead futures contract listed on the German market from 2006 to 2008; in particular, an annual periodicity can be observed in the log-price. Differently, there is no evidence of annual seasonality for the yearly contracts (see, e.g., Di Poto and Fanone [2012]).

Another main feature of the electricity markets, which makes them completely different from others, is the overlapping of delivery periods. This means that a position in a quarterly futures can be replicated with a portfolio of three monthly futures positions, and in an analogous way, a yearly contract can be replicated with four quarterly futures. In the HJM framework the model describes the continuous forward curve dynamics, and the swaps obtained by the forward curve have to satisfy many no-arbitrage conditions. This makes the HJM approach complicated as discussed in Benth and Koekebakker (2005). This problem can be resolved by describing directly the swap dynamics in a market model framework, because in this case the non-overlapping swaps are directly modeled by choosing the appropriate *building block*[3]: monthly, quarterly, or yearly. Therefore, a smoothing procedure have to be implemented to delete the overlapping of delivery periods.

Different smoothing procedures were developed in the academic literature, Fleten and Lemming (2003), Benth et al. (2007) and Borak and Weron (2008). In this section, we apply the smoothing algorithm developed in Benth et al. (2007), where the forward curve can be written as the sum of a seasonal function and an adjustment function that measures the forward curve deviation from the seasonal component, respectively.

$$f(t) = s(t) + \epsilon(t) \tag{4}$$

By using the forward curve in Equation (4), we might build the swap prices of any delivery period $[\tau_s, \tau_e]$ as follows:

$$F(t, \tau_s, \tau_e) = \int_{\tau_s}^{\tau_e} du f(u) w(u, \tau_s, \tau_e) \tag{5}$$

where $w(u, \tau_s, \tau_e)$ is some kind of normalized weight function. The objective function of this algorithm is to maximize the smoothness of the adjustment function, which means:

$$\min \int_{\tau_s}^{\tau_e} dt [\epsilon''(t)]^2 \tag{6}$$

In this way, the swap market price provided in Equation (5) shall be obtained. The objective function (6) means that the goal of the algorithm is to find a continuous forward curve that smooths, according to the market, as far as possible. This algorithm allows us to build up swap prices for every delivery period that needs to be highlighted and not only for those traded in the market. Furthermore, we can create swap prices for any building block, and in that way they refer to the same time of the delivery period.

We use fourth-order polynomials for adjusting the function $\epsilon(t)$. This means that we can write the adjustment function as

$$\epsilon(t, \mathbf{x}) = \begin{cases} a_1 u^4 + b_1 u^3 + c_1 u^2 + d_1 u^1 + e_1 & t \in [t_0, t_1] \\ a_2 u^4 + b_2 u^3 + c_2 u^2 + d_2 u^1 + e_2 & t \in [t_1, t_2] \\ \ldots & \\ \ldots & \\ a_n u^4 + b_n u^3 + c_n u^2 + d_n u^1 + e_n & t \in [t_n - 1, t_n] \end{cases}$$

ESTIMATING ELECTRICITY FUTURES

and the parameters

$$\mathbf{x}^T = \Big[a_1, b_1, c_1, d_1, e_1;\quad a_2, b_2, c_2, d_2, e_2;\quad \ldots\ldots; a_n, b_n, c_n, d_n, e_n\Big]$$

are estimated solving the convex quadratic programming problem (6) with the following constraints:

$$\begin{cases} (a_{j+1} - a_j)u_j^4 + (b_{j+1} - b_j)u_j^3 + (c_{j+1} - c_j)u_j^2 + (d_{j+1} - d_j)u_j \\ \qquad + (e_{j+1} - e_j) = 0 \\ 4(a_{j+1} - a_j)u_j^3 + 3(b_{j+1} - b_j)u_j^2 + 2(c_{j+1} - c_j)u_j \\ \qquad + (d_{j+1} - d_j) = 0 \\ 12(a_{j+1} - a_j)u_j^2 + 6(b_{j+1} - b_j)u_j + (c_{j+1} - c_j) = 0 \\ \epsilon'(T_n, \mathbf{x}) = 0 \\ F_i^{mkt} = \displaystyle\int_{T_i^s}^{T_i^e} w(r,t)(s(t) + \epsilon(t, \mathbf{x})) \end{cases} \quad (7)$$

with $j=1,\ldots,n-1$.

The result of the smoothing algorithm applied to EEX closing futures prices of March 10, 2009 are presented in Figure 5.2. The root mean square

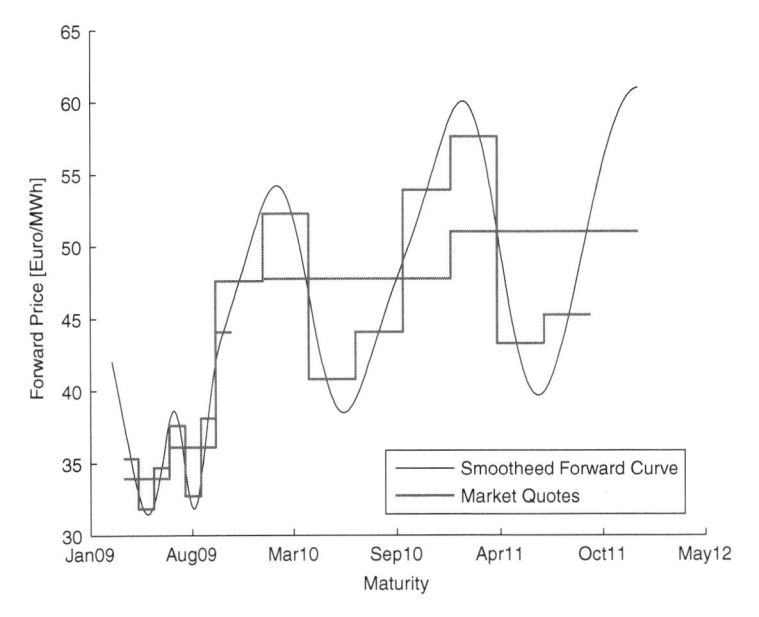

Figure 5.2 Smoothing forward curve. Example of the smoothing procedure for EEX futures on March 10, 2009.

error (RMSE) between the swap market prices and the extrapolated ones is equal to 0.3 percent.

Another important characteristic of futures prices is also their mean-reversion behavior. One cane define "mean-reversion" as the property of reverting to a certain constant or time-varying level with limited variance around it. After that the seasonal function in Equation (3) is estimated, we can remove the effect of this component by subtracting it from the log-price. Then, the existence of a mean-reversion component can be tested using the autocorrelation function (ACF) and partial autocorrelation function (PACF) functions. The ACF of the de-seasonalized data and the PACF of the filtered data (Figure 5.3) clearly indicate that we need a mean-reverting component to explain the evolution of the time series.

Last but not least, a feature of electricity futures prices is that the return distribution of forward prices is leptokurtic (see the right graph of Figure 5.1), that is, it has a high center peak and heavy tails (see, for example, Frestad et al. (2010) or Benth et al. (2008) for discussions). This suggests that Gaussian-based models will have shortcomings in representing the risk related to substantial market movements observed in electricity markets. Since risk measures and option prices depend on the

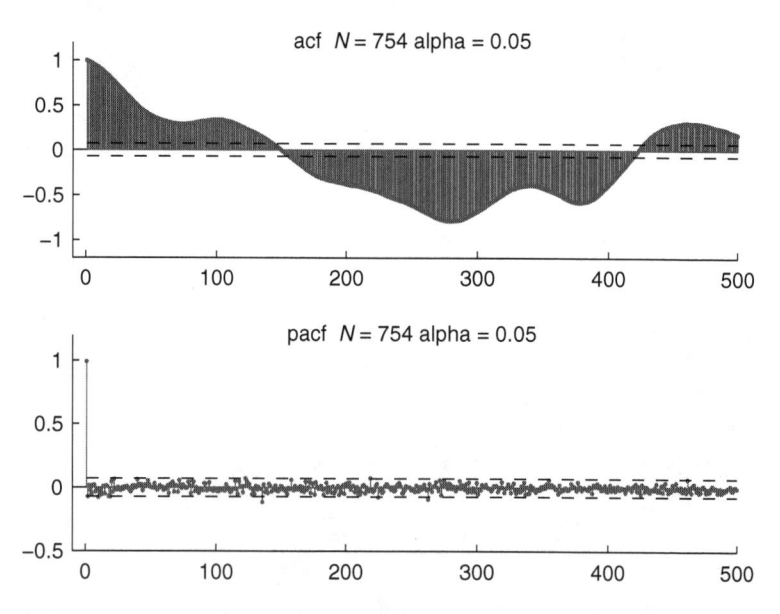

Figure 5.3 Autocorrelation of prices. The panel plots the autocorrelation (ACF – upper graph) and partial autocorrelation (PACF—lower graph) of the first deseasonalized monthly futures log-prices. The dashed line is the 5% of confidence interval.

distribution used in a model, it is important to develop models that are able to handle the non-Gaussian nature of electricity prices.

To consider this features of futures prices, we analyze Gaussian and Lévy-based models in the following sections. Furthermore, we also present two different methodologies to estimate the model parameters: principal (PCA) and independent (ICA) component analyses.

3 Modeling Electricity Futures Term Structures in a Gaussian World

Following Kiesel et al. (2009) and Boerger (2008), a simple log-normal market model representation in the filtered probability space $(\Omega, \mathcal{F}, (\mathcal{F}_t)_{t \in [0,T']}, \mathbb{P})$ is given by the following stochastic differential equation (SDE):

$$d \ln F_c(t) = \Psi_c(t)dt + \sum_{k=1}^{n} \Sigma_{c,k}(t)dB_k(t) \qquad (8)$$

where $F_c(t) = F_c(t, \tau_s^c, \tau_e^c)$ is the price at time t for an electricity future with delivery period $[\tau_s^c, \tau_e^c]$. We assume Ψ and Σ to be sufficiently regular functions such that the swap dynamic $\ln F_c$ is square integrable.

In Equation (8), two parameters have to be defined: n, the number of factors necessary to explain the variance for each contract c (i.e., $n = 2$ means a two-factor model) and, $\Sigma_{c,k}$, the volatility function.

The first parameter can be obtained by using a reduction technique (e.g. PCA), where n is chosen in such a way as to explain a fixed amount of volatility; for the second parameter we have to assume a functional form that depends on the time to the start of the delivery period, $\tau_s - t$, and that allows us to capture the volatility term structure movements, that is, the level, the slope, and the curvature. An example of an ad hoc functional form of volatility that allows us to consider these changes is given by

$$\Sigma_{c,k}(t) = \sigma_0^{(k)} + \left(\sigma_1^{(k)} + \sigma_2^{(k)}(\tau_c^s - t)\right)e^{-\lambda^{(k)}\left(\tau_c^s - t\right)} \qquad (9)$$

The next step is to estimate for each factor n the parameters of Equation (9). A common and very popular method to estimate models with several components (multifactor models) is the PCA.

A PCA is mathematically defined as an orthogonal linear transformation that transforms the data to a new coordinate system such that the greatest variance by any projection of the data comes to lie on the first coordinate (called the first principal component), the second greatest variance on the second coordinate, and so on. This means that by applying a

PCA we necessarily assume that the information we are searching for is provided by the variance in the data.

The main hypothesis to apply this method is the Gaussian distribution of returns. Even though this is often violated in financial markets, PCA is still used for dimensionality reduction in a data set, C, by retaining those characteristics of the data set that contribute most to its variance, by keeping the first few principal components, n, and ignoring higher-order ones. Therefore, PCA allows us to obtain $n < C$ needed to explain the dynamic of the variables.

Considering a sample of N observations and C futures price returns, the $N \times C$ data matrix $\mathbf{X}_{N \times C}$ is specified as

$$\mathbf{X}_{N \times C} = \begin{pmatrix} x_{11} & x_{12} & \cdots & x_{1C} \\ x_{21} & x_{22} & \cdots & x_{2C} \\ \vdots & \vdots & \ddots & \ddots \\ \vdots & \vdots & \ddots & \ddots \\ x_{N1} & x_{N2} & \cdots & x_{NC} \end{pmatrix}. \tag{10}$$

The corresponding sample covariance matrix Ψ of dimension $C \times C$ is

$$\Psi_{C \times C} = P \Lambda P', \tag{11}$$

where

$$\mathbf{P}_{C \times C} = \begin{pmatrix} p_{11} & p_{12} & \cdots & p_{1C} \\ p_{21} & p_{22} & \cdots & p_{2C} \\ \vdots & \vdots & \ddots & \ddots \\ \vdots & \vdots & \ddots & \ddots \\ p_{C1} & p_{C2} & \cdots & p_{CC} \end{pmatrix}$$

and

$$\Lambda_{C \times C} = \begin{pmatrix} \lambda_{11} & 0 & \cdots & 0 \\ 0 & \lambda_{22} & \cdots & 0 \\ \vdots & \vdots & \ddots & \ddots \\ \vdots & \vdots & \ddots & \ddots \\ 0 & 0 & \cdots & \lambda_{CC} \end{pmatrix}.$$

Matrices $\mathbf{P}$ and Λ are the diagonal matrix of eigenvalues λ_{ii} with $i = 1, \ldots, C$ of Ψ and the orthogonal matrix of eigenvector p_i corresponding to λ_{ii}, respectively, which satisfies $\mathbf{PP'} = \mathbf{I}_N$ where $\mathbf{I}$ is the identity matrix.

Performing the PCA yields C uncorrelated factors z_i of size $N \times 1$, $\mathbf{Z} = (z_1 z_2 \ldots z_C)$, called the principal components of X, each component being a simple linear combination of the original normalized returns

$$\mathbf{z}_i = X p_i = x_1 p_{1i} + x_2 p_{2i} + \cdots + x_M p_{Mi}$$

The sample covariance of the principal components follows:

$$\text{var}(\mathbf{Z}) = P'\Lambda P = P'P\Lambda P'P = \Lambda. \qquad (12)$$

Hence, the principal components are uncorrelated and the variance of the i-th component z_i is λ_{ii}.

The principal components are by convention ordered according to the size of the eigenvalue so that $\lambda_{11} \geq \lambda_{22} \ldots \geq \lambda_{CC}$. The first principal component, corresponding to the largest eigenvalue, explains most of the variation. To explain all the variation in $\mathbf{X}$, all C principal components are necessary. In particular, the theoretical covariance matrix in Equation (11) can be approximated using only the first $M < C$ eigenvalues in Λ while putting the remaining equal to zero. Thus, it is possible to measure the proportion of total variance by a simple criterion called percentage of variance criterion.[4] This criterion is based on the following procedure: additional factors are added until the cumulative percentage of the variance explained, $\left(\sum_{i=1}^{M} \lambda_i / \sum_{i=1}^{C} \lambda_i\right)$, reaches a specified level.

The PCA method cannot be applied for all commodity markets. For example, on the one hand, in the case of intercontinental exchange (ICE) Brent futures term structure,[5] we are able to explain 99.96 percent of the variance of 12 monthly contracts by using only three factors of the model (8). Figure 5.4 displays the PCA results for the Brent futures term structure. In the top part of Figure 5.4, we plot the eigenvalues and the cumulative contribution of the first M factors. We see that the first three factors account for 99.96 percent of the total randomness. The middle and lower graphs display the fitting of the first three loading factors to the data and a comparison between theoretical and empirical maturity volatilities, respectively.

The theoretical maturity volatilities can be computed by using the eigenvectors p_{Mi} corresponding to the eigenvlaues $\lambda_i i$, as follows:

$$\hat{\sigma}_i(t, t_m) = \sqrt{\lambda_{ii} p_{Mi}}$$

where (t_m) is the time to delivery of i-th futures contract.

This simple application of the PCA to the oil market permits us to assert that it is enough to capture the shifting, tilting and bending factors to

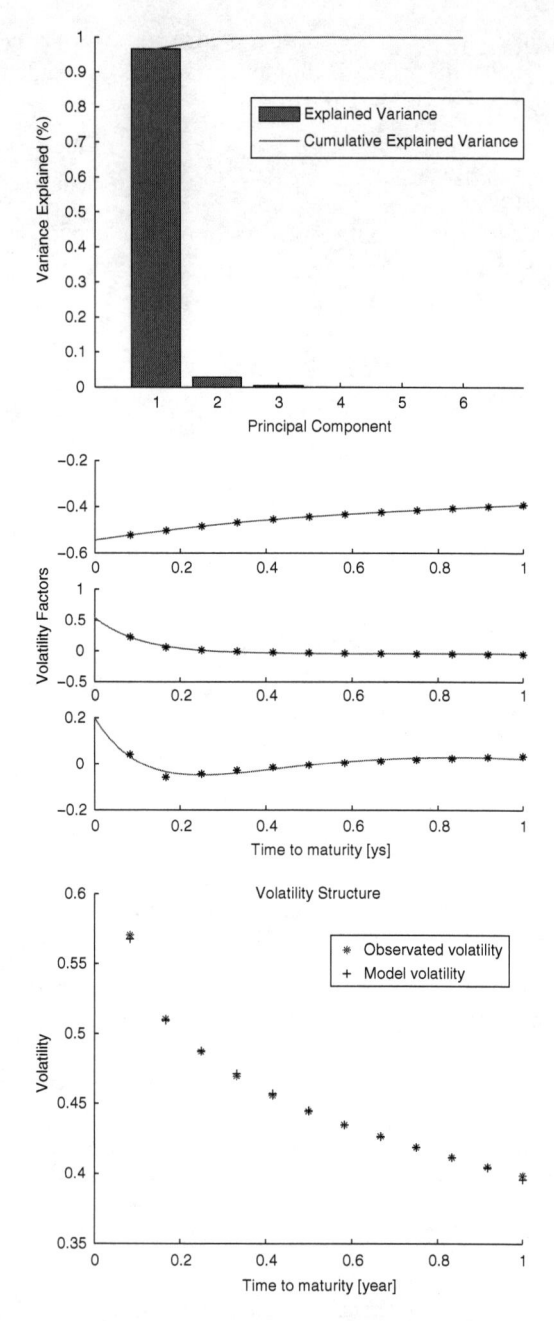

Figure 5.4 Principal component analysis. Results of the PCA on Brent futures price returns.

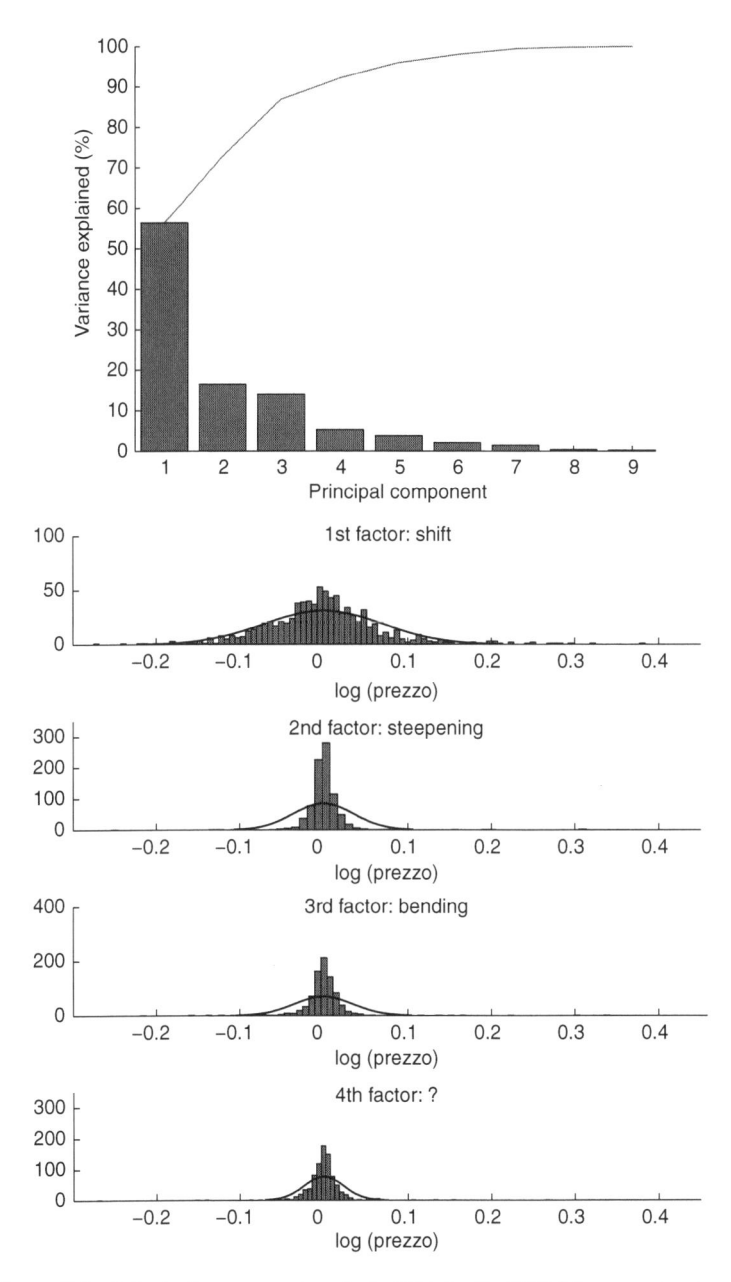

Figure 5.5 Principal component analysis. PCA for the TTF futures contracts.

model the term structure of this commodity. The other moments of the data are not considered here; because the PCA is a second-order method, it tries to capture only the variance of the process, since it is the unique factor needed to model the return, by hypothesis normal distributed.

On the other hand, this is unfortunately not the case for the electricity and gas markets. Figure 5.5 displays the PCA results for the TTF futures term structure.

From the upper graph, we can see that more than three factors are needed to explain the same amount of variance that we have explained for Brent. This means that the volatility parametrization in Equation (9) is no longer useful, and for this reason we need to introduce a more general one; in particular, we can use a polynomial function of degree 5.[6] In the lower graph we plot the histogram of the observed values of each factor, which is a proxy for their respective marginal distributions, with a normal density function. From a visual inspection it becomes clear that we cannot model the joint distribution of the factors as a normal distribution. Thus, we introduce a Lévy multifactor model to deal with non-normal returns in the next section.

4 Lévy LIBOR Market Models for Commodity Markets

4.1 Lévy Processes

Following the same approach as the LMM for interest rates, the model (8) can be generalized in the framework of Lévy processes as follows:

$$d \ln F_c(t) = \Psi_c(t)dt + \sum_{k=1}^{n} \Sigma_{c,k}(t)dL_k(t) \qquad (13)$$

where, as in the Brownian case, we assume Ψ and Σ to be sufficiently regular functions such that $\ln F_c$ is square integrable, and $dL_k, k = 1, \ldots, n$ are independent Lévy increments. The mean-reverting component $\Psi_c(t)$ can be modeled by assuming

$$\Psi_c(t) = \frac{ds_c(t)}{dt} + \alpha_c(s_c(t) - \ln F_c(t)) \qquad (14)$$

This component allows us to capture the typical behavior that we have analyzed in detail in previous sections, that is, the mean-reversion in the direction of seasonality.

Describing the Lévy components $L(t)$ in more detail, we can make the following assumptions. For $dL_k(t)$, we suggest using a Lévy process with marginal distributions in the class of generalized hyperbolic (GH) distributions, see Barndorff-Nielsen (1977) and Eberlein and Keller (1995). This is a very flexible family of distributions which can model skewness and heavy tails. The GH density is given by

$$f(x; \lambda, \upsilon, \alpha, \beta, \delta) = c\big(\delta^2 + (x-\upsilon)^2\big)^{(\lambda-1/2)/2} \exp\big(\beta(x-\upsilon)\big)$$
$$\times K_{\lambda-1/2}\Big(\alpha\sqrt{\delta^2-(x-\upsilon)^2}\Big) \qquad (15)$$

where $K_\lambda(\cdot)$ is the modified Bessel function of the third kind with index λ; the normalizing constant c is given as

$$c = \frac{(\alpha^2-\beta^2)^{\lambda/2}}{\sqrt{2\pi}\alpha^{\lambda-0.5}\delta^\lambda K_\lambda\big(\delta\sqrt{\alpha^2-\beta^2}\big)}. \qquad (16)$$

υ is the location parameter of the distribution; α controls the steepness; β represents the skewness; and δ denotes the scaling parameter. The GH Lévy process is a pure jump process with the Lévy measure:

$$\ell_{GH} = |z|^{-1} e^{\beta z} \left\{ \frac{1}{\pi^2} \int_0^\infty \frac{\exp(-\sqrt{2y+\alpha^2}|z|)}{J_\lambda^2(\delta\sqrt{2y}) + Y_\lambda^2(\delta\sqrt{2y})} \frac{dy}{y} + \lambda e^{-\alpha|z|} \right\} dz \qquad (17)$$

if $\lambda \geq 0$, and

$$\ell_{GH} = |z|^{-1} e^{\beta z} \frac{1}{\pi^2} \int_0^\infty \frac{\exp(-\sqrt{2y+\alpha^2}|z|)}{J_{-\lambda}^2(\delta\sqrt{2y}) + Y_{-\lambda}^2(\delta\sqrt{2y})} \frac{dy}{y}$$
$$+ \lambda e^{-\alpha|z|} dz \qquad (18)$$

if $\lambda < 0$. $J_\lambda(\cdot)$ and $Y_\lambda(\cdot)$ denote the Bessel functions of the first and second type with index λ, respectively.

The Lévy measure ℓ is defined as the unique positive measure on $\mathbb{R}$ that counts the number of jumps of all sizes per unit of time, see Benth et al. (2008).

Equation (13) is properly defined when the Lévy component has finite variance. By setting $\lambda = -1/2$ in Equation (15) in order to describe the $dL_k(t)$ process with NIG marginal distributions, to obtain the finite variance of the returns $\ln F_c$, we have to impose the integrability condition:

$$\mathbb{E}\left[\int_0^t \int_{\mathbb{R}\setminus\{0\}} |\ln F_c(s)|^2 \ell(ds, dz) \right] < \infty, \qquad (19)$$

where $\ell(\mathrm{d}s, \mathrm{d}z)$ is the Lévy-measure:

$$\ell(\mathrm{d}s, \mathrm{d}z) = \mathrm{d}s\, \ell_{NIG}(\mathrm{d}z) = \mathrm{d}s\, \frac{\alpha \delta}{\pi |z|} K_1(\alpha |z|) e^{\beta z} \mathrm{d}z. \tag{20}$$

We point out that the Lévy-measure (20) is the product between the time and jump activity axis; thus, the existence condition (19) is satisfied for $\delta > 0$ and $|\beta| \leq \alpha$, which are the conditions for the existence of the NIG measure. In fact, we can go deeper in the analysis defining our deseasonalized process:

$$X(t) = \ln F_c(t) - s_c(t), \tag{21}$$

which solves the SDE

$$\mathrm{d}X(t) = -\alpha X(t) \mathrm{d}t + \Sigma(t) \mathrm{d}L(t). \tag{22}$$

We focus this analysis on $n = 1$ Lévy components. The generalization for more components is straightforward. By using Ito's formula we obtain the solution

$$X(t) = \int_0^t e^{-\alpha(t-s)} \Sigma(t) \mathrm{d}L(s) \tag{23}$$

given $X(0) = 0$. The characteristic function of the process (23) is

$$\psi \equiv \mathbb{E}\left[\exp(i\theta X(t))\right] = \exp\left[\int_0^t \phi_{NIG}(\theta e^{-\alpha(t-s)} \Sigma(s)) \mathrm{d}s\right], \tag{24}$$

where ϕ_{NIG} is the log-characteristic of the NIG process $L(1)$:

$$\phi_{NIG}(\theta) = \delta(\sqrt{\alpha^2 - \beta^2} - \sqrt{(\alpha^2 - (\beta + i\theta))}). \tag{25}$$

Given the characteristic function (24) for the process (23), we are able to write the second moment, which is:

$$m_2 \equiv (-i)^2 \frac{\mathrm{d}^2 \psi(0)}{\mathrm{d}\theta^2} = \left[\int_0^t \phi'_{NIG}(0) e^{-\alpha(t-s)} \Sigma(s) \mathrm{d}s\right]^2$$
$$+ \int_0^t \phi''_{NIG}(0) \Sigma^2(s) e^{-2\alpha(t-s)} \mathrm{d}s. \tag{26}$$

If $\phi'_{NIG}(0)$ and $\phi''_{NIG}(0)$ are finite, the second moment (26) is finite as well, as in the case $\delta > 0$ and $|\beta| \leq \alpha$. These are the conditions to have a finite variance process (23).

By assuming the Lévy dynamic (13) for the returns, PCA cannot be applied to estimate the model since the Gaussian assumption is violated and the ICA must be used.

4.2 From PCA to ICA

In many fields researchers are interested in reliable methods and techniques enabling the extraction or separation of useful information from signals (prices) corrupted by non-normal distributed noise. The identification of original signals or factors from a given data set is the focus of blind source separation (BSS). The term "blind," in this context, means that both the original factors (sources) and the mixing process are unknown. With the assumption that the observed data are given by a linear combination of mutually independent factors, we can apply ICA to solve this source separation problem. Therefore, the ICA method is used to separate the independent components (ICs) that build up the observed process.

Let us assume we have the vector $s \in \mathbb{R}^n$ and a matrix A, which is the mixture constant $n \times m$ matrix. Using s and A, we can construct the observed random vector $x \in \mathbb{R}^m$:

$$x = As \qquad (27)$$

The main assumptions of this model are:

1. The number of observed variables has to be greater than the number of independent components $m \geq n$,
2. The mixture matrix A has to be of full column rank,
3. There is non-Gaussianity of each ICs_j; $j = 1, \ldots, n$, with just one exception allowed,
4. There is mutual independence of the original factors.

The last assumption needs a detailed analysis with respect to the others. The objective of ICA is therefore to identify these factors by searching for components that are as statistically independent as possible, not only uncorrelated. "Independence" means that the values of one component provide no information about the values of others. This is a stronger condition than the pure noncorrelation condition in PCA, where the values of one component can still provide information about the values of another component in case of non-Gaussian distributions. In addition, the components of ICA are not restricted to being orthogonal.

In our case, and for the rest of this chapter, we assume that $m = n$. The aim of ICA is to solve the system, finding the sources s and the mixing matrix **A**. In general, ICA provides a vector of independent component **y** and demixing matrix **W** such that:

$$\begin{aligned} \mathbf{y} &= \mathbf{W}\mathbf{x} \\ &= \mathbf{W}\mathbf{A}\mathbf{s} \end{aligned} \tag{28}$$

When $\mathbf{W} = \mathbf{A}^{-1}$, ICA provides a perfect separation and $\mathbf{y} = \mathbf{s}$. There are different ways to identify the ICs, but they all have the main purpose of maximizing the non-Gaussianity of the sources and minimizing the mutual information of each component. These methods differ from each other by the objective function and the algorithm used for the optimization. It is possible to build up the objective function by using the differential entropy of a random variable **y** distributed with law $f(\mathbf{y})$. The entropy definition is given by

$$H(\mathbf{y}) = -\int f(\mathbf{y})\log f(\mathbf{y})d\mathbf{y} \tag{29}$$

As explained in Cover and Thomas (1991), information theory indicates that a Gaussian variable has the largest entropy among all random variables with equal variance, so we can define the negentropy $J(\mathbf{y})$ as a "distance" from Gaussianity by

$$J(\mathbf{y}) = H(\mathbf{y}_{\text{Gaussian}}) - H(\mathbf{y}) \tag{30}$$

where $\mathbf{y}_{\text{Gaussian}}$ is a Gaussian random vector with the same covariance matrix as **y**. J is always non-negative, and it is zero if and only if **y** is a Gaussian random variable, see Comon (1994). By using negentropy it is possible to take into account the mutual information by the following definition:

$$I(y_1,\ldots,y_n) = J(\mathbf{y}) - \sum_{i=1}^{n} J(y_i) + \frac{1}{2}\log\frac{\prod C_{i,i}}{|\mathbf{C}|} \tag{31}$$

where **C** is the covariance matrix of y_i, and $\prod C_{i,i}$ is the product of its diagonal elements. The third term vanishes when **C** is diagonal, that is the y_i are uncorrelated: this does not mean they are statistically independent. In fact, to make the optimization algorithm simpler, **y** are decorrelated by a linear transformation. This step is called *whitening*.

Given Equation (31) without the third term, it is possible to find the ICA formulation, see Hyvärinen and Oja (2000), a minimization of mutual information, $I(\mathbf{y})$, which is equivalent to find the directions $J(y_i)$ alongside the negentropy $J(\mathbf{y})$ is maximized.

The estimation of the negentropy is a difficult task. To solve this problem, we might use an approximation of the negentropy; for example in Hyvärinen (1998) the author uses the approximation:

$$J(y) \approx c[\mathbb{E}[G(y)] - \mathbb{E}[G(y_{\text{Gaussian}})]]^2 \qquad (32)$$

where $G(.)$ could be any of nonquadratic functions and c is a constant that is irrelevant to maximise $J(\mathbf{y})$. In this chapter, we use the algorithm developed in Hyvärinen (1997) and Hyvärinen (1999).[7]

In order to estimate the model (13) by applying an ICA, it is useful to write it as

$$d \ln F_c(t) - \Psi_c(t)dt = \sum_{k=1}^{n} \Sigma_{c,k}(t)dL_k(t) \qquad (33)$$

Equation (33) has to be read in the same way as Equation (27), where the Lévy increment vector $dL_k(t)$ is the source, which is mixed with the volatility matrix $\Sigma_{c,k}(t)$, to obtain the observed log-returns (clean of the mean-reverting component) $d \ln F_c(t) - \Psi_c(t)dt$.

5 Implementation of a Lévy Electricity Model

5.1 Estimation of EMM by ICA

In order to estimate the EMM model (13), we use the EEX term structure evolution during the period 2006–2008. Considering monthly, quarterly and yearly futures contracts traded on EEX during the sample period, the smoothing procedure showed in the previous section is applied. More specifically, we consider nonoverlapping synthetic forward contracts obtained from a smoothed forward curve. The forward contracts that we use are obtained by first constructing a smooth forward curve from traded forward contracts, and then computing synthetic forward contracts from the smooth forward curve. In this way we can construct a data set based on six monthly, six quarterly, and three yearly swap contracts. Instead of modeling all electricity futures in the market, we divide it in three segments according to the length of the delivery period.

We estimate the parameters in Equation (3) by using the least squares approach for each futures contract. Since there is no evidence of annual seasonality for the yearly contracts, we use only the linear trend of Equation (3). After estimating the seasonal function, we remove the effect of this component by subtracting it from the log-price. The acf function of the deseasonalized log price (see Figure 5.3) shows a strong memory effect. Figure 5.3 refers just to the first monthly contract, but this is a common feature among all the contracts. As suggested by the pacf function in the lower graph of the Figure 5.3, we remove the AR(1) component.

Now we have to estimate the mean-reverting component (14) of our model. The estimated mean-reversion parameters $\hat{\alpha}_i$ are very close to zero, meaning that the speed of mean-reversion is rather slow. This means that electricity futures price time-series have long memory. Fanone et al. (2013) analyze the presence of long memory in the time-series of prices by first-order fractional autoregressive process, or FAR(1) for short.

The long memory effect is confirmed by analyzing the mean-reverting parameters reported in Table 5.1.

We have to point out that not all of the estimated parameters are significantly (5 percent significance level) different from zero; that means we cannot reject the unit root hypothesis for the time-series of the de-seasonalized log price, and in fact the augmented Dickey-Fuller (ADF) test confirms this for several forward contracts. Nevertheless, we decided to use a mean-reversion model for two main reasons. First, the mean-reversion component allows us to force the prices to stay close enough to the seasonal level. Second, we have tested the power of the ADF test by Monte Carlo simulation. We have simulated mean-reverting samples with parameters of the same order of magnitude of those estimated, and conducted an ADF test for each of 10,000 paths simulated. The test rejected the null hypothesis 12 times out of 100, basically saying that according to a sample of 750 observations involved, included in our historical sample, we obtained an error of the second type with 88 percent probability. Consequently, we prefer to use a mean-reverting model.[8]

Once we have removed the seasonal and the auto-regressive components, we have to manage the residuals. In order to reduce the dimensionality of the model we could apply PCA. Figure 5.6 shows the variance explained by the number of principal factors for monthly and quarterly contracts, and we can see an explanation of only 90 percent of variance by

Table 5.1 Estimated mean-reversion parameters

Parameter	Monthly	Quarterly	Yearly
α_1	0.0082	0.0051	0.0069
α_2	0.0056	0.0069	0.0053
α_3	0.0036	0.0089	0.0037
α_4	0.0031	0.0072	
α_5	0.0046	0.0085	
α_6	0.0092	0.0105	

Note: Estimated parameters of the AR(1) process for futures contracts with different maturity.

using the first three factors; this means that we should expect a roughly 10 percent error between the observed and the fitted volatility. For yearly contracts the situation is slightly better, because the number of contracts is lower than the monthly and quarterly ones.

We could consider all the factors involved to increase the accuracy of fitting. Even for all the components, we do not need to improve it too much,

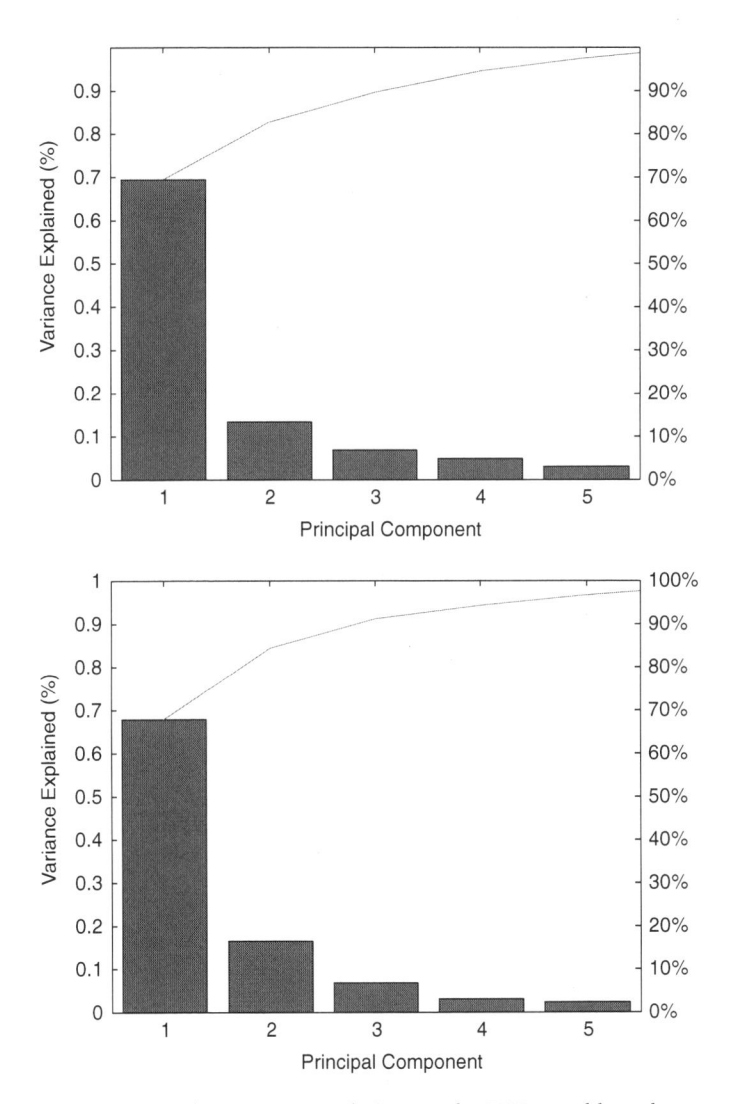

Figure 5.6 Principal component analysis. PCA for EEX monthly and quarterly futures contracts.

because we are using the volatility structure (9) to fit the loading factors. This is an ad-hoc parametrization used to fit suitably the first three factors: level, slope, and curvature. By applying the ICA method, these three movements are lost. Therefore, a more general parametrization should be defined. We decided to use a polynomial parametrization to fit the loading factors by fixing the degree n in order to get the desired approximation.

Furthermore, the residuals $\boldsymbol{x} = \mathrm{d}\ln F_c(t) - \Psi_c(t)\mathrm{d}t$ are far from being normally distributed, as shown in the two examples in Figure 5.1, with kurtosis values equal to 6.68 (upper case) and 6.08 (lower case).[9] The non-normality hypothesis of residuals is confirmed by the Jarque–Bera test. The large deviations from normality of the residuals produce a biased volatility estimation by PCA. For all these reasons we assume a Lévy-type process for the source component $\boldsymbol{s} = \mathrm{d}L_k$, and we apply the ICA algorithm to the residuals $\boldsymbol{x}$, to decompose them in the mixing matrix $\boldsymbol{A} = \Sigma_{c,k}$ and sources $\boldsymbol{s}$.

Figure 5.7 shows independent components (ICs) obtained by applying the ICA algorithm on the residuals of monthly futures. In Figure 5.8, we fit the first three sources, obtained from the application of ICA on monthly futures, with the NIG and Normal distribution. This figure shows a better fitting of the NIG distribution than the Normal one.

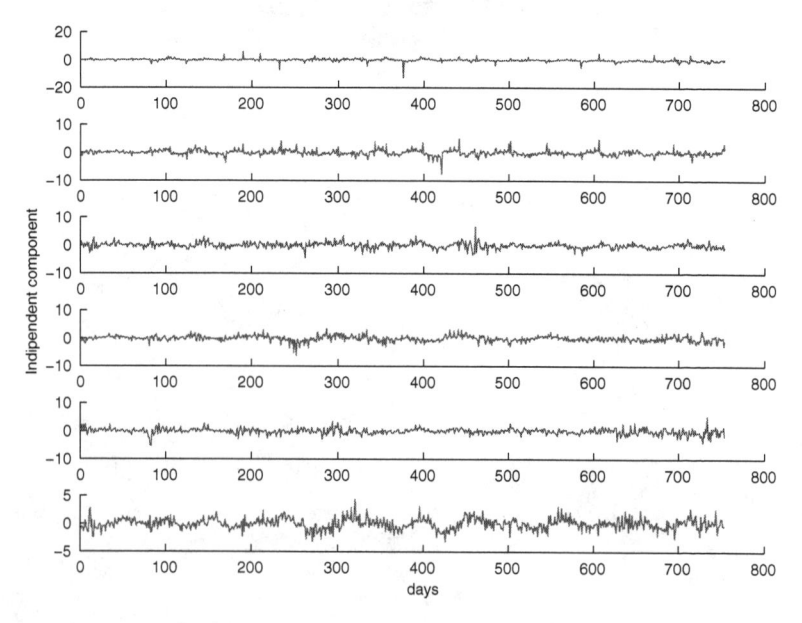

Figure 5.7 Independent component analysis. ICs of EEX monthly futures returns.

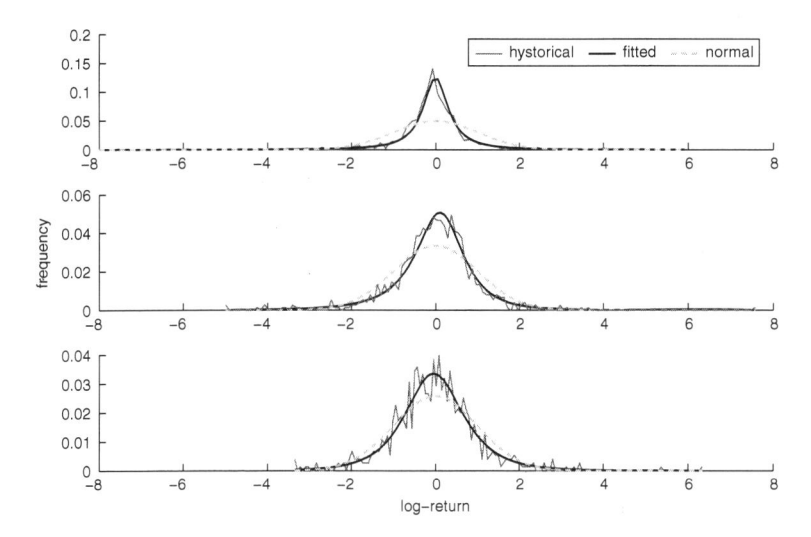

Figure 5.8 Fitted normal and NIG density. Comparison of empirical density to the fitted normal and NIG distributions of the first three sources $dL_k(t)$ computed on EEX monthly futures.

The Kolmogorov–Smirnov test confirms that we cannot reject the NIG distribution for the residuals.

The sources $dL_k(t)$ within each market segment (monthly, quarterly and yearly) are independent by definition, therefore we estimate the NIG distribution for each independent source. The parameters are estimated by maximum likelihood, and the results are shown in Table 5.2.

Once we have estimated the model, we are able to compare the observed volatilities with those obtained by the estimated model. Figure 5.9 shows the results for monthly, quarterly, and yearly futures. These figures show a good fit for monthly and yearly forwards; in fact the RMSE are 1.3 and 1.5 percent, respectively. The IC should have a variance close to one, but we get 0.57 by using the estimated parameters. We have tried to add further constraints on the parameters in the maximum likelihood procedure, but the algorithm becomes extremely time-consuming.

The correlation among the EEX contracts are provided in Tables 5.3–5.5. We observe a decreasing correlation with the lag period of the contracts, for the monthly and the yearly case. This monotone behavior is lost for the quarterly case.

Comparing Tables 5.3–5.5 we can see that the results are similar to those obtained for the volatilities. We get quite a good fit for the monthly and yearly forwards contracts, but not for the quarterly ones. This is strictly related to the volatility mismatch.

Table 5.2 Estimated GH parameters

Product	Maturity	$\hat{\mu}$	$\hat{\alpha}$	$\hat{\beta}$	$\hat{\delta}$
Monthly	1M	1.810^{-3}	0.422	2.110^{-3}	0.360
	2M	0.138	0.814	−0.147	0.749
	3M	0.072	1.048	−0.073	1.024
	4M	0.076	0.954	−0.076	0.942
	5M	−0.012	1.066	0.012	1.056
	6M	0.146	1.595	−0.147	1.580
Quarterly	1Q	0.011	0.931	−0.028	0.275
	2Q	−0.075	0.969	0.075	0.959
	3Q	0.011	0.616	−0.012	0.591
	4Q	−0.129	0.714	0.172	0.517
	5Q	3.810^{-3}	0.745	-3.910^{-3}	0.730
	6Q	−0.040	1.045	0.039	1.038
Yearly	1Y	−0.007	0.436	0.007	0.456
	2Y	−0.011	0.718	0.013	0.638
	3Y	0.127	1.169	−0.134	1.103

Note: Estimated parameters of the NIG distribution divided by product and maturity.

Table 5.3 Empirical and fitted correlation matrix for EEX monthly futures

	Maturity	1M	2M	3M	4M	5M	6M
Empirical	1M	1					
	2M	0.7143	1				
	3M	0.6834	0.7722	1			
	4M	0.5969	0.7115	0.7509	1		
	5M	0.5664	0.6320	0.6839	0.7384	1	
	6M	0.3926	0.5081	0.4925	0.5923	0.5599	1
Model	1M	1					
	2M	0.7202	1				
	3M	0.6830	0.7746	1			
	4M	0.6044	0.7111	0.7565	1		
	5M	0.5641	0.6334	0.6873	0.7455	1	
	6M	0.4291	0.5342	0.5323	0.6121	0.6070	1

We conclude this section with a simulation study where futures price paths are simulated by using the model (13) and the estimated parameters as given in Tables 5.1 and 5.2. In particular, the Lévy component $L(t)$ is represented by a NIG distribution; therefore, we need a sampling method

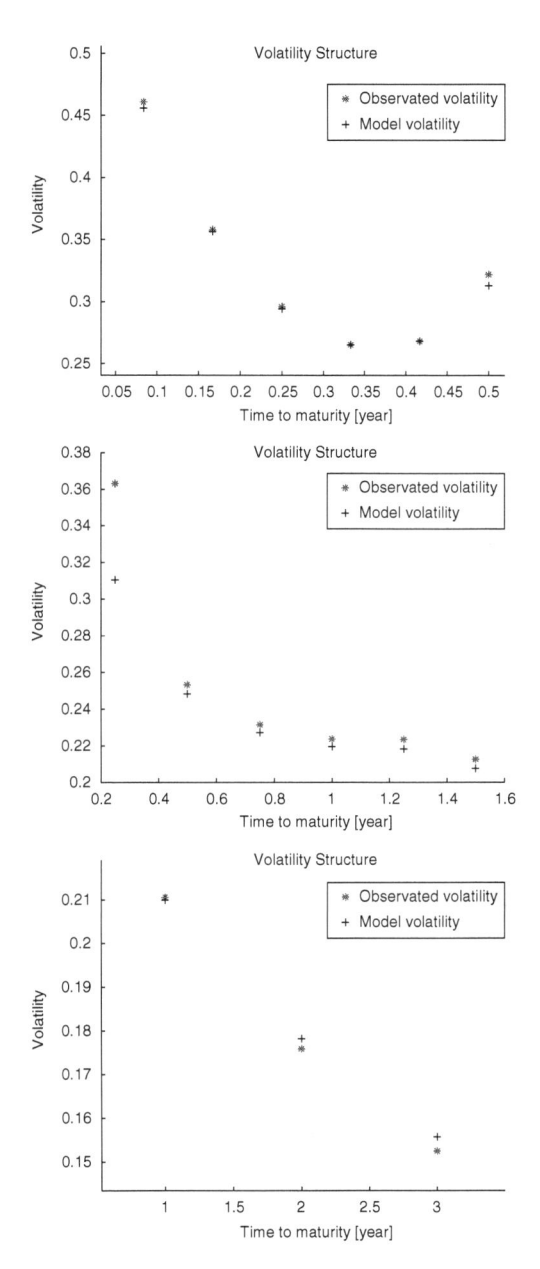

Figure 5.9 Empirical and fitted volatilities. This figure displays empirical and fitted volatility term structures for EEX (upper graph) monthly (left graph), quarterly (middle graph) and yearly (right graph) futures contracts.

Table 5.4 Empirical and fitted correlation matrix for EEX quarterly futures

	Maturity	1Q	2Q	3Q	4Q	5Q	6Q
Empirical	1Q	1					
	2Q	0.4661	1				
	3Q	0.6003	0.8256	1			
	4Q	0.4604	0.8096	0.8327	1		
	5Q	0.5745	0.7843	0.8405	0.8443	1	
	6Q	0.4101	0.8078	0.8009	0.8298	0.8081	1
Model	1Q	1					
	2Q	0.6115	1				
	3Q	0.6506	0.8404	1			
	4Q	0.5670	0.8058	0.8369	1		
	5Q	0.6363	0.7950	0.8355	0.8420	1	
	6Q	0.5389	0.8002	0.8090	0.8211	0.8100	1

Table 5.5 Empirical and fitted correlation matrix for EEX yearly futures

Product	Maturity	1Y	2Y	3Y
Empirical	1Y	1		
	2Y	0.9086	1	
	3Y	0.8459	0.9431	1
Model	1Y	1		
	2Y	0.9179	1	
	3Y	0.8554	0.9461	1

to draw random numbers from this distribution. This can be achieved by the algorithm proposed by Rydberg (1997):

$$L = \upsilon + \beta Z + \sqrt{Z} Y$$
$$\sim \text{NIG}(\alpha, \beta, \upsilon, \delta), \tag{34}$$

where Z is drawn from the Inverse Gaussian (IG) distribution, IG(δ^2, $\alpha^2 - \beta^2$), and Y from the standard Normal distribution.

The sampling of Z consists of first drawing a random variable V, which follows a χ^2 distribution with one degree of freedom and then defining a new random variable

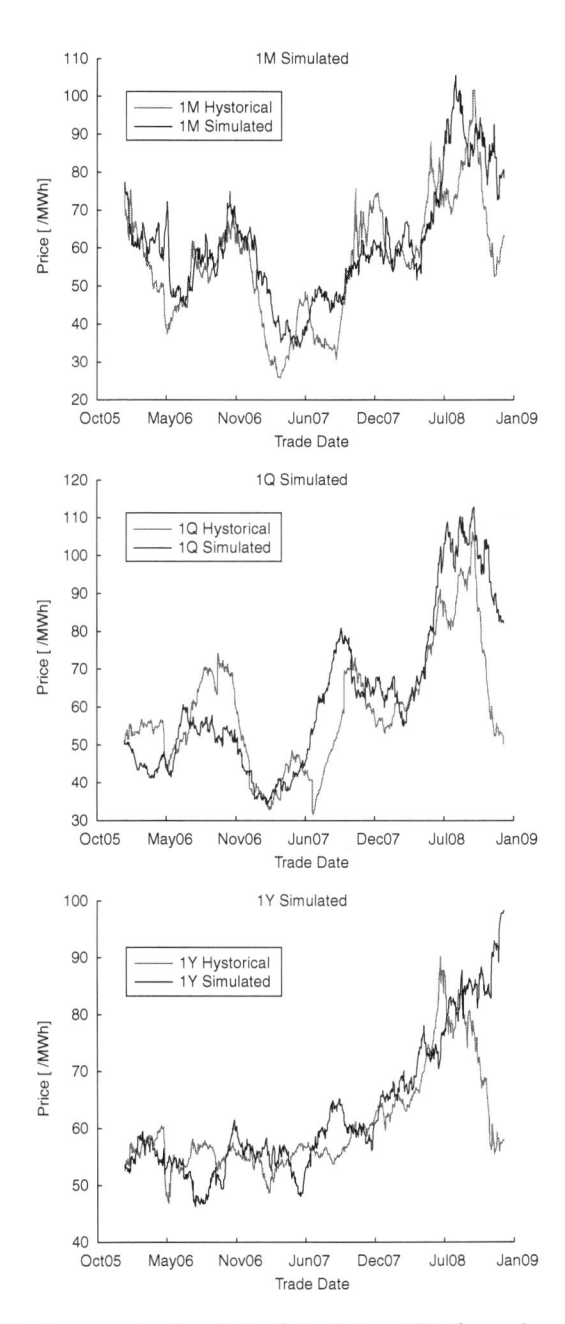

Figure 5.10 Cross-sectional analysis of simulations. This figure shows simulated prices paths of German futures prices with monthly (upper graph), quarterly (middle graph), and yearly (lower (graph) delivery period.

$$W = \zeta + \frac{\zeta^2 V}{2\delta^2} - \frac{\zeta}{2\delta^2}\sqrt{4\zeta\delta^2 V + \zeta^2 V^2} \qquad (35)$$

and letting

$$Z = W\mathbb{I}_{U_1 \leq \frac{\zeta}{\zeta+W}} + \frac{\zeta^2}{W}\mathbb{I}_{U_1 \geq \frac{\zeta}{\zeta+W}}, \qquad (36)$$

with U_1 being uniformly distributed and $\zeta = \delta/\sqrt{\alpha^2 - \beta^2}$. The above procedure generates random numbers from a NIG$(\alpha, \beta, \upsilon, \delta)$ distributed random variable L.

In Figure 5.10, we compare the historical and simulated EEX paths realizing a very similar evolution; joined to the volatility and correlation fitting makes the EMM suitable to manage the risk of electricity futures portfolios.

6 Conclusions

Our goal in this chapter was to model electricity forward/futures prices directly in a non-Gaussian world. This assumption does not permit to apply the PCA to estimate the parameters of models based on the Libor market model framework.

In detail, we have analyzed a multifactor Lévy model for the electricity future market developed in Di Poto and Fanone (2012). The purpose of the model is to capture the main features of electricity markets—such as cross-section and time-series seasonality, fat tails—and to fit the observed volatility term structure and correlations.

The correlation structure in place between futures is achieved by combining independent Lévy-type process in a linear way. Each IC is separated by the ICA in the estimation step. This is similar to the PCA, but unlike that, it can deal with non-Gaussian processes.

Future work could be to calibrate the model to option market prices, but this is a very difficult task for a multifactor Lévy model. Boerger (2008) calibrates a two-factor Lévy model to electricity futures options, but no attempt has been made for a multifactor model. A second issue we do not face in this chapter is the existence of an equivalent martingale measure. This is a nontrivial issue but since we are here not interested in pricing derivatives contracts, we do not face it and leave it for future work. The last open issue is to calibrate the cross-correlation structure (e.g., if we use the multifactor Lévy model analyzed for optimizing a power plant and so the clean spark spread options). One attempt has been made int his direction Andresen et al. (2012) present a discrete random-field model for forward prices driven by the multivariate normal inverse Gaussian distribution but more work is needed.

Notes

1. The Samuelson effect decribes the observation that volatility is decreasing with maturity.
2. Empirical analyses of the futures term structure show fewer spikes than in spot prices, both in terms of intensity and size.
3. The building blocks mean that the "smallest" forward contracts are extrapolated and then modeled.
4. In the statistical literature there does not exist a solid criterion as to how many factors should be used to approximate the theoretical covariance well enough. Hair et al. (1992) discuss three possible criteria that can be used to select the number of loading factors:
   1. Eigenvalue criterion: Only eigenvalues greater than one are considered.
   2. Scree test criterion: A graphical method where the eigenvalues are plotted as a diminishing series and where the position of relatively sharp breaks in the series determines the number of factors.
   3. Percentage of variance criterion.
5. We can make the same considerations regarding gasoline or emissions futures term structures.
6. We apply the *polyfit* function in Matlab. The polynomial degree is chosen in such a way to reach the desired fit of the volatility term structure.
7. A MatLab algorithm, that permits us to estimate the negentropy, can be downloaded from the following web site www.cis.hut.fi/projects/ica/fastica/.
8. It would be interesting to analyze the model (13) by assuming a FAR(1) process (or in general an autoregressive fractional integrated moving-average (ARFIMA) process) to model the mean-reverting component.
9. The kurtosis value assumes different ranges according to the length of the delivery period. For monthly futures, the kurtosis value assumes values between 4.52 and 11.05; for quarterly futures, the range of value is between 6.08 and 41.34 and last but not least for yearly futures is between 9.90 and 12.94

References

Andresen, A., Koekebakker, S., and Westgaard, S. (2012). Modeling electricity forward prices using the multivariate normal inverse Gaussian distribution. *Journal of Energy Markets*, 3:3–25.

Barndorff-Nielsen, O. E. (1977). Exponentially decreasing distribution for the logarithm of particle size. *Proc. R. Stat. Soc. London A*, 353:401–419.

Benth, F., Benth, J., and Koekebakker, S. (2008). *Stochastic modeling of electricity and related markets*. World Scientific.

Benth, F. E. and Koekebakker, S. (2005). Stochastic modeling of financial electricity contracts. *Energy Economics*, 30:1116–1157.

Benth, F. E., Koekebakker, S., and Ollmar, F. (2007). Extracting and applying smooth forward curves from average based contracts with seasonal variation. *Journal of Derivatives*, 15:52–66.

Bjerksund, P., Rasmussen, H., and Stensland, G. (2000). Valuation and risk management in the nordic electricity market. Working paper, Norwegian School of Economics and Business Administration.

Boerger, R. H. (2008). *Energy-related commodity futures: Statistics, Models and Derivatives*. VDM.

Borak, S. and Weron, R. (2008). A semiparametric factor model for electricity forward curve dynamics. *Journal of Energy Markets*, 1:3–16.

Brace, A., Gatarek, D., and Musiela, M. (1997). The market model of interest rates dynamics. *Mathematical Finance*, 7:127–155.

Comon, P. (1994). Independent component analysis – a new concept? *Signal Processing*, 36:287–314.

Cover, T. M. and Thomas, J. A. (1991). *Elements of information theory*. John Wiley.

Di Poto, G. and Fanone, E. (2012). Estimating a lévy multifactor market model for electricity futures markets by using independent component analysis. *Journal of Energy Markets*, 5:33–62.

Eberlein, E. and Keller, U. (1995). Hyperbolic distribution in finance. *Bernoulli*, 1:281–299.

Fanelli, V. and Musti, S. (2008). Modeling electricity forward curve dynamics in the Italian market. Working paper, University of Foggia.

Fanone, E., Gamba, A., and Prokopczuk, M. (2013). The case of negative day-ahead electricity prices. *Energy Economics*, 35:22–34.

Fleten, S. and Lemming, J. (2003). Constructing forward price curves in electricity markets. *Energy Economics*, 25:409–424.

Hair, J., Anderson, R., Tatham, R., and Black, W. (1992). *Multivariate Data Analysis*. Macmillan Publishing Company.

Heath, D., Jarrow, R., and Morton, A. (1992). Bond pricing and the term structure of interest rates: a new methodology for contingent claim valuation. *Econometrica*, 60:77–105.

Hyvärinen, A. (1997). A fast fixed-point algorithm for independent component analysis. *Neural Computation*, 9:1483–1492.

Hyvärinen, A. (1998). Fast and robust fixed-point algorithm for independent component analysis. *IEEE Trans. on Neural Networks*, 10:626–635.

Hyvärinen, A. (1999). New approximations of differential entropy for independent component analysis and projection pursuit. *Advances in Neural Information Processing Systems*, 10:273–279.

Hyvärinen, A. and Oja, E. (2000). Independent component analysis: Algorithms and applications. *Neural Networks*, 13:411–430.

Kiesel, R., Schindlmayr, G., and Börger, R. H. (2009). A two-factor model for the electricity forward market. *Quantitative Finance*, 9:279–287.

Koekebakker, S. (2003). An arithmetic forward curve for the electricity market. Working paper, Agder University College.

Koekebakker, S. and Ollmar, F. (2005). Forward curve dynamics in the Nordic electricity market. *Managerial Finance*, 31:73–94.

Lucia, J. and Schwartz, E. (2002). Electricity prices and power derivatives: Evidence from the nordic power exchange. *Review of Derivatives Research*, 5:5–50.

Rydberg, T. (1997). The normal inverse gaussian lÂť'evy process: Simulation and approximation. *Communications in Statistics: Stochastic Models*, 13:887–910.

6

Hourly Resolution Forward Curves for Power: Statistical Modeling Meets Market Fundamentals

Michael Coulon, Christian Jacobsson, and Jonas Ströjby

1 Introduction

Electricity markets represent the ultimate challenge for an avid modeler of financial markets and prices. Their complexity and ever-changing structure requires understanding and capturing a huge range of different factors and effects. Thus, weaknesses can always be found in existing models, and consensus on which model is best can rarely be reached. And yet, the fundamental transparency of the electricity price-setting mechanism, the large amount of available data, and the rapidly growing literature all tempt the modeler to try a bit harder: perhaps that one elusive model that ticks all the boxes is out there somewhere, just beyond reach.

Of course, we must be realistic, and certainly we do not claim to present the perfect model here. Indeed, as every electricity market is different and every modeling goal is different too, the ultimate prize will (and should rightly) always remain out of reach. However, we do hope to make a contribution in a very promising direction, presenting a flexible stack-based approach, which incorporates as much as possible of the crucial market fundamentals while still retaining user-friendliness and computational tractability. We aim to exploit the growing number of mathematical modeling ideas emerging from academia in this direction, but complement these with a healthy dose of practical industry experience, substantial data analysis, and a realistic focus on what really matters for practitioners in these markets.

Our aim is thus to strike the right balance between the heavy fundamental models traditionally used in the energy industry, and the nimble reduced-form approaches that often migrate across from quantitative finance and econometrics. The former approach can be described for many reasons by the word "slow." Data collection is often messy and painfully slow, involving large amounts of information on individual generators and their operational constraints, in order to build up a very detailed supply stack. More importantly, implementation of such giant models tends to rely on large-scale optimization techniques, rendering them too slow to handle stochasticity well, particularly when attempting to calibrate the outputs of spot price scenarios to observed market forward quotes. Analyzing model output or parameter sensitivity for rapid trading, hedging, or derivative pricing decisions is not feasible, relegating these slow models instead more toward the realm of scenario testing, price forecasting, and long-term investment planning.

At the other end of the spectrum, classical reduced-form stochastic models for spot and forward prices are fast in many ways. Writing down a model is fast, estimating parameters usually fast, and if the chosen stochastic processes are sufficiently convenient, calibration to forwards, and even options can potentially be very fast. On the other hand, speed and convenience can come at a very high price in power markets. Reduced-form models typically tell you to throw away all your detailed data on weather forecasts, demand patterns, changes in the generation mix, and perhaps most worryingly also your common sense that parameters estimated from price histories are no longer reliable given the fundamental market changes underway. Having to wait for years for today's market news to make it into our historical price data and corresponding parameter estimates is an issue on which our so-called "fast" models are arguably relegated to being the slowest of all. This is not to say that there is no use for either the "fast" or the "slow" models, but simply that both have significant disadvantages that can hopefully be limited by looking for a hybrid approach. This idea is certainly not new, and forms part of a growing branch of 'structural' models in the literature, as discussed for example in the recent survey paper of Carmona and Coulon (2014).

1.1 The Challenge: Hourly Forward Curve Construction

Before we outline our specific contribution to the literature here, let us briefly address the question of why any of it matters. Why is it fundamentally important for an energy company to have a realistic, reliable, flexible, and tractable approach to generating spot price dynamics and forward curves? Why is this particularly crucial nowadays, suggesting the need for new and innovative approaches? First, it is well known that electricity spot prices can be extremely volatile and difficult to predict, with dramatic but short-lived spikes frequently occurring in both the upwards and downwards directions, as illustrated later in Figure 6.2a for the German market (EEX). Together with the correlated risk of shocks to load itself, this produces substantial risk management challenges for utilities and power generators, particularly as hedging weather or outage-related risk may be impossible. Trading in forward contracts over various maturities is a natural first step to managing electricity spot price risk. However, not all maturity forwards are traded, some suffer from illiquidity, and even the most liquid of contracts have delivery periods of a week, a month, or longer, nowhere near the hourly granularity of spot. In sum, the forward curve that the market provides is often far from ideal for many practical applications.

Instead, hourly granularity forward curves can be constructed by averaging over scenarios from an hourly granularity spot price model. This is a very common and yet challenging task for many energy companies. Hourly spot price simulations and hourly forward curves are needed as inputs for a wide range of applications, from risk evaluation and P&L calculations (mark to market) to virtual contract evaluation or the optimal operation and valuation of a physical asset. Managing hydro plants requires hourly prices to accurately capture the "optionality" embedded in the plant's operation, whereby water can be pumped up when power is cheap and released again just hours later for a profit. Similarly, flexible gas plants can rapidly switch on and off to exploit hourly price swings and require hourly price curves for both gas and electricity.

Industry experience suggests that there is much room for improvement on this topic, making it a very suitable testing ground for new modeling ideas. The short and long ends of the forward curves require different considerations, which can rarely be managed by a single model. For example, a reduced-form stochastic model can often capture quite effectively the volatility term structure of power forwards (i.e., the Samuelson effect), intra-day and seasonal price patterns, and long-term forward curve shapes. However, to accurately construct a realistic forward curve for the coming days and weeks, it is vital that known weather forecasts are used as inputs, impossible for a pure reduced-form approach. On the other hand, models for demand, wind and solar typically focus on getting the best day-ahead or short-term forecast, and are less amenable to long-term hourly simulations needed for multiyear forward curves. At the long end of the curve, it is often desirable to extrapolate beyond the liquid market quotes to construct a power curve going out five to ten years or more. In this case, the extra information at one's disposal may be long maturity fuel forward quotes, and growth forecasts for new capacity (both renewable and conventional), which can only be realistically used as inputs in conjunction with a model for the progression of the merit order over time. Moreover, while the heavy full fundamental models can project forward a forecasted merit order over many years, they crucially fail to handle the randomness: various different merit order scenarios are possible over long time horizons, each with different probabilities attached, and each affecting power prices in different ways via the highly nonlinear supply stack structure.

The challenges described above have become increasingly complex in recent years, due to a number of major ongoing changes in the European electricity markets. For example, together with rapid growth of renewables, high gas prices in Europe have kept many gas generators high up the stack and "out-of-the-money," leading to risk of closures. At the same time, ongoing market coupling to integrate European electricity markets has led to lower price spreads between countries, as we shall mention again in Section 5. Such developments demand new modeling ideas to handle price fluctuations rarely seen in historical data. Finally, an ever-increasing amount of historical and forward-looking data are now publicly available, making it even more advantageous to build a flexible enough model to allow for more inputs such as detailed demand and capacity forecasts (e.g., see Fuss et al., 2013a; Cartea et al., 2008; Benth et al., 2013). Structural models can fairly easily adapt to these market changes and to new information, as each component of the model can be adjusted to reflect current conditions and then bolted back into place.

In this work, we adapt and extend the existing literature in this field by applying a multi-fuel structural stack model to the challenging German power market, illustrating its ability to calibrate to market data and capture key characteristics of the market. We demonstrate a novel approach to obtain a stable fit of the stack model to *both* bid and offer curve data, as required due to the large demand-side elasticity on EEX, which we shall explore. Furthermore, we pay specific attention to the rapidly growing wind and solar capacity in Germany, and more generally describe the impact of the various types of generator capacity entering at different points in the stack. Importantly, we also demonstrate how to choose stochastic processes for each of the fuel prices and for residual demand (after removing renewable supply) such that a closed-form approximation to power forward prices can be obtained as a function of fuel forwards. In this manner, we facilitate rapid calibration to market quotes, without needing to resort to a reduced-form price model, and we construct hourly forward curves going out many years. Finally, we discuss future challenges to be faced in the evolving market environment.

1.2 Market Fundamentals: The Case of the German Power Market

The first step to building an effective spot price model is to understand the fundamental supply and demand factors that determine prices. These market fundamentals differ somewhat from region to region, but strong commonalities exist, with weather, fuel prices, generation mix, and bidding rules always important to understand. In this work we choose Germany as a case study, and argue that it reflects a very wide selection of modeling challenges upon which to demonstrate the merits of our approach. If we can obtain a promising fit to data here, we have a decent chance of doing the same or better elsewhere, of course assuming that enough care is taken to manage the idiosyncrasies of different markets when adapting a model.

Firstly, the German power market is possibly the most complicated European market in terms of production types. The mix consists of: wind, solar, run-of-river hydro, reservoir hydro, nuclear, combined heat and power, lignite-, coal-, gas-, and oil-fired plants. None of these production types dominate (and none is insignificant enough to ignore!), and in recent years the proportional mix has changed dramatically, with a massive increase in wind and solar. Figure 6.1 illustrates both of these points, showing the overall percentages of generated production (right plot), and also the rapid increase in wind and solar generation in recent years (left plot).[1]

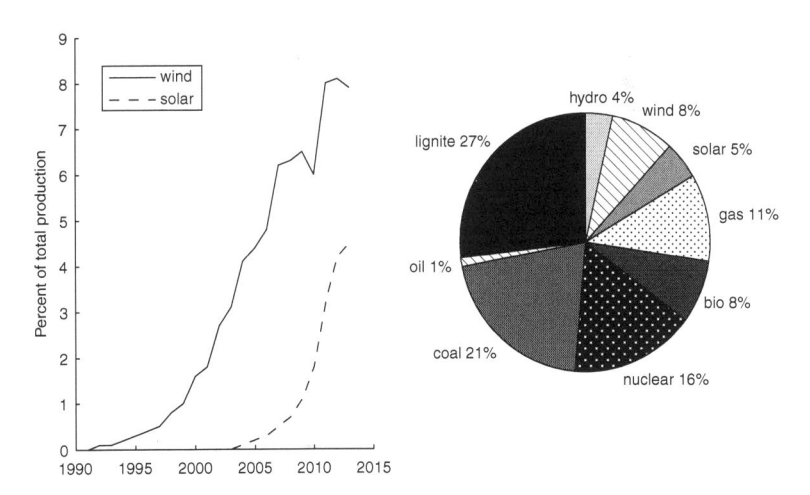

Figure 6.1 Changing fuel mix in the German power market: growth of production from renewables (left) and national production totals by fuel type for 2013 (right).

It is important to understand that on any given hour the production mix may be very different than these annual averages suggest. In particular, the intermittency of renewables (lack of solar at night, and periods of low wind) implies that other hours must have much higher proportions in order to produce the averages shown.

To further complicate matters, the clearing volume on the German power exchange (EEX) is typically only around 25–30 percent of total German power consumption, with the remainder traded bilaterally. As we shall investigate, the size and composition of this exchange-traded volume can vary significantly from day to day or even hour to hour. Generators in the thermal part of the stack engage in many bilateral contracts, but jump in and out of the EEX spot market as prices move, sometimes buying from the market, and sometimes selling to it. In addition to high demand-side elasticity (and the lack of a convenient single demand number), this creates an interesting correlation between supply and demand curves which is crucial to model correctly.

For wind and solar, things are different. Wind and solar power are handled by the transmission systems operators (TSOs), who estimate the amount of day-ahead supply available nationally and offer the entire volume at very low prices (often at −€3,000), since in practice they cannot shut down. This implies a much larger impact on spot price dynamics from renewables than one might expect from the numbers in Figure 6.1 (i.e. all 13 percent belong to the 25–30 percent range), Figure 6.2 illustrates the significant impact of renewables on price dynamics in recent years. First, Figure 6.2a shows that the risk of sudden positive spikes has sharply declined, and been replaced by a risk of negative price spikes due to excess wind at night. Another key change over this

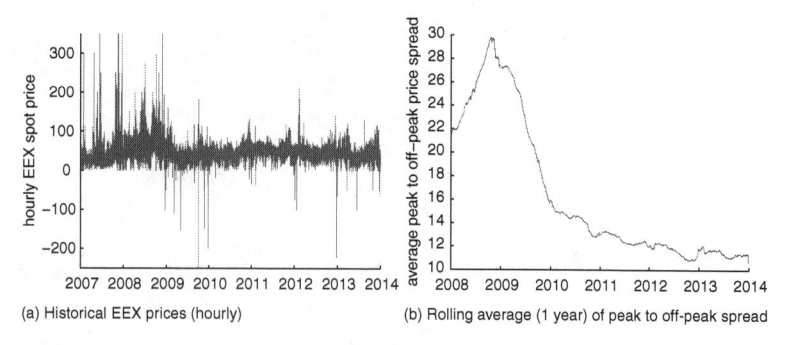

Figure 6.2 Historical EEX hourly spot prices and peak to off-peak price spread (1 year rolling average).

period is a substantial narrowing of the spread between average peak time prices (hours 8–20 of weekdays) and average off-peak prices (all others), as shown in Figure 6.2b. Note that the early increase is clearly linked to the record high prices witnessed throughout commodity markets in 2008, while the steady decrease thereafter can be especially attributed to solar, whose daily production profile is similar to that of demand. Thus, the growing renewable capacity in Germany continues to complicate the modeling of EEX price dynamics, while also causing significant balancing challenges for the grid operators, as both wind and solar can contribute 25,000 MW or more of capacity, which then disappears to zero at other times of the day or night. In addition, it is worth noting that renewables can cause significant volatility increases on the intraday market due to their intermittency and to forecasting difficulties, but we shall not explore this further here as we focus instead on the day-ahead market.

1.3 Statistical Modeling: Existing Techniques and New Ideas

The field of mathematical finance provides us with a rich array of statistical modeling tools with which to describe electricity price dynamics. Much work has been done in the last decade, as described for example in textbooks such as (Eydeland and Wolyniec, 2003; Burger et al., 2007; Benth et al., 2008; Swindle, 2014). Most traditional approaches in this branch of the literature begin by specifying a stochastic differential equation (SDE) for spot or forward prices directly, avoiding all the messy market details described above. These reduced-form models then estimate parameters from historical prices, and optimistically hope that the future will not be too different from the past. Convenient tools for handling uncertainty (like Brownian motions or Levy processes) and convenient formulas for forward and options help to try to justify the oversimplifications needed, as does the sheer complexity of electricity market structure.

However, various authors gradually began to experiment with ways of using these same mathematics, but moving closer to the fundamentals. Why not apply these same stochastic processes to demand or capacity directly, and then transform back to prices in step two? Barlow (2002) is often credited with the birth of such structural models, but similar early ideas were also proposed by (Eydeland and Wolyniec, 2003; Skantze et al., 2000; Pirrong and Jermakyan, 2008) and others. The literature has continued to grow in recent years, with more sophisticated techniques needed particularly to handle multi-fuel markets with possible merit order changes (see Coulon and Howison, 2009; Aïd et al., 2009, 2012; Carmona et al., 2013) or to handle especially "spikey" markets (see Kanamura and Ohashi, 2007; Anderson and Davison, 2008; Coulon et al., 2013). A big part of the challenge is the choice of function that maps underlying factors to prices, serving as an approximation to the generation stack and its constraints. Many of these papers argue for the need to retain closed-form solutions for forwards (and possibly options) as much as possible. This reflects a desire to keep the best of both worlds: the tractability and computational speed of a reduced-form model, and the market insight and data exploitation of a fundamental one.

In this vein, we continue to push the boundaries of how much of the fundamentals can be squeezed into a tractable structural model. In some sense, this could be viewed as working backwards, starting with a closed-form formula for forward prices, and carefully adding more of the necessary pieces of the puzzle without losing the computational benefits. We build on the work of (Carmona et al., 2013; Carmona and Coulon, 2014) who demonstrated that exponential bid curves, Gaussian demand, and lognormal fuel prices can be combined in a two-fuel structural model for power prices, with closed-form solutions available for forwards and spread options. Crucially, this approach allows for overlapping bids from different fuels as well as merit order changes (and resulting changes in correlation structures). For example, gas generators may be pushed up the stack ("out-of-the-money") by lower coal and carbon prices or by higher gas prices, as we have witnessed in Europe in recent years. We extend this approach by an approximation technique for handling many more than two fuel types, as well as handling demand elasticity, both of which are necessary for EEX.

We also devote attention to the practicalities of data fitting and the messy details of calibration to the market, which is sometimes ignored in the existing literature. Coulon and Howison (2009), Coulon et al. (2013), and Lyle and Elliott (2009) provide data fitting exercises for somewhat simpler North American markets, and Aïd et al. (2009) do a simple fit to the French market. For EEX in particular, Wagner (2013) and He et al. (2013) both provide nice analysis of fitting a structural model to the German market, but focus primarily on capturing renewable infeed accurately and less on forward curve construction. Fuss et al. (2013a) also looks at EEX from a structural approach, but this time with a focus on the added benefit of incorporating supply and demand forecasts. On the whole, despite promising advances, more work is certainly needed to properly quantify the performance of structural models and encourage their widespread adoption in industry. We aim to contribute in this respect by illustrating the performance of our approach for the important task of building hourly resolution forward curves.

2 The Stack Model

The key ingredient in all structural, hybrid or fundamental models for electricity markets is the treatment of the stack: the transformation from underlying stochastic factors to power prices. In most literature, power demand is considered price inelastic, so the stack transformation simply consists of the supply stack function,[2] which is strictly increasing, generally convex and can lead to dramatic price spikes due to its very steep finish. Broadly speaking, there are three ways of constructing this transformation:

1. From auction data directly
2. From cost data directly
3. Indirectly inferred from historical price and demand data only

We shall not discuss the last of these at all, since it clearly relies heavily on historical price series and struggles to accurately describe sections of the stack that only rarely set the price. We shall briefly touch on the second, primarily since there are some power markets for which auction data are not released. However, we shall focus heavily on the first, since bypassing cost data is advantageous in many ways. First, it avoids any assumption that bids (offers) actually equal costs, since profit margins and other differences are built into the auction data on which the model is estimated. Second, and by the same logic, any strategic bidding is effectively built into the model already, assuming such behavior is fairly consistent over time. And finally, in markets such as EEX where auction data are released *after* adjustment for transmission and operational constraints (such that the intersection of bid and offer curves precisely equals the market clearing price), we get an added benefit of also bypassing these challenging constraints, again subject to the assumption that they are fairly stable over time.

The approach using auction data directly can also be split into two subcategories, depending on how these data are released. In markets like EEX, no information is given about which bids or offers come from which types of production. All data are anonymous. In this case, the statistical techniques used to fit the stack must try to infer this from its behavior over time. In contrast, in some markets (like Italy), more information is provided, such that we can identify exactly which parts of the stack come from which production type, potentially simplifying the fitting procedure.

2.1 Supply Curves, Demand Curves, and Price Curves

For the day-ahead market (typically called spot), EEX provides supply and demand curves from the electricity auction for each hour of every day, and the intersection of these offer and bid curves exactly matches the market clearing price (MCP). The allowed price range for bids and offers is currently from −€3000 to +€3000 (previously 0 to 3000). Prices of offered production volumes are of course related to running costs for fossil fuel plants (be they based on lignite, coal, gas, or oil), while for wind, solar and other "must-run" generators, all expected capacity is typically offered at or near the bottom of the stack.

Figure 6.3 shows an example from hour 13, 2013/03/04. The first thing to notice is the strong elasticity of the demand curve, with demand dropping substantially as price increases. At first this is rather surprising, since it is well known that very few consumers of power are price-sensitive. An example might be aluminum plants, but they certainly cannot account for the elasticity seen, which for many hours (including the one shown) is greater even than the supply-side elasticity. We must look elsewhere to find an explanation.

If the EEX market covered the total national volume of power needed each hour, then the demand curve would be almost inelastic, and the

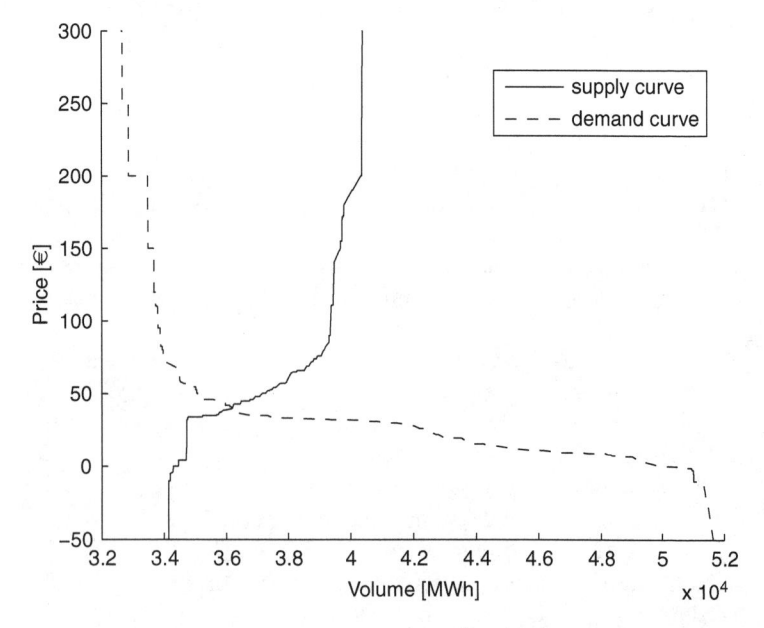

Figure 6.3 Sample supply and demand curves from EEX for hour 13, 2013/03/04.

cleared volume would be a good approximation of total national power demand. However, since EEX only covers some 25–30 percent of national demand, a big bilateral market exists, where energy providers are contracted to deliver power to a certain customer. If the prices on EEX happen to be lower than the contracted price, the provider can choose to buy power from the market instead of producing it himself, so-called make-or-buy behavior. This option to switch from selling to buying explains the very elastic demand curve we observe, with some generators even simultaneously submitting both supply and demand bids, separated by some spread.

The complication of having an exchange-based market and a bilateral market in parallel, with interchanging volumes, forces us to model not just an elastic supply stack, but also an elastic demand stack. This causes a major headache for traditional structural models, but can be avoided by constructing what we call a price curve. The entire elasticity from the demand side is transferred to the supply side to create the price curve. As a result, we get a perfectly inelastic (vertical) demand curve, and of course, the clearing price stays the same, as shown in Figure 6.4. Describing this transformation mathematically, since volumes are added together in the x direction of our plots, we can represent the price curve $y = p(x)$ in terms of the supply curve $s(x)$ and demand curve $d(x)$ via their inverses:[3]

$$y = p(x), \quad \text{where } x = s^{-1}(y) + d^{-1}(-3000) - d^{-1}(y) \qquad (1)$$

Note that our inelastic demand value is now simply $x = d^{-1}(-3000)$, since $y = p(x)$ then leads to $s(x) = d(x)$ in (1), thereby matching supply and demand. This procedure simplifies matters and also leads to some quite interesting and nice features. In particular, by moving the elastic "make-or-buy" volumes from the demand curve into the supply curve, we obtain a single price curve that is much more stable than either of the original curves. Furthermore, the remaining inelastic demand is also much more stable, or rather predictable, than the market clearing volume of the supply and demand curves.

Figures 6.5a and 6.5b, respectively, depict the supply and demand curves for seven consecutive days, all at hour 13. All curves have been shifted so that they start at the same volumes (zero) at the lowest permitted price of −€3000. Figure 6.5c depicts the same plot for the price curve. As can be seen, the seven price curves look more similar to each other, at least in the mid-price region, than the seven supply and demand curves. It is only the price curves from Saturday and Sunday that deviate at higher prices, indicating that some expensive production types are not offered on weekends when the expected spot price is lower. Except for high

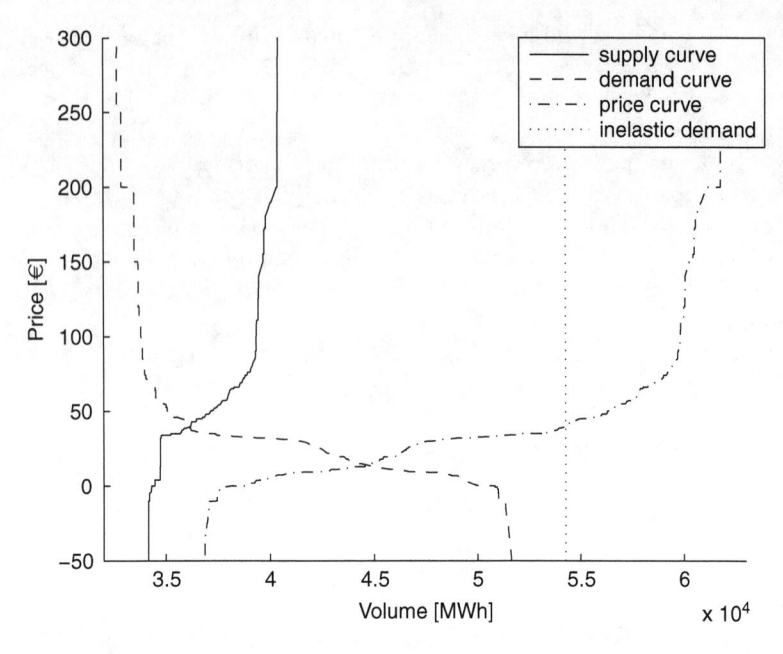

Figure 6.4 An illustration of the transformation to the price curve using Equation (1). Although not visible on this zoomed-in plot, note that by definition the supply and price curves both start at the same volume level for the lowest bid of −€3000. The price curve grows more slowly because of accumulating the demand-side volumes as well.

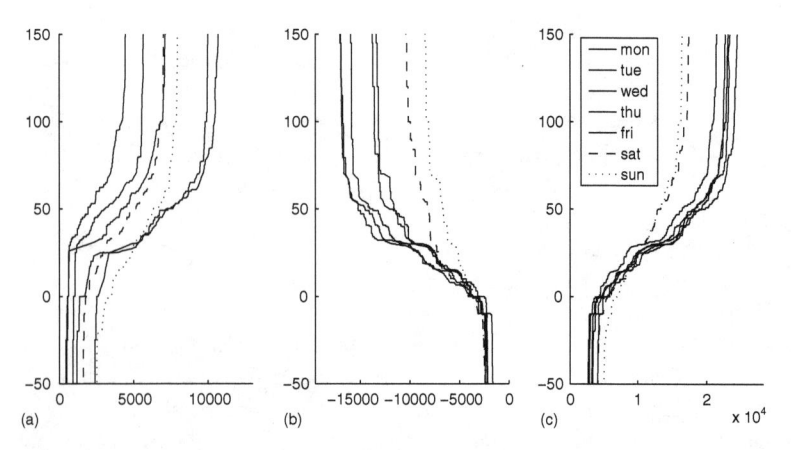

Figure 6.5 (a) Supply curves, (b) demand curves, and (c) price curves, from seven consecutive days (27/05/13-02/06/13).

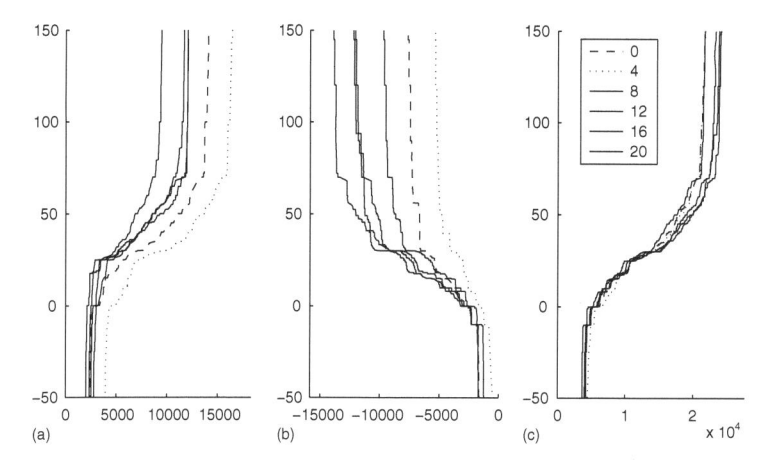

Figure 6.6 (a) Supply curves, (b) demand curves, and (c) price curves, from six representative hours during one day (Friday 31/05/2013).

prices/volumes, far above the typical clearing price, the price curve looks reasonably stable for modeling purposes.

Similarly let us look at a sequence of hours within a day, as shown in Figure 6.6. Here again price curves show remarkably more stable behavior than supply and demand curves. Only for high prices/volumes do some hours deviate, and the deviating hours are the weak off-peak hours (0 and 4 here), where prices tend to be the lowest of the day. For these hours some of the expensive production is again apparently not offered.

Longer horizon comparisons also reveal that this added stability persists over time as we would hope, with the only significant variation in the price curves hopefully ascribable to changing fuel prices. Finally in Figure 6.7, we compare the inelastic demand produced by our transformation with the original market clearing volume. In particular, we are interested in determining how strongly they correlate to national power demand, which is relatively straightforward to model and predict. In Figure 6.7b we clearly see a much stronger correlation between inelastic and national demand than between clearing volume and national demand in Figure 6.7a.

2.2 The Composition of the Stack

Figure 6.8a shows an example of a price stack again taken from EEX 03/04/2013, hour 13. Here we see the same information as in Figure 6.3 transformed into a histogram style, with price bins along the x-axis and

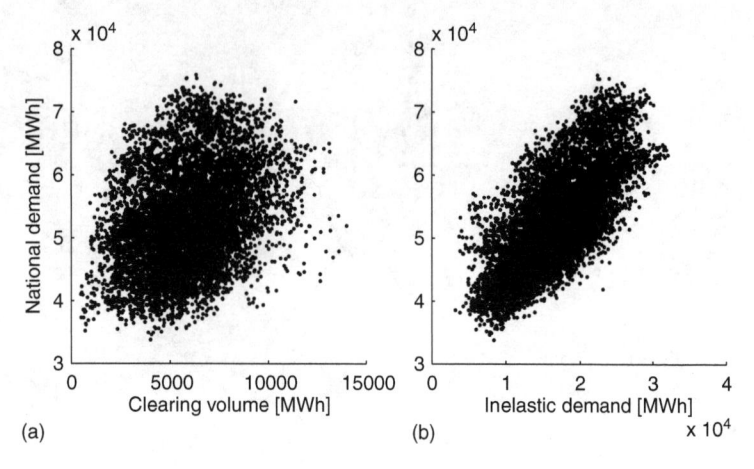

Figure 6.7 (a) National demand vs. market clearing volume; (b) National demand vs. "inelastic" demand (following transformation).

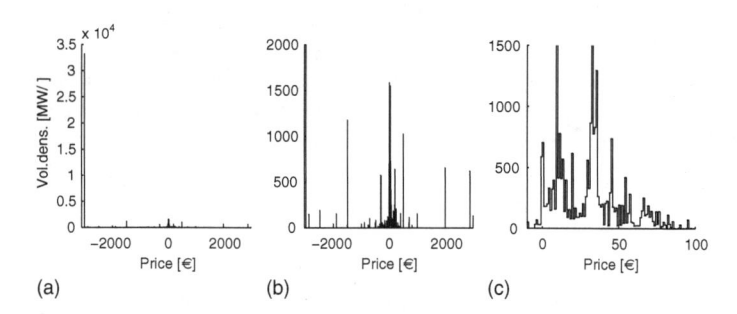

Figure 6.8 A histogram view of the stack on hour 13, 03/04/2013: (a) entire dataset; (b) truncated y axis; (c) further truncated y axes.

volumes along the y-axis, an approach for analysing bid data advocated in Coulon and Howison (2009). In this case, we see little more than a huge volume offered at −€3000 and a small "bump" of volumes just above zero euros. If we zoom in, as in Figure 6.8b, we also notice smaller volumes scattered in the price range between −3000 and zero. From zero up to around €300 we have the thermal stack, and above 300 there might be expensive production units offering volumes that will be used only under special circumstances, due to an unexpected shortage of production. Figure 6.8c is yet another zoom-in around the thermal stack, that reveals a structure we will look into in more detail soon.

2.3 The "Must-Run" Stack

In Figure 6.9a we see the volume being offered at −3000 as an hourly time series of about 8–9 days (solid line), and compared to the measured/estimated wind and solar production for the same period (dashed line). It is interesting to observe that during some of the nights, the production drops to zero, while during other (windy) nights, it can be a significant quantity. It is clear that the dynamics of the volume at −3000 resemble the dynamics of renewable production. In Figure 6.9b we see a much larger amount of the same data (all of 2013) as a scatter plot, indicating the rather strong correlation. The residual volume (around 15,000 MW for this sample) is likely to come from other types of must-run production like nuclear and combined heat and power plants.

Although it looks like a clear majority of wind and solar production is offered at −€3000, we suspect that it could also be offered at higher prices, still negative and negative enough to avoid the risk of not being below a clearing price. Thus a safer approach to capturing the offered volume from −€3000 up to near zero would be to assume that it all comes from a combination of wind, solar, nuclear and combined heat and power production. Since we have numbers of wind and solar production, as well as nuclear production, and further assume that their entire volume is offered to the market, we can simply subtract this volume from the total. The residual we label as combined heat and power (chp) and model separately. This combination of wind, solar, nuclear, and chp is what we call the "must-run" stack.

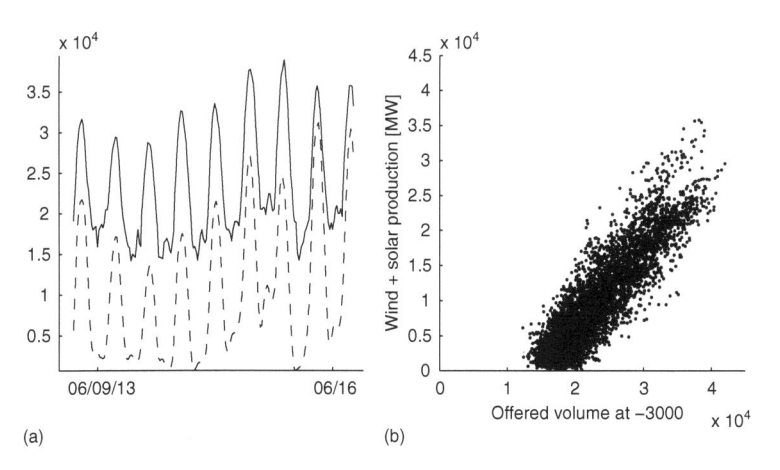

Figure 6.9 The relationship between volume offered at −3000 and total production from renewables shown via: (a) an hourly time series of 8–9 days (b) a scatter plot for all of 2013.

2.4 The Thermal Stack

We define the thermal stack as the production volumes offered from slightly below zero to a few hundred euros.[4] This is the price range where we normally find the offers from lignite-, coal-, gas-, and oil-based production types. When observing the price stack in this region, again in histogram style, we find clustered volumes, starting with one around zero euros, followed by two to four bigger and smaller clusters up to around €200. Figure 6.10a provides an insightful view of these clusters of volumes, and their movements over a one-year period. The price stack for hour 13 of every day is plotted as a sequence of histograms, with the x-axis (horizontal) representing price, the y-axis the time in days, and the z-axis the volume density. The mid-2008 to mid-2009 time period analyzed here is an interesting one to examine, as it starts with relatively high fuel prices where the clusters of bids/offers are well separated and ends with relatively low prices where the clusters are also lower and overlap heavily.

These clusters of volumes can be assumed to arrive from the different types of production, driven by different fuels, and thus have different running costs. Our aim is to identify and model how these clusters vary in offered price with varying running costs, and how their respective magnitudes vary over time, typically with day-of-week and time-of-day patterns. We expect expensive production types like gas and oil to be offered at relatively high prices and most often on peak hours. Lignite on the other hand is more likely to also be offered on off-peak hours, and maybe even at prices below running cost to avoid the additional costs associated with ramping down and up too often.

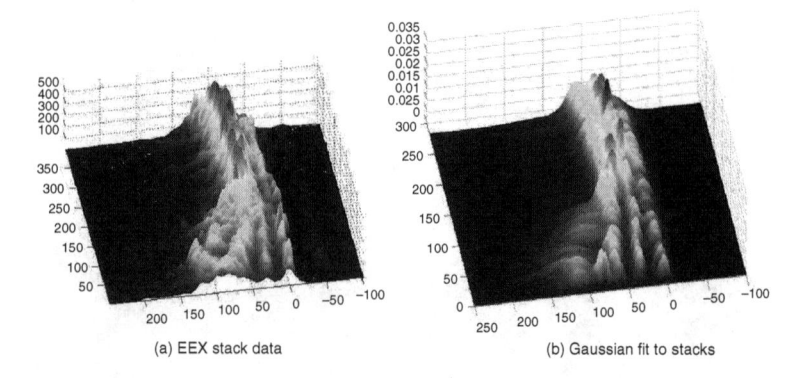

(a) EEX stack data

(b) Gaussian fit to stacks

Figure 6.10 One year of stack data from EEX and the corresponding fit using a Gaussian mixture model.

The running cost r we calculate as

$$r = \frac{1}{e}\left(f + 3.6cA\right) \tag{2}$$

where e is the efficiency of a plant, f is the fuel price, A is the price of a CO_2 allowance and c is the number of tons of CO_2 emitted per GJ of fuel consumed. The factor 3.6 converts from GJ to MWh.

Motivated by the clear long-term links between the movements of volume clusters and their associated fuel costs, we follow the approach of Coulon and Howison (2009) by fitting densities to these clusters each day (and hour), and analyzing the movements of the parameters. Figure 6.10b illustrates the result from fitting Gaussian densities to clusters each day, and clearly parallels the behavior seen in Figure 6.10a over the same one-year period. We use a mixture density network (MDN) model (see Bishop [1994] for details), in principle a weighted sum of density functions with three parameters per component: the mean, the variance, and the relative weight. We let the mean be given as a linear function of the running cost in (2) for each fuel type. We then estimate the mean parameters, variance, and weight for each component. Figure 6.11a shows an example of a price stack on a certain day and hour (dashed line), fitted with a set of Gaussian distributions (solid line). Although the fitted stack may not look particularly convincing in this histogram form, in the end what we are using is the price curve (produced by integrating and inverting the densities), which comes out reasonably well, as shown in Figure 6.11b. It is only for very high prices, clearly above typical market clearing prices, that the fitted line deviates significantly from the observed data.

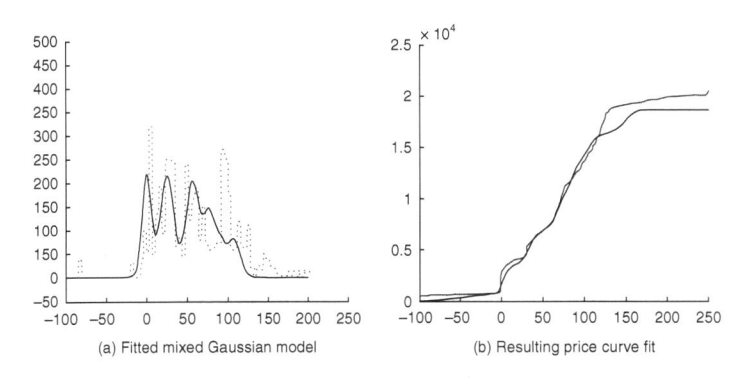

Figure 6.11 Illustration of converting an MDN model fit to a price curve fit.

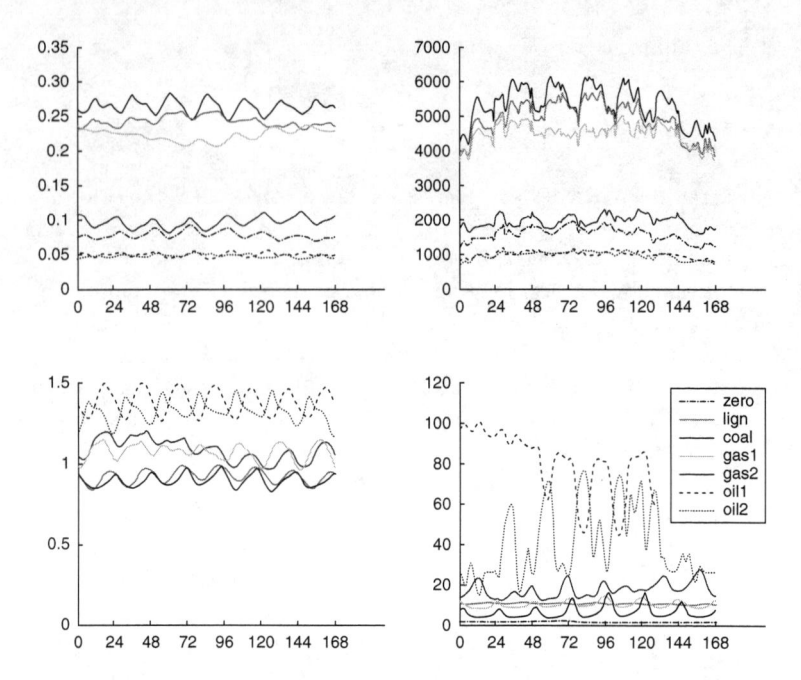

Figure 6.12 Weekly patterns output from the MDN model: relative magnitudes of the seven Gaussians (top left), their absolute magnitudes (top right), their means relative to running costs (bottom left), and their variances (bottom right).

Figure 6.12 illustrates how the three outputs of the MDN model look as a function of time. Since we model the distributions as a function of time-of-day and time-of-week, we provide output for a period of one week. The top left plot shows the relative volumes of each of the seven different distributions. The order from top to bottom is: coal, lignite, gas1, gas2, the "zero hump,"[5] oil1 and oil2. Notice that we have two distributions for gas and two for oil. This is motivated by the fact that in Germany we have a modern set of gas/oil plants with relatively high efficiency and thus low running cost (gas1/oil1), and another older set of gas/oil plants with lower efficiency and thus higher running costs (gas2/oil2). As can be seen, the highest relative volumes in the EEX price stack seem to correspond to coal plants, closely followed by lignite and modern gas plants, roughly in line with production volumes in Figure 6.1. The top right plot in Figure 6.12 shows the same results but in absolute volumes. In the bottom left plot, we then have the marginal price of the different types, where 1 means their calculated running cost. This time from top to bottom we have: oil2 and oil1 partly overlapping, gas2 and gas1 also partly overlapping, and coal and lignite also partly overlapping (no zero hump in this case as the mean is fixed). We notice here that lignite and coal are often offered below their running costs, as expected, and gas plants go down to their running costs but not below. Oil fired plants ask for a high margin. Finally, the bottom right plot shows the variances of the Gaussian clusters, which are significantly less stable than the other model parameters. This is to be expected given their sensitivities to outliers in the tails, and also the challenge of fitting overlapping clusters.

3 The Fundamental Factors

The stack model provides the core of our approach and much of our original contribution here. However, it is only one half of the picture, since all the randomness in the model comes from the treatment of the underlying factors. It is important to note that many different choices can be made here while retaining the same stack methodology above, for example by making deterministic factors stochastic or vice versa (generation capacities are a good example here). There is little doubt that fuel prices, demand and renewable supply should, however, all remain stochastic to try to capture the majority of the variation seen in EEX prices. However, we begin in this section by addressing their nonstochastic components, before adding randomness in the next section. We now introduce our approach for each fundamental factor in turn, starting with the demand side and moving towards the supply side, by way of wind and solar which in some sense sit in the middle.

When modeling demand, wind and solar production, we need weather data. Demand is dependent on temperature, wind power on wind speed and solar power on solar irradiation. Weather forecasts, and also reanalysis data (as close as you can get to measurements), are provided in their rawest form as so called grib-files. From these grib-files one can extract the temperature, the wind speed at ground level and solar irradiation for a specified region. We have been using Global Forecast System (GFS) from the US National Weather Service as a provider since their grib-files are free of charge. Another provider is European Centre for Medium-Range Weather Forecasts (ECMWF). Measurements, or rather estimates, of demand, wind and solar production are provided by the four TSOs for their respective areas. This means we can construct models for each area to improve performance, instead of just looking at the entire country.

When we model wind and solar, we do this in Coordinated Universal Time (UTC), and then afterward transform back to Central European Time (CET), as weather data are always given in UTC. This is to exclude complications with daylight saving shifts in spring and autumn. The weather and thus the wind and solar production do not care about humans shifting the clocks! Demand, on the other hand, has a strong component from social behavior: when do we get up and make breakfast, what working hours are normal, when do we cook dinner in the evening, and so on. So for demand modeling purposes we have to consider the time shift.

3.1 Demand

Power cannot be stored in any significant amounts. So when we need power, it is a demand that is immediate. If it gets cold we demand more power immediately to heat our houses. When factories start up in the morning they do not take it from some storage in the basement. They demand it to be produced and delivered through the grid immediately. Unlike other commodity markets which can rely on inventories to smooth out demand, the nonstorability of power thus gives power demand a specific structure, or rather periodicity, that comes from the periodicity of both temperature and social behavior. The holiday calendar sometimes breaks this symmetry and needs to be taken care of explicitly. Christmas takes place on a different weekday every year, Easter can shift in time by up to a month, and so on.

The periodicities seen in a time-series of demand are rather complex. The shape of the daily periodicity will change over a year, mainly because of the sun rising and setting at different times, causing lights to be switched on at different times of the day depending on time-of-year. So the shape of the daily periodicity (and the timing of the morning and evening peak) will change gradually with time-of-year: a periodic periodicity. To model this correctly is important, since these periodicities, due to the nonstorability of power, are also observed in electricity spot prices.

The periodicity can be modeled as a function of time: hour-of-day, day-of-week, time-of-year. But time, as we measure it with clocks, is not good for mathematical modeling in general, and in particular not as an input to the neural network approach we shall use below. Imagine something that has a daily periodicity and needs to be modeled using the hour of the day: 1 till 24. Hour 24 is very close to hour 1, as close as hour 1 to hour 2, but the numerical difference is 23, instead of 1. We need a periodic clock, something that uniquely defines the hour of the day, and with equidistant intervals between all consecutive hours. This cannot be achieved with only one variable, but instead by two variables that we call x and y:

$$x = \sin(2\pi t), \qquad y = \cos(2\pi t)$$

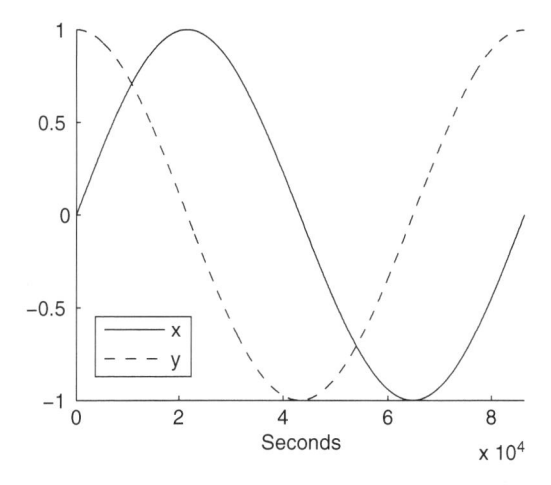

Figure 6.13 An illustration of the periodic (x, y) clock.

where t is calendar time measured in days. Here the pair (x, y) serves as our periodic clock (as illustrated in Figure 6.13), still uniquely defining the time of the day, but having a period of 24 hours. This method of representing time can be applied not only to hour-of-day, but also to day-of-week and time-of-year, or whatever period is appropriate for the problem at hand. For power demand we need all three periodic clocks.

The power demand we need to model is not the total power demand of Germany, but the power demand we see in the day-ahead market at EEX, which constitutes about 25–30 percent of national demand. As we saw in the previous section, the demand (clearing volume at EEX) is far from inelastic. However, after the specified transformation to a price curve in (1), we get another time series of "inelastic demand" that resembles much more closely the national demand, and can thus be modeled according to the reasoning made above. We use a conventional neural network to model the dependence on temperature and periodicities (see Bishop [1995] for background on this approach), since it is well suited to handle periodic behavior and we have enough data to avoid any risk of overfitting.

In addition to its dependence on fundamental factors of temperature and social behavior periodicities, demand will also gradually increase and decrease with time. Normally, for the national demand, this would be related to the business cycle. In our case, modeling the inelastic demand calculated from the day-ahead market will also capture the slowly changing volumes traded at EEX (but we will still call it "business cycle"). So when calibrating our model using historical data, we need to incorporate something to handle the dependence on the business cycle. Moreover, when simulating future demand, we need a "handle" to adjust the future demand level accordingly. We do this by adding to the previous fundamental neural network another component: a very limited (few hidden nodes) neural network dependent on linear time:

$$d = f_1(t) + f_2(T, p, H)$$

where f_1 is the business-cycle neural network dependent on linear time t, and f_2 is the fundamental neural network dependent on temperature T, periodicities p (x and y variables earlier) and a holiday calendar H.

In Figure 6.14 (top left), we see the calibrated daily mean values as a solid line, compared to the inelastic demand as calculated from the supply and demand curves provided by EEX, in a dotted line. We see that the volumes have steadily increased over the period shown, 2011 to 2014. This increase has been captured by the "business cycle" part of the model, as shown in the top right. The bottom left shows hourly values during one week illustrating the weekly pattern captured by the model. Finally, the bottom right shows hourly demand patterns during two days, both Wednesdays, chosen at roughly the brightest and darkest periods of a year. This is included to illustrate how the model captures the shift in the evening peak to earlier afternoon hours when it is dark earlier.

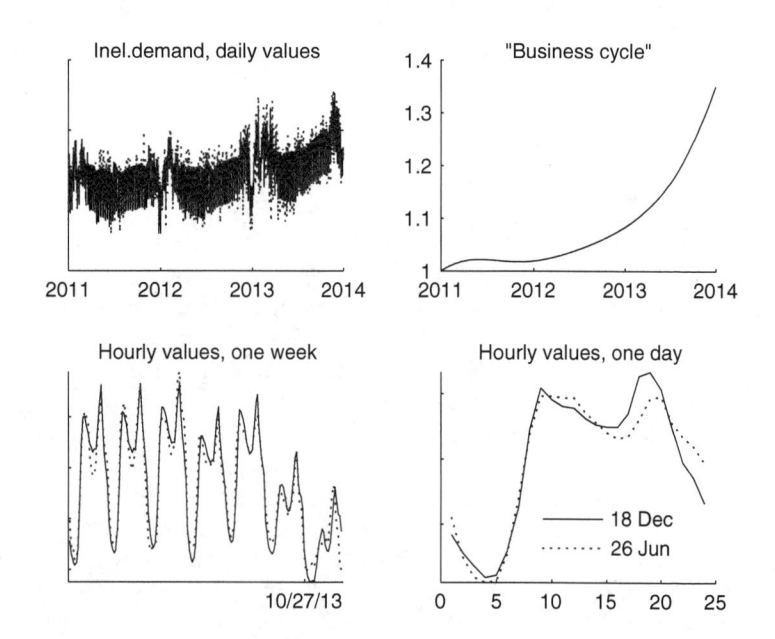

Figure 6.14 Analysis of the (transformed) inelastic demand process in EEX.

Although it is important to back out the "business cycle" from history when fitting, it will of course be impossible to make realistic assumptions about its development in the future. Therefore, as will be shown in more detail later, the "business cycle" is used when we calibrate our simulated spot prices to forward quotes.

3.2 Wind

We need to model generated wind power both as a short-term forecast, and to simulate long-term production. Since the installed capacity has increased massively over the years, and might continue to increase, we need to construct a model that takes this into account.

When modeling wind power (normally the production from a single wind park), one might try to model even individual wind turbines with their characteristic power curve (wind power against wind speed), and also take into account wind direction, topography, temperature, and air pressure. We need the produced wind power on a national level, and thus aim for a simpler model where we mainly take into account the wind speed.

The wind power curve of a turbine tells how much power is produced at a certain wind speed at hub level. The shape is sigmoidal and reaches a maximum level of production for around 10–15 m/s. If the wind goes higher, a wind turbine will try to avoid damage by rotating its blades, will thus produce less power for these high wind speeds, and will even at some level turn off. A function (for power p vs wind speed w) that can nicely reproduce this shape is the beta function:

$$p = \frac{\left(\frac{w}{w^{\max}}\right)^{\alpha-1}\left(1 - \frac{w}{w^{\max}}\right)^{\beta-1}}{\left(\frac{1-\alpha}{2-\alpha-\beta}\right)^{\alpha-1}\left(1 - \frac{1-\alpha}{2-\alpha-\beta}\right)^{\beta-1}}$$

We modify it slightly so it covers a range $[0, w^{\max}]$ instead of the normal $[0, 1]$. The α and β parameters are the normal parameters to calibrate the shape. We also normalized it in such a way that the maximum of the curve is set to 1. This is done to ensure that the installed capacity can be appropriately interpreted as a multiplicative factor C. (The installed capacity of a wind turbine is the maximum possible production.) The weighted sum over n different beta functions enables a higher flexibility when calibrating wind speeds at several locations within a TSO area to just one measurement of wind power, P. For example, shapes may differ for older and newer turbines, but n can and should be kept small to avoid overfitting. We assume the rate of capacity increase is the same for all locations n within each TSO area, but it is also possible to have one for each location i.

$$P = C(t) \sum_{i=1}^{n} \omega_i p_i \qquad \text{where } \sum_{i=1}^{n} \omega_i = 1$$

The installed capacity $C(t)$ is a function of time. We can get historical values of installed capacity from Bundesnetzagentur but they do not reveal exactly when this capacity started operating. We therefore aim to also calibrate $C(t)$ using historical data. Since we know that the installed capacity has grown, we restrict the model for $C(t)$ to be a monotonically increasing function of time t. In the equation below, a, b, c, and v are all free parameters, and m should be kept small to avoid overfitting.

$$C(t) = a^2 + \sum_{i=1}^{m} c_i^2 h(b + v_i^2 t), \qquad \text{where } h(x) = \frac{1}{1 + e^{-x}}$$

Figure 6.15 shows the result of calibrating the wind power generated in the RWE region over a three-year period. The top left shows the two beta functions used (summing up to a max of 1 as they should). The top right shows the estimated installed capacity increase during this period. The bottom left shows the hourly wind power generated and forecasted, and

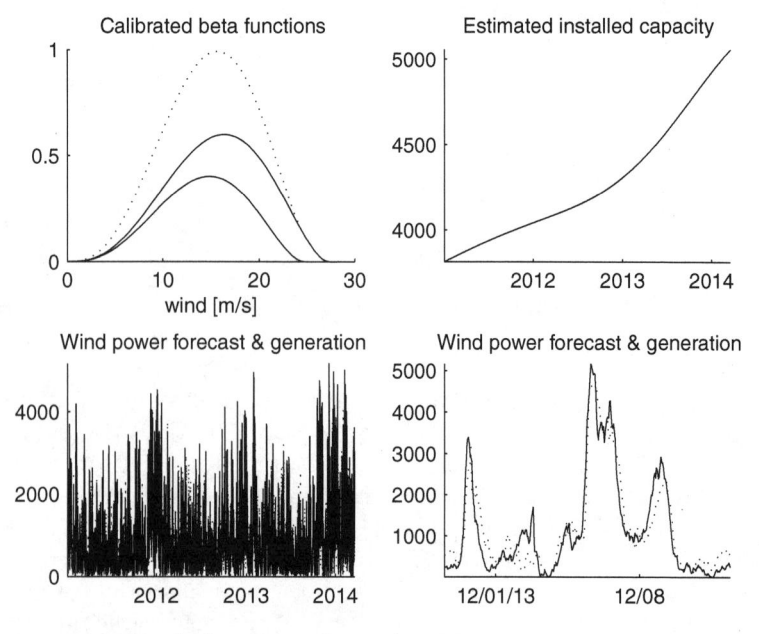

Figure 6.15 Results from fitting the wind model.

finally the bottom right zooms in on a two-week period to more clearly illustrate how the calibrated model compares to measurements provided by the TSO.

3.3 Solar

Solar panels are distributed across all of Germany, even though solar radiation is highest in the south. Solar power production is a function of solar irradiation, installed capacity, and to some extent temperature. (e.g., see Huld 2005 Williams et al. 2005) High temperatures have a negative impact on the efficiency of a panel. Since, as for wind, we need to capture the solar power production for the entire country (or at least for each of the four TSO areas) we need to use a simple model. The function below is a simplified version of the function suggested in Huld, 2005; Williams et al., 2005.

$$P = C(t)(\alpha I + \beta I^2)$$

Here $C(t)$ is the installed capacity and, as before, modeled using a strictly positive, monotonically increasing function of time and calibrated against measured solar power and solar irradiation. α and β are free parameters

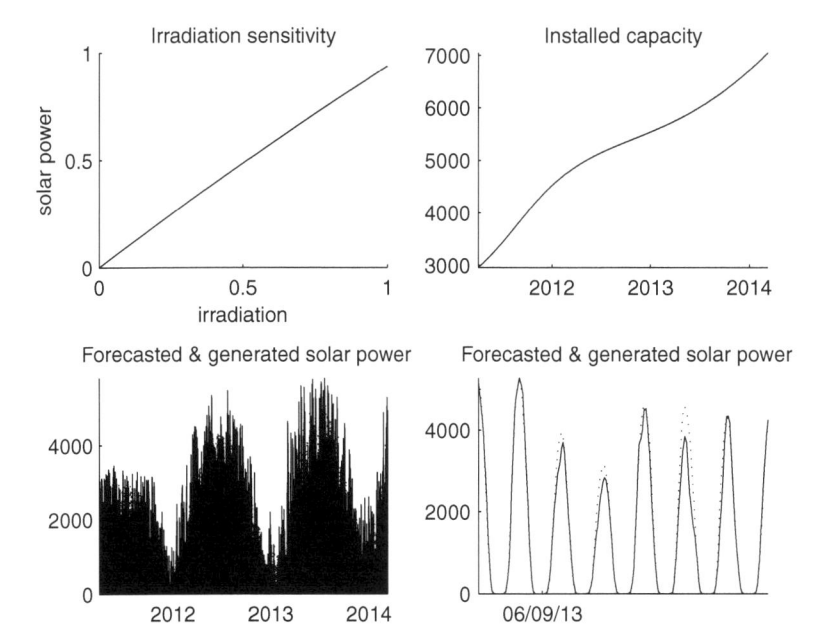

Figure 6.16 Results from fitting the solar model.

and I is the solar irradiation falling vertically on one square meter. This means we do not need to keep track of the sun's declination and its possible effect on the mostly fixed solar panels that do not follow the movements of the sun.

Figure 6.16 in the top left plot shows the sensitivity to irradiation, in scaled units of irradiation and solar power generated. As can be seen we get an almost linear dependence. The slight downward bend for higher irradiation levels might be an indirect temperature dependence: high irradiation implies high temperature which causes a less efficient panel. The top right plot shows the estimated increase in installed capacity during the three-year period. The bottom left plot shows the generated and modeled solar power for the full period and finally, the bottom right plot zooms in on one week to illustrate the model's capacity to capture varying production in different days.

3.4 Nuclear and Combined Heat and Power

Nuclear power production we regard as "must-run" for Germany. The nuclear power plants are run according to available long-term plans with scheduled maintenance periods. However, the historically realized production is noticeably always lower than the planned production. Using historical data, a simple model can be used to make this adjustment as a function of planning horizon, typically with greater downwards adjustment the further out we look.

Combined heat and power (chp) production is generated in winter as a bi-product to heat, and hence the volumes offered are not related to expected power prices but more to outdoor temperatures. In summer, though, when heat is in of less demand, power can still be produced, at least for those plants with a so-called heat-sink. But in this case power will only be produced if prices are high enough, which we typically achieve only when we have low volumes offered from wind and solar. An appropriate model for chp production in winter requires a dependence on temperature and time (typically time-of-day and day-of-year). To handle the different behavior in the summer, we can add expected wind and solar production as additional factors. We model this using a neural network.

3.5 Fossil Fuels: Lignite, Coal, Gas, and Oil

The last of our fundamental factors to model is the set of fossil fuel prices. As described in Section 2.4, each fuel price is converted to approximate running costs in (2) as part of the fitting procedure for the thermal stack. We then model joint running cost dynamics in a reduced-form manner as correlated stochastic processes, to be discussed further in the next section. Recalling that our primary goal is hourly forward curve construction for power, instead of trying to forecast long-term mean levels for fuels, we logically let the mean fuel prices be set by the fuel forward prices in the market. As carbon forward prices are also available, we can easily obtain a "forward running cost" value. As we shall see, having explicit formulas for power forwards as a function of fuel forwards greatly facilitates the calibration procedure.

4 Forward Curve Construction

In all commodity markets, accurately capturing the shape and dynamics of the forward curve is crucial, as forwards and futures represent the most liquidly available traded assets and the dominant hedging tools for many companies. Furthermore, the forward curve serves as a vital set of information about the market's views of the future spot price, blurred somewhat by the addition of possible risk premia linked to the strength of hedging demand. A model that misprices observed forward contracts is bound to fail at other tasks as well, not least because all other derivatives are priced by no arbitrage relative to known forward prices. Therefore, not only should mathematical models of commodity prices *take advantage* of forward quotes in data-fitting procedures, they should go as far as *exactly matching* the observed prices, also known as "calibrating to the forward curve." In practice, this task becomes increasingly challenging as models become increasingly sophisticated, with computation time often rapidly exploding in the absence of convenient formulas for forward prices. In this section, we summarize our approach to forward curve construction and calibration in the model introduced above.

4.1 From Spot to Forward

Standard finance theory tells us that a forward contract struck at time t, with maturity T, has a forward price $F(t, T)$ and a corresponding payoff $S_T - F(t, T)$, where S_T is the underlying spot price. By risk neutral pricing, since there is no cost to enter into the contract at t, we must have

$$F(t, T) = \mathbb{E}_t^{\mathbb{Q}}[S_T]$$

where $\mathbb{E}_t^{\mathbb{Q}}$ is the time t conditional expectation under the risk neutral pricing measure $\mathbb{Q}$. Note that we do not debate the uniqueness of $\mathbb{Q}$, but make the usual assumption that an appropriate $\mathbb{Q}$ can be inferred from the market given available quotes. Indeed, calibrating to the forward curve identifies for us the $\mathbb{Q}$ distribution of S_T that is consistent with both our model and the market.

In electricity markets, forward contracts typically have delivery periods of one week, month, or quarter, with power scheduled for delivery every hour of that period, or in some cases only every peak hour, or every off-peak hour. Assuming the payment of F is made at a single time point (to avoid adjustments for discounting), the forward price now satisfies

$$F(t, [T_L, T_U]) = \frac{1}{N} \sum_{T_i \in \mathcal{H}}^{N} F(t, T_i) = \frac{1}{N} \sum_{T_i \in \mathcal{H}}^{N} \mathbb{E}_t^{\mathbb{Q}}[S_{T_i}]$$

where $\mathcal{H}$ represents the appropriate bucket of hours during the delivery period $[T_L, T_U]$, for example, all weekday hours between 8 and 20 in January.

Given a spot price model, the task of forward curve construction therefore boils down to taking an expectation over the spot price distribution in the future, or more precisely, many many such expectations. In particular, as we are interested in hourly granularity forwards here, we need to calculate almost 9,000 such expectations for each year of the forward curve we build. For a full fundamental model which mimics the hourly dispatch optimization, just generating a single hourly price path over several years can be computational demanding, let alone averaging over many such paths (and many sources of randomness) to produce a reliable forward curve. Even a reasonably fast algorithm to *generate* a forward curve, may not be good enough to *calibrate to* a forward curve, as this second step requires tuning some component of the model until all market and model prices line up.

It is for this reason that closed-form formulas for forwards (or derivatives more generally in finance) remain very valuable. The modeling approach we introduced in Sections 2 and 3 is undoubtedly a complicated model, with many different periodicities, many stochastic factors, many parameters, and much data required, but through an approximation technique described in the next section, we still retain tractability for forward curve computations. In particular, we rely heavily on the techniques discussed in Carmona and Coulon (2014) and Carmona et al. (2013), who show that closed-form formulas can be found through the right combination of Gaussian random variables and exponential bid curves. However, we need to extend their results to handle the large number of fuel types in the German market, and hence propose a new approximation technique for handling the merit order changes possible in a complex multifuel stack.

4.2 Mixtures of Exponential Stacks

Recall from Section 2.4 that the thermal part of the stack in EEX (where the price is most often set) can be represented as in Coulon and Howison (2009) by a mixture of clusters of bids/offers from different fuel types, each driven by a different fuel price. Alternatively, we can view these clusters or "substacks" as parameterized price curves, which merge to form the market price curve. In particular, employing a mixture of exponential functions (as in Carmona et al., 2013) leads conveniently to a piecewise exponential function for the overall stack (more precisely, the transformed "price curve"). Note that strictly speaking, this approach is still a special case of the mixture density model, but with the rather unusual choice of a density function matching that of the exponential of a uniform random variable. In order to fit this variation of the earlier approach, one can either repeat a similar fitting exercise, or more crudely transform parameter estimates by a simple technique like moment matching. Finally, for markets where no auction data are available at all, we might choose to fit these exponential curves directly to cost (and efficiency) data.

Thus, following the approach and notation of Carmona et al. (2013), we assume that (at some given time t) each fuel type i produces a price curve of the form

$$b_i\left(\xi_t^i, S_t^i\right) := S_t^i \exp\left(k_i + m_i \xi_t^i\right), \tag{3}$$

for $i \in \{1, \ldots, n\}$ and $0 \leq \xi_t^i \leq \bar{\xi}^i$. For each fuel i, S^i is its spot price,[6] ξ^i is the supply from that fuel (determined using demand D) and $\bar{\xi}^i$ is the maximum capacity for that fuel. Fixed parameters m_i and k_i determine the shape of the curve.

Then the power spot price S_t^p, obtained by creating the total combined market stack (or price curve) and then matching residual demand D_t (with wind, solar, nuclear, chp, and other "must-run" units feeding into D_t), can be written as

$$S_t^p = \left(\prod_{i=1}^n (S_t^i)^{\alpha_i}\right) \exp\left\{\beta + \gamma\left(D_t - \sum_{i=1}^n \bar{\xi}^i \mathbf{1}_{\{\delta_i=2\}}\right)\right\}, \tag{4}$$

where

$$\alpha_i = \mathbf{1}_{\{i \in \mathcal{M}\}} \frac{\prod_{j \in \mathcal{M}, j \neq i} m_j}{\sum_{l \in \mathcal{M}} \prod_{j \in \mathcal{M}, j \neq l} m_j}, \quad \beta = \frac{\sum_{l \in \mathcal{M}} k_l \prod_{j \in \mathcal{M}, j \neq l} m_j}{\sum_{l \in \mathcal{M}} \prod_{j \in \mathcal{M}, j \neq l} m_j},$$

$$\gamma = \frac{\prod\limits_{j \in \mathcal{M}} m_j}{\sum\limits_{l \in \mathcal{M}} \prod\limits_{j \in \mathcal{M}, j \neq l} m_j}, \tag{5}$$

with $\mathcal{M} = \{i : \delta_i = 1\}$ and

$$\delta_i := \begin{cases} 0 & \text{if } S_t^p < b_i(0) \\ 1 & \text{if } b_i(0) < S_t^p < b_i(\bar{\xi}^i) \\ 2 & \text{if } S_t^p > b_i(\bar{\xi}^i) \end{cases}$$

The main step in applying the formula above is determining which fuels are at the margin at any time (i.e., the set $\mathcal{M}$), which depends on both demand and the fuel prices. This is easy to do in a spot price simulation (ordering the endpoints of the bid curves and summing the capacity up the curve), but causes a challenge for explicit forward price derivations due to the vast number of permutations of the bids curves and their overlap regions. The number of possible expressions for P is

$$\sum_{i=1}^{n} \binom{n}{i} \left[\sum_{j=0}^{n-i} \binom{n-i}{j} \right].$$

For two fuels ($n = 2$) we have 5 expressions while for three we already have 19. Clearly the complexity increases rapidly, and for a six-fuel market, we reach 665 cases. In order to obtain closed-form expressions for forward prices, we must evaluate an expectation over all possible fuel price and demand states, so each permutation must contribute some terms to the final expression. Even for simple choices of distributions like multivariate Gaussians, such calculations quickly become infeasible.

However, under the assumption of a Gaussian distribution for D and jointly lognormal fuel prices $\{S^c, S^g\}$ (say, coal and gas), in the bivariate case we have a manageable closed-form expression for power forwards, as given in Carmona et al. (2013) and provided in the appendix here. Moreover, this expression can conveniently be split into three components (F^L, F^M, F^H), corresponding to the contribution of the low, middle, and high regions of the two-fuel stack:

$$F(t, T) = \mathbb{E}_t^{\mathbb{Q}}[S_T] = F^L + F^M + F^H$$

This split is easy to perform because the derivation of the full result for $F(t, T)$ relies on first calculating the expectation conditional on D before integrating over three demand regions in the final step. If, for example, coal has more capacity than gas ($\bar{\xi}^c > \bar{\xi}^g$) then these three regions correspond to $[0, \bar{\xi}^g]$, $[\bar{\xi}^g, \bar{\xi}^c]$ and $[\bar{\xi}^c, \bar{\xi}^g + \bar{\xi}^c]$. Then F^L, for example, corresponds to

$$F^L = \mathbb{E}_t^{\mathbb{Q}}\left[S_T 1_{\{0 \leq D_T \leq \bar{\xi}^g\}}\right]$$

and analogously for F^M and F^H. These expressions of course account for merit order changes and capture the probabilities of either (or both) of the two fuels being marginal in the given region of the stack.

4.3 Pairwise Overlap Approximation

We now exploit the decomposition above to construct an approximation of the forward price in the general n fuel case (as needed for EEX), based on the argument that we are most likely to only see overlap and merit order changes between *neighboring* pairs of fuels. Thus, we begin with an initial merit order for the stack at time T, and propose for this purpose $F^i(t, T)e^{k_i + \frac{1}{2}m_i \bar{\xi}^i}$, the median of the bids from fuel type i with fuel price set equal to the known fuel forward price.[7] Assuming $i = 1, \ldots, n$ is now the *ordered* set of fuel types, we can divide the market stack into n demand regions as follows:

$$0 < D < \bar{\xi}^1$$

$$\bar{\xi}^1 < D < \bar{\xi}^1 + \bar{\xi}^2$$

$$\ldots$$

$$\sum_{j=1}^{n-1} \bar{\xi}^j < D < \sum_{j=1}^{n} \bar{\xi}^j$$

For each demand region i, we now implicitly assume that fuel type i is always present, and that it can be mixing pairwise either with fuel type $i - 1$ or fuel type $i + 1$ (except for regions 1 and n where only one pairwise mixing is possible). We hence approximate the component of the forward price for region i by a (weighted) average of the corresponding pairwise two-fuel expressions for pair $(i, i - 1)$ and for pair $(i, i + 1)$. This requires selecting the appropriate F^L, F^M and F^H terms for each region, and is described in detail in the appendix.

The big simplification provided by this "pairwise overlap technique" is evident when we consider the number of possible permutations of fuel types which are now being captured in our calculation. The number of expressions for the power price is dramatically reduced to only

$$5(n-1)$$

cases (i.e., $n-1$ pairs, for which each of the 5 two-fuel cases can occur). In the six-fuel case, this is a reduction from 665 cases to only 25. While this approximation may seem too crude, recall that the vast majority of permutations are completely unrealistic in practice (hence contributing virtually zero to forward prices), and only fuels near each other in the stack have a realistic chance of swapping positions or overlapping significantly. Clearly, the approximation becomes weaker for very long maturities or when fuel price volatilities are very high, but numerical tests suggest it to be reliable in most practical applications.

4.4 The Stochastic Factors

There are several sources of uncertainty (i.e., randomness) to consider when we simulate electricity spot prices for the future, on both the supply and the demand side. We distinguish between two types of uncertainty: stationary and nonstationary. Important nonstationary ones include the future installed capacity of wind and solar production, and long-term trends in demand. In contrast, stationary ones are typically fast-moving processes such as the short-term variability of wind and solar production and of power demand, all stemming from variability in the weather, which, adjusted for periodicity, is typically considered ergodic. In addition, fuel prices are crucial sources of uncertainty on the supply side, which feed into the merit order of the stack and are also often considered mean-reverting over longer time horizons.

As is typical for a structural model, we only attempt to model the *stochastic* behavior of the faster-moving processes (weather, demand, and fuels), which explain the vast majority of power price volatility. For gradual long-term effects, we instead rely on accurately capturing their expected levels. Hence, we make an assumption about the future installed capacity growth rates of solar and wind power, based on numbers provided by various sources, for instance Bundesnetzsagentur, but we do not include any assumptions on the uncertainty in these provided forecasts. For long-term demand levels, we note that the part of Germany's demand traded on EEX has changed (mainly increased) slowly over the years, as we saw in Section 3.1. How it will change in the future is very hard to estimate. We therefore opt to use this nonstationary uncertainty as the element that we adjust in the calibration of spot prices against forward quotes, as will be described in Section 4.5.

For the stationary uncertainties, we first consider those related to weather: temperature for demand, wind speed for wind power, and solar irradiation for solar power production. The ultimate approach would be to fully simulate weather using stochastic weather generators. This would provide seasonal variations, short-term variability, and also the correlation structure between temperature, wind, and solar irradiation. For example, a high-pressure dominated winter will typically have cold temperatures, lower than normal wind and higher than normal irradiation. The simulated weather would then be used as an input to our demand, wind and solar power models.

A very much simpler and more practical approach, which we have taken, is to make use of long-term weather averages or so-called "normals." Meteorologists provide 30-year average values of weather variables that can be used, or if you have long enough time-series, you can generate these normals yourself. The weather normals are used as inputs to our demand, wind and solar power models, and we obtain normals of inelastic demand, wind and solar production. These normals of demand and supply can then be compared to corresponding historical measurements to estimate the stationary stochastic components. Another simplification can be made here, by recalling our definition of "residual demand" as the difference between inelastic demand and total wind and solar production. Although each of the individual components of residual demand (e.g., wind production at one location) may be very non-Gaussian, the aggregation across the market and the merging of several factors into one produces a stationary stochastic component of this residual demand, which can be well represented by a Gaussian distribution and most easily by an Ornstein-Uhlenbeck (OU) process. As was described in Section 4.2, this is precisely what is needed to use our closed-form expressions for forwards.

Similarly, we also saw that we require an assumption of lognormal fuel prices (or, more precisely, running costs), which is a natural choice consistent with many classical commodity price models (e.g., see Schwartz 1997; Schwartz and Smith 2000; Swindle 2014). However, crucially, we do not need to attempt to forecast these fuel prices, since the expected values we need (under the risk neutral measure $\mathbb{Q}$) are provided to us by the observable fuel forward quotes. Indeed, our expressions for power forwards $F^p(t, T)$ are given explicitly as functions of all the fuel forwards (see Appendix A).[8] Therefore, we only need to estimate a covariance structure (volatilities and correlations) for fuel spot prices, for which either historical price data or observed option prices could be used. Here we use the former, and fit exponential OU processes (the Schwartz one-factor model) to each fuel S^i, for $i = 1, \ldots, n$:

$$dS_t^i = \kappa_i \left(\mu_i - \log S_t\right) S_t dt + \sigma_i S_t dW_t^{(i)}$$

where $W_t^{(i)}$, $W_t^{(j)}$ are correlated Brownian Motions, with correlation ρ_{ij}.

4.5 Calibration to the Quotes

When calibrating the spot price model against forward quotes, we choose to adjust the residual demand, defined in Section 4.4. In order to fit to both base and peak quotes, we need to make adjustments to the overall demand level as well as the peak to off-peak spread. This is achieved by using one multiplicative and one additive part:

$$D_i^{adj} = (D_i + \alpha_i)\beta_i$$

where D_i^{adj} is adjusted demand, D_i is actual demand, α_i and β_i are scalars and i represents a certain period in time.

While it may at first seem unnatural to artificially adjust the demand process in this way to reproduce observed forward prices, it is in fact quite consistent with standard finance theory regarding risk premiums. As mentioned above, fuel price distributions under $\mathbb{Q}$ are already identified directly from fuel forwards, but our model for residual demand is entirely under the physical (true) probability measure $\mathbb{P}$. Hence a shift in the dynamics of residual demand from $\mathbb{P}$ to $\mathbb{Q}$ is needed, and corresponds to an assumption about the market price of risk for this factor. A constant market price of risk would produce a simple shift in the long-term mean level (as produced by α_i above), but a state-dependent market price of risk can lead to a change in the width of the demand distribution as well (as produced by β_i above). For example, risk premiums might be assumed higher at times of high demand, potentially contributing to a wider peak to off-peak spread in forwards.[9]

Forward quotes have different delivery periods and they can overlap. In the case of complete overlap like three monthly contracts vs a quarterly one, the months of course provide a more detailed picture (without loss of any information) and should therefore be chosen. In the case of partial overlap (a week within a month, say), the quotes can be reconstructed into virtual quotes that no longer overlap. When calibrating hourly spot prices to the nonoverlapping quotes, the simplest approach is to have one

α and one β parameter per set of base and peak quotes. The disadvantage with this approach is that we can end up with discontinuities when moving from one set of quotes to the next: the forward curve might be "step-like." To mitigate this issue, we can define shorter periods for each pair (α, β), typically a week long. As we then have infinitely many solutions, we have to insert something into the objective function to select the most suitable one. A natural approach here is to keep the αs and βs as close as possible to zero and one respectively (minimal adjustment to original model output) while also minimizing the size of the discontinuities in α and β to keep the forward curve as smooth as possible. A more elegant approach to this smoothness criteria is to minimize the second derivative of the αs and βs with respect to time via spline techniques, sometimes called the "thin-plate" method (Duchon, 1976).

Figure 6.17 (left plot) shows a set of base and peak quotes to calibrate against. There are forward quotes from spring 2012, covering one year ahead. We clearly see the nearest short-term weekly products, followed by months and quarters and we have partial overlaps of weeks within months, and months within quarters. In the bottom right plot, we see the residual demand plotted on top of dotted lines representing stacked available

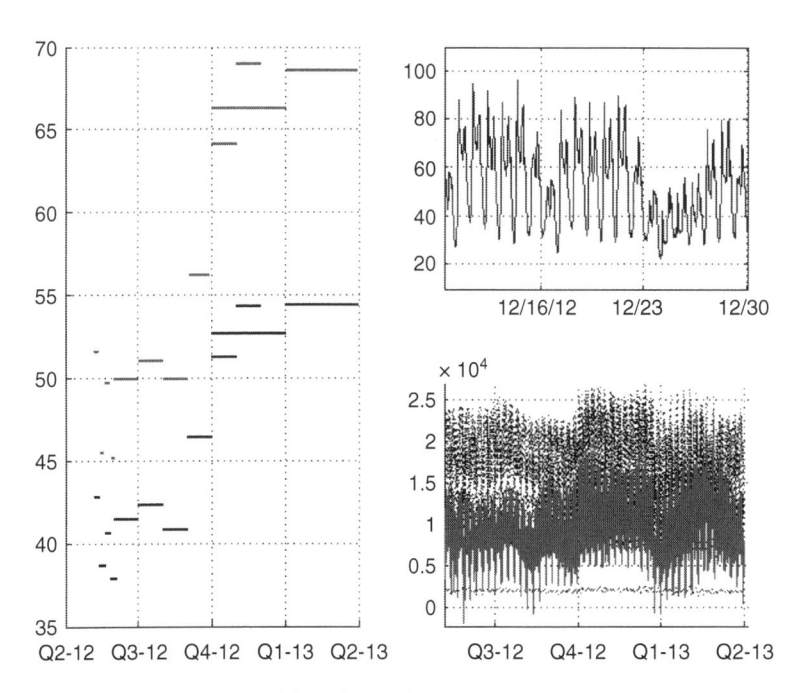

Figure 6.17 Illustration of fit to forward quotes.

production per fuel type, thus showing how residual demand will have a clearing price at different production types at different points in time. Finally, in the top right plot, we see a resulting calibrated *hourly* forward curve produced by the model, zoomed in during December 2012. Not only do we see the intraday patterns predicted by the residual demand model, but this time period illustrates how the holiday calendar used in the demand model provides substantially lower prices over Christmas. While this is only one sample date for illustration purposes, it is a good example of the level of detail captured in our hourly forward curve construction, which reflects a wide variety of information about the key market fundamentals.

5 Discussion and Conclusion

In this work we have aimed to provide both newcomers and experienced modelers with some original ideas on how to tackle modern electricity markets, with all their messy details, ongoing structural changes, and rather uncertain future behavior. Although we have described a comprehensive modeling framework for which our own experience with the German market gives promising results, we have opted to not extend this chapter with a rigorous analysis of model performance or a comparison with other approaches. Ultimately, we hope instead to encourage readers to try some of these ideas out themselves, perhaps merging some of our suggestions with their own ideas or existing models. Clearly, every electricity market requires a different set of considerations, as do different time periods or different modeling goals within the same market. Some of the pieces of our overall picture may fit another case well, while others may require substantial modification, or even redesigning from scratch.

To summarize some of our key contributions here, we have extended existing structural models to handle several important challenges of the German power market. Firstly, the high demand-side elasticity caused by "make-or-buy" bidding was tackled by a transformation of bids and offers to a single "price curve." Thorough data analysis of the dynamics of the price curve (relative to those of the supply and demand curves) clearly illustrated the added value of the proposed transformation for modeling purposes. Next, we demonstrated practical approaches to handling the rapidly growing renewable presence in Germany, piecing together separate solar, wind, and demand models (and aggregating across the country) to produce a combined residual demand model estimated from history. For this piece of the model, we proposed using neural networks to identify short-term periodic patterns and long-term trends in the "business cycle" of demand or the capacity growth of renewables. Moving on from the must-run stack to the thermal stack, we then showed how to capture the complex correlation structure between power and all its fuels, using statistical techniques to identify and parameterize the behavior of clusters of bids/offers from different fuel types. In particular, we have extended existing work by incorporating as many as seven different clusters (driven by four different fuels), and yet still retain closed-form expressions for forward prices via a rather complicated pairwise approximation technique. Although ugly on paper, these formulas provide a vital step toward our stated goal of constructing hourly forward price curves that can both match market quotes and reflect as much detail as possible on market fundamentals, their well-known periodicities and their volatility and correlation structures. Having determined our computational tractability requirements from the outset, our modeling philosophy has always been a practical industry-orientated one of incorporating as much as possible when the mathematics allows it, but making compromises where necessary.

Of course, there is much further work that could be done in this direction, both in analyzing this particular framework and in building related ones. For example, an important question following the calibration procedure suggested in Section 4.5 is how stable the α and β values are across maturities and also through time. Any calibration procedure which exactly replicates market prices should ideally lead to relatively low and stable tuning or adjustment factors (assuming low and stable risk premia) in order to inspire confidence in the approach. From our experience in Germany, we find that at the short end of the curve much more stable adjustment factors are obtained simply by including short-term weather forecasts as inputs to the residual demand model. Other stability and predictability tests are also possible—for example, looking at option prices, or at model-implied numbers for quantities such as production by fuel type.

For our main goal of forward curve construction, the timing and magnitude of upward and downward spikes is not the highest priority, since these get averaged over delivery periods to produce forwards. However, for the secondary goal of simulating the most realistic spot price time-series possible, more work could certainly be done in analyzing how best to treat periodicities in the volatility (not just the mean) of residual demand, and also how best to treat the shape of the stack in the negative price region. As negative bids and offers have only been a feature of EEX in recent years and the renewables sector continues to develop and mature, such questions will require extra care going forward. One could also anticipate possible changes due to policy decisions, as renewables may no longer enjoy the same benefits they currently do in Germany as technologies become more cost competitive and also as volumes become more problematic for grid operators. In some countries like Italy, renewable generators already face penalties for supplying volumes which deviate too much from their stated offers.

While we may only be interested in modeling one particular market (like EEX in Germany), another ongoing fundamental change in European electricity markets suggests that an isolated regional or national perspective may no longer be feasible. Market coupling is as a new and expanding system for integrating the allocation of cross-border transmissions into the daily electricity auction, such that power flows optimally between neighboring countries each hour, thus bringing prices closer together. Indeed since coupling was introduced between Germany and France in November 2010, about 65 percent of hourly prices are now identical, although large price differentials can still occur when the capacity limit on cross-border flows is reached. Markets such as France and Belgium are even more closely linked (over 90 percent of hours identical) due to their smaller sizes relative to border capacity. Such price behavior is particularly challenging to model and once again represents a structural change, which renders reduced-form historical parameter estimates unreliable. The literature on modeling prices under market coupling is still rather limited for now and we have chosen not to include our initial investigations into the methodology presented here, but some promising structural approaches have been proposed, for example in Fuss et al. (2013b).

More importantly, market coupling is yet another clear example of a challenge that demands new modeling ideas in order to capture the ever-changing link between prices and market fundamentals. As coupling extends throughout Europe, profit opportunities and bidding strategies of generators may also change significantly. For example, Scandinavia and Switzerland's abundant flexible hydro power could provide a valuable form of battery, helping to balance unpredictable wind and solar growing in other countries. In addition, anticipated developments in smart grid technology and flexible demand management are likely to further increase the elasticity of the demand curve, this time requiring different modeling considerations to the "make-or-buy" effect. Political decisions, market participant behavior, investments in grid capacity, and fuel price dynamics will all play an important role going forward. While some will attempt to understand this multitude of factors via full fundamental stack models built up from individual generator characteristics, trade-offs undoubtedly exist. Such complex and slow approaches already face difficulties differentiating between the mix of generators bidding into EEX and those active in the entire German production park. Adding an extra layer of interaction between bids in neighboring countries further weakens the link between the constructed national generation stack and the true price formation mechanism. On the other hand, using auction data directly gives us more hope of adapting to such changes. As we have seen, a key advantage of the structural approach we have advocated here is its flexibility to be stretched, twisted, and remolded in innovative ways. As challenges continue to multiply, it remains to be seen how well the modeling innovations are able to keep up.

A. Appendix: Details of Pairwise Overlap Approximation

Here we provide further technical details on our closed-form approximation to forward prices to accompany Section 4.3.

We begin with the bivariate case, as described in Carmona et al. (2013). Coal and gas prices are assumed to be jointly lognormal and demand is Gaussian but truncated at the top and bottom of the stack, that is, we have (under $\mathbb{Q}$):

$$\begin{pmatrix} \log S_T^c \\ \log S_T^g \end{pmatrix} \sim N\left(\begin{pmatrix} \mu_c \\ \mu_g \end{pmatrix}, \begin{pmatrix} \sigma_c^2 & \rho\sigma_c\sigma_g \\ \rho\sigma_c\sigma_g & \sigma_g^2 \end{pmatrix} \right)$$

and $D_T = \max\left(0, \min\left(\bar{\xi}, X_T\right)\right)$, where $X_T \sim N(\mu_d, \sigma_d^2)$. Then power forwards $F_t^p = F^p(t,T)$ are given in terms of fuel forwards F_t^c and F_t^g by

$$\begin{aligned} F_t^p = & \sum_{i \in I} e^{\frac{m_i^2 \sigma_d^2}{2}} \left\{ b_i\left(\mu_d, F_t^i\right) \Phi_2^{2\times1}\left(\begin{bmatrix} \bar{a}^i - m_i\sigma_d \\ \bar{a}_0 - m_i\sigma_d \end{bmatrix}, \frac{\hat{R}_i(\mu_d, 0, m_i^2)}{\sigma_{i,d}}; \frac{m_i\sigma_d}{\sigma_{i,d}} \right) \right. \\ & \left. + b_i\left(\mu_d - \bar{\xi}^j, F_t^i\right) \Phi_2^{2\times1}\left(\begin{bmatrix} \bar{a} - m_i\sigma_d \\ \bar{a}^j - m_i\sigma_d \end{bmatrix}, \frac{\hat{R}_i\left(\mu_d - \bar{\xi}^j, \bar{\xi}^j, m_i^2\right)}{-\sigma_{i,d}}; \frac{-m_i\sigma_d}{\sigma_{i,d}} \right) \right\} \\ & + \sum_{i \in I} \delta_i e^{\eta} b_{cg}(\mu_d, \mathbf{F}_t) \left\{ -\Phi_2^{2\times1}\left(\begin{bmatrix} \bar{a}^i - \gamma\sigma_d \\ \bar{a}_0 - \gamma\sigma_d \end{bmatrix}, \frac{\hat{R}_i(\mu_d, 0, \gamma m_i) + \alpha_j\sigma^2}{\delta_i \sigma_{i,d}}; \frac{m_i\sigma_d}{\delta_i \sigma_{i,d}} \right) \right. \\ & \left. + \Phi_2^{2\times1}\left(\begin{bmatrix} \bar{a} - \gamma\sigma_d \\ \bar{a}^j - \gamma\sigma_d \end{bmatrix}, \frac{\hat{R}_i\left(\mu_d - \bar{\xi}^j, \bar{\xi}^j, \gamma m_i\right) + \alpha_j\sigma^2}{\delta_i \sigma_{i,d}}; \frac{m_i\sigma_d}{\delta_i \sigma_{i,d}} \right) \right\} \\ & + \Phi(\bar{a}_0) \sum_{i \in I} b_i\left(0, F_t^i\right) \Phi\left(\frac{R_i(0,0)}{\sigma} \right) + \Phi(-\bar{a}) \sum_{i \in I} b_i\left(\bar{\xi}^i, F_t^i\right) \Phi\left(\frac{-R_i\left(\bar{\xi}^i, \bar{\xi}^j\right)}{\sigma} \right), \end{aligned}$$

where $I = \{c, g\}$ is the set of fuels, $j = I \setminus \{i\}$, and $\delta_i = (-1)^{1\{\bar{\xi}^i \geq \bar{\xi}^j\}}$. Parameters $\alpha_c, \alpha_g, \beta, \gamma$ are given by (5), and simplify to

$$\alpha_c = \frac{m_g}{m_c + m_g}, \quad \alpha_g = 1 - \alpha_c = \frac{m_c}{m_c + m_g},$$

$$\beta = \frac{k_c m_g + k_g m_c}{m_c + m_g}, \quad \gamma = \frac{m_c m_g}{m_c + m_g}$$

Price curves b_c and b_g are given in (3), and the combined price curve for where coal and gas bids overlap is given by (4):

$$b_{cg}(\xi, \mathbf{S}) := (S^c)^{\alpha_c} (S^g)^{\alpha_g} \exp(\beta + \gamma \xi)$$

Other parameters and functions are defined as

$$\sigma^2 = \sigma_c^2 - 2\rho\sigma_c\sigma_g + \sigma_g^2,$$

$$\sigma_{i,d}^2 = m_i^2 \sigma_d^2 + \sigma^2,$$

$$\eta = \frac{1}{2}\left(\gamma^2 \sigma_d^2 - \alpha_c \alpha_g \sigma^2\right),$$

$$R_i(\xi_i, \xi_j) = k_j + m_j \xi_j - k_i - m_i \xi_i + \log\left(F_t^j\right) - \log\left(F_t^i\right) - \frac{1}{2}\sigma^2,$$

$$\hat{R}_i(\xi_i, \xi_j, y) = k_j + m_j \xi_j - k_i - m_i \xi_i + \log\left(F_t^j\right)$$

$$- \log\left(F_t^i\right) - \frac{1}{2}\sigma^2 - y\sigma_d^2,$$

capacity thresholds normalized by demand distribution parameters are

$$\bar{a}_0 := \frac{-\mu_d}{\sigma_d}, \quad \bar{a}^c := \frac{\bar{\xi}^c - \mu_d}{\sigma_d}, \quad \bar{a}^g := \frac{\bar{\xi}^g - \mu_d}{\sigma_d}, \quad \bar{a} := \frac{\bar{\xi} - \mu_d}{\sigma_d},$$

and finally $\Phi(\cdot)$ and $\Phi_2(\cdot, \cdot; \rho)$ the cumulative distribution functions (cdfs) of the univariate and bivariate (correlation ρ) standard Gaussian distributions respectively, while to further shorten notation

$$\Phi_2^{2\times 1}\left(\begin{bmatrix} x_1 \\ x_2 \end{bmatrix}, y; \rho\right) := \Phi_2(x_1, y; \rho) - \Phi_2(x_2, y; \rho).$$

In order to obtain closed-form approximations to the power forwards in the case of $n > 2$ fuels, we will continually reuse the two-fuel expression above, based on the idea that in any given region of the stack, only two fuels are likely to be overlapping (jointly at the margin) in most cases. As discussed in Section 4.3, the first step in the pairwise approximation approach is to define an initial ordering of fuels in the stack, and for this purpose we choose the median of each fuel's bids. Hence we now refer to fuel $i \in \{1, \ldots, n\}$ as the fuel for which $F^i(t,T)e^{k_i + \frac{1}{2}m_i \bar{\xi}^i}$ is the i-th lowest. Demand region i corresponds to the event that

$$\sum_{j=1}^{i-1} \bar{\xi}^j < D < \sum_{j=1}^{i} \bar{\xi}^j$$

and represents a region where fuel i is dominant and mixes with only fuels $i - 1$, and $i + 1$, giving us two terms to calculate: one for pair $(i, i - 1)$ and one for pair $(i, i + 1)$ (or only one for the simpler top and bottom regions $i = n$ and $i = 1$).

To adapt and generalize the bivariate (coal and gas) result above to handle the pairwise overlap and mixing of any two neighboring fuels a and b in the stack, we first split the expression above into three components F^L, F^M, and F^H, corresponding to low, medium, and high demand within the region of interest. Without loss of generality, we assume that $\bar{\xi}^a > \bar{\xi}^b$ and we also introduce $\bar{\xi}^\star$ to represent all capacity already used up by fuels lower than both a and b in the merit order. We define for example $F^L(\bar{\xi}^a, \bar{\xi}^b, \bar{\xi}^\star)$ as

$$F^L = \sum_{i \in I} e^{\frac{m_i^2 \sigma_d^2}{2}} \left\{ b_i \left(\mu_d - \bar{\xi}^\star, F_t^i \right) \Phi_2^{2 \times 1} \left(\begin{bmatrix} \bar{a}^b - m_i \sigma_d \\ \bar{a}_0 - m_i \sigma_d \end{bmatrix}, \frac{\hat{R}_i(\mu_d - \bar{\xi}^\star, 0, m_i^2)}{\sigma_{i,d}}; \frac{m_i \sigma_d}{\sigma_{i,d}} \right) \right\}$$

$$+ \sum_{i \in I} \delta_i e^{\eta} b_{ab}(\mu_d - \bar{\xi}^\star, \mathbf{F}_t) \left\{ -\Phi_2^{2 \times 1} \left(\begin{bmatrix} \bar{a}^b - \gamma \sigma_d \\ \bar{a}_0 - \gamma \sigma_d \end{bmatrix}, \frac{\hat{R}_i(\mu_d - \bar{\xi}^\star, 0, \gamma m_i) + \alpha_j \sigma^2}{\delta_i \sigma_{i,d}}; \frac{m_i \sigma_d}{\delta_i \sigma_{i,d}} \right) \right\}$$

where all notation is analogous to earlier, but with $I = \{a, b\}$ replacing $I = \{c, g\}$, with the exception of the normalized capacity threshold values for which μ_d is replaced by $\mu_d - \bar{\xi}^\star$, that is,

$$\bar{a}_0 := \frac{\bar{\xi}^\star - \mu_d}{\sigma_d}, \quad \bar{a}^b := \frac{\bar{\xi}^\star + \bar{\xi}^b - \mu_d}{\sigma_d}.$$

The basic idea is that F^L corresponds to integrating demand over $[\bar{\xi}^\star, \bar{\xi}^\star + \bar{\xi}^b]$ only, which produces only a subset of the terms in our earlier equation for F_t^p, and all containing the pair of thresholds $[\bar{a}_0, \bar{a}^b]$. Similarly, expressions for $F^M(\bar{\xi}^a, \bar{\xi}^b, \bar{\xi}^\star)$ and $F^L(\bar{\xi}^a, \bar{\xi}^b, \bar{\xi}^\star)$ can be written out, which each contain four terms in $\Phi_d^{2 \times 1}$ from the original result and contain thresholds $[\bar{a}^b, \bar{a}^a]$ and $[\bar{a}^a, \bar{a}]$, respectively.[10]

Now we explain how to use these expressions to approximate the component of the forward price from demand region i in our multifuel stack, by considering pairwise mixing / overlap between fuels $i-1$, i and $i+1$. First, consider the pair $(i, i-1)$. If $\bar{\xi}_i > \bar{\xi}_{i-1}$, then the contribution to the forward power price is

$$f_{i,-} = F^M\left(\bar{\xi}^i, \bar{\xi}^{i-1}, \sum_{j=1}^{i-2}\bar{\xi}^j\right) + F^H\left(\bar{\xi}^i, \bar{\xi}^{i-1}, \sum_{j=1}^{i-2}\bar{\xi}^j\right)$$

while if $\bar{\xi}_i < \bar{\xi}_{i-1}$, then we have instead

$$f_{i,-} = F^H\left(\bar{\xi}^{i-1}, \bar{\xi}^i, \sum_{j=1}^{i-2}\bar{\xi}^j\right)$$

Second, consider the pair $(i, i+1)$. If $\bar{\xi}_i > \bar{\xi}_{i+1}$, then the contribution to the forward power price is

$$f_{i,+} = F^M\left(\bar{\xi}^i, \bar{\xi}^{i+1}, \sum_{j=1}^{i-1}\bar{\xi}^j\right)$$

while if $\bar{\xi}_i < \bar{\xi}_{i+1}$, then we have instead

$$f_{i,+} = F^L\left(\bar{\xi}^{i+1}, \bar{\xi}^i, \sum_{j=1}^{i-1}\bar{\xi}^j\right) + F^M\left(\bar{\xi}^{i+1}, \bar{\xi}^i, \sum_{j=1}^{i-1}\bar{\xi}^j\right)$$

Note that the in some cases above $a = i$, while in other cases $b = i$ (where a is the larger fuel type), so the ordering of the $\bar{\xi}$s is swapped in the functions F^L, F^M, and F^H.

Note finally that for region 1 instead, since there is no pair $(i, i-1)$ we have instead a term representing the starting point of the entire stack (when $D = 0$). Then

$$f_{1,-} = F_t^1 e^{k_1} \Phi\left(\frac{R_1(0,0)}{\sigma}\right) + F_t^2 e^{k_2} \Phi\left(\frac{R_3(0,0)}{\sigma}\right)$$

Similarly for the n-th region, we have

$$f_{n,+} = F_t^n e^{k_n + m_n \bar{\xi}^n} \Phi\left(\frac{-R_3(\bar{\xi}^n, \bar{\xi}^{n-1})}{\sigma}\right)$$
$$+ F_t^{n-1} e^{k_{n-1} + m_{n-1} \bar{\xi}^{n-1}} \Phi\left(\frac{-R_1(\bar{\xi}^n, \bar{\xi}^{n-1})}{\sigma}\right).$$

The last step is to combine all the terms $f(i,-)$ and $f(i,+)$ and sum over regions $i = 1, \ldots, n$. Here we have some flexibility in how we create the weighted average of the two pairs for regions $i = 2, \ldots, n-1$. The simplest is equal weighting, in which we always take a simple average. Then we have the final result

$$F_t^p = f(1,-) + f(1,+) + f(n,-) + f(n,+) + \sum_{i=2}^{n-1} \frac{f(i,-) + f(i,+)}{2}.$$

Alternatively we instead weight them differently and set

$$F_t^p = f(1,-) + f(1,+) + f(n,-) + f(n,+) + \sum_{i=2}^{n-1} \left[w_i f(i,-) + (1-w_i) f(i,+)\right].$$

One possibility for w_i is a weighting based on the ratio of quantity of bids from fuel $i-1$ vs quantity from fuel $i+1$ in region i of the initial stack based on forward prices (which was used to find the ordering). To be precise,

$$w_i = \frac{Q_i^{i-1}}{Q_{i-1}^i + Q_{i+1}^i}$$

where

$$Q_j^i = \max\left(0, \min\left(\bar{\xi}^j, \frac{\log(P_+^i / m_j) - k_j}{m_j}\right)\right)$$
$$- \max\left(0, \min\left(\bar{\xi}^j, \frac{\log(P_-^i / m_j) - k_j}{m_j}\right)\right)$$

is the quantity of bids in region i from fuel j, and hence

$$P_+^i = b\left(\sum_{k=1}^i \bar{\xi}^k\right) \qquad P_-^i = b\left(\sum_{k=1}^{i-1} \bar{\xi}^k\right)$$

are the endpoints of region i in price terms (with $b(\cdot)$ the market bid stack, or more precisely "price curve"). The advantage of this approach is that, for example if there is a complete separation between certain fuel types in the stack (i.e., no overlap at all), then the pairwise component which would bridge this gap is weighted to zero. In other words pairs that are more likely to actually overlap are given more weight in the pairwise approximation. Other variations are this approach could of course be tested.

Figure 6.18 illustrates the results of some basic numerical tests comparing the closed-form pairwise overlap technique with simulated forwards. It can be seen that divergence of the technique (left plots) only occurs when the probability (right plots) that three or more fuel types appear at the margin (as calculated by simulation) becomes very high. This is to be expected of course, and only happens with either fuel prices become highly volatile (bottom plots), or when the parameters m_i all become larger (top plots), stretching the stacks so that there is plenty of overlap even for low-volatility fuel prices.

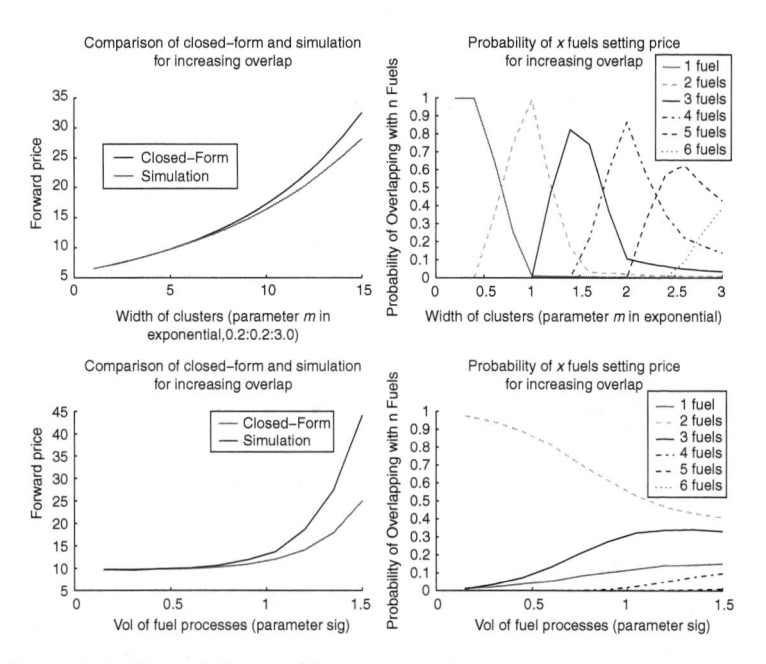

Figure 6.18 Numerical tests of the approximation.

Notes

1. Data from AG Energiebilanzen, http://commons.wikimedia.org/wiki/File: Energiemix_Deutschland.svg
2. Sometimes called the bid stack function, but more appropriately the offer stack function.
3. We do not need to worry about the mathematical technicality of the inverses s^{-1} and d^{-1} potentially not existing (due to flat sections in the stack) since we are simply inverting a second time to get back to the price curve.
4. We find −€10 to be a good choice in terms of a stable fit for the thermal part of the stack. The top of the stack is hard to set a fixed threshold for and we let this limit vary as the highest cluster of bids varies.
5. Adding an additional cluster (or hump) of volumes with mean fixed at or near zero and not driven by fuel prices is found to significantly improve the results. This cluster of miscellaneous bids is likely to contain a variety of different production types, and could be related to operational constraints.
6. Note that in practice we use the running cost here instead of the spot price, as described in (2), which allows us to potentially capture dependence on carbon prices and even exchange rates. We would then interpret $[\exp(k_i), \exp(k_i + m_i \bar{\xi}^i)]$ as describing the range of deviations between average market running costs and bids.
7. Note that like power forward contracts, fuel forwards also have delivery periods (typically monthly), but constructing smooth daily fuel forward curves from the market quotes is a fairly common and straightforward exercise.
8. As we replace fuels with running costs via (2), we in fact calculate "running cost forwards" as appropriate combinations of fuel and carbon forward prices. As gas and oil are split into two clusters (i.e., gas1, gas2, oil1, oil2) in our model, we reuse the same fuel forwards in these cases, but different efficiencies produce different running cost forwards.
9. More specifically, for an OU process, if the market price of risk is assumed to be linear in the process itself, then the risk neutral dynamics for the process are still OU, but with a different mean and different speed of mean-reversion, which produces a different variance.
10. To save space we do not write these out fully here, but leave it as a little challenge for the keen reader. As a hint, note that for F^M no summations appear in the result, since in this middle region the lower capacity fuel b is never marginal by itself, so $i = a, j = b$ throughout the four terms.

References

Aïd, R., Campi, L., Huu, A. N., and Touzi, N. (2009). A structural risk-neutral model of electricity prices. *International Journal of Theoretical and Applied Finance*, 12:925–947.

Aïd, R., Campi, L., and Langrené, N. (2012). A structural risk-neutral model for pricing and hedging power derivatives. *Mathematical Finance*, 23(3):387–438, July 2013.

Anderson, C. and Davison, M. (2008). A hybrid system-econometric model for electricity spot prices: Considering spike sensitivity to forced outage distributions. *IEEE Transactions on Power Systems*, 23:927–937.

Barlow, M. (2002). A diffusion model for electricity prices. *Mathematical Finance*, 12(4):287–298.

Benth, F., Benth, J., and Koekebakker, S. (2008). *Stochastic Modeling of Electricity and Related Markets*, volume 11 of *Advanced Series in Statistical Science & Applied Probability*. World Scientific.

Benth, F. E., Biegler-Koenig, R., and Kiesel, R. (2013). An empirical study of the information premium on electricity markets. *Energy Economics*, 36:55–77.

Bishop, C. (1994). Mixture density networks. Technical report, Neural Computing Research Group.

Bishop, C. (1995). *Neural Networks for Pattern Recognition*. Oxford University Press, Oxford, UK.

Burger, M., Graeber, B., and Schindlmayr, G. (2007). *Managing Energy Risk: An Integrated View on Power and Other Energy Markets*. Finance. Wiley.

Carmona, R. and Coulon, M. (2014). A survey of commodity markets and structural models for electricity prices. In Benth, F. E., Kholodnyi, V. A., and Laurence, P., editors, *Quantitative Energy Finance: Modeling, Pricing and Hedging in Energy and Commodity Markets*. Springer.

Carmona, R., Coulon, M., and Schwarz, D. (2013). Electricity price modeling and asset valuation: a multi-fuel structural approach. *Mathematics and Financial Economics*, 7(2):167–202.

Cartea, A., Figueroa, M., and Geman, H. (2008). Modelling electricity prices with forward looking capacity constraints. *Applied Mathematical Finance*, 32:2501–2519.

Coulon, M. and Howison, S. (2009). Stochastic behaviour of the electricity bid stack: from fundamental drivers to power prices. *Journal of Energy Markets*, 2:29–69.

Coulon, M., Powell, W., and Sircar, R. (2013). A model for hedging load and price risk in the texas electricity market. *Energy Economics*, 40:976–988.

Duchon, J. (1976). Splines minimizing rotation invariant semi-norms in sobolev spaces. In *Constructive Theory of Functions of Several Variables*, Lecture Notes in Mathematics, pages 85–100. Springer.

Eydeland, A. and Wolyniec, K. (2003). *Energy and Power Risk Management: New Developments in Modeling, Pricing and Hedging*. Finance. Wiley.

Fuss, R., Mahringer, S., and Prokopczuk, M. (2013a). Electricity derivatives pricing with forward-looking information. working paper.

Fuss, R., Mahringer, S., and Prokopczuk, M. (2013b). Electricity spot and derivatives pricing when markets are interconnected. working paper.

He, Y., Hildmann, M., Herzog, F., and Andersson, G. (2013). Modeling the merit order curve of the european energy exchange power market in germany. *IEEE Transactions on Power Systems*, 28(3):3155–3164.

Huld, T. (2005). Estimating pv performance over large geographical regions. *Photovoltaic Specialists Conference, 2005. Conference Record of the Thirty-first IEEE*, pages 1679–1682.

Kanamura, T. and Ohashi, K. (2007). A structural model for electricity prices with spikes: measurement of spike risk and optimal policies for hydropower plant operation. *Energy Economics*, 29(5):1010–1032.

Lyle, M. and Elliott, R. (2009). A "simple" hybrid model for power derivatives. *Energy Economics*, 31:757–767.

Pirrong, C. and Jermakyan, M. (2008). The price of power: The valuation of power and weather derivatives. *Journal of Banking and Finance*, 32:2520–2529.

Schwartz, E. (1997). The stochastic behaviour of commodity prices: Implications for valuation and hedging. *The Journal of Finance*, 3:923–973.

Schwartz, E. and Smith, J. (2000). Short-term variations and long-term dynamics in commodity prices. *Management Science*, 46:893–911.

Skantze, P., Gubina, A., and Ilic, M. (2000). Bid-based stochastic model for electricity prices: the impact of fundamental drivers on market dynamics. MIT E-lab report.

Swindle, G. (2014). *Energy Markets: Valuation and Risk Management*. Economics. Cambridge University Press.

Wagner, A. (2014). Residual Demand Modeling and Application to Electricity Pricing. *The Energy Journal*, 35(2).

Williams, S., Betts, T., Gottschalg, R., Infield, D., van der Borg, N., Burgers, A., de Moor, H., Warta, W., Friesen, G., Chianese, D., Guerin de Montgareuil, A., Zdanowicz, T., Stellbogen, D., Herrmann, W., Pietruzko, S., Krustok, J., and Dunlop, E. (2005). Evaluating the state of the art of photovoltaic performance modelling in europe. *20th European Photovoltaic Solar Energy Conference*.

7

Modeling Price Spikes in Electricity Markets—The Impact of Load, Weather, and Capacity*

Rangga Handika, Chi Truong, Stefan Trück, and Rafał Weron

1 Introduction

In recent decades, many countries have transformed the electricity power sector from monopolistic, government-controlled systems into deregulated, competitive markets. Like other commodities, electricity is now traded under competitive rules using spot and derivative contracts. Electricity prices are far more volatile than other commodity prices, as pointed out by, for example, Eydeland and Wolyniec (2012), Huisman (2009), or Weron (2006). The volatility of electricity, measured by the daily standard deviation of returns, can be as high as 50 percent, while the maximum volatilities of stocks are usually lower than 4 percent (Weron, 2000). Therefore, the risk of extreme outcomes in electricity spot markets is of significant concern to market participants.

Electricity prices often exhibit unique behavior compared to other commodity markets. Typical features include mean-reversion, seasonality, extreme volatility, and so-called price spikes (Bierbrauer et al., 2007; Higgs and Worthington, 2008; Huisman et al., 2007; Janczura and Weron, 2010; Kanamura and Ohashi, 2008; Lucia and Schwartz, 2002). The latter usually describe abrupt, short-lived, and generally unanticipated extreme changes in the spot price and can be considered as one of the most pronounced features of electricity spot markets. Despite their rarity, spikes account for a large part of the total variation of changes in the spot price and are therefore an important component of the risk faced by market participants. Spikes are also a key reason for designing derivatives contracts such as futures and options that have been introduced to allow electricity buyers and sellers to hedge against extreme price movements in the spot market (Anderson et al., 2007; Shawky et al., 2003). For example, in Australia, next to yearly and quarterly futures contracts, option contracts or so-called 300 cap products are also traded in the ASX Australian Electricity Futures and Options Market. For these contracts, the payoff is determined based on both the frequency and magnitude of observed half-hourly price spikes during a calendar quarter. To evaluate these instruments accurately and to facilitate price spike risk management, it is necessary to understand the impacts of different factors on the occurrence and magnitude of price spikes.

From a modeling perspective, price spikes are one of the most serious reasons for including discontinuous components in econometric models of electricity price dynamics. The literature suggests a variety of approaches to achieve this—including, for example, autoregressive time-series models with thresholds (Misiorek et al., 2006), mean reverting jump-diffusion models (Cartea and Figueroa, 2005; Clewlow and Strickland, 2000; Geman and Roncoroni, 2006; Knittel and Roberts, 2005) or Markov-switching models incorporating spikes by proposing different price regimes (Becker et al., 2007; Bierbrauer et al., 2007; De Jong, 2006; Huisman and Mahieu, 2003; Janczura, 2014; Janczura and Weron, 2010; Kanamura and Ohashi, 2008; Kosater, 2008; Weron et al., 2004). For further references and discussions we refer to a comprehensive review by Weron (2014).

Factors explaining the large variation of electricity prices in general, and the occurrence of price spikes in particular, have also been analyzed in a number of studies. Escribano et al. (2002) and Knittel and Roberts (2005) suggest a jump-diffusion model with a time-varying intensity parameter, where the intensity of the jump process is modelled as being dependent on deterministic seasonal and diurnal factors. Kanamura and Ohashi (2007) provide a structural model for electricity prices taking into account the nonlinear relationship between supply and demand in the market and spot electricity prices. In particular they focus on modeling the relationship between demand and occurring price spikes by formulating the supply function as a hockey-stick shape curve and by incorporating the demand seasonality explicitly. Mount et al. (2006) confirm the hockey stick shape of the electricity supply curve and argue that supply is elastic when demand is lower than a certain threshold, but when demand exceeds this threshold, supply is virtually infinitely inelastic, which leads to price spikes. Due to the different phases of price behavior for electricity prices, the authors suggest using a regime-switching model with two different states where the price process itself as well as the transition probabilities between the regimes are dependent on explanatory variables such as demand and the reserve margin. Kanamura and Ohashi (2008) follow a similar approach and employ a regime-switching model with a nonspike and a spike regime. Transition probabilities are then dependent on the relationship between demand levels and the threshold of supply capacity, changes in demand as well a trend caused by the deviation of temporary demand fluctuation from its long-term mean. Huisman (2008) introduces a temperature dependent regime-switching model, where either price levels or both price levels and the probability for a transition to the spike regime are dependent on the temperature deviation from its mean level. Kosater (2008) in particular focuses on the impact of weather on the price behavior in different regimes while Cartea et al. (2009) and Maryniak and Weron (2014) relate the occurrence and magnitude of price spikes to forward looking capacity constraints. On the other hand, Maciejowska (2014) reports for the UK market that fundamental drivers (wind generation, demand, gas price) play a minor role, while speculative or spot price shocks are responsible for up to 95% of the price volatility.

Generally, the literature agrees that electricity spot prices behave quite differently in the spike regime compared to the normal regime, see, for example, Huisman (2009) and Janczura and Weron (2010). Also, studies by, for example, Cartea et al. (2009), Kanamura and Ohashi (2007, 2008), and Mount et al. (2006), seem to provide evidence that the relationship between determinants of electricity spot prices and the price itself is also quite different when prices are extreme than under a normal regime. Therefore, when modeling the relationship between explanatory variables such as load, weather or capacity constraints and the magnitude of price spikes, a model that focuses on spike observations only and not the entire sample of spot electricity prices may be more appropriate. This idea motivated us to conduct this study.

The contribution of this chapter is twofold. First, this is one of the few studies to concentrate in particular on explaining and modeling the magnitude of price spikes in electricity spot markets. Many models that have been suggested in the literature for the behavior of spot electricity prices feature components that have been designed to include price spikes, such as, for example, a jump-diffusion component or a separate regime for price spikes. However, often the suggested models do not include additional explanatory variables besides the price process itself (Bierbrauer et al., 2007; De Jong, 2006; Huisman and Mahieu, 2003) or the relationship between exogenous variables and electricity prices is modelled using the entire sample (Kanamura and Ohashi, 2007; Kosater, 2008; Mount et al., 2006). Given the changing nature of the relationship between exogenous variables and electricity prices, it may well be that a model that attaches all weight to spike observations and zero weight to nonspike observations may perform better in modeling and forecasting the spikes. In a similar line of thought, Christensen et al. (2009, 2012) suggest that the intensity of the occurrence of price spikes is not homogenous, but is also driven by additional exogenous variables. Building on this fact, the authors suggest focusing on forecasting extreme price events only instead of modeling the entire price trajectory. Note, however, that these authors are only concerned with modeling the occurrence of price spikes and not with modeling the actual magnitude of the extreme prices, which is the focus of our study. Clearly, market participants will not only be interested in the occurrence of a price spike, but would also like to obtain an estimate for the size or magnitude of the extreme observation.

Second, to our best knowledge, in this chapter we provide the first application of the Heckman selection model to electricity markets in order to determine appropriate models for the occurrence and magnitude of price spikes. Following Hill et al. (2008), the application of this technique can be used to appropriately estimate the relationship between an exogenous and a dependent variable for a nonrandom subset of the observations. For our application of modeling electricity price spikes, this means that we are able to estimate the relationship between the considered explanatory variables and the subsample of observed electricity prices spikes since potential selection bias has been controlled for. Note that a similar approach has been applied to modeling losses from operational risk in a recent paper by Dahen and Dione (2010). However, to our best knowledge, this study presents the first application of the technique to electricity spot markets.

The remainder of the chapter is organized as follows. In Section 2 we present a brief overview of regional Australian electricity markets, focusing on market price caps and products available to hedge the risk of price spikes occurring. Section 3 describes the theoretical basis for the inclusion of the considered explanatory variables. Section 4 reviews the Heckman selection model and illustrates how it can be applied to model the magnitude of electricity price spikes. Section 5 reports the estimation results for the Heckman selection model, different ordinary least squares (OLS) models and evaluates their performance. Finally, in Section 6, we conclude and discuss future work.

2 The Australian National Electricity Market

Since the late 1990s the Australian electricity market has experienced significant changes. At that point in time, to promote energy efficiency and reduce the costs of electricity production, the Australian government commenced a significant structural reform. The key objectives of this reform were the separation of transmission from electricity generation, the merger of 25 electricity distributors into a smaller number of distributors, and the functional separation of electricity distribution from the retail supply of electricity. Retail competition was also introduced through the reform such that states' electricity purchases could be made through a competitive retail market and customers were free to choose their retail supplier.

As a wholesale market, the National Electricity Market (NEM) in Australia began operating in December 1998. It is now an interconnected grid comprising several regional networks that provide supply of electricity to retailers and end-users. The NEM includes the states of Queensland (QLD), New South Wales (NSW), Victoria (VIC), and South Australia (SA), while Tasmania (TAS) is connected to VIC via an undersea interconnector. The link between electricity producers and electricity consumers is established through a pool, which is used to aggregate the output from all generators in order to meet the forecasted demand. The pool is managed by the Australian Energy Market Operator (AEMO). Unlike many other markets, the Australian spot electricity market is not a day-ahead market but electricity is traded in a constrained real-time spot market where prices are set each 5 minutes by AEMO. Therefore, generators are able to submit their offers every 5 minutes. This information is used to select generators to produce electricity in the most cost-efficient way. The final price is determined in half-hour intervals for each of the regions as an average over the 5-minute spot prices for each trading interval. AEMO determines the half-hourly spot prices for each of the regional markets separately. Note that for Australian electricity markets, until June 30, 2010, the market price cap was 10,000 AUD/MWh. The market price cap determines the maximum possible bidding price and therefore, also the highest possible outcome for a half-hourly price. On July 1, 2010, the bid-cap was increased to 12,500 AUD/MWh, while it was further increased to 12,900 AUD/MWh on July 1, 2012, and to 13,100 AUD/MWh on July 1, 2013. Price spikes play an important role in hedging decisions for NEM market participants, since Australian electricity markets can be considered as being significantly more volatile and spike-prone than other comparable markets (Higgs and Worthington, 2008). There have been several occasions in the regional markets when the determined half-hourly price was close to or even reached the determined market price cap. Therefore, research on the determinants of the occurrence and magnitude of price spikes is of significant importance for market participants.

In recent years, the market for electricity derivatives has also developed rapidly including electricity forward, futures, and option contracts being traded at the Sydney Futures Exchange (SFE). Next to the futures contracts that are priced with respect to average electricity spot prices during a delivery period, the SFE also offers a number of alternative derivative contracts. These include, for example, option contracts or so-called AUD 300 cap products for a calendar quarter. For these contracts, the payoff is determined by the sum of all base load half-hourly spot prices for the region in the calendar quarter greater than AUD 300 (e.g., the severity of the spikes) and the total number of half-hourly spot prices for the region in the calendar quarter greater than AUD 300 (e.g., the frequency of the spikes). While in this study we do not price these products, our results will be of great interest in particular with respect to modeling the payoff distribution of these contracts in future work.

Note that for electricity markets, derivative contracts typically do not require physical delivery of electricity but are settled financially. Therefore, market participants can participate in electricity derivatives markets and increase market liquidity without owning physical generation assets.

3 Explanatory Variables

Generally, the reasons for the occurrence of a price spike can be manifold and may include the unexpected outage or shutdown of power plants, problems with the network transmission grid, extreme temperature events, unanticipated high loads, or they may be a result of the bidding behavior of market participants (see, e.g., Eydeland and Wolyniec, 2012, Weron, 2006). Therefore, as pointed out by Misiorek et al. (2006) the spot electricity price can be considered as the outcome of a vast number of variables including fundamentals (like loads and network constraints) but also unquantifiable psychological and sociological factors that can cause an unexpected and irrational buyout of certain contracts, leading to price spikes.

The empirical literature suggests a number of variables that may have a significant impact on the occurrence and magnitude of price spikes (see, e.g., Becker et al. 2007, Cartea and Figueroa 2005, Huisman 2008, Kosater 2008, Lu et al. 2005, Mount et al. 2006, Weron and Misiorek 2008). Generally, these variables can be grouped into three classes: (i) factors related to electricity demand and load, (ii) factors related to weather conditions, and (iii) factors related to the capacity of the system and the reserve margin.

The load measures electricity demand and given that electricity supply is constrained in the short run, the load usually has a significant impact on wholesale electricity prices. Load patterns typically exhibit seasonality throughout the day, week, and year. The load has been determined as one of the key factors determining spot electricity prices in many studies. For example, Lu et al. (2005) suggest that electricity load is a significant variable in determining the probability of the occurrence of a price spike. Misiorek et al. (2006) conclude that day-ahead load forecasts issued by the system operator in California (CAISO) lead to more accurate day-ahead spot price forecasts than the actual load. They explain this phenomenon by the fact that the prices are an outcome of the bids, which in turn are placed with the knowledge of load forecasts but not actual future loads. Indeed, electricity suppliers generally do not know the exact system load by the time they enter their bids. Instead, they often have to rely on weather variables and/or past observations of load (Mount et al., 2006; Weron, 2014).

Weather conditions will have also a significant impact on electricity consumption. It can be expected that during a cold winter or a hot summer, electricity consumption will increase due to the use of heating or air-conditioning, respectively. Various weather variables can be considered, but temperature and humidity are the most commonly used load predictors. Hippert et al. (2001) report that of the 22 research publications considered in their electricity load prediction survey, 13 made use of temperature only, three made use of temperature and humidity, three utilized additional weather parameters, and three used only load parameters. Generally, with respect to temperature, electricity demand and hence spot prices depend more on the deviation from the normal temperature, rather than the temperature itself (Huisman, 2008). For this reason, in our empirical analysis we will use the absolute or squared deviation of the air temperature from 18°C.

Finally, the reserve margin measures the relationship between the available capacity in the system and peak demand. It provides a measure for the aptitude of the market to maintain reliable operation while meeting unforeseen increases in demand (e.g., extreme weather) and unexpected outages of existing capacity. It has been found to be a significant factor in determining the occurrence of price spikes in previous studies, see, e.g., Cartea et al. (2009), Lu et al. (2005), Maryniak and Weron (2014), Mount et al. (2006), Weron (2014), Zareipour et al. (2006), to mention only a few. For this reason, we also consider the reserve margin as an explanatory variable for the occurrence and magnitude of price spikes in this study.

4 Methodology

This section discusses the Heckman correction that can be applied in order to overcome a selection bias in the modeling procedure when estimating the relationship between the considered explanatory variables and the magnitude of price spikes. We will also briefly review the so-called Box–Cox transformation technique that is applied to the raw price data in order to obtain the approximate normality of the variables that is required by the Heckman selection model. We also provide an overview of measures for comparing the forecast ability of the different models that are applied in this chapter.

4.1 The Heckman Selection Model

The Heckman selection model is a statistical approach developed by Heckman (1979) to correct for selection bias. Standard econometric literatures (Greene, 2008; Hill et al., 2008; Verbeek, 2008) argue that when the majority of the observations for the dependent variable takes on a value of 0, a standard OLS regression approach is not appropriate (for a detailed proof see, e.g., Kennedy, 2003). Under these circumstances, an alternative approach for regression analysis is required. In this chapter, the dependent variable of interest is the magnitude of observed price spikes in our sample. As argued by several authors (see, e.g., Cartea et al., 2009; Kanamura and Ohashi, 2007, 2008; Mount et al., 2006), the relationship between explanatory variables such as load, weather, or capacity constraints and spot electricity prices may be very different for price spikes than for price observations under a normal price regime. Therefore, one of the motivations of this study is that we believe that a model that focuses on spike observations only and not the entire sample of spot electricity prices may be more appropriate to quantify this relationship for extreme observations. However, including observations of price spikes only in the analysis is somehow critical due to the bias of preselecting data based on whether observations are classified as a price spike or not. Such a systematic preselection violates the random sample principle and, therefore, we need to apply an econometric technique that is able to correct estimates for the sample selection bias. in this chapter we decide to use the Heckman correction for this task.

The Heckman (1979) selection model is essentially a two-stage procedure and the resulting model can generally be described by a system of two equations. The first equation determines the probability of the occurrence of an event, that is, a binary choice model, while the second equation estimates the relationship between the explanatory variables and the outcome of the dependent variable. The first step, that is, the occurrence of an event is typically modeled using a Probit equation and is estimated using maximum likelihood. Then for each observation the so-called inverse Mills ratio (IMR) is calculated as the standard normal density function divided by the cumulative standard normal distribution function of the Probit model for the occurrence of the event. In a second step, the dependent variable, for example, the size or magnitude of an event, is regressed on the explanatory variables and the IMR using standard OLS. Then a test to detect the presence of a sample selection bias can be conducted by testing whether the coefficient of the IMR is significantly different from zero (Hill et al., 2008). If the coefficient of the IMR is significantly different from zero, a selection bias is present and the Heckman correction is favorable to applying standard OLS to the selected data. Note that the full model, that is, the selection equation (the binary choice model) and the final regression equation (the standard OLS equation) are typically estimated jointly using maximum likelihood.

4.2 The Lognormal and Box-Cox Transformation

In the Heckman selection model, it is assumed that error terms are normally distributed such that large deviations of the dependent variable from normality would possibly provide spurious results. Spot electricity prices, however, usually exhibit positive skewness and excess kurtosis, indicating that the empirical distribution is far more heavy-tailed than the normal distribution. Therefore, a transformation of the observed spot prices is often conducted before the estimation of an econometric model (see, e.g., Bierbrauer et al., 2007; Huisman, 2009; Weron and Misiorek, 2008). The most popular transformation in the econometric literature for electricity markets is to use the logarithm of the actually observed prices in order to dampen the extreme volatility, skewness, and excess kurtosis. In our empirical analysis, we therefore also consider log-transformed spot electricity prices for estimation of the model instead of the originally observed prices.

An alternative and a more general technique for the transformation of heavy-tailed price data is to apply the Box and Cox (1964) transformation in order to obtain approximate normality of the considered variables (Davidson and MacKinnon, 1993). The Box–Cox transformation of a variable y is defined as

$$y(\lambda) = \begin{cases} \frac{y^\lambda - 1}{\lambda} & (\lambda \neq 0) \\ \log(y) & (\lambda = 0) \end{cases} \qquad (1)$$

where y denotes the original observation, λ is the so-called transformation parameter and $y(\lambda)$ denotes the transformed variable. Clearly, this technique offers a more flexible way of transforming data, depending on the choice of the parameter. Note that for the special case when λ is chosen to be zero, the Box–Cox transformation becomes the logarithmic transformation. To estimate the optimal value for λ that generates transformed observations as close as possible to a normal distribution, maximum likelihood estimation is used (see, e.g., Davidson and MacKinnon, 1993, for further details). Due to the popularity of the log-transformation in the literature on modeling electricity spot prices, in our empirical analysis we will provide the results for models based on the logarithm transformation as well as the Box-Cox transformation with $\lambda \neq 0$.

4.3 Measures to Compare Forecast Accuracy

In our empirical analysis we will compare the performance of different models with respect to their ability to appropriately model the magnitude of a spike. In particular, we will compare the results for the estimated Heckman correction-based model in comparison to standard OLS regression approaches. Clearly, there has been a variety of measures suggested in the literature in order to compare the performance of econometric models. Given that we are mainly interested in the ability of the models to appropriately quantify or forecast price spikes, we will focus on the following three measures: the mean absolute error (MAE), the mean absolute percentage error (MAPE), as well as the log-likelihood of the estimated models. Note that we decided to rather use the MAE instead of the mean squared error (MSE), since the latter is usually much more dominated by a few large outliers. Since price spikes can be of quite extreme magnitude and for the considered time period take on values up to AUD 10,000, it is likely that a comparison of models based on the MSE would be dominated by the few really extreme observations only. The MAE is defined as

$$\text{MAE} = \frac{1}{T} \sum_{t=1}^{T} |y_t - f_t| \qquad (2)$$

where T denotes the number of observations, y_t the transformed spot price (either using the natural log or Box–Cox transformation), and f_t the model forecast for the transformed price. In a similar manner the MAPE is defined as

$$\text{MAPE} = \frac{100}{T} \sum_{t=1}^{T} \left| \frac{y_t - f_t}{y_t} \right| \qquad (3)$$

Clearly, the MAPE focuses more on the relative forecast error and will, therefore, give less weight to extreme spike observations that are also expected to coincide with large model forecast errors.

5 Empirical Results

5.1 Data and Models

We consider data on price spikes for four Australian regional markets, namely NSW, QLD, SA, and VIC. Note that these are the states with the highest electricity demand in Australia (Higgs, 2009), while SFE offers a variety of derivatives contracts, including futures as well as AUD 300 cap options in those states only. Electricity spot prices and system loads at the half-hourly frequency are obtained from AEMO. We use data from the period April 1, 2002, to June 30, 2010, the time period where the market price cap had been set to 10,000 AUD/MWh (AEMO, 2012). As mentioned previously, from July 1, 2010, onward the cap was increased to 12,500 AUD/MWh, while it was further increased to 12,900 AUD/MWh on July 1, 2012, and to 13,100 AUD/MWh on July 1, 2013, such that data on price spikes from later periods may exhibit different properties due to the revised market price caps. We therefore decided to exclude all price observations from July 1, 2010, onward from the conducted analysis.

Half-hourly weather data are obtained from the Bureau of Meteorology (BOM) and include relative air temperature, wet bulb temperature, dew point temperature, relative humidity, and mean sea level pressure (Australia Government Bureau of Meteorology, 2012). We decided to use observations on weather that are measured at airport weather stations in Sydney for NSW, Brisbane for QLD, Adelaide for SA, and Melbourne for VIC. Data on the capacity in the system is obtained from AEMO. Based on the information provided on the capacity and load in the market, we define the reserve margin as $r = [\text{capacity/load}] - 1$. Clearly, with this specification, values of r close to zero indicate that there is only little reserve capacity available. On the other hand, larger values of r illustrate more reserve capacity in the market. Note, however, that we have data on the so-called supply capacity only, which reflects the installed capacity for each market, rather than the actual operational capacity.

To illustrate the extremely spiky behavior in the Australian NEM, consider Figure 7.1. The figure provides a plot of half-hourly electricity prices in QLD for the considered time period April 1, 2002, to June 30, 2010, and illustrates that half-hourly electricity prices exhibit extreme variation and a high number of spikes. We also observe that for the QLD market, half-hourly prices reach the bid-cap of 10,000 AUD/MWh in a few cases. There are also occasions on which prices are negative. This situation occurs when the cost of turning off electricity generators is high and producers are willing to put negative bids into the system to ensure that they can dispatch the generated electricity.

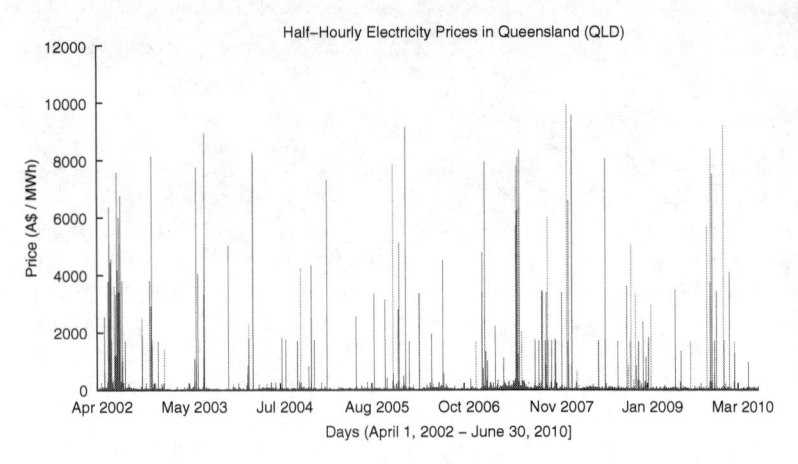

Figure 7.1 Half-hourly electricity price (AUD/MWh) for the QLD market during the considered time period April 1, 2002–June 30, 2010.

Table 7.1 provides detailed descriptive statistics for half-hourly electricity prices in the four states, both for the entire sample as well as for the pre-selected sample that only contains price spikes. Note that in this study we classify all price observation greater than 300 AUD/MWh as price spikes. Recall that in Australia, option contracts or so-called AUD 300 cap options are traded in the Australian Securities Exchange (ASX) Australian Electricity derivatives market. The payoff for these products is determined based on both the frequency and magnitude of observed half-hourly prices in excess of 300 AUD/MWh during a calendar quarter. Therefore, given these products available in the market, we believe that the most natural definition of a spike is an observation greater than 300 AUD/MWh.

For the entire sample we find that the average price is around 35–45 AUD/MWh, while the maximum half-hourly price during the sample period is 10,000 AUD/MWh or very close to 10,000 AUD/MWh for each of the four markets. The standard deviation can be as high as 296 AUD/MWh for SA, but is greater than four times the average spot price for each of the markets. As it is typical for spot electricity prices, data are heavily skewed to the right and exhibit excess kurtosis. For the selected sample of price spikes only, we find that with 408 observations VIC exhibits the lowest number of spikes during the sample period, while in NSW for the same period 743 spikes can be observed. The average magnitude of a spike ranges from 2,037 AUD/MWh in NSW to 3,253 AUD/MWh

Table 7.1 Descriptive statistics of half-hourly electricity prices for NSW, QLD, SA, VIC for the period April 1, 2002–June 30, 2010.

Descriptive Statistics	NSW	QLD	SA	VIC
All Prices				
Mean	41.16	37.33	46.29	36.84
Standard Deviation	229.96	198.85	296.32	170.21
Minimum	−264.31	−675.46	−1,000.00	−496.71
Maximum	10,000.00	9,920.99	9,999.92	10,000.00
Skewness	29.71	30.30	29.37	41.71
Kurtosis	1,005.33	1,076.61	924.00	2,043.70
Number of Observations	144,624	144,624	144,624	144,624
Price Spikes (Prices >300 AUD/MWh) Only				
Mean	2,037.29	2,176.19	3,252.93	2,057.05
Standard Deviation	2,488.34	2,228.11	3,556.68	2,448.91
Minimum	300.03	300.04	300.82	300.13
Maximum	10,000.00	9,920.99	9,999.92	10,000.00
Skewness	1.65	1.52	1.04	1.94
Kurtosis	4.74	4.56	2.45	6.02
Number of Observations	743	590	549	408

Note: The upper panel contains descriptive statistics for the entire sample, while the lower panel provides descriptive statistics for the pre-selected sample of spikes, e.g., price observations greater than 300 AUD/MWh.

in SA. As mentioned before, in each state there are spikes that reach the 10,000 AUD/MWh market price cap during the considered sample period.

Figure 7.2 shows the relationship between the log transformed price spikes in the QLD market (e.g., the plot contains only price observations greater than 300 AUD/MWh) and the explanatory variables market load, relative air temperature, reserve margin, and humidity for this market. At first glance, the plots do not indicate a strong relationship between the explanatory variables and the observed magnitude of price spikes in the QLD market. We now specify the following model for a more detailed analysis of the relationship between the considered explanatory variables and observed spot electricity prices. For our analysis, the Heckman selection model can be specified by equations (4) and (5) given below. Equation (4) denotes the Probit model, for example, the first stage of the Heckman selection procedure. The Probit model is concerned with the determinants of the occurrence of a price spike and, therefore, is estimated using all

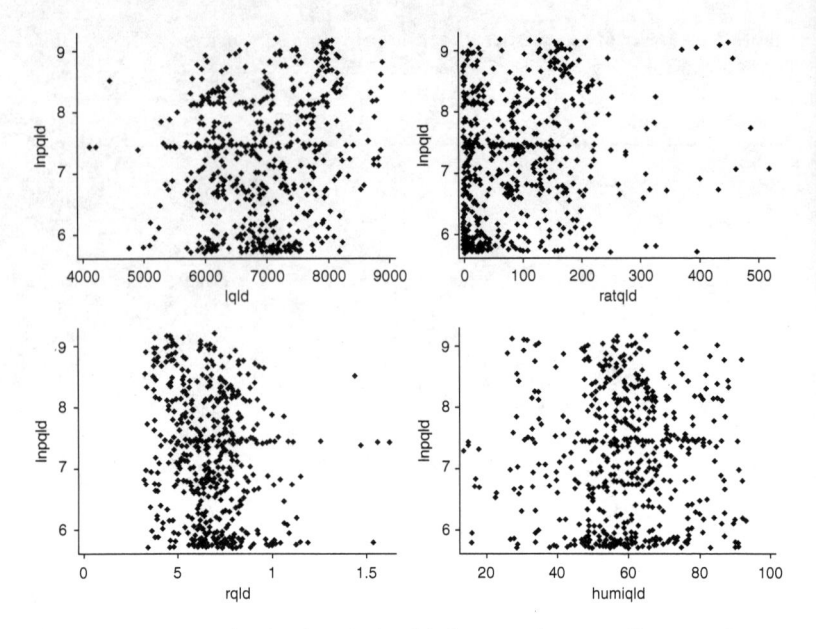

Figure 7.2 Scatter plot for the relationship between the natural log transformation of observed price spikes (dependent variable) and the explanatory variables' market load (upper left panel), relative air temperature (upper right panel), reserve margin (lower left panel), and humidity (lower right panel) for the QLD market.

observations on price data:

$$\text{DPS}_t = \gamma_0 + \gamma_1 L_t + \gamma_2 r_t + \gamma_3 rat_t + \gamma_4 webt_t + \gamma_5 dwpt_t \\ + \gamma_6 humi_t + \gamma_7 selp_t + \epsilon \qquad (4)$$

$$\text{DPS} = \begin{cases} 1 & \text{when a price spike occurs} \\ 0 & \text{otherwise} \end{cases}$$

DPS is a dummy variable for the occurrence of a price spike, L is the market load, and r is the reserve margin that is defined as $r = [\text{capacity} / \text{load}] - 1$. Further, *rat* denotes the relative air temperature that is based on the deviation of the temperature from 18°C that is, $rat = [\text{air temperature} - 18]^2$, *webt* denotes the wet bulb temperature measured using a standard mercury-in-glass thermometer, *dwpt* is the dew point temperature, that is, a measure of the moisture content of the air and the temperature to which air must be cooled in order for dew to form. Finally, *humi* denotes the air humidity and *selp* is the sea level pressure that is affected by changing weather conditions.

Table 7.2 Sample size (number of observations) details for each state

	State			
	NSW	QLD	SA	VIC
Observations (no missing data)	141,358	143,853	142,666	140,505
Censored observations	140,645	143,267	142,128	140,108
Uncensored observations	713	586	538	397

Equation (5) denotes the second stage of the estimation procedure, that is, the model for the magnitude of the occurred price spikes:

$$LNP_t = \beta_0 + \beta_1 L_t + \beta_2 rat_t + \beta_3 r_t + \beta_4 IMR_t + v \qquad (5)$$

LNP denotes the log transformation (alternatively, the Box–Cox transformation) of the observed electricity price spikes, L is the market load, rat the relative air temperature (as defined earlier), $r = [capacity/load]-1$ is the reserve margin and IMR denotes the so-called inverse Mills ratio that is specified as

$$IMR = \frac{\phi(\gamma_0 + \gamma_1 L + \gamma_2 r + \gamma_3 rat + \gamma_4 webt + \gamma_5 dwpt + \gamma_6 humi + \gamma_7 selp)}{\Phi(\gamma_0 + \gamma_1 L + \gamma_2 r + \gamma_3 rat + \gamma_4 webt + \gamma_5 dwpt + \gamma_6 humi + \gamma_7 selp)} \qquad (6)$$

and can be calculated for each observation based on Equation (5). Table 7.2 shows the number of observations for each market for the original sample and the censored sample that only contains observations of price spikes greater than 300 AUD/MWh. Obviously, for all markets, the sample size for the Probit model is quite large, since all price observations greater than 0 are included, while the sample size for the second step in the Heckman selection model, Equation (5), is much smaller but is still reasonable to provide reliable estimation results. Note that we excluded negative and zero prices from the analysis, since both the logarithmic and the Box-Cox transformation can only be applied to positive numbers.

5.2 Estimation Results

5.2.1 Heckman Selection Model with Log Transformation

Table 7.3 reports the estimation results of the Heckman selection model with log-transformed data for the spot electricity prices. We find that for

Table 7.3 Estimation results for Heckman selection method for the log transformation of spot electricity prices.

							State						
	NSW			QLD			SA			VIC		
Variable	Coef	t-Stat	Sign	Coef	t-Stat	Sign	Coef	t-Stat	Sign	Coef	t-Stat	Sign
Dependent Variable: LNP												
Cons	1.0252	0.50		4.8838	5.13	***	−3.3654	−1.26		5.0556	2.95	***
L	0.0004	3.10	***	0.0002	2.58	***	0.0029	4.33	***	0.0002	1.46	
rat	0.0026	2.99	***	0.0015	2.50	**	0.0025	3.22	***	0.0007	1.26	
r	0.4989	1.22		−0.6766	−1.54		0.3381	0.44		2.7471	4.01	***
IMR	0.3958	1.53		0.3838	2.98	***	1.5296	2.10	**	−0.1988	−0.61	
Dependent Variable: DPS												
Cons	14.2095	4.78	***	38.9371	10.28	***	2.8418	0.80		−7.7089	−2.29	**
L	0.0006	26.24	***	0.0003	7.41	***	0.0012	10.32	***	0.0005	12.82	***
r	−1.3859	−10.33	***	−1.4679	−10.17	***	−0.9129	−7.48	***	−1.7051	−9.42	***
rat	0.0033	10.14	***	0.0031	8.88	***	0.0012	4.07	***	0.0031	10.46	***
webt	0.0615	3.12	***	−0.1481	−5.70	***	−0.0133	−0.85		−0.0301	−1.63	
dwpt	−0.0545	−3.22	***	0.0569	2.45	**	−0.0070	−0.63		0.0529	3.47	***
humi	0.0122	4.51	***	−0.0031	−0.89		0.0028	1.13		0.0016	0.55	
selp	−0.0231	−8.05	***	−0.0397	−11.11	***	−0.0065	−1.89	*	0.0019	0.59	
Adj-R^2	0.05			0.06			0.14			0.08		

Note: The upper panel reports results for Equation (5) referring to the model for the magnitude of the observed price spikes, while the lower panel provides results for the Probit model for the occurrence of a spike specified in Equation (4).

the estimated Probit model the variables load, relative air temperature, and reserve margin are significant. As expected, load and relative air temperature have a positive impact on the probability of occurrence of a price spike while the reserve margin has a negative impact, that is, the closer the system is to full capacity (reserve margin r close to zero), the higher is the probability of a price spike.

In Equation (5) for the magnitude of price spikes, the IMR is significant for the QLD and SA market, while it is almost significant at the 10 percent level for NSW. The Heckman correction for sample selection bias is therefore important when examining factors affecting the magnitude of price spikes in electricity spot markets. Also, the variables load L and relative temperature *rat* are significant and have the expected positive sign in all markets except for VIC. Note, however, that the reserve margin r is only significant in VIC and yields a coefficient with a positive sign for three of the regional markets. This is counterintuitive, since it suggests that price spikes are of greater magnitude with more reserve capacity in the system. These results may be due to the low quality of data on supply capacity which reflects only the installed capacity, rather than the actual operational capacity. In general, the estimated models do not have a very high explanatory power and yield adjusted-R^2 coefficients of determination between 0.05 for NSW and 0.14 for SA. This is not surprising since, by definition, price spikes are rather unexpected events and can be considered as the outcome of a vast number of variables including fundamentals (like loads and network constraints) but also unquantifiable psychological and sociological factors that can cause an unexpected and irrational buyout of certain contracts (Misiorek et al., 2006). Therefore, for example, an R^2 of 14 percent as is obtained for the SA market can be considered quite high, since it explains a significant fraction of the variation in the magnitude of the spikes.

5.2.2 Heckman Selection Model with Box–Cox Transformation

Table 7.4 reports the estimation of the Box–Cox transformation parameter λ, based on Davidson and MacKinnon (1993), for each of the considered states, while Table 7.5 presents the estimation results for the Heckman selection model after applying the Box–Cox transformation. We obtain results very similar to when the log transformation was used for the observed spot electricity prices. Note that in the estimated model, the two variables load, L, variable air temperature *rat* are significant for all markets and show the expected sign. Also the reserve margin r is significant for three of the four markets and yields the expected negative coefficient for QLD and SA, while the coefficient is positive and significant for VIC. Results for the explanatory power of the model are also very similar to

Table 7.4 Optimal Box–Cox parameter estimates for each state based on maximum likelihood estimation (Davidson and MacKinnon, 1993)

State	λ
NSW	−0.6608
QLD	−0.5643
SA	−0.2189
VIC	−0.2405

those obtained for the log transformation. Interestingly, the explanatory power of the model with the Box–Cox transformation is slightly lower than when the log transformation is applied.

5.2.3 OLS Model Estimated with All Electricity Prices
Table 7.6 reports the estimation results for a standard OLS regression model when all transformed electricity prices are regressed on the explanatory variables (load and reserve margin, and relative air temperature). The results are presented both for the log transformation (upper panel) as well as for the Box–Cox transformation (lower panel). The results indicate that all three explanatory variables are significant for each of the considered markets and for both transformations. The coefficient for load always has the expected sign while relative air temperature yields a negative sign for QLD when the log transformation is used and for QLD and SA when the Box–Cox transformation is employed. Surprisingly, the coefficient for the reserve margin is also positive for QLD for both types of transformation. The explanatory power of the models measured by the adjusted-R^2 is quite high, indicating that the considered variables provide significant explanatory power for the level of spot electricity prices. However, since all price observations are considered in this model, results for the coefficient of determination are not really comparable to the Heckman selection model that is applied to observed price spikes in excess of 300 AUD/MWh only.

5.2.4 Standard OLS Results for Price Spike Subsample
Table 7.7 presents the estimation results for the transformed price spikes on the considered explanatory variables, ignoring the selection bias. The results are quite similar to those for the Heckman selection procedure with significant and positive coefficients for the variables load L and relative

Table 7.5 Estimation results for Heckman selection method for the Box–Cox transformation of spot electricity prices.

	State											
	NSW			QLD			SA			VIC		
Variable	Coef	t-Stat	Sign	Coef	t-Stat	Sign	Coef	t-Stat	Sign	Coef	t-Stat	Sign
Dependent Variable: LNP												
Cons	1.4317	70.42	***	1.6943	92.68	***	1.3069	2.32	**	3.0458	9.85	***
L	0.0000	3.22	***	0.0000	2.09	**	0.0006	4.26	***	0.0000	1.28	
rat	0.0000	3.08	***	0.0000	3.00	***	0.0006	3.53	***	0.0001	1.23	
r	0.0067	1.65	*	−0.0172	−2.03	**	−0.0407	−0.25		0.4687	3.79	***
IMR	0.0044	1.72	*	0.0098	3.95	***	0.3916	2.53	**	−0.0316	−0.54	
Dependent variable: DPS												
Cons	14.2095	4.78	***	38.9371	10.28	***	2.8418	0.80		−7.7089	−2.29	**
L	0.0006	26.24	***	0.0003	7.41	***	0.0012	10.32	***	0.0005	12.82	***
r	−1.3859	−10.33	***	−1.4679	−10.17	***	−0.9129	−7.48	***	−1.7051	−9.42	***
rat	0.0033	10.14	***	0.0031	8.88	***	0.0012	4.07	***	0.0031	10.46	***
webt	0.0615	3.12	***	−0.1481	−5.70	***	−0.0133	−0.85		−0.0301	−1.63	
dwpt	−0.0545	−3.22	***	0.0569	2.45	**	−0.0070	−0.63		0.0529	3.47	***
humi	0.0122	4.51	***	−0.0031	−0.89		0.0028	1.13		0.0016	0.55	
selp	−0.0231	0.00	***	−0.0397	−11.11	***	−0.0065	−1.89	*	0.0019	0.59	
Adj-R^2	0.06			0.06			0.11			0.07		

Note: The upper reports results for Equation (5) referring to the model for the magnitude of the observed price spikes, while the lower panel provides results for the Probit model for the occurrence of a spike specified in Equation (4).

Table 7.6 Estimation results using OLS for the entire sample of electricity spot prices from April 1, 2002 to June 30, 2010.

						State						
	NSW			QLD			SA			VIC		
Variable	Coef	t-Stat	Sign	Coef	t-Stat	Sign	Coef	t-Stat	Sign	Coef	t-Stat	Sign
Dependent Variable: LNP, All Prices												
Cons	1.3997	107.74	***	0.9257	36.47	***	1.6226	89.14	***	0.6716	49.19	***
L	0.0002	183.77	***	0.0004	121.33	***	0.0012	154.19	***	0.0005	238.43	***
rat	0.0016	53.96	***	−0.0001	−4.09	***	0.0002	7.47	***	0.0004	20.88	***
r	−0.1278	−26.37	***	0.1253	15.57	***	−0.0525	−12.94	***	−0.0920	−18.04	***
Adj–R^2	0.44			0.28			0.48			0.49		
Dependent Variable: BCP, All Prices												
Cons	1.1393	988.33	***	1.1416	338.17	***	1.7190	212.00	***	1.1080	189.88	***
L	0.0000	215.73	***	0.0001	136.07	***	0.0005	143.08	***	0.0002	246.87	***
rat	0.0001	21.15	***	−0.0001	−20.84	***	−0.0001	−10.98	***	0.0000	4.80	***
r	−0.0154	−35.72	***	0.0095	8.91	***	−0.0596	−33.00	***	−0.0462	−21.21	***
Adj-R^2	0.50			0.34			0.48			0.50		

Note: that the results on the explanatory power of the model cannot be compared to Table 7.3 and 7.5, since the estimation refers to a much larger data set that contains mainly price observations from a 'normal' price regime.

Table 7.7 Estimation results using OLS for the subsample of price spikes, i.e., prices greater than 300 AUD/MWh only

	State											
	NSW			QLD			SA			VIC		
Variable	Coef	t-Stat	Sign	Coef	t-Stat	Sign	Coef	t-Stat	Sign	Coef	t-Stat	Sign
Dependent Variable: LNP, Price Spikes Only (Prices > 300 AUD/MWh)												
Cons	4.0378	7.91	***	6.2360	7.43	***	1.9256	2.57	**	4.0665	7.35	***
L	0.0002	5.16	***	0.0001	1.58		0.0016	6.79	***	0.0003	4.10	***
rat	0.0014	4.12	***	0.0014	2.37	**	0.0013	3.04	***	0.0010	2.67	***
r	0.9574	3.44	***	−0.2017	−0.49		1.7630	5.52	***	2.4064	6.06	***
Adj−R^2	0.07			0.05			0.17			0.12		
Dependent Variable: BCP, Price Spikes Only (Prices > 300 AUD/MWh)												
Cons	1.4654	287.26	***	1.7288	107.47	***	2.6651	17.57	***	2.8885	28.91	***
L	0.0000	5.01	***	0.0000	0.67		0.0003	5.77	***	0.0000	3.59	***
rat	0.0000	3.91	***	0.0000	2.85	***	0.0003	3.19	***	0.0002	2.53	**
r	0.0119	4.29	***	−0.0051	−0.64		0.3223	4.99	***	0.4145	5.78	***
Adj−R^2	0.07			0.04			0.14			0.11		

air temperature *rat* for most of the regional markets. Interestingly, load is no longer significant for the QLD market. However, the reserve margin r is significant for three of the four markets (NSW, SA, VIC) but in each case yields a counterintuitive positive sign. As indicated by the results for the Heckman selection model where the IMR was significant for several of the considered markets, estimation results of a simple OLS model are not reliable because they are biased. However, results on adjusted-R^2 are very similar to the results we obtain for the Heckman selection model.

5.3 Comparing the Forecasting Ability of the Models

In the following, we compare the forecasting ability of the three estimated models (Heckman selection model, OLS model using all prices, OLS model using price spikes only) for the observed price spikes in the sample. As pointed out in Section 4.3, we focus on the following three performance measures: MAE, MAPE, and log likelihood of the estimated models. The results for all three models and performance criteria are shown in Table 7.8. We find that for each of the considered measures and markets, the Heckman selection model yields the best performance. This is true both for the logarithmic and the Box–Cox transformation of the price data. For all markets, the estimated OLS model that uses price spikes only performs second best, while the OLS model using all prices performs significantly worse.

The poor performance of the standard OLS model that is estimated using all prices can be explained by the fact that the model is calibrated using mainly nonspike observations and only gives a small weight to actual price spikes. It also points towards the nonlinear relationship between wholesale prices and the considered explanatory variables, as has been suggested, e.g. by Kanamura and Ohashi (2008), Mount et al. (2006), or Weron (2006). These studies also suggest that the relationship between load or demand and electricity wholesale prices can be characterized by a hockey-stick shape. Overall, the weaker performance of a standard OLS model for quantifying the magnitude of price spikes is not very surprising.

More interestingly, the estimated Heckman selection model also outperforms an OLS model that is estimated using price spikes only. This indicates that a correction for the selection bias in the estimation as well as the inclusion of the IMR in the model plays an important role and should be further examined in future studies.

Table 7.8 MAE, MAPE, and log likelihood of the estimated models for the OLS using the entire sample, OLS applied to price spikes only, and the Heckman selection model.

Natural Log Transformation for Price			
Method	(1) OLS - All Prices	(2) OLS - Price Spikes	(3) Heckman Selection
NSW			
MAE	2.75	0.94	0.94
MAPE	38.20	13.57	13.54
Log Likelihood	−1,784.76	−1,067.90	−1,067.05
QLD			
MAE	3.57	0.87	0.86
MAPE	48.81	12.39	12.26
Log Likelihood	−1,600.50	−833.97	−829.90
SA			
MAE	2.81	0.95	0.94
MAPE	36.80	13.43	13.28
Log Likelihood	−1,362.85	−820.71	−814.70
VIC			
MAE	2.75	0.84	0.84
MAPE	37.92	12.03	12.08
Log Likelihood	−993.98	−557.55	−557.21
Box-Cox Transformation for Price			
Method	1) OLS - All Prices	2) OLS - Price Spikes	3) Heckman Selection
NSW			
MAE	0.08	0.01	0.01
MAPE	5.25	0.65	0.65
Log Likelihood	764.57	2,217.11	2,217.85
QLD			
MAE	0.21	0.02	0.02
MAPE	11.96	0.96	0.95
Log Likelihood	77.47	1,483.25	1,490.47
SA			
MAE	0.76	0.19	0.19
MAPE	20.64	5.40	5.33
Log Likelihood	−651.99	38.92	46.39
VIC			
MAE	0.69	0.15	0.15
MAPE	20.31	4.54	4.54
Log Likelihood	−443.89	121.95	122.29

Note: That results are reported for log transformation and Box-Cox transformation of the original prices.

6 Summary and Conclusions

In this chapter, we proposed the Heckman selection model framework to examine factors driving the frequency and magnitude of price spikes. Using this framework, estimation results are not influenced by low (or normal) electricity prices while the selection bias due to random sampling is overcome. The literature suggests that electricity spot prices behave quite differently in the spike regime compared to the normal regime (for a review see, e.g., Weron, 2014). Studies by, for example, Cartea et al. (2009), Kanamura and Ohashi (2007, 2008), Mount et al. (2006), seem to provide further evidence that also the relationship between determinants of electricity spot prices and the price itself is quite different when prices are extreme than under a normal regime. Therefore, when modeling the relationship between explanatory variables such as load, weather, or capacity constraints and the magnitude of price spikes, a model that focuses on spike observations only and not the entire sample of spot electricity prices may be more appropriate.

The Heckman procedure is applied to four regional electricity markets in Australia and it is found that for each of these markets, load, relative air temperature, and reserve margins are significant variables for the occurrence of price spikes, while load and relative air temperature have a significant impact on the magnitude of a price spike. We also find that the IMR is significant for several of the considered markets, which indicates that application of a standard OLS model to preselected data of price spikes will generally lead to biased results. The performance of the Heckman selection model for the quantification of price spikes is also compared with the performance of an OLS model using all prices and an OLS model using price spikes only. We find that for all of the considered measures the Heckman selection model performs best. Our results encourage further application of the Heckman selection model to electricity markets.

Note

* This work was partially supported by funds from the Australian Research Council (ARC) through grant no. DP1096326 and the National Science Centre (NCN, Poland) through grant no. 2011/01/B/HS4/01077.

References

AEMO (2012). AEMO Submission to the Review of the Reliability and Emergency Reserve Trader (RERT) Issues Paper.

Anderson, E., Hu, X., and Winchester, D. (2007). Forward Contracts in Electricity Markets: The Australian Experience. *Energy Policy*, 65:329–344.

Australia Government Bureau of Meteorology (2012). Climate Glossary Index.

Becker, R., Hurn, S., and Pavlov, V. (2007). Modelling Spikes in Electricity Prices. *The Economic Record*, 35:371–382.

Bierbrauer, M., Menn, C., Rachev, S., and Trück, S. (2007). Spot and Derivative Pricing in the EEX Power Market. *The Journal of Banking & Finance*, 31:3462–3485.

Box, G. and Cox, D. (1964). An Analysis of Transformations. *Journal of the Royal Statistical Society Series B (Methodological)*, 26(2):211–252.

Cartea, A. and Figueroa, M. (2005). Pricing in Electricity Markets: A Mean Reverting Jump Diffusion Model with Seasonality. *Applied Mathematical Finance*, 12(4).

Cartea, A., Figueroa, M., and Geman, H. (2009). Modelling Electricity Prices with Forward Looking Capacity Constraints. *Applied Mathematical Finance*, 16(2):103–122.

Christensen, T., Hurn, A., and Lindsay, K. (2009). It Never Rains but It Pours: Modelling the Persistence of Spikes in Electricity Prices. *Energy Journal*, 30(1):25–48.

Christensen, T., Hurn, A., and Lindsay, K. (2012). Forecasting Spikes in Electricity Prices. *International Journal of Forecasting*, 28(2):400–411.

Clewlow, L. and Strickland, C. (2000). *Energy Derivatives—Pricing and Risk Management*. Lacima Publications, London.

Dahen, H. and Dione, G. (2010). Scaling Models for the Severity and Frequency of External Operational Loss Data. *The Journal of Banking & Finance*, 34:1484–1496.

Davidson, R. and MacKinnon, J. (1993). *Estimation and Inference in Econometrics*. University Press, Oxford, Cambridge.

De Jong, C. (2006). The Nature of Power Spikes: A Regime-Switching Approach. *Studies in Nonlinear Dynamics and Econometrics*, 10(3):1–26.

Escribano, A., Pena, J., and Villaplana, P. (2002). Modelling Electricity Prices: International Evidence.

Eydeland, A. and Wolyniec, K. (2012). *Energy and Power Risk Management*. Wiley, Hoboken, NJ, 2nd edition.

Geman, H. and Roncoroni, A. (2006). Understanding the fine structure of electricity prices. *The Journal of Business*, 79(3):1225–1261.

Greene, W. (2008). *Econometric Analysis*. Pearson Prentice Hall, Upper Saddle River, NJ, 6th edition.

Heckman, J. (1979). Selection Bias as a Specification Error. *Econometrica*, 47(1):153–161.

Higgs, H. (2009). Modeling Price and Volatility Inter-Relationship in the Australia Wholesale Spot Electricity Markets. *Energy Economics*, 31:748–756.

Higgs, H. and Worthington, A. (2008). Stochastic Prices Modeling of High Volatility, Mean Reverting, Spike-Prone Commodities: The Australia Wholesale Spot Electricity Market. *Energy Economics*, 30:3172–3185.

Hill, R., Griffiths, W., and Lim, G. (2008). *Principles of Econometrics*. Wiley, Hoboken, NJ, 3rd edition.

Hippert, H., Pedreira, C., and Souza, R. (2001). Neural Networks for Short Term Load Forecasting: A Review and Evaluation. *IEEE Transactions on Power Systems*, 16(1):44–55.

Huisman, R. (2008). The Influence of Temperature on Spike Probability in Day-Ahead Power Prices. *Energy Economics*, 30:2697–2704.

Huisman, R. (2009). *An Introduction to Models for the Energy Markets*. Risk Books, London.

Huisman, R., Huurman, C., and Mahieu, R. (2007). Hourly Electricity Prices in Day-Ahead Markets. *Energy Economics*, 29:240–248.

Huisman, R. and Mahieu, R. (2003). Regime Jumps in Electricity Prices. *Energy economics*, 25(5):425–434.

Janczura, J. (2014). Pricing Electricity Derivatives within a Markov Regime-Switching Model: A Risk Premium Approach. *Mathematical Methods of Operations Research*, 79(1):1–30.

Janczura, J. and Weron, R. (2010). An Empirical Comparison of Alternate Regime-Switching Models for Electricity Spot Prices. *Energy Economics*, 32:1059–1073.

Kanamura, T. and Ohashi, K. (2007). A Structural Model for Electricity Prices with Spikes Measurement of Spike Risk and Optimal Policies for Hydropower Plant Operation. *Energy Economics*, 29:1010–1032.

Kanamura, T. and Ohashi, K. (2008). On Transition Probabilities of Regime Switching in Electricity Prices. *Energy Economics*, 30:1158–1172.

Kennedy, P. (2003). *A Guide to Econometrics*. Pearson Prentice Hall, Upper Saddle River, NJ, 5th edition.

Knittel, C. and Roberts, M. (2005). An Empirical Examination of Restructured Electricity Prices. *Energy Economics*, 27:791–817.

Kosater, P. (2008). On the Impact of Weather on German Hourly Power Prices. *Energy Economics*, 30:2697–2704.

Lu, X., Dong, Z., and Li, X. (2005). Electricity Market Price Spike Forecast with Data Mining Techniques. *Electric Power Systems Research*, 73:19–29.

Lucia, J. and Schwartz, E. (2002). Electricity Prices and Power Derivatives: Evidence from the Nordic Power Exchange. *Review of Derivatives Research*, 5:5–50.

Maciejowska, K. (2014). Fundamental and Speculative Shocks, what Drives Electricity Prices? IEEE conference proceedings – EEM14, http://dx.doi.org/10.1109/EEM.2014.6861289.

Maryniak, P. and Weron, R. (2014). Forecasting the Occurrence of Electricity Price Spikes in the UK Power Market, submitted. Working paper version available from RePEc: http://ideas.repec.org/p/wuu/wpaper/hsc1411.html.

Misiorek, A., Trück, S., and Weron, R. (2006). Point and Interval Forecasting of Spot Electricity Prices: Linear vs Non-Linear Time Series Models. *Studies in Nonlinear Dynamics and Econometrics*, 10(3), Article 2.

Mount, T., Ning, Y., and Cai, X. (2006). Predicting Price Spikes in Electricity Markets Using a Regime-Switching Model with Time-Varying Parameteres. *Energy Economics*, 28:62–80.

Shawky, A., Marathe, A., and Barrett, C. (2003). A First Look at the Empirical Relation between Spot and Futures Electricity Prices in the Unites States. *The Journal of Futures Markets*, 23(10):931–955.

Verbeek, M. (2008). *A Guide to Modern Econometrics*. Wiley, Chichester, 3rd edition.

Weron, R. (2000). Energy Price Risk Management. *Physica A*, 285:127–134.

Weron, R. (2006). *Modelling and Forecasting Loads and Prices in Deregulated Electricity Markets*. Wiley, Haboken, NJ.

Weron, R. (2014). Electricity Price Forecasting: A Review of the State-of-the-Art with a Look into the Future. *International Journal of Forecasting*, 30(4):1030–1081.

Weron, R., Bierbrauer, M., and Trück, S. (2004). Modelling Electricity Prices: Jump Diffusion and Regime Switching. *Physica A*, 336:39–48.

Weron, R. and Misiorek, A. (2008). Forecasting Spot Electricity Prices: A Comparison of Parametric and Semiparametric Time Series Models. *International Journal of Forecasting*, 24(744–763).

Zareipour, H., Canizares, C.A., Bhattacharya, K., and Thomson, J. (2006). Application of Public-Domain Market Information to Forecast OntarioŠs Wholesale Electricity Prices. *IEEE Transactions on Power Systems*, 21(4):1707–1717.

8
Indifference Pricing of Weather Futures Based on Electricity Futures

Fred Espen Benth, Stephan Ebbeler, and Rüdiger Kiesel[1]

1 Introduction

Increasing the share of renewable energies within the energy supply of European countries and the United States poses various challenges to energy markets, regulatory bodies, and capital markets. In particular, with the emergence of renewable power sources such as wind and photovoltaic, weather factors now also have a substantial impact on the supply side in the power market. Previously, temperature has played a crucial role in determining the demand side of power, as households require heating in the winter and cooling in the summer. As the risk in operating in power markets has a strong relation to weather factors, it is of crucial importance to understand the interplay between weather and power prices and how these risk factors can be hedged.

The Chicago Mercantile Exchange (CME) provides a wide range of weather-linked futures contracts that can be used for hedging weather risk in power markets. At the CME, futures contracts are written on weather indices measured in locations worldwide. The most important futures are written on temperatures recorded in several cities in the United States, Europe, Canada, and Asia.

As the underlying of derivative contracts on weather is typically not tradable we are facing an incomplete market situation in which we need to use an appropriate pricing approach. In this chapter, we propose a framework for pricing temperature futures based on the indifference pricing approach. As temperature drives the demand of power, we suggest using power futures as a correlated asset in our pricing approach and derive "fair prices" of temperature futures (as a side effect this also increases the liquidity of the contracts used for pricing). The indifference approach sets up two stochastic control problems of an agent to compare maximizing the expected utility of trading in power futures to first issuing a weather derivative and then trading optimally in power futures. The indifference price will be the one that makes the agent indifferent between the two. We derive both a seller and a buyer price based on this approach.

We model temperature using a continuous-time autoregressive model, which has turned out to explain the stochastic evolution of temperatures very well (see Benth et al., 2007; Härdle and Cabrera 2012). Power spot prices are modeled by a seasonally varying Ornstein–Uhlenbeck process (OU), from which we can compute explicit power forward prices. We derive, using an exponential utility function, analytic temperature futures prices by solving the corresponding Hamilton–Jacobi–Bellman (HJB) equations arising from the stochastic control problems, introducing a factorization of the solution.

We apply our results to pricing temperature futures written on the city of Essen, Germany. We use power spot and forward prices collected from the German power exchange EEX, and analyze our results with a view toward the actually observed futures prices at CME for this German city.

The indifference pricing approach is a well-established technique for derivatives pricing in incomplete markets (see Henderson and Hobson (2009) and further articles collected in Carmona (2009) and references therein). It has been applied to price rainfall derivatives by Carmona and Diko (2005). The novelty of this chapter is that we apply the approach to temperature derivatives, and can test the conclusions on actually traded weather derivatives in the market. Our theoretical solution also requires very different models and some new results regarding forwards and optimal control.

Furthermore, due to the explicit solution of the CAT futures price process, we will be able to calculate the price process for the whole trading period of a CAT contract and compare these results to the real data observed at the CME. Based on the results of the comparison it will be possible to develop strategies for the investor/hedger as to whether he should be active at the exchange or rather go to the over-the-counter market. From our point of view, this is the first time that the results of a mathematical model can be compared to real CME data for different contracts and that strategies for investors can be deduced. Additionally, from the indifference pricing approach, we will be able to analyze the risk preferences of the market participants as well as any implied risk premiums.

The remainder of this chapter is structured as follows. In Section 2 we give an overview of the market for temperature derivatives and the most important derivative structures. Section 3 is devoted to introduce our modeling approach. We then use the indifference approach to price the relevant futures contracts. In the following Section 4 we perform an empirical analysis of the relevant data with a focus on the correlation of temperature and power prices. In Section 5, we then use our approach to calculate prices for various derivatives and compare them with market prices. Section 6 then gives a sensitivity analysis of important model parameters. Section 7 draws some conclusions.

2 The Temperature Derivative Market

Weather-related derivatives present a relatively newly developed class of derivatives compared to derivatives based on other financial assets (e.g., currency swaps etc.). The first weather derivatives were traded in 1997 probably due to the impact of the weather phenomenon El Niño on some industries. The first weather derivatives that are mentioned in the literature were traded by Aquila Energy (a weather option embedded in a power contract; Considine, 2000) and Enron Corp. which structured a weather-related bond with Koch Industries, Inc. In this contract, Enron agreed to pay $10,000 for every degree that was below the normal temperature index for Milwaukee, United States, for the winter period 1997–1998.

The CME in Chicago is currently the only exchanges offerings weather derivatives. The largest part of weather derivatives that are traded at the CME are related to the temperature indices HDD, CDD, and CAT (see below). The temperature indices differ in the way the daily average temperature is accumulated over the observation period:

- Heating-degree-day
  The *heating-degree-day* (HDD) approach originates from the heating industry in the United States, which found out that the demand for heating and cooling in households depends strongly on the deviation of the daily average temperature from 65 degrees Fahrenheit (°F) or 18 degrees Celsius (°C). The HDD of day i measures the degrees of daily average temperatures which are below 18°C on day i, or, mathematically

  $$\text{HDD}_i = \max\{18 - T_i, 0\}$$

  where T_i is the average temperature on day i. The HDD of a given observation period with N days is then defined as the sum of the

HDD$_i'$s of the N days or

$$\text{HDD} = \sum_{i=1}^{N} \text{HDD}_i.$$

In the following, we will synonymously use the term HDD for either the HDD of one day or of an observation period.

- Cooling-degree-day
  Similar to the definition of the HDD, the *cooling-degree-day* (CDD) describes the days on which the daily average temperature exceeds 18°C, which are typically the days where a higher load consumption of US households is expected due to the use of air conditioning. Consequently, the CDD of the day i is defined as

$$\text{CDD}_i = \max\{T_i - 18, 0\}$$

and the CDD of a period of N days is given by

$$\text{CDD} = \sum_{i=1}^{N} \text{CDD}_i.$$

- Cumulative average temperature
  For Europe, the cumulative average temperature index (CAT-index) is used instead of the CDD index in the summer months, which is the sum of the daily average temperatures. The cumulative average temperature index (CAT-index) for the period of N days is defined as

$$\text{CAT} = \sum_{i=1}^{N} T_i.$$

For the Asia-Pacific region a slight modification of the CAT temperature index, the PRim-index (Pacific Rim index), is used for both time periods, winter and summer.

As seen in the example of Enron and Aquila Energy, the main purpose of weather derivatives is to hedge the risks that a company is facing and which are correlated to the influence of weather. It is estimated that about 80 percent of the global economy is directly or indirectly affected by the weather (Auer, 2003).

Currently the CME offers temperature futures for 24 US cities, six cities in Canada, ten cities in Europe, and three cities in Australia and the Pacific Rim region (CME Group, 2009). For most cities monthly and seasonal contracts as well as options of European style are available. For the US cities, HDD and CDD futures whereas for Europe HDD and CAT contracts are offered. All US futures are settled with a tick size of $20 whereas the European futures are settled with €20 or £20 for London. The HDD contracts are tradable for the winter months November to March whereas both the CDD and CAT contracts are available for May to September. For the months October and April, both CDD/CAT and HDD contracts are available (CME Group, 2009). All contracts are financially settled and the last trading day is the first business day, which is at least five days after the end of the contract month.

3 Indifference Pricing of Temperature Futures

As mentioned in the introduction, we focus on deriving an explicit and closed form expression for a weather derivative based on the indifference pricing approach. In the following we introduce the pricing framework and the assumed dynamics for the temperature process as well as the process of the correlated asset, the electricity futures contract. The advantage of the electricity futures contract traded, for example, at the European Power Exchange (EPEX) are that there are contracts available with the same delivery period as weather derivatives (e.g., monthly contracts).

3.1 The Pricing Framework

Let $T < \infty$ be a fixed time in the future denoting the end of the planning horizon which covers all times of interest and $(\Omega, \mathcal{F}, \mathbb{P}, \mathbb{F})$ be a probability space with an augmented filtration $\mathbb{F} = \{\mathcal{F}_t\}_{0 \leq t \leq T}$ (satisfying the usual conditions) generated by the two Brownian motions W^{temp} and W^{elect}. Furthermore, let $t \in [0, T]$ denote the current time and T_1, T_2 be the beginning and the end of the measurement period of the CAT futures contract, that is, $t \leq T_1 < T_2 \leq T$. Hence, we require a real measurement period instead of a one-time event. Additionally, the focus lies on the price process of the CAT futures before the start of the measurement period.

For the dynamics of the temperature process we follow Benth et al. (2007), who propose to use the continuous-autoregressive process (CAR) model. The advantage of the CAR models lies in the implementation procedure. CAR models are continuous time models for which closed form expressions for various derivatives can be derived using standard techniques from financial mathematics. In order to estimate the parameters of the model, the close relation to the analogous autoregressive (AR) model is used. In a first step, the parameters of the AR model are estimated, which is convenient as temperature data are usually available on a daily basis and a broad range of fitting procedures for time series data exist.

Our analysis of daily temperatures in Germany concludes that the model of Benth et al. (2007) which was also applied by Härdle and Cabrera (2012) fits best for temperatures in Germany. The model has the following structure. Let $T(t)$ be the temperature at time t, which is driven by the dynamics of a CAR(p) process of the following form:

$$T(t) = \Lambda^{\text{temp}}(t) + \mathbf{X}_1(t) \tag{1}$$

where $\Lambda^{\text{temp}}(t)$ is a deterministic and seasonal function and $\mathbf{X}_1(t)$ is the first coordinate of a state space vector, which is driven by a mean-reverting OU process with dynamics:

$$d\mathbf{X}(t) = A\mathbf{X}(t)dt + e_p \eta(t)\, dW^{\text{temp}}(t) \tag{2}$$

where e_k is the kth-unit vector of $\mathbb{R}^p$, $p \in \mathbb{N}_+$, $\eta(t)$ a positive and square-integrable function such that the Itô integral is well defined and A and $\mathbf{X}(t)$ given by

$$A = \begin{pmatrix} 0 & 1 & 0 & \cdots & 0 \\ 0 & 0 & 1 & \cdots & 0 \\ \vdots & \vdots & \ddots & \ddots & \vdots \\ 0 & 0 & 0 & \cdots & 1 \\ -\alpha_p & -\alpha_{p-1} & -\alpha_{p-2} & \cdots & -\alpha_1 \end{pmatrix}; \quad \mathbf{X}(t) = \begin{pmatrix} X(t) \\ X^{(1)}(t) \\ \vdots \\ X^{(p-2)}(t) \\ X^{(p-1)}(t) \end{pmatrix} \tag{3}$$

with $\alpha_i > 0$ for $i = 1 \ldots p$ and $X^{(k)}(t)$ denoting the kth derivative of $X(t)$. For the special case $p = 1$ the matrix A reduces to the constant $-\alpha_1$.

For a constant volatility function $\eta(t) \equiv \eta$ the process $\mathbf{X}(t)$ is stationary if and only if the eigenvalues of A have all strictly negative real parts and $\mathbf{X}(0)$ is Gaussian distributed with variance $\eta^2 \int_0^\infty e^{At} e_p^\top e_p e^{A^\top t} dt$ where $A_p^\top$ denotes the transpose of the matrix A (for a proof, see Brockwell and Hyndman, 1992; Brockwell, 2009). For the setting above the requirements are slightly more restrictive (for the proof of the following proposition we refer to Benth et al. (2007)).

Proposition 1 *The solution of the process $\mathbf{X}(t)$ is stationary if all eigenvalues of A have strictly negative real parts and the volatility function $\eta(t)$*

is bounded which ensures that the variance matrix converges,

$$\lim_{t \to \infty} \int_0^t \eta^2(t-u) e^{Au} e_p^\top e_p e^{A^\top u} du < \infty$$

where $A^\top$ denotes the transpose of the matrix A.

In order to derive a closed form expression for the price process we assume a rather simple spot price process, which is based on the arithmetic model of Benth et al. (2008b) and is similar to the model of Lucia and Schwartz (2002). We assume that the dynamics of the spot price are mainly driven by a mean-reverting OU process with time dependent and strictly positive volatility (i.e., $\sigma(t) \geq \delta$ for a constant $\delta > 0$):

$$S(t) = \Lambda^{\text{arith}}(t) + Z(t) \quad \text{with}$$

$$dZ(t) = -\kappa Z(t) dt + \sigma(t) dW^{\text{elect}}(t). \tag{4}$$

If, instead of the spot price, the log spot price is used, this is often called a geometric spot price model. Before we can start with the indifference price framework we need to derive the dynamics of electricity futures based on the given spot price models. In order to obtain a closed form expression for the indifference price we concentrate on the *arithmetic model* in Equation (4). For this part, we simplify the notation by suppressing the superscript "elect" in W^{elect} as we deal only with the Brownian motion driving the spot price process here.

Following Benth et al. (2008b) the futures price at time t with delivery period $[T_1, T_2]$ is given as

$$F(t, T_1, T_2) = \mathbb{E}_\mathbb{Q} \left[\int_{T_1}^{T_2} \frac{1}{T_2 - T_1} S(u) du \Big| \mathcal{F}_t \right]$$

assuming a constant risk free interest rate r, a pricing measure $\mathbb{Q}$ and financial settlement at the end of the delivery period.

Let θ be constant, then by the Girsanov theorem (see Bingham and Kiesel (2004); Karatzas and Shreve, 1997) the process

$$W^\theta(t) = W(t) - \theta t \quad \text{for } 0 \leq t \leq T$$

is a Brownian motion and the measure $\mathbb{Q}$ is equivalent to $\mathbb{P}$ with *Radon-Nikodym* derivative

$$\frac{d\mathbb{Q}}{d\mathbb{P}} \Big|_{\mathcal{F}_t} = \exp\left\{ -\theta W(t) - \frac{1}{2}\theta^2 t \right\}.$$

Moreover, the explicit solution of the spot price dynamic under the pricing measure $\mathbb{Q}$ is given by

$$Z(t) = e^{-\kappa(t-u)}Z(u) + \int_u^t e^{-\kappa(t-s)}\sigma(s)dW^\theta(s)$$
$$+ \int_u^t \theta e^{-\kappa(t-s)}\sigma(s)ds$$

for $0 \leq u \leq t \leq T$.

After the introduction of a pricing measure we can proceed with the valuation of electricity futures

Theorem 2 *Let the spot price dynamics given by Equation (4). Furthermore, assume that the pricing measure $\mathbb{Q}$ is given by the Radon-Nikodym derivative $\frac{d\mathbb{Q}}{d\mathbb{P}}|_{\mathcal{F}_t} = \exp\{-\theta W(t) - \frac{1}{2}\theta^2 t\}$ where θ is a constant measuring the market-price-of-risk. Then the price of a futures contract at time t with delivery period $t \leq T_1 \leq T_2 \leq T$, constant interest rate r and financial settlement at the end of the delivery period is given by*

$$F(t, T_1, T_2) = \frac{1}{T_2 - T_1}\left\{\int_{T_1}^{T_2}\Lambda(u)du + Z(t)\int_{T_1}^{T_2}e^{-\kappa(u-t)}du\right.$$
$$\left. + \theta\int_t^{T_2}\int_{\max\{T_1,s\}}^{T_2}e^{-\kappa(u-s)}\sigma(s)du\,ds\right\}.$$

A detailed proof of the theorem can be found in Benth et al. (2008b). As a consequence we obtain the following two propositions.

Proposition 3 *The $\mathbb{Q}$-dynamics for the futures price $F(t, T_1, T_2)$ is given by*

$$dF(t, T_1, T_2) = \tilde{\sigma}(t, T_1, T_2)\,dW^\theta(t) \tag{5}$$

with

$$\tilde{\sigma}(t, T_1, T_2) = \frac{\sigma(t)}{T_2 - T_1}\int_{T_1}^{T_2}e^{-\kappa(u-t)}du.$$

Proposition 4 *The $\mathbb{P}$-dynamics of the futures price is given by*

$$dF(t, T_1, T_2) = \tilde{\theta}(t, T_1, T_2)dt + \tilde{\sigma}(t, T_1, T_2)dW(t) \tag{6}$$

with

$$\tilde{\sigma}(t, T_1, T_2) = \frac{\sigma(t)}{T_2 - T_1} \int_{T_1}^{T_2} e^{-\kappa(u-t)} du \quad \text{and} \tag{7}$$

$$\tilde{\theta}(t, T_1, T_2) = -\theta \tilde{\sigma}(t, T_1, T_2). \tag{8}$$

Note that $\tilde{\sigma}(t, T_1, T_2)$ is a deterministic, strictly positive, and bounded function due to the characteristic of $\sigma(t)$ and the fact that $T_1 < T_2$.

Furthermore, we assume that the two Brownian motions W^{temp} and W^{elect} are correlated with coefficient ρ, which is a valid assumption for Germany, as we will show empirically later. For the investor we assume an exponential utility function with risk aversion coefficient $\gamma > 0$,

$$U(x) = 1 - e^{-\gamma x}. \tag{9}$$

Moreover, the interest rate $r \geq 0$ is assumed to be constant and hence the bank account dynamics $R(t)$ are given by

$$dR(t) = rR(t)dt \tag{10}$$

with $R(0) = 1$.

3.2 Optimal Futures Investment

Let us consider the investment into electricity futures contracts with a financial settlement. Suppose the investor is long $\xi(t) \in \mathbb{R}$ futures, all with the same delivery period, at time t and has $\zeta(t)$ monetary units in the bank account. Hence we allow for the purchase or sale of parts of futures. Let us now look at the value of the portfolio between time t and $t + dt$. Assume that the investor closes the futures position by going short at time $t + dt$, then the investor gains/loses $\xi(t)dF(t)$. On the other hand, the value of the bank account increases by $\zeta(t) r R(t)dt$. Furthermore, assume that the investor can close the futures position at every time and transfers the gain/loss to/from the bank account (and if necessary borrowing money from the bank unconstrained). This means that every change in the futures price is continuously transferred to the accounts of both parties. The dynamics of the wealth process $Y(t)$ of the portfolio at time t, with $t_0 < t < T_1$ is then given by

$$dY(t) = \xi(t)dF(t) + \zeta(t)rR(t)dt \quad \text{with} \quad Y(t_0) = y_{t_0}. \tag{11}$$

where y_{t_0} denotes the initial investment.

Due to the fact that it is costless to enter a futures contract and the marking-to-market of the futures position, the wealth of the portfolio at every time t with $t_0 \leq t \leq T_1$ can be written as:

$$Y(t) = \zeta(t)R(t). \tag{12}$$

Note that the dynamics of the wealth process implies that the futures position is finally closed at the start of the delivery period T_1 since we get the proceeds from the futures position by canceling out the position.

Let us assume that the number of futures contracts in the portfolio is limited in order to avoid an infinite investment in futures. Hence, the set of admissible trading strategies can be defined as follows.

Definition 5 *An investment strategy process* $\pi \in \{\pi(t) | 0 \leq t \leq T_1\}$ *is called admissible and we write* $\pi \in \mathcal{A}$ *if* $\pi(t)$ *is progressively measurable and* $|\pi(t)| < K$ *a.s. for* $K \in \mathbb{R}_+$.

Note that the boundedness of the investment strategy ensures that the wealth process has a unique and strong solution. We can simplify the dynamics of the wealth process by inserting (12) into (11) and using the futures dynamics in order to derive for an investment strategy π:

$$\begin{aligned}
dY^\pi(t) &= \pi(t)dF(t) + \frac{Y^\pi(t)}{R(t)} rR(t)dt \\
&= \left(\pi(t)\tilde{\theta}(t) + rY^\pi(t)\right)dt + \pi(t)\tilde{\sigma}(t)\,dW^{\text{elect}}(t) \tag{13}
\end{aligned}$$

where we used for simplification $\tilde{\theta}(t)$ and $\tilde{\sigma}(t)$ instead of $\tilde{\theta}(t, T_1, T_2)$ and $\tilde{\sigma}(t, T_1, T_2)$, respectively. For an admissible control $\pi(t)$ and $\tilde{\sigma}$ as defined in (7) the Itô integral is well defined. Based on the definition the wealth process also depends on the portfolio strategy π. Due to the boundedness of π, the wealth process $Y^\pi(t)$ has a unique t-continuous solution (see for details Ebbeler, 2012).

In order to maximize the expected utility of the investor based on the chosen (exponential) utility function, the stochastic control problem has to be solved:

$$\sup_{\pi(t)\in\mathcal{A}} \mathbb{E}[U(Y^\pi(T_1))|Y(t) = y]$$
$$= \sup_{\pi(t)\in\mathcal{A}} \mathbb{E}[1 - \exp(-\gamma Y^\pi(T_1))|Y(t) = y]$$

which is analog to

$$\Phi(t,y) := \sup_{\pi(t)\in\mathcal{A}} \mathbb{E}[-\exp(-\gamma Y^\pi(T_1))|Y(t)=y]$$
$$= \sup_{\pi(t)\in\mathcal{A}} \mathbb{E}[\tilde{U}(Y^\pi(T_1))|Y(t)=y] \quad (14)$$

with the reduced utility function $\tilde{U}: y \mapsto -\exp\{-\gamma y\}$.

3.2.1 Hamilton-Jacobi-Bellman Equations and the Verification Theorem

We use the HJB (see Øksendal, 1998, Ch.11) to solve the stochastic control problem (14). For all functions $\phi(t,y) \in C^{2,2}([0,T]\times\mathbb{R})$ and $\pi \in \mathcal{A}$ we introduce the functional operator

$$(L^\pi\phi)(t,y) = (\pi(t)\tilde{\theta}(t) + ry)\phi_y(t,y) + \frac{1}{2}\pi^2(t)\tilde{\sigma}^2(t)\phi_{yy}(t,y).$$

Then the HJB equation for the wealth process $Y^\pi(t)$ is given by

$$\Phi_t(t,y) + \sup_\pi\{(L^\pi\Phi)(t,y)\} = 0 \quad (15)$$

for all $t \in [0,T_1]$ and $y \in \mathbb{R}$, with terminal condition

$$\Phi(T_1,y) = -\exp(-\gamma y) = \tilde{U}(y) \text{ for all } y \in \mathbb{R}. \quad (16)$$

where $\phi_t, \phi_y, \phi_{yy}$ denote the partial derivatives of the function ϕ with respect to t, resp. y.

In order to ensure that the solutions obtained are the solutions to the optimal control problem in (14) we state the following HJB verification theorem (see Øksendal, 1998, Ch. 11; Benth et al., 2003).

Theorem 6 (Verification Theorem I) *Let $\phi(t,y) \in C^2([0,T_1]\times\mathbb{R})$ be a solution of the HJB equation* (15) *with terminal condition* (16). *Assume that*

$$\int_0^{T_1} \mathbb{E}[\pi^2(s)\tilde{\sigma}^2(s)\phi_y^2(s,Y(s))]ds < \infty$$

for all admissible controls $\pi(t) \in \mathcal{A}$.

Then $\phi(t,y) \geq \Phi(t,y)$ for all $(t,y) \in [0,T_1]\times\mathbb{R}$.

Moreover, if π^* is a maximizer of the HJB equation (15) *and π^* is an admissible trading strategy, then*

$$\phi(t,y) = \Phi(t,y) \text{ for all } (t,y) \in [0,T_1]\times\mathbb{R}$$

and π^* is an optimal trading strategy.

Proof: Using Itô's formula for ϕ and the fact that ϕ is a solution of the HJB equation (15) proves that $\phi(t, y) \geq \Phi(t, y)$. If π^* is a maximizer of (15) then $\phi \leq \Phi$, which shows the equality.

3.2.2 Reduction of HJB Equation

Let us assume that $\Phi_{yy} < 0$. Then the mapping $\pi \mapsto (\pi\tilde{\theta}(t) + ry)\Phi_y(t, y) + \frac{1}{2}\pi^2\tilde{\sigma}^2(t)\Phi_{yy}(t, y)$ is concave and so $\pi^* \in (-K, K)$. ($K > 0$ can always be chosen such that the function lies inside the interval.) The first-order condition for an optimal control policy is found by differentiating the HJB equation with respect to π which leads to

$$\Phi_y(t, y)\tilde{\theta}(t) + \pi\tilde{\sigma}^2(t)\Phi_{yy}(t, y) = 0$$

which implies that the maximizer is given by

$$\pi^*(t, y) = -\frac{\tilde{\theta}(t)\Phi_y(t, y)}{\tilde{\sigma}^2(t)\Phi_{yy}(t, y)}.$$

Inserting the optimal control π^* into (15) gives the nonlinear partial differential equation

$$\Phi_t(t, y) + ry\Phi_y(t, y) - \frac{1}{2}\frac{\tilde{\theta}^2(t)\Phi_y^2(t, y)}{\tilde{\sigma}^2(t)\Phi_{yy}(t, y)} = 0. \qquad (17)$$

We try to find a solution of the value function of the form

$$\Phi(t, y) = h(t)\exp\{-\gamma g(t)y\}$$

with suitable functions h, g (i.e., we assume $h(t) \neq 0$). Inserting into the partial differential equations of Φ solutions for g and h are given by

$$g(t) = \exp\{r(T_1 - t)\} \quad \text{and} \quad h(t) = -\exp\left\{-\int_t^{T_1} \frac{1}{2}\frac{\tilde{\theta}^2(s)}{\tilde{\sigma}^2(s)}ds\right\}.$$

Summing up all the results we obtain that the value function Φ is given by

$$\Phi(t, y) = -\exp\{-\int_{T_1}^{T_2} \frac{1}{2}\frac{\tilde{\theta}^2(s)}{\tilde{\sigma}^2(s)}ds - \gamma e^{r(T_1-t)}y\}$$

and the optimal trading strategy π^*:

$$\pi^* = \frac{\tilde{\theta}(t)e^{-r(T_1-t)}}{\tilde{\sigma}^2(t)\gamma}.$$

Clearly, it is possible to chose K such that the optimal strategy lies within the interval $(-K, K)$.

Before we state the final theorem that proves the existence and uniqueness of the solution to the HJB equation and the optimal control strategy we state an important characteristic of the value function that is used in the proof of the existence and uniqueness theorem.

Proposition 7 *Let $Y^\pi(t)$ be the wealth process as described in (13) and π be an admissible and deterministic trading strategy i. e. the strategy only depends on the time t.*

Consider the following stochastic process $Z(t) = \exp\{-\gamma e^{r(T_1-t)} Y^\pi(t)\}$. Then (see Benth et al., 2003)

$$\mathbb{E}[|Z(t)|^m] < \infty \quad \forall t \in [0, T_1] \quad m \geq 2.$$

Proof: For the proof see Ebbeler (2012).

Proposition 7 shows that due to the Lipschitz and bounding conditions of volatility and drift term the exponential of the wealth process possesses finite moments. This fact will be used in the following theorem, which shows that the value function obtained is unique and optimal.

Theorem 8 (Existence and Uniqueness) *Let the wealth process $Y^\pi(t)$ be given by (11) and let (15) be the corresponding HJB equation with terminal condition (16). Then the optimal control is given by*

$$\pi^*(t) = \frac{\tilde{\theta}(t)}{\gamma \tilde{\sigma}^2(t)} e^{-r(T_1-t)}. \tag{18}$$

Moreover the solution of the HJB equation is given by

$$\Phi(t, y) = -\exp\left\{-\frac{1}{2}\int_t^{T_1} \frac{\tilde{\theta}(s)}{\tilde{\sigma}(s)} ds - \gamma e^{r(T_1-t)} y\right\}. \tag{19}$$

Proof: The control π^* is independent of y and deterministic. Additionally, for $K \in \mathbb{R}_+$ large we have $\pi^* \in [-K, K]$ and so we obtain that $\pi^* \in \mathcal{A}$. Obviously, $\Phi \in C^2([0, T_1] \times \mathbb{R})$ and a solution to the HJB equation. Furthermore, the process $Y^\pi(t)$ has a unique and continuous solution with $\mathbb{E}[\int_0^{T_1} |Y^\pi(t)|^2 dt] < \infty$ for all $\pi \in \mathcal{A}$. Additionally, Prop. 7 shows that $Z(t) = \exp\{-\gamma e^{r(T_1-t)} Y^\pi(t)\}$ possesses finite moments i.e. $\mathbb{E}[\int_0^{T_1} |Z(t)|^2 dt] < \infty$. As $\tilde{\theta}$ and $\tilde{\sigma}$ are bounded functions, $\int_0^{T_1} (\int_t^{T_1} \frac{\tilde{\theta}(s)}{\tilde{\sigma}(s)} ds)^2 \, dt < \infty$ and therefore

$$\Phi_y(t, Y(t)) = \gamma e^{r(T_1-t)} \exp\{-\frac{1}{2}\int_t^{T_1} \frac{\tilde{\theta}(s)}{\tilde{\sigma}(s)} ds\} Z(t)$$

is square-integrable. Consequently

$$\int_0^{T_1} \mathbb{E}[\pi^2(t)\tilde{\sigma}^2(t)\Phi_y^2(t, Y(t))] dt < \infty.$$

Hence the requirements of the verification theorem 6 are fulfilled, which concludes the proof.

Remark 9 *The optimal portfolio strategy π^* is independent of the wealth process but changes over time. Plugging in the formula for $\tilde{\theta}(t) = -\theta\tilde{\sigma}(t)$ leads to*

$$\pi^*(t) = \frac{-\theta}{\gamma\tilde{\sigma}(t)} e^{-r(T_1-t)}$$

which presents the optimal control as a linear function in the market-price-of-risk θ.

3.3 Futures Portfolio Optimization Extended by CAT Futures

Let us suppose that the futures portfolio is extended with a long position in a CAT futures, and $G(t)$ denotes the CAT futures price with time period $[T_1, T_2]$. From the temperature model in Equation (1), the index amount $I(T_1, T_2)$ the buyer receives is given by

$$I(T_1, T_2) = \int_{T_1}^{T_2} T(s) ds = \int_{T_1}^{T_2} \Lambda(s) + e_1^\top \mathbf{X}(s) ds.$$

Considering Equation (13) the following value function is optimized over the set of admissible trading strategies $\pi \in \mathcal{A}$:

$$\Gamma_p(t) = \sup_{\pi \in \mathcal{A}} \mathbb{E}\Big[-\exp\{-\gamma(Y^\pi(T_1) - e^{-r(T_2-T_1)}(G(t) \\ - \int_{T_1}^{T_2} \Lambda(s) + e_1^\top \mathbf{X}(s) ds))\} | \mathcal{F}_t\Big]$$

$$= \exp\left\{-\gamma e^{-r(T_2-T_1)} \int_{T_1}^{T_2} \Lambda(s)ds\right\} \tilde{\Gamma}^p(t)$$

with

$$\tilde{\Gamma}^p(t) = \sup_{\pi \in \mathcal{A}} \mathbb{E}\Big[-\exp\{-\gamma(Y^\pi(T_1) - e^{-r(T_2-T_1)}(G(t)$$

$$-\int_{T_1}^{T_2} e_1^\top \mathbf{X}(s)ds))\}|\mathcal{F}_t\Big]$$

where we use the superscript p in order to highlight that we are dealing with a p-dimensional case. Using the solution of $\mathbf{X}(t)$ for a fixed T_1 we obtain

$$\int_{T_1}^{T_2} e_1^\top \mathbf{X}(s)ds = \bar{A}(T_2 - T_1)\mathbf{X}(T_1) + \eta \int_{T_1}^{T_2} \bar{A}(T_2 - u)e_p \, dW^{\text{temp}}(u)$$

where $\bar{A}: \mathbb{R} \mapsto \mathbb{R}^{1 \times p}$ is defined as $\bar{A}(u) = e_1^\top[A^{-1}(\exp\{Au\} - I_p)]$ and I_p denotes the identity matrix of $\mathbb{R}^{p \times p}$. Using double conditioning and the fact that the stochastic integral is independent of $\mathcal{F}_{T_1}$ the value function can be rewritten as

$$\tilde{\Gamma}^p(t) = \sup_{\pi \in \mathcal{A}} \mathbb{E}\Big[\mathbb{E}\big[-\exp\{-\gamma(Y^\pi(T_1) - e^{-r(T_2-T_1)}(G(t)$$

$$-\bar{A}(T_2 - T_1)\mathbf{X}(T_1)$$

$$-\eta \int_{T_1}^{T_2} \bar{A}(T_2 - u)e_p \, dW^{\text{temp}}(u)))\}|\mathcal{F}_{T_1}\big]|\mathcal{F}_t\Big]$$

$$= \exp\{\frac{1}{2}\gamma^2 e^{-2r(T_2-T_1)}\eta^2 \int_{T_1}^{T_2} (\bar{A}(T_2-s)e_p)^2 ds\} \bar{\Gamma}^p(t)$$

with

$$\bar{\Gamma}^p(t) = \sup_{\pi \in \mathcal{A}} \mathbb{E}\Big[-\exp\{-\gamma(Y^\pi(T_1) - e^{-r(T_2-T_1)}(G(t)$$

$$-\bar{A}(T_2 - T_1)\mathbf{X}(T_1)))\}|\mathcal{F}_t\Big].$$

The CAT futures price $G(t)$ is based on information up to time t and therefore adapted to $\mathcal{F}_t$. Consequently, the term $G(t)$ can be factored out of the expectation and hence

$$\bar{\Gamma}^p(t) = \exp\{\gamma e^{-r(T_2-T_1)} G(t)\} \, \Psi^p(t,x,y)$$

where

$$\Psi^p(t,x,y) = \sup_{\pi \in \mathcal{A}} \mathbb{E}\Big[- \exp\{-\gamma(Y^\pi(T_1)$$
$$+ e^{r(T_2-T_1)} \bar{A}(T_2 - T_1)\mathbf{X}(T_1))\} | \mathbf{X}(t) = x, Y(t) = y\Big]. \quad (20)$$

Note that the last part of the value function $\bar{A}(T_2 - T_1)\mathbf{X}(T_1)$ can be seen as a sum of the components of $\mathbf{X}(t)$ (i.e., $\bar{A}(T_2 - T_1)\mathbf{X}(T_1) = \sum_{k=1}^{p} \bar{A}_i \mathbf{X}_i(T_1)$ where the ith subscripts denote the ith component of the vector).

It is sufficient to optimize the value function Ψ^p (20).

3.4 Reduction of the HJB Equation

Again the optimal trading strategy π^* is bounded (i.e., $\pi^* \in [-K, K]$) in order to avoid an optimization, which goes to infinity. Note that the vector $y \in \mathbb{R}$ whereas x is p-dimensional with components $x_1, x_2, \ldots, x_p$. The gradient of the function Ψ^p with respect to the vector x is denoted by $\nabla_x \Psi = (\frac{\partial \Psi}{\partial x_1}, \ldots, \frac{\partial \Psi}{\partial x_p})^\top$ and Ψ_{x_i} denotes the partial derivative of Ψ with respect to x_i. Let the value function Ψ^p be given as above, then the HJB equation is defined as

$$\Psi_t^p + \sup_{\pi \in \mathcal{A}} \left\{ (\pi \tilde{\theta}(t) + ry)\Psi_y^p + \frac{1}{2}\pi^2 \tilde{\sigma}^2(t)\Psi_{yy}^p + \pi \tilde{\sigma}(t)\eta \rho \Psi_{yx_p}^p \right\}$$
$$+ \sum_{i=1}^{p-1} x_{i+1} \Psi_{x_i}^p + \sum_{i=1}^{p} -a_i x_{p-i+1} \Psi_{x_p} + \frac{1}{2}\eta^2 \Psi_{x_p x_p}^p = 0$$

or using the vector notation

$$\Psi_t^p + \sup_{\pi \in \mathcal{A}} \left\{ (\pi \tilde{\theta}(t) + ry)\Psi_y^p + \frac{1}{2}\pi^2 \tilde{\sigma}^2(t)\Psi_{yy}^p + \pi \tilde{\sigma}(t)\eta \rho \Psi_{yx_p}^p \right\}$$
$$+ (Ax)^\top \nabla_x \Psi^p + \frac{1}{2}\eta^2 \Psi_{x_p x_p}^p = 0. \quad (21)$$

The terminal condition for $t = T_1$ is given by

$$\Psi^p(T_1, x, y) = -\exp\{-\gamma(y + e^{-r(T_2-T_1)}\bar{A}(T_2 - T_1)x)\}. \quad (22)$$

Theorem 10 (Verification Theorem II) *Let $\psi^p(t,x,y) \in C^2([0,T_1] \times \mathbb{R}^p \times \mathbb{R})$ be a solution of the HJB Equation (21) with terminal condition (22). Assume that*

$$\int_0^{T_1} \mathbb{E}[\pi^2(s)\tilde{\sigma}^2(s)\big(\psi_y^p(s,\mathbf{X}(s),Y^\pi(s))\big)^2] ds < \infty$$

$$\int_0^{T_1} \mathbb{E}[\eta^2 \big(\psi_{x_p}^p(s,\mathbf{X}(s),Y^\pi(s))\big)^2] ds < \infty$$

for all admissible controls $\pi(t) \in \mathcal{A}$.

Then $\psi^p(t,x,y) \geq \Psi^p(t,x,y)$ for all $(t,x,y) \in [0,T_1] \times \mathbb{R}^p \times \mathbb{R}$. Moreover, if π^* is a maximizer of the HJB equation (21) and π^* is an admissible trading strategy, then

$$\psi^p(t,x,y) = \Psi^p(t,x,y) \text{ for all } (t,x,y) \in [0,T_1] \times \mathbb{R}^p \times \mathbb{R}^2$$

and π^* is an optimal trading strategy.

Proof: The proof is analogous to the proof of 6.

If $\Psi_{yy}^p < 0$ the mapping $\pi \mapsto (\pi\tilde{\theta}(t) + ry)\Psi_y^p + \frac{1}{2}\pi^2\tilde{\sigma}^2(t)\Psi_{yy}^p + \pi\tilde{\sigma}(t)\eta\rho\Psi_{yx_p}^p$ is concave and hence the optimal trading strategy π^* lies in the open interval $(-K,K)$. The first-order condition for the optimality is given by

$$\pi^*(t,x,y) = -\frac{\tilde{\theta}(t)\Psi_y^p + \tilde{\sigma}(t)\eta\rho\Psi_{yx_p}^p}{\tilde{\sigma}^2(t)\Psi_{yy}^p}.$$

Inserting the optimal portfolio strategy π^* into the HJB equation (21) and simplifying the expression leads to the following equation:

$$\Psi_t^p - \frac{\tilde{\theta}^2(t)(\Psi_y^p)^2}{\tilde{\sigma}^2(t)\Psi_{yy}^p} - \frac{\tilde{\theta}(t)\eta\rho\Psi_{yx_p}^p\Psi_y^p}{\tilde{\sigma}(t)\Psi_{yy}^p}$$

$$+ ry\Psi_y^p + \frac{1}{2}\frac{(\tilde{\theta}(t)\Psi_y^p + \tilde{\sigma}(t)\rho\eta\Psi_{yx_p}^p)^2}{\tilde{\sigma}^2(t)\Psi_{yy}^p} - \frac{\tilde{\theta}(t)\eta\rho}{\tilde{\sigma}(t)}\frac{\Psi_y^p\Psi_{yx_p}^p}{\Psi_{yy}^p}$$

$$- \frac{\eta^2\rho^2(\Psi_{yx_p}^p)^2}{\Psi_{yy}^p} + (Ax)^\top \nabla_x \Psi^p + \frac{1}{2}\eta^2 \Psi_{x_px_p}^p = 0. \quad (23)$$

Let $a(t), c(t)$ be suitable functions from $\mathbb{R} \mapsto \mathbb{R}$ and $b: \mathbb{R} \mapsto \mathbb{R}^p$ a p-dimensional function with components $b_i(t)$ $1 \leq i \leq p$. Then we try to identify a solution of the value function of the form

$$\Psi^p(t,x,y) = -\exp\{a(t) + c(t)y + (b(t))^\top x\}$$

$$= -\exp\{a(t) + c(t)y + \sum_{i=1}^{p} b_i(t)x_i\} \quad (24)$$

where $(b(t))^\top$ denotes the transpose of the function $b(t)$. If $b_p(t) = e_p^\top b(t)$ the pth component of $b(t)$ exists and is integrable then $a(t)$ and $c(t)$ possess unique solutions of the form

$$c(t) = -\gamma \exp\{r(T_1 - t)\} \quad (25)$$

$$a(t) = -\frac{1}{2}\int_t^{T_1}\left(\frac{\tilde{\theta}^2(s)}{\tilde{\sigma}^2(s)} - \eta^2 b_p^2(s)(1-\rho^2) + 2\frac{\tilde{\theta}(s)}{\tilde{\sigma}(s)}\eta\rho b_p(s)\right)ds. \quad (26)$$

Since the differentiation is with respect to the time t, the unique solution of $b(t)$ is given by

$$b(t) = e^{-(t-T_1)A^\top}b(T_1)$$

$$= -\gamma e^{-r(T_2-T_1)}(\bar{A}(T_2 - T_1)e^{-(t-T_1)A})^\top. \quad (27)$$

Summing up all the results above we can conclude that the function Ψ^p of the form

$$\Psi^p(t,x,y)$$

$$= -\exp\{-\gamma e^{r(T_1-t)}y - \gamma e^{-r(T_2-T_1)}\bar{A}(T_2-T_1)e^{-(t-T_1)A}x + a(t)\}$$

$$= \Phi(t,y)\exp\left\{-\gamma e^{-r(T_2-T_1)}\bar{A}(T_2-T_1)e^{-(t-T_1)A}x\right.$$

$$\left. + \frac{\eta^2(1-\rho^2)}{2}\int_t^{T_1}b_p^2(s)ds - \eta\rho\int_t^{T_1}\frac{\tilde{\theta}(s)}{\tilde{\sigma}(s)}b_p(s)ds\right\}$$

with $a(t)$ as defined above, solves the HJB Equation (21). The optimal trading strategy is given by

$$\pi^*(t,x,y) = \frac{\tilde{\theta}(t)}{\tilde{\sigma}^2(t)\gamma}e^{-r(T_1-t)} + \frac{\eta\rho}{\tilde{\sigma}(t)\gamma}e^{-r(T_1-t)}b_p(t)$$

$$= \pi_0^*(t) + \frac{\eta\rho}{\tilde{\sigma}(t)\gamma}e^{-r(T_1-t)}b_p(t)$$

Theorem 11 *Let the process $Y^\pi(t)$ and $\mathbf{X}(t)$ be defined as in Equation (13), respectively. (1), and let (21) be the corresponding HJB equation with terminal condition (22). Then the optimal control is given by*

$$\pi^*(t) = \frac{\tilde{\theta}(t)}{\tilde{\sigma}^2(t)\gamma} e^{-r(T_1-t)} + \frac{\eta\rho}{\tilde{\sigma}(t)\gamma} e^{-r(T_1-t)} b_p(t)$$

with $b_p(t)$ as defined in (27). Moreover, the solution of the HJB equation is given by

$$\Psi^p(t, \mathbf{X}(t), Y^{\pi^*}(t)) = -\exp\{-\gamma e^{r(T_1-t)} Y^{\pi^*}(t)$$
$$- \gamma e^{-r(T_2-T_1)} \bar{A}(T_2-T_1) e^{-(t-T_1)A} \mathbf{X}(t) + a(t)\}$$

with $a(t)$ as defined in (26).

Proof: The control π^* is independent of y and deterministic. Additionally, for $K \in \mathbb{R}_+$ large we have $\pi^* \in [-K, K]$ and so we obtain that $\pi^* \in \mathcal{A}$. Obviously, $\Psi \in C^2([0, T_1] \times \mathbb{R}^{p+1})$ and a solution to the HJB equation. In order to apply the verification theorem we need to show

(i) $\int_0^{T_1} \mathbb{E}[\pi^2(s)\tilde{\sigma}^2(s)(\psi_y^p(s, \mathbf{X}(s), Y^{\pi^*}(s)))^2] ds < \infty$

(ii) $\int_0^{T_1} \mathbb{E}[\eta^2(\psi_{x_p}^p(s, \mathbf{X}(s), Y^{\pi^*}(s)))^2] ds < \infty$

Observe that $\mathbf{X}_t = e^{A(t-T_1)}\mathbf{X}(T_1) + \int_{T_1}^t e^{A(t-u)} e_p \eta \, dW^{temp}(u)$ is normally distributed due to the stochastic integral and hence $\exp\{X(t)\}$ possesses finite moments. The rest of the proof is similar to the proof of Theorem 8.

The indifference price of a CAT futures can be derived by setting $\Phi(t, y) = \Gamma_p(t, x, y)$ and solving for the price $G(t)$. Observe that the optimized wealth process for the portfolio of electricity futures and CAT futures is

$$\Gamma_p(t, x, y) = \exp\left\{ -\gamma e^{-r(T_2-T_1)} \int_{T_1}^{T_2} \Lambda(s) ds + \frac{1}{2}\gamma^2 \eta^2 e^{-2r(T_2-T_1)} \right.$$

$$\left. \int_{T_1}^{T_2} (\bar{A}(T_2-s)e_p)^2 ds \right\}$$

$$\times \exp\{\gamma e^{-r(T_2-T_1)} G(t)\} \Psi^p(t, x, y).$$

Hence, the CAT price is given by

$$G(t) = \int_{T_1}^{T_2} \Lambda(s)ds - \frac{1}{2}\gamma e^{-r(T_2-T_1)}\eta^2 \int_{T_1}^{T_2} (\bar{A}(T_2-s)e_p)^2 ds$$

$$+ \frac{1}{\gamma} e^{r(T_2-T_1)} \ln\left(\frac{\Phi(t,y)}{\Psi^p(t,x,y)}\right).$$

Recall the fact that the function Ψ^p is a multiple of the function Φ:

$$\Psi^p(t,x,y) = \Phi(t,y) \exp\Big\{ -\gamma e^{-r(T_2-T_1)} \bar{A}(T_2-T_1) e^{-(t-T_1)A} x$$

$$+ \frac{\eta^2(1-\rho^2)}{2} \int_t^{T_1} b_p^2(s)ds - \eta\rho \int_t^{T_1} \frac{\tilde{\theta}(s)}{\tilde{\sigma}(s)} b_p(s)ds \Big\}.$$

Using $b_p(t) = e_p^\top b(t) = -\gamma e^{-r(T_2-T_1)} e_p^\top (e^{-(t-T_1)A})^\top \bar{A}(T_2-T_1)^\top$ the CAT price can be simplified further to

$$G(t) = \int_{T_1}^{T_2} \Lambda(s)ds + e_1^\top [A^{-1}(e^{A(T_2-t)} - e^{A(T_1-t)})]\mathbf{X}(t) \quad (28)$$

$$- \eta\rho \int_t^{T_1} \frac{\tilde{\theta}(s)}{\tilde{\sigma}(s)} e_p^\top e^{-A^\top(s-T_1)} ds \bar{A}(T_2-T_1)^\top$$

$$- \frac{1}{2}\gamma e^{-r(T_2-T_1)}\eta^2 \Big(\int_{T_1}^{T_2} (\bar{A}(T_2-s)e_p)^2 ds$$

$$+ (1-\rho^2) \int_t^{T_1} (e_p^\top e^{-A^\top(s-T_1)} \bar{A}(T_2-T_1)^\top)^2 ds\Big).$$

In view of Equation (28), the price of the CAT temperature futures at time t consists of four parts, the integral of the seasonal function over the measurement period, the stochastic price process of the deseasonalized temperature process $\mathbf{X}$ at time t, and two adjustment factors, which are driven by the market-price-of-risk of the electricity market and the volatility factor of the temperature dynamics, respectively. If we analyze the first two components of the CAT price more precisely and consider the results of Benth et al. (2007), we obtain that these two components describe the expected CAT temperature futures price. Therefore, Equation (28) can be rewritten as

$$G(t) = \mathbb{E}\left[\int_{T_1}^{T_2} T(s)\,ds \Big| \mathcal{F}_t\right] - \rho R_p^{\text{el}}(t, T_1, T_2) - \gamma R_p^{\text{temp}}(t, T_1, T_2)$$

where the risk premium for hedging in electricity futures R^{el} is defined as

$$R_p^{el}(t, T_1, T_2) = \eta \int_t^{T_1} \frac{\tilde{\theta}(s)}{\tilde{\sigma}(s)} e_p^\top e^{-A^\top(s-T_1)} ds \bar{A}(T_2 - T_1)^\top \tag{29}$$

and the risk premium from the risk aversion towards the trading of CAT futures R^{temp} is given by

$$R_p^{temp}(t, T_1, T_2) = \frac{1}{2}\eta^2 e^{-r(T_2-T_1)} \left(\int_{T_1}^{T_2} (\bar{A}(T_2 - s)e_p)^2 ds \right. \tag{30}$$

$$\left. + (1-\rho^2) \int_t^{T_1} (e_p^\top e^{-A^\top(s-T_1)} \bar{A}(T_2 - T_1)^\top)^2 ds \right). \tag{31}$$

Moreover, using Equation (8) the risk premium R^{el} can be simplified to

$$R_p^{el}(x, y, z) = \eta \theta e_p^\top [(A^\top)^{-1}(e^{-A^\top(t-T_1)} - I)]\bar{A}(T_2 - T_1)^\top$$

which shows that the risk premium is proportional to the market-price-of-risk. Furthermore, the premium is scaled by the "mean reversion coefficient" A of the temperature process, the time-to-measurement as well as the length of the measurement period. The sign of R_p^{el} mainly depends on the sign of θ as η is naturally positive. If θ is positive R_p^{el} is negative and vice versa. If the time-to-measurement converges to zero, that is, t goes to T_1, the risk premiums will converge to zero which is what we would expect, as the influence of the trade in electricity should vanish close to the start of the measurement period.

The risk premium R^{temp} depends on the volatility of the temperature and some averaging of the speed of mean reversion, discounted with the interest rate back to the start of the measurement period. R^{temp} is always positive due to the definition of $\bar{A}$ and the fact that $\rho \leq 1$ and consequently the risk premium contributes negatively to the CAT price. Furthermore, for t converging to T_1 the risk premium does not converge to zero but rather

$$\lim_{t \to T_1} R^{temp} = \frac{1}{2}\eta^2 e^{-r(T_2-T_1)} \int_{T_1}^{T_2} \bar{A}^2(T_2 - u) du.$$

This shows that, driven by the utility function, the price the investor is willing to pay for a CAT contract is below the risk neutral price of the CAT at the start of the measurement period (t close to T_1). Hence, the investor wants to have a discount for bearing the risk of the CAT futures.

Combine the two risk premia from above and define the overall risk premium R as

$$R(t, T_1, T_2) = -\rho R^{\text{el}}(t, T_1, T_2) - \gamma R^{\text{temp}}(t, T_1, T_2) \tag{32}$$

which describes the difference between the CAT price and the predicted payments of a long position in the CAT futures.

If ρ and θ are positive the first component R_ρ^{el} of R is negative and it will be a matter of relative size of the two terms if R is positive or not. This will depend on the length of the measurement period as well as the time-to-measurement. For $t = T_1$, that is, at the start of the measurement period, the overall risk premium is negative as the first component vanishes.

Consider the situation of no correlation between temperature and spot price, the CAT price $G(t)$ is different from the expected discounted payments of the futures. The risk premium reduces mainly to R_ρ^{temp}, which is due to the exponential nature of the utility function and nature of the aggregated temperatures over the measurement period.

For the case $p = 1$, the temperature process is driven by an OU process, the CAT price reduces to

$$\begin{aligned}
G(t) = & \int_{T_1}^{T_2} \Lambda^{\text{temp}}(s)ds + \frac{1}{\alpha}(e^{-\alpha(T_1-t)} - e^{-\alpha(T_2-t)})X(t) \\
& - \rho\eta\bar{\alpha}(T_2 - T_1) \int_t^{T_1} \frac{\tilde{\theta}(s)}{\tilde{\sigma}(s)} e^{-\alpha(T_1-s)} ds \\
& - \frac{1}{2}\gamma\eta^2 e^{-r(T_2-T_1)} \left(\frac{1}{2}\bar{\alpha}^2(T_2 - T_1)(1 - \rho^2)\bar{\alpha}(2(T_1 - t))\right. \\
& + \left. \int_{T_1}^{T_2} \bar{\alpha}^2(T_2 - u)du \right), \tag{33}
\end{aligned}$$

with the notation $\bar{\alpha}(u) = \frac{1}{\alpha}(1 - e^{-\alpha u})$.

3.5 Indifference Selling Price of CAT Futures

In a similar way a CAT futures price for the selling side can be derived. Analogous to the previous setting the optimization problem is extended by a short position in a CAT futures and given by

$$\Gamma_p^s(t) = \sup_{\pi \in \mathcal{A}} \mathbb{E}\big[-\exp\{-\gamma(Y^\pi(T_1) + e^{-r(T_2-T_1)}(G^s(t)$$
$$- I(T_1, T_2)))\}|\mathcal{F}_t\big] = \sup_{\pi \in \mathcal{A}} \mathbb{E}\big[-\exp\{-\gamma(Y^\pi(T_1)$$
$$+ e^{-r(T_2-T_1)}(G^s(t) - \int_{T_1}^{T_2} \Lambda(s) + e_1^\top \mathbf{X}(s)ds))\}|\mathcal{F}_t\big].$$

With a similar calculation as before the selling price of the CAT futures is given by

$$G^s(t) = \int_{T_1}^{T_2} \Lambda(s)ds + e_1^\top [A^{-1}(e^{A(T_2-t)} - e^{A(T_1-t)})]\mathbf{X}(t)$$
$$- \eta\rho \int_t^{T_1} \frac{\tilde{\theta}(s)}{\tilde{\sigma}(s)} e_p^\top e^{-A^\top(s-T_1)} ds \bar{A}(T_2-T_1)^\top$$
$$+ \frac{1}{2}\gamma e^{-r(T_2-T_1)}\eta^2 \bigg(\int_{T_1}^{T_2} (\bar{A}(T_2-s)e_p)^2 ds$$
$$+ (1-\rho^2)\int_t^{T_1} (e_p^\top e^{-A^\top(s-T_1)} \bar{A}(T_2-T_1)^\top)^2 ds\bigg)$$
$$= \mathbb{E}[\int_{T_1}^{T_2} T(s)ds|\mathcal{F}_t] - \rho R_p^{el} + \gamma R_p^{temp}.$$

4 Parameter Estimation and Correlation Analysis

4.1 Parameter Estimation of the Temperature Model

For the empirical analysis of temperature we select eight German cities (Munich, Stuttgart, Frankfurt, Essen, Leipzig, Berlin, Hannover, and Hamburg), which represent a comprehensive grid of the temperature landscape in Germany. Additionally to the eight time-series of temperature data, we also calculated an artificial Germany average temperature, which is the (unweighted) average temperature of the eight cities. In the following we will denote this time-series as Germany-Average or Germany. All temperature data are obtained from the Deutsche Wetterdienst (DWD).[2] For each weather station we use temperature data from January 1, 1993, to June 30, 2010. In order to have equally sized years we removed all data points of February 29, which leads to a total of 6386 data points except for Munich, for which we observe one missing value on January 20, 1999.

The best fit for the seasonal function Λ^{temp} to the data is obtained by the following form:

$$\Lambda^{temp}(t) = b_1 + b_2 t + b_3 \cos\left(\frac{2\pi}{365}(t-b_4)\right). \tag{34}$$

The parameters are obtained using the least-square estimation and are presented in Table 8.1 (for more details see Ebbeler, 2012).

Conducting the augmented Dickey-Fuller (ADF) and Kwiatkowski-Phillips-Schmidt-Shin (KPSS) test we observe that the remaining deseasonalized temperature data are stationary. Analyzing the autocorrelation function (ACF) and the partial autocorrelation function (PACF) of the deseasonalized temperatures conclude that an AR(p) process should be used. Using the Schwarz information criteria and the plots of the PACF an AR(3) model ist most suitable for the data, which is in line with the results of Härdle and Cabrera (2012). The results of the parameters and the related CAR parameters ($\alpha_1, \alpha_2, \alpha_3$) can be found in Table 8.2.

The remaining residuals are best modeled by a volatility function $\eta^2(t)$ which is based on a truncated Fourier series of the form

$$\eta^2(t) = c_1 + \sum_{k=1}^{K} c_{2k} \cos\left(\frac{2k\pi t}{365}\right) + c_{2k+1} \sin\left(\frac{2k\pi t}{365}\right). \tag{35}$$

For the different cities in Germany, we accept that the number of Fourier terms is different as the residuals show significant differences in the plots. In order to determine the appropriate length K of the Fourier series the parameters are estimated with different length $K = 1, 2, \ldots, T$. K is then chosen to be the maximum value for which all parameters c_{2k} and c_{2k+1} are significant at the 5% significance level, i.e. $K = \max\{J = 1, 2, \ldots | c_{2j}, c_{2j+1}$ are significant $\forall j \in \mathbb{N}$ and $j \leq J\}$. In the case, $K = 0$, the variance function is modeled by a constant $\eta^2(t) \equiv \eta^2$, which is given by the variance of the white noise term derived by the AR regression. This procedure is conservative regarding the number of parameters in the model as the model is reduced to the smallest number of Fourier Series terms, which contribute significantly to the variance function. The results are shown in Table 8.3 (for details see Ebbeler, 2012).

4.2 Parameter Estimation of the Electricity Model

Analyzing the EPEX spot prices we obtain the best fit for the seasonal function Λ as

$$\Lambda(t) = \beta_0 + \beta_1 \mathbf{1}_{\{t=\text{Sat,Sun}\}}$$
$$+ \beta_2 t + \beta_3 \cos\left(\frac{2\pi}{365}(t+\beta_4)\right) + \beta_5 \cos\left(\frac{6\pi}{365}(t+\beta_6)\right). \tag{36}$$

Table 8.1 Parameter estimation for the seasonal temperature function Λ^{temp} with the corresponding p-values in parentheses below

	Munich	Stuttgart	Frankfurt	Essen	Leipzig	Berlin	Hannover	Hamburg	Germany
b_1	8.827	9.724	10.730	10.395	9.478	9.746	9.428	9.255	9.698
	(<0.001)	(<0.001)	(<0.001)	(<0.001)	(<0.001)	(<0.001)	(<0.001)	(<0.001)	(<0.001)
b_2	6.00×10^{-05}	1.95×10^{-05}	5.35×10^{-05}	2.58×10^{-05}	7.52×10^{-05}	1.06×10^{-04}	1.14×10^{-04}	8.86×10^{-05}	6.77×10^{-05}
	(0.021)	(0.439)	(0.030)	(0.300)	(0.004)	(<0.001)	(<0.001)	(<0.001)	(0.004)
b_3	9.867	9.269	9.333	8.163	9.513	9.758	8.592	8.523	9.124
	(<0.001)	(<0.001)	(<0.001)	(<0.001)	(<0.001)	(<0.001)	(<0.001)	(<0.001)	(<0.001)
b_4	−167.598	−166.810	−167.420	−164.275	−165.523	−166.084	−163.893	−163.277	−165.691
	(<0.001)	(<0.001)	(<0.001)	(<0.001)	(<0.001)	(<0.001)	(<0.001)	(<0.001)	(<0.001)

Source: Own calculations.

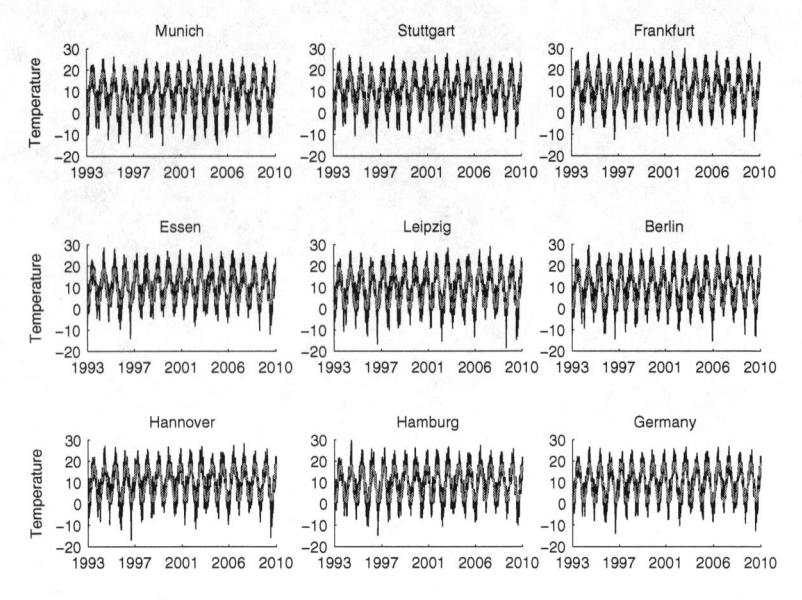

Figure 8.1 Daily average temperature (black solid line) and the estimated deterministic, seasonal function Λ^{temp} (dashed line).
Source: Own calculations based on DWD data.

In this function t is measured in days and **1** denotes the indicator function which is equal to one if t is Saturday or Sunday. This model accounts for the weekly pattern by using the dummy variable and hence creates different price levels for the weekend and the week. Furthermore, the two cosine functions account for the annual seasonality and the semi-annual peaks in the data. In order to receive stable parameter estimates, outliers are excluded from the parameter estimation. Data points that are above or below four standard deviations from the mean are defined as outliers. This leads to an exclusion of 16 data points which is less than 0.5 percent of the data sample. The parameters are estimated using the least-square regression.[3] The results of the parameters are shown in Table 8.4.

All parameters are significant at the 1 percent level except for the parameter β_6 which is significant at the 10 percent level (see Ebbeler, 2012 for more details). We also tested a seasonal function with a 4π cosine term, which is used in Benth et al. (2008a) but we obtained a better fit with the chosen function (36). The ADF test and the Phillips–Perron test show that the deseasonalized power prices are stationary time series.

For simplification, we further assume that the volatility is constant. Considering the unique solution of Equation (4) the parameters can be estimated using the procedures for AR processes.

Table 8.2 Parameter estimation for the autoregression coefficients a_1, a_2, a_3 with the corresponding p-values in parentheses below

	Munich	Stuttgart	Frankfurt	Essen	Leipzig	Berlin	Hannover	Hamburg
a_1	0.952	0.969	0.927	0.993	0.959	0.957	0.939	0.892
	(<0.001)	(<0.001)	(<0.001)	(<0.001)	(<0.001)	(<0.001)	(<0.001)	(<0.001)
a_2	−0.222	−0.241	−0.200	−0.297	−0.246	−0.230	−0.226	−0.183
	(<0.001)	(<0.001)	(<0.001)	(<0.001)	(<0.001)	(<0.001)	(<0.001)	(<0.001)
a_3	0.056	0.063	0.060	0.110	0.095	0.081	0.091	0.088
	(<0.001)	(<0.001)	(<0.001)	(<0.001)	(<0.001)	(<0.001)	(<0.001)	(<0.001)
α_1	2.048	2.031	2.073	2.007	2.041	2.043	2.061	2.108
α_2	1.318	1.303	1.346	1.311	1.327	1.316	1.348	1.400
α_3	0.214	0.209	0.213	0.194	0.191	0.192	0.196	0.204
λ_1	−0.244	−0.239	−0.232	−0.207	−0.199	−0.205	−0.201	−0.200
$\lambda_{2,3}$	−0.902	−0.896	−0.920	−0.900	−0.921	−0.919	−0.930	−0.954
	±0.254i	±0.268i	±0.267i	±0.358i	±0.335i	±0.309i	±0.330i	±0.328i

Note: CAR parameter estimates $\alpha_1, \alpha_2, \alpha_3$ and the corresponding eigenvalues $\lambda_1, \lambda_2, \lambda_3$ of the coefficient matrix A.
Source: Own calculations.

Table 8.3 Parameter estimation of the variance function $\eta^2(t)$ with the corresponding p-values in parentheses below

	Munich	Stuttgart	Frankfurt	Essen	Leipzig	Berlin	Hannover	Hamburg
c_1	4.955	4.543	4.561	4.246	4.779	4.633	4.691	4.606
	(<0.001)	(<0.001)	(<0.001)	(<0.001)	(<0.001)	(<0.001)	(<0.001)	(<0.001)
c_2	1.465	1.041	0.830		0.530	0.383	0.764	0.491
	(<0.001)	(<0.001)	(0.030)		(<0.001)	(0.002)	(<0.001)	(<0.001)
c_3	0.498	0.322	0.361		0.566	0.700	0.401	0.561
	(<0.001)	(0.011)	(0.003)		(<0.001)	(<0.001)	(0.001)	(<0.001)
c_4						0.572		0.721
						(<0.001)		(<0.001)
c_5						−0.304		−0.236
						(0.015)		(0.036)
K	1	1	1	0	1	2	1	2

Note: The number of truncated Fourier Series terms K is given in the last line.
Source: Own calculations.

Table 8.4 Results of the parameter estimation of the seasonal function for arithmetic spot price model and the corresponding p-values in parentheses below

β_0	β_1	β_2	β_3	β_4	β_5	β_6
21.386	−12.985	0.010	3.474	41.118	−2.116	6.068
(<0.001)	(<0.001)	(<0.001)	(<0.001)	(<0.001)	(<0.001)	(0.042)

Source: Own calculations.

Table 8.5 Results of the parameter estimation for the mean reversion and volatility of the spot price model

κ	σ
0.323	13.127

Source: Own calculations.

In order to estimate the market-price-of-risk parameter θ we use the approach proposed by Cartea and Figueroa (2005) based on monthly electricity contracts (EEX baseload contracts) for the time period 2006–2009 under the assumption of a constant volatility σ. The resulting market-price-of-risk for the indifference pricing approach is calculated as the average of each monthly θ_i (see Ebbeler, 2012). For the observed time period we obtain a market-price-of-risk of $\theta = 0.233$, which we will use later in the indifference pricing valuation.

4.3 Correlation Analysis between Temperature and Electricity Spot Price

Many papers have analyzed the relationship between temperatures and the electricity demand in different countries. Peirson and Henley (1994) analyze the effect of temperature on load in Great Britain. They observe that the influence of temperature on load is statistical significant irrespective if the model considers autocorrelation or not. Similarly Pardo et al. (2002) analyze the influence of temperature and seasonality on the load in Spain and observe that both parameters are significant. Weron (2006) uses a slightly different approach to analyze the dependency between temperature and electricity load in California. In his study, he calculates the Pearson correlation coefficient between the load and the temperature in California for the years 1999–2002. The results show that the correlation between temperature and load is significant and the correlation coefficient is even higher if the weekly pattern in the load series is considered.

While all the papers mentioned above analyze the relation between air temperature and system load, explaining the relation to the demand side of the electricity price evaluation, a different approach is used by Lucia and Torró (2005). They analyze, among other weather variables, the influence of air temperature to the electricity spot price at NordPool. This approach differs in the way that going from the system load to the price traded at an exchange can change the dependency structure, since known demand patterns might be considered in the capacity forecast and hence have no effect on the spot price. They calculate the correlation between the average of the 168 hourly spot system prices and the maximum of the difference between the heating degree of the week and its historical average and 0. The results show a correlation of about 40 percent, showing that significant abnormal cold weather waves (over at least one week or more) have an impact on the average spot price in Norway. Similar results are also observed by Weron and Misiorek (2008) for four 5-week periods between the hourly log-price at NordPool and the hourly air temperature.

The approach that is chosen here differs significantly from all other approaches. For the correlation analysis between temperature and spot price we define for each time series an appropriate stochastic model and analyze the correlation between the stochastic components of both time series and not between the price and the temperature itself. In this way, we can exclude that the correlation is affected by the deterministic and a priori known temperature and spot price movements within a year. The fact that the air temperature is lower in Germany in the winter months compared to summer is obvious and therefore already priced-in the spot price, which generally has higher prices in winter compared to summer. Consequently, analyzing the temperature and the spot price directly without removing the deterministic part leads to a correlation effect, which is only caused by the general effect of colder temperature and higher spot prices in winter. From our point of view, such a correlation effect is not adequate to decide if electricity contracts can be used to price weather derivatives. Moreover, utility companies usually set up a capacity plan for their production facilities in advance, which should cover the expected electricity demand. This plan is especially important for the nuclear and older coal plants. Short-term changes in the demand are mostly covered by gas turbine plants or similar plants, which are more flexible in the capacity loads. The drawback of this flexibility lies in the higher running costs of these plants. As a consequence we could expect that deviations from the expected level, for example caused by unexpected temperatures, lead to price movements at the spot price (away from the expected spot price). Due to these reasons we estimate the deterministic components of the temperature time series and the spot price time series. After removing the seasonal component from the data, the obtained time series show the deviations of the temperature and the spot price from the expected values. Based on these data, the correlation between the stochastic processes driving the time series can be analyzed. In the given situation, this means that the effect of deviations of the daily average temperatures in Germany on the spot price traded at the EPEX is analyzed.

The following correlation analysis is split into two parts. The first part deals with the correlation between the deseasonalized daily average temperatures and the deseasonalized spot prices in winter whereas the second part analyzes the correlation effect in the summer months.

In order to avoid that negative correlation effects of the winter months are counterbalanced by positive correlation effects in the summer, the correlation is calculated separately for winter and summer. Additionally, the analysis of the correlation is conducted for each year separately in order to gain further insights about the development of the correlation over time.

4.3.1 Correlation Analysis: Winter

As the primary reason for additional energy consumption in winter months is heating, the analysis concentrates on the heating period in Germany. For most parts of Germany, the heating period starts in November and goes until end of February or mid March. Consequently, the considered time period in the winter is from November 1 until February 28 of the following year. If we also included March in the analysis, the results change only marginally. The Pearson and the Spearman correlation coefficient are calculated for each year separately, that is, we calculate the correlation for the time period 2009/11/01–2010/02/28 and 2008/11/01–2009/02/28, etc. separately. As during the Christmas break (December 24–January 1), many industry companies shut down their production, the energy demand differs significantly from the usual demand level. This often leads to very unusual spot prices at the EPEX. In order to ensure that the measured correlation effects are not driven by these effects we excluded the Christmas break from our data set for each year. As a consequence, the sample for each year consists of 111 data points, which is an adequate sample size for the calculations and to obtain reliable results.

For the calculations, the deseasonalized German average temperature is used, which is the average of the daily average temperatures of all eight cities. On the other side, we used the deseasonalized arithmetic spot price in Equation (4) as well as the log-price (the geometric model). In the correlation analysis the temperature of a specific day is compared to the EPEX spot price of the same day. In general the temperature forecasts for Germany are very precise for the next 24 hours with only an error rate of less than a few percent. Therefore the comparison of the real temperatures measured on day t and the spot price on the same day does not possess a strong bias although the spot price for day t is already determined on the day before.

The results of the correlation analysis for the winter periods can be seen in Table 8.6. We obtain correlation coefficients for both models that are all significant at the 2 percent level. Most of them are even significant at the 0 percent level. Concentrating on the arithmetic case the Pearson correlations mainly are between 31 percent and 57 percent with a very high correlation in the period 2004–2005 and 2009–2010. On the other hand, the lowest correlation coefficient is calculated for the period 2008/2009, which is probably due to the financial crisis and the uncertainty in the commodity markets. The deviations between the Spearman and the Pearson coefficient can, in large, be explained by two effects. Firstly (especially in 2001–2002 and 2002–2003) the dependence structure between temperature and spot price is not linear but rather quadratic; secondly in 2007–2008 the introduction of the CO_2 emissions certificates led to some

Table 8.6 Results of the correlation analysis for the winter period 11/01–02/28 excluding the Christmas break

Timeframe	Arithmetic Model		Geometric Model	
	Pearson r	Spearman ρ	Pearson r	Spearman ρ
2009/11/01–2010/02/28	−73.46%	−73.67%	−69.80%	−69.38%
	(0.00)	(0.00)	(0.00)	(0.00)
2008/11/01–2009/02/28	−25.89%	−22.76%	−28.30%	−23.35%
	(0.01)	(0.02)	(0.00)	(0.01)
2007/11/01–2008/02/28	−35.43%	−28.84%	−30.36%	−30.64%
	(0.00)	(0.00)	(0.00)	(0.00)
2006/11/01–2007/02/28	−33.67%	−39.75%	−40.28%	−41.76%
	(0.00)	(0.00)	(0.00)	(0.00)
2005/11/01–2006/02/28	−39.51%	−38.40%	−49.64%	−47.13%
	(0.00)	(0.00)	(0.00)	(0.00)
2004/11/01–2005/02/28	−56.60%	−57.04%	−58.01%	−59.33%
	(0.00)	(0.00)	(0.00)	(0.00)
2003/11/01–2004/02/28	−33.18%	−24.78%	−36.86%	−30.02%
	(0.00)	(0.01)	(0.00)	(0.00)
2002/11/01–2003/02/28	−43.07%	−51.84%	−47.83%	−48.27%
	(0.00)	(0.00)	(0.00)	(0.00)
2001/11/01–2002/02/28	−31.54%	−68.94%	−57.17%	−73.29%
	(0.00)	(0.00)	(0.00)	(0.00)

Note: The results of the Pearson and Spearman coefficient for the arithmetic model are presented in columns 2 and 3 respectively with the p-values in parentheses below. The correlation results for the geometric model are stated in columns 4 and 5.
Source: Own calculations.

price movements in first days of 2008, which weakens the correlation coefficient.

The picture in the geometric case is slightly different. In general, both correlations are slightly higher compared to the arithmetic case for most years. Additionally, all coefficients are significant at the 1 percent level.

4.3.2 Correlation Analysis Summer

Similar to the correlation analysis of the winter, the correlation for the summer period is calculated for each year separately. The time period that is analyzed each year starts on June 1 and ends on August 31. Hence the sample of each year consists of 92 data points. We expect that, on warmer days, the electricity demand increases, which would lead to a positive correlation between temperature and spot price.

The Pearson correlation for the summer varies between 25 percent and 46 percent for the arithmetic case and between 25 percent and 58 percent in the geometric case (see Table 8.7). The years 2008 and 2009 show significantly lower correlation results for both models, which could be based on the financial crisis. The 2008 results in particular differ from the other

Table 8.7 Results of the correlation analysis for the summer period June 1–August 31 separately for each year

Timeframe	Arithmetic Model		Geometric Model	
	Pearson r	Spearman ρ	Pearson r	Spearman ρ
2009/06/01–2009/08/31	22.60%	25.33%	15.97%	21.49%
	(0.03)	(0.02)	(0.13)	(0.04)
2008/06/01-2008/08/31	17.26%	15.57%	13.82%	13.48%
	(0.10)	(0.14)	(0.19)	(0.20)
2007/06/01–2007/08/31	29.47%	35.29%	28.59%	31.47%
	(0.00)	(0.00)	(0.01)	(0.00)
2006/06/01–2006/08/31	46.44%	47.81%	58.29%	49.23%
	(0.00)	(0.00)	(0.00)	(0.00)
2005/06/01–2005/08/31	40.72%	40.07%	37.34%	36.69%
	(0.00)	(0.00)	(0.00)	(0.00)
2004/06/01-2004/08/31	31.11%	36.97%	37.65%	37.67%
	(0.00)	(0.00)	(0.00)	(0.00)
2003/06/01–2003/08/31	25.44%	32.83%	25.30%	27.46%
	(0.01)	(0.00)	(0.01)	(0.01)
2003/06/01–2003/08/31	27.52%	28.77%	29.10%	27.38%
	(0.01)	(0.01)	(0.00)	(0.01)

Note: The results of the Pearson and Spearman coefficient for the arithmetic model are presented in columns 2 and 3 respectively with the p-values in parentheses below. The correlation results for the geometric model are stated in columns 4 and 5.
Source: Own calculations.

results, which coincide with the peak of the financial crisis in the summer 2008 and therefore are probably caused by the high insecurity in the commodity markets. Excluding the years 2008 and 2009, all estimated Pearson correlation results are significant at the 1 percent level, confirming our assumption of the dependence structure.

Moreover, the results of the Spearman correlation coefficients are similar to the values of the Pearson correlation, clearly indicating that the dependence structure exists and is not driven by one-time effects or special effects in the different years.

The results of the correlation analysis for the winter and the summer period demonstrates that a correlation structure exists between the deseasonalized temperatures and the deseasonalized spot price in Germany. This effect is significant for most of the years (only excluding 2008). Additionally, the effect is independent of the chosen model for the electricity spot price. The correlation values indicate that the use of electricity-based derivatives are appropriate as an hedging instrument for weather derivatives. In comparison to the winter period, the correlation values are slightly smaller, supporting the hypothesis that the "air conditioning effect" in Germany has a smaller impact on the spot price compared to the "heating effect" in the winter.

5 Empirical Analysis of Indifference Prices

5.1 CAT Price Models

The empirical analysis is conducted for two scenarios of the temperature process, the OU process (which is a CAR process with $p = 1$) and a CAR process with $p = 3$, which is the result of the temperature analysis in Germany. Based on the derived CAT prices 33 and 28 and based on the derived parameter estimates CAT prices for Essen. Figures 8.2–8.4 show the results of the price models for the months May–September of 2010 and 2011. For each measurement month the CAT prices are calculated for at least the last three months before the start of the measurement period. The prices are compared to the CAT price of the corresponding month traded at the CME in Chicago (solid line).[4] In addition to the CME price shows the CAT of Essen for the corresponding measurement month and is calculated a posteriori, that is, the CAT is calculated at the end of the measurement period. This value represents the value that is chosen by the clearing house to balance the traded futures contracts.

The indifference CAT prices are very similar in all analyzed months. The prices are stable in the first part of the observation period. In this time period the prices are dominated by the seasonal function component

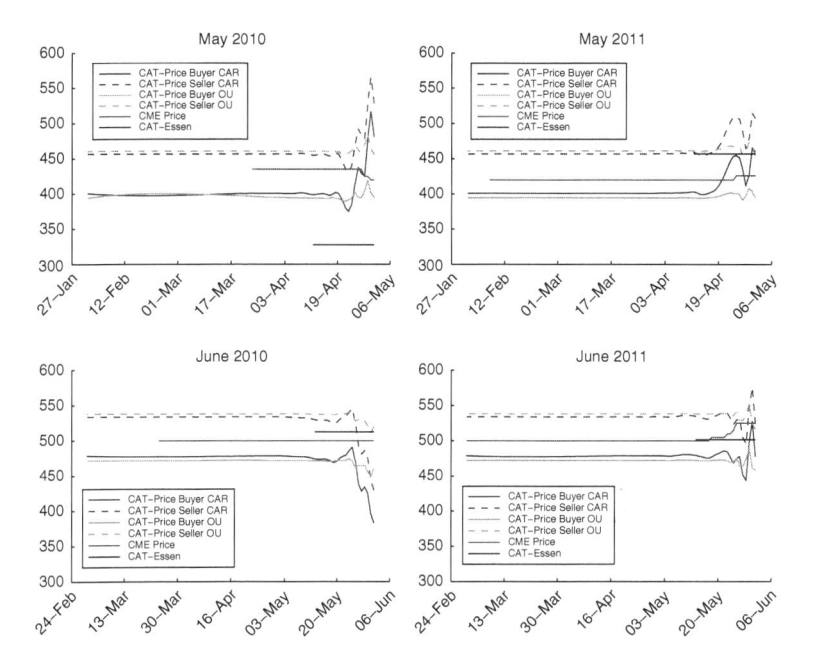

Figure 8.2 Comparison of the calculated CAT prices of the two analyzed models (OU model and CAR model) compared to the CAT prices traded at the CME and the observed CAT for Essen (a-posteriori) for May 2010 (left top), May 2011 (right top), June 2010 (left bottom), and June 2011 (right bottom) with parameters: $r = 3\%$, $\rho = 30\%$, $\theta = 0.23$ and $\gamma = 5.0\%$.
Source: Own calculations and Reuters data.

and the risk premium. Since the seasonal component is independent of t, this is a constant value throughout the observation period. The risk premium, on the other hand, is dependent in both models on t but due to the exponential function, variations are only detectable shortly before the measurement period. In both models we obtain that the selling price is higher compared to the buying price due to the different sign of R^{temp}, which is as expected due to the bid-ask spread. The differences in the price processes are based on the different values of the risk premiums, which is higher (in absolute values) in the OU model. In the last two weeks before the measurement, the behavior of the indifference prices changes from almost constant to more volatile behavior. This behavior is driven by two effects. First, the influence of the second component of the price equation, which depends on $X(t)$, increases. Depending on the values of the deseasonalized temperatures on the current day (OU model) and additionally the last two days in the CAR model ($p = 3$), this component adds a positive or negative shift to the price process. Second, the risk premium

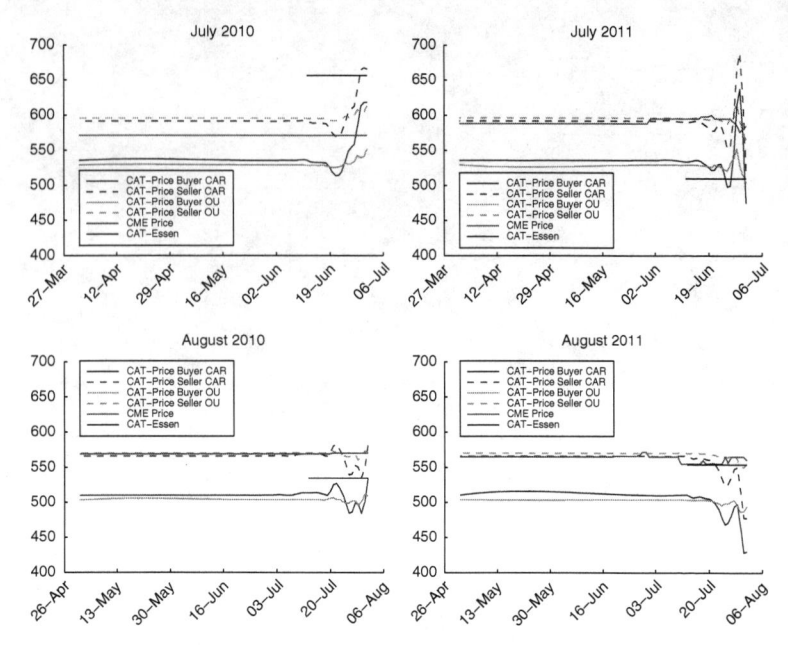

Figure 8.3 Comparison of the calculated CAT prices of the two analyzed models (OU model and CAR model) compared to the CAT prices traded at the CME and the observed CAT for Essen (a-posteriori) for July 2010 (left top), July 2011 (right top), August 2010 (left bottom) and August 2011 (right bottom) with parameters: $r = 3\%, \rho = 30\%, \theta = 0.23$ and $\gamma = 5.0\%$.
Source: Own calculations and Reuters data.

changes close to the measurement period as the R^{el} component converges to zero, reducing the risk premium to the negative component R^{temp}. Comparing the two price models it is observable that the CAR model is more volatile. The reason for this lies in the fact that the deseasonalized temperatures of three days are considered and taken into account as a weighted sum whereas in the other model only the temperature of one day is considered. Consequently, the CAR model possesses larger price movements in the last days before the start of the measurement period. Hence, in the OU model the derived prices are closer to the value of the seasonal component (the expected CAT based on the seasonal function). Consequently, this model can be seen as more conservative.

Analyzing the eight months under consideration, we observe that the indifference price models are adequate to price weather derivatives on the buyer and seller side. The derived mathematical price models possess a clear structure consisting of the expected CAT value (incl. a seasonal component) and a risk premium which only varies in the sign of the

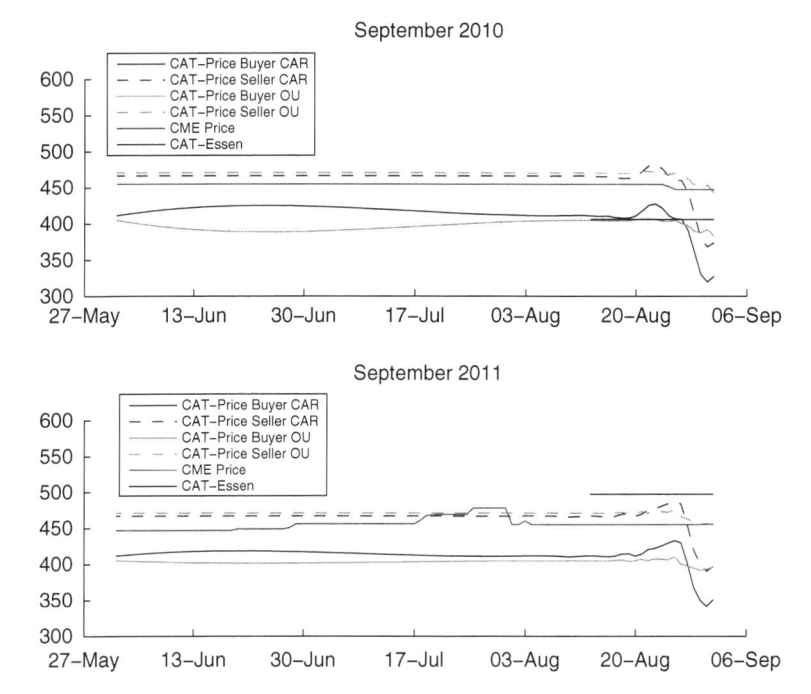

Figure 8.4 Comparison of the calculated CAT prices of the two analyzed models (OU model and CAR model), the CAT prices traded at the CME and the observed CAT for Essen (a-posteriori) for September 2010 and 2011 with parameters: $r = 3\%, \rho = 30\%, \theta = 0.23$ and $\gamma = 5.0\%$.

Source: Own calculations and Reuters data.

R^{temp} between the seller and buyer price. Due to this clear structure, all price models can be implemented without the use of Monte-Carlo simulations or other approximations. Furthermore, and more importantly, the obtained prices for Essen are in a similar price range compared to the traded CME prices as well as the real Essen CAT. This shows the adequacy of the derived models.

Considering all the analyzed months, it can be summarized that the buying prices for both models are mainly lower than the corresponding CME price. As a consequence, investors would try to find a counterparty at the OTC market rather than buying at the CME.

A similar picture is observable for the selling prices, which are higher compared to buying price due to the change in the sign of R^{temp}. For most of the observed months, the selling prices of both models (OU and CAR model) are higher compared to the CME price, which again leads to the situation where the investor sells the CAT OTC rather than at the CME.

A further characteristic of the presented price models can be seen, if the prices are compared to the real and a posteriori calculated Essen CAT values. Considering the derived CAT prices for the buyer of a contract, it can be obtained that the price models show a better prediction of the Essen CAT compared to the CME. In particular, the CAR(3) model shows an appropriate fit to the Essen CAT. In cases where the CAR(3) price differs from the CAT value, the buying price is below the Essen CAT, which implies a profit for the investor.

Based on the chosen approach it is also possible to derive an indication about the implied risk aversion of the current market participants. Using the proposed model, the best fit with the CME data is obtained with a small risk aversion coefficient γ (<1 percent), as a decrease in risk aversion leads to an upward shift of the prices in the buying models. However, even with a very small γ the CME price is still above the buying CAT prices of the models for most months. Hence, the above conclusions are still valid.

All the price models show the expected characteristic of temperature futures with an almost constant price at the beginning of the trading period and an increase in volatility close to the measurement period, the so called Samuelson effect (see also Benth et al., 2007). The selling prices of both models is clearly higher than the proposed buying prices, which display the typical bid-ask spread. Moreover, the observed CME price is in most cases between the selling and buying price, which would imply for investors using the indifference pricing approach and the assumed risk aversion that they would not trade at the exchange but go to the OTC market. Furthermore, the observed prices are appropriate for trading as the processes either predict the real CAT value quite well or produce a positive payoff in the case of deviations from the CAT value.[5]

6 Sensitivity Analysis of the Pricing Model

In the previous sections the derived CAT price models were analyzed based on estimations from market data (EPEX spot market, EEX futures market, and weather data). In order to show the robustness of the CAT price model sensitivity analyses for the risk aversion factor γ, the market-price-of-risk θ and the correlation factor ρ are conducted.

6.1 Risk Aversion Coefficient γ

The risk aversion coefficient γ describes the investor's caution to enter a risky investment compared to a certain cash flow. The larger γ, the higher the aversion of the investor to buy a risky asset and to prefer a riskless and certain investment. A value for γ close to zero consequently implies that the investor is more willing to accept a fair game. In the CAT price model, the risk aversion coefficient is introduced through the utility function of the investor which is assumed to be negatively exponential in our setting. In the derived CAT price model γ is part of the risk premium R and the leading coefficient of R^{temp}. As discussed before the two components of the risk premium possess different signs and therefore the interaction between these two components determines the structure of R. Therefore, the sensitivity analysis primarily focuses on the impact of different values for γ on the risk premium. The obtained structure of R is then transferred unchanged to the CAT price due to the linear structure of R in $G(t)$.

Figure 8.5 shows the risk premium for the values $\gamma = 0.1$ percent, $1, 2.5, 5, 7.5$ and 10 percent for the last 50 days before the start of the measurement period (T_1) of the CAT contract. The case $\gamma = 0.1$ percent describes the case in which the investor is almost risk neutral. In this case, the risk premium is positive and almost constant for the first days and decreases sharply to zero close to T_1. The positivity of R is caused by the fact that for small γ the influence of R^{temp} in the risk premium is only marginal, which contributes negatively to R. This described structure of R and especially the positive value of R implies that the investor is willing to pay an extra premium to enter the CAT futures contract. This

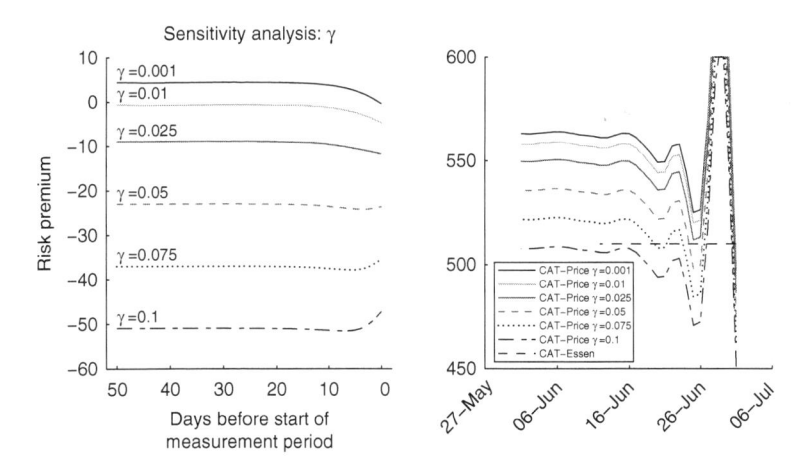

Figure 8.5 The results of the sensitivity analysis for the risk aversion coefficient parameter γ. The impact of different values for γ on the risk premium (R) (left) and the corresponding impact on the overall CAT price (right) exemplary for the CAT July 2011 contract.
Source: Own calculations.

willingness for the extra premium is mainly driven by the hedging effect of the electricity contracts considered in the model. Hence, for the investor, the advantages of the hedging effect dominates their own risk aversion. As in this setting we deal with an investor that is almost risk neutral, the additional hedging effect (additional information) through the futures contracts leads to a higher attractiveness for the CAT futures, which is usually displayed in an higher bid price, which coincides here with the observations in the sensitivity analysis and the CAT prices.

An increase in γ has two main effects. Firstly, the risk premium is vertically shifted in the direction of negative values of R (for the constant part) and secondly, the behavior close to T_1 changes. For values close to zero, the risk premium is decreasing in the last days whereas for larger values R firstly decreases slightly before it sharply increases in the last five days. The turning point for the last days can be observed for a value of $\gamma = 3.2$ percent in which R is almost constant. For $\gamma = 10$ percent the risk premium is around -50, which, in the context of the CAT contract, implies a reduction of more than $1.5°C$ per day in the measurement period in order to buy the contract. The increase in R in the last days before T_1 implies that the investor requires a smaller discount in order to buy the CAT. This is in line with the expectations. As the aversion should reduce as more information about the temperatures in the observation period are available, which is the case close to T_1. Hence, the structure of the risk premium R displays in an appropriate way the characteristic of both, a risk averse investor as well as a risk neutral investor.

6.2 Market Price of Risk θ

Note that this parameter represents the market-price-of-risk of the electricity market and not the market-price-of-risk of the weather derivatives market. The empirical analysis showed that the market-price-of-risk varies between the contracts and is mainly in the range between –0.5 and 0.5, which therefore also represents the analyzed value range in the following sensitivity analysis.

Figure 8.6 shows the structure of the risk premium R for different values of θ and depending on the last days before the start of the measurement period at T_1. A number of characteristics are observable. For the time period 15 days and more before T_1, R is linear increasing in θ.

6.3 Spot Temperature Correlation ρ

The correlation parameter ρ in the CAT price model describes the correlation between the electricity spot price and the temperature. As described

INDIFFERENCE PRICING OF WEATHER FUTURES 263

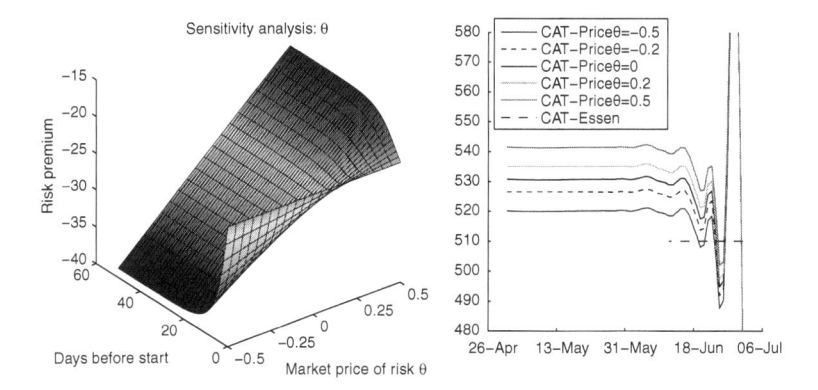

Figure 8.6 The results of the sensitivity analysis for the market-price-of-risk coefficient θ on the risk premium (R) (left) and the corresponding CAT price (right) exemplary for the CAT July 2011 contract.
Source: Own calculations.

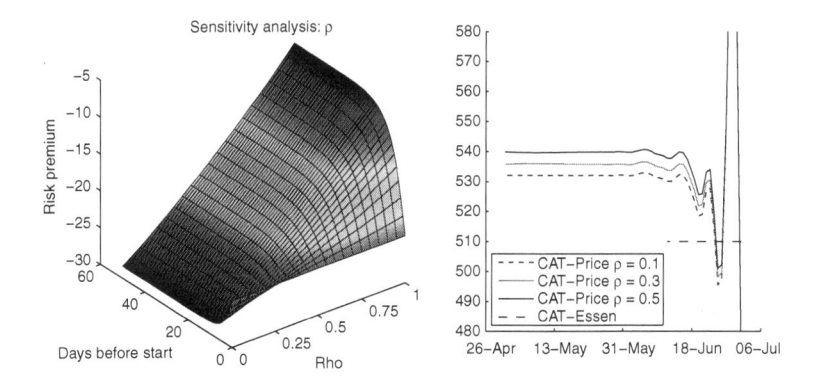

Figure 8.7 The results of the sensitivity analysis for the correlation ρ on the risk premium (R) (left) and the corresponding CAT price (right) exemplary for the CAT July 2011 contract.
Source: Own calculations.

above, it seems natural to assume that the spot price and the temperature is positively correlated in the summer months. Consequently, the value range of $[0, 1]$ for ρ is considered in the analysis where $\rho = 1$ represents a perfect correlation between spot price and temperature whereas $\rho = 0$ implies that both times series are uncorrelated. In the CAT price model obtained, the parameter ρ influences both parts of the risk premium R. On the one hand ρ is the leading coefficient of the electricity risk R^{el} and on the other hand, one summand of the temperature risk R^{temp}.

The results show that the risk premium R is smallest in absolute values for $\rho = 1$ for the time period 10 or more days before T_1 and increases sharply (in absolute values) in the last days before T_1. This characteristic is in line with what we would expect from a market point of view for an indifference price model of weather derivatives. For $\rho = 1$ a strong correlation between spot price and temperature is assumed, which should give the investor a perfect hedge of its weather derivative position by the electricity futures portfolio. Consequently, the investor requires only a small risk premium. Simply in the last days before T_1 new and more precise information about the temperatures in $[T_1, T_2]$ are available and therefore the hedging effect decreases and hence the investor asks for a higher risk premium. Put simply, in contrary to this, if it is assumed that spot price and temperature are uncorrelated ($\rho = 0$), no hedging effect is expected in the portfolio through the electricity futures position and hence the investor requires a high risk premium. This effect is well displayed in the risk premium of the weather derivative pricing model (see Figure 8.7), which has the highest risk premium (in absolute values) for $\rho = 0$. In this situation, the risk premium is almost six times higher compared to the case of $\rho = 1$. Another effect that was also observable in the sensitivity analysis of the market-price-of-risk is visible here as well. The risk premium is independent of ρ in T_1 since $R^{el} \to 0$ for $t \to T_1$ as well as the summand of R^{temp} which possesses the factor $1 - \rho^2$. As a consequence, R is either increasing or decreasing sharply in the last days before T_1, depending on the chosen correlation. For the CAT price, we observe that the prices are different for different values of ρ at the beginning but converges to the same CAT price in T_1 as the risk premia coincide.

7 Conclusion

In our analysis, we studied the relation of electricity futures and CAT temperature futures and the applicability of the indifference pricing approach for CAT contracts using electricity futures. We conducted an empirical analysis of average daily temperatures, which are best modeled by a deterministic function covering the seasonal effects, and a stochastic component, which is driven by a CAR(3) process. After taking appropriate care of seasonalities, a significant correlation structure between the deseasonalized temperature and the deseasonalized spot price is observable for winter and summer months independently of the chosen spot price model. Furthermore, using the indifference pricing approach and electricity futures as the tradable asset, a closed-form expression for the CAT price is derived, which consists of the expected payments of the CAT and a risk premium. We show that the derived CAT prices for both models are adequate for pricing temperature derivatives and, after conducting a thorough sensitivity analysis that CAT price models are robust under changes in key parameters.

Future lines of research could be an extension of the modeling approach by using different electricity price models, in particular models that include jumps as described in Benth et al. (2008b). Also, we could apply our approach to other temperature derivatives such as HDD and CDD contracts. The HDD contracts are traded for the winter period and hence are the counterpart of the CAT contracts for the cities in Europe. As the HDD of one day is defined by $HDD_t = \max\{18 - T(t), 0\}$ (with $T(t)$ as the daily average temperature), the independence properties used in the simplification of the HJB equation are not applicable. However, with some modifications in the approach presented it should be possible also to derive the price process of a HDD contract, which could be at least solved numerically. Carmona and Diko (2005) solved a similar problem for precipitation-based derivatives using a transformation formula for the payoff function. Another interesting extension would be the analysis of wind speed and rainfall derivatives (of which the latter is traded at CME, but the former does not yet exist).

Notes

1. Acknowledgments: F.E. Benth and R. Kiesel acknowledge financial support from the project "Managing Weather Risk in Electricity Markets" (MAWREM), funded by the Norwegian Research Council.
2. The DWD is part of the Bundesministerium für Verkehr, Bau und Stadtentwicklung and is running 181 weather stations in Germany (see www.dwd.de for details).
3. Since the first day of the observation period is not January 1 we adapt the parameter t in parameter estimation in the form that $t = 167$ for the first observed data on June 16, 2000. In this way, every multiple of 365 for t denotes January 1.
4. All CME data are obtained from Reuters.
5. A detailed view towards the risk premium can be found in Ebbeler (2012).

References

Auer, J. (2003). Weather derivatives heading for sunny times. *Deutsche Bank Research*.

Benth, F. E., Cartea, Á., and Kiesel, R. (2008a). Pricing forward contracts in power markets by the certainty equivalence principle: Explaining the sign of the market risk premium. *Journal of Banking & Finance*, 32(10):2006–2021.

Benth, F. E., Karlsen, K. H., and Reikvam, K. (2003). Merton's portfolio optimization problem in a Black and Scholes market with non-Gaussian stochastic volatility of Ornstein-Uhlenbeck type. *Mathematical Finance*, 13(2):215–244.

Benth, F. E., Šaltytė-Benth, J., and Koekebakker, S. (2007). Putting a price on temperature. *Scandinavian Journal of Statistics*, 34:746–767.

Benth, F. E., Šaltytė-Benth, J., and Koekebakker, S. (2008b). *Stochastic modelling of electricity and related markets*, volume 11 of *Advanced series on statistical science & applied probability*. World Scientific, Singapore [u.a.].

Bingham, N. H. and Kiesel, R. (2004). *Risk neutral valuation: Pricing and hedging of financial derivatives*. Springer finance. Springer Finance, London [u.a.], 2 edition.

Brockwell, P. J. (2009). Lévy–driven continuous–time ARMA Processes. In Mikosch, T., Kreiß, J.-P., Davis, R. A., and Andersen, T. G., editors, *Handbook of financial time series*, pages 457–480. Springer Berlin and Heidelberg.

Brockwell, P. J. and Hyndman, R. J. (1992). On continuous-time threshold autoregression. *International Journal of Forecasting*, 8(2):157–173.

Carmona, R. (2009). *Indifference pricing: Theory and applications*. Princeton series in financial engineering. Princeton Univ. Press, Princeton [u.a.].

Carmona, R. and Diko, P. (2005). Pricing precipitation based derivatives. *International Journal of Theoretical and Applied Finance*, 8(7):959–988.

Cartea, Á. and Figueroa, M. G. (2005). Pricing in electricity markets: A mean reverting jump diffusion model with seasonality. *Applied Mathematical Finance*, 12(4):313–335.

CME Group (20.05.2009). Weather products. www.cmegroup.com/trading/weather/files/WT-124_WeatherBrochure.pdf.

Considine, G. (2000). Introduction to weather derivatives. www.cmegroup.com/trading/weather/files/WEA_intro_to_weather_der.pdf.

Deutscher Wetterdienst (DWD) (2011). Wetter und Klima – Deutscher Wetterdienst. www.dwd.de/.

Ebbeler, S. (2012). *Indifference pricing of weather derivatives based on electricity futures*. PhD thesis, University of Duisburg-Essen.

Härdle, W. K. and Cabrera, B. L. (2012). The Implied Market Price of Weather Risk. *Applied Mathematical Finance*, 19(1):59–95.

Henderson, V. and Hobson, D. (2009). Utility indifference pricing: An overview. In Rene Carmona, editor, *Indifference pricing*, Princeton series in financial engineering, pages 45–73. Princeton University Press, Princeton.

Karatzas, I. and Shreve, S. E. (1997). *Brownian motion and stochastic calculus*, volume 113 of *Graduate texts in mathematics*. Springer, New York, study ed., 2. ed., corr. softcover ed., 4. print. edition.

Lucia, J. J. and Schwartz, E. S. (2002). Electricity prices and power derivatives: Evidence from the nordic power exchange. *Review of Derivatives Research*, 5(1):5–50.

Lucia, J. J. and Torró, H. (2005). Short-term electricity futures prices: Evidence on the time-varying risk premium. www.ivie.es/downloads/docs/wpasec/wpasec-2008-08.pdf.

Øksendal, B. K. (1998). *Stochastic differential equations: An introduction with applications*. Universitext. Springer, Berlin [u.a.], 5 edition.

Pardo, A., Meneu, V., and Valor, E. (2002). Temperature and seasonality influences on Spanish electricity load. *Energy Economics*, 24(1):55–70.

Peirson, J. and Henley, A. (1994). Electricity load and temperature: Issues in dynamic specification. *Energy Economics*, 16(4):235–243.

Weron, R. (2006). *Modeling and forecasting electricity loads and prices: A statistical approach*. Wiley, Chichester.

Weron, R. and Misiorek, A. (2008). Forecasting spot electricity prices: A comparison of parametric and semiparametric time series models. *International Journal of Forecasting*, 24(4):744–763.

Index

ASX, 196, 206
Australian electricity derivatives market, 206
Australian Securities Exchange. See ASX

Baseload, 118, 251
BEKK, 46, 61, 62, 63, 69, 70, 88
BOM, 205
Box–Cox transformation, 27, 29, 30, 31, 33, 36, 39, 201, 203, 204, 211
Brownian motion, 22, 26, 116, 153, 180, 227
BTU, 98–9
Bureau of Meteorology. See BOM

CAISO, 201
California, 201, 251
CAR, 227, 256
CCC-GARCH, 62, 63
CDD, 225–7
CEV, 21
CGARCH, 45
Chicago Mercantile Exchange. See CME
CME, 98, 104, 223, 224, 225
CO_2, 163, 253
Cointegration, 44, 46, 47, 61, 74–87
combined-cycle unit, 99
constant elasticity of variance. See CEV
convenience yield, 3, 6, 22, 36
cooling-degree-day. See CDD
copula, 46, 97
    Archimedean, 102, 107

Clayton, 101, 102, 104, 106–10
density, 100, 102
empirical, 102
function, 100
Gaussian, 101
Gumbel, 101, 102
implicit, 101
model, 97
normal, 101
normal mixture, 101
parametric, 103
Student-t, 101
theory, 100
crude oil
    benchmark, 57
    Brent, 59, 83
    Canadian, 55
    data, 1, 102
    derivatives, 10
    diversity of, 47
    dynamics of, 74
    fundamentals of, 47
    futures, 1, 10, 70, 100
    grade of, 47
    as input, 97
    inventories, 55
    light sweet, 48, 58
    market, 15, 43, 44, 46, 81
    model for, 22
    from NYMEX, 104
    prices, 2, 17, 45, 46–54, 76, 97, 99
    production, 55
    role of, 43
    supply, 50
    volatility of, 45
    WTI, 33, 36, 59, 83

deregulation, 21
derivative
  commodity, 3, 5
  crude oil, 10
  electricity, 199
  energy, 1, 17
  energy spread, 111
  exchange-traded, 17
  nonlinear, 6
  rainfall, 224
  temperature, 224, 225
  trading, 47
  weather, 224

EEX, 117, 149, 152, 224
EGARCH, 45
EIA, 48, 53, 57
electricity
  auction, 156, 184
  Australian market, 198
  buyers and sellers, 196
  consumers, 199
  demand, 118, 200, 201, 205, 251, 252, 255
  derivatives, 200, 205
  distribution, 199
  futures, 115, 116, 117, 123, 133, 223, 227–31
  generators, 205
  half-hourly electricity prices, 205
  hourly price curves, 149
  load, 251
  market, 98, 115, 116, 119, 147, 150, 174, 195, 199, 242
  models for, 24, 155
  price dynamics, 153, 196
  prices, 21, 97, 98, 99, 106, 111, 117, 149, 178, 195, 251
  price-setting mechanism, 147
  producers, 199
  production, 198
  spikes, 197, 198, 208
  supply, 199, 200
  supply curve, 196
  swap prices, 116
  term structure, 123
  volatility of, 195

electricity spot prices. *See* electricity prices
European energy exchange. *See* EEX
EWMA, 105
exponential-weighted moving average. *See* EWMA

FIGARCH, 45
fossil fuels, 172
Fourier
  Fourier-based pricing, 1, 17
  inversion, 9
  series, 117, 246
  transform, 9, 10
futures
  Brent, 46, 125
  CAT, 224, 236
  crude oil, 1, 10, 58, 100, 104
  curve, 3, 5
  Dubai, 46
  dynamics of, 6, 115, 232
  EEX, 118, 260
  electricity, 115, 117, 123, 196, 227
  energy, 33
  heating oil, 23, 104
  ICE, 47, 59
  natural gas, 33
  options on, 2, 8
  power, 116, 224
  temperature, 223, 224, 227
  term structure of, 1
  trading in, 7
  volatility of, 7, 10, 117
  weather, 223
  WTI, 46, 54

GARCH, 22, 29, 44, 45, 61
generalized autoregressive conditional heteroscedasticity. *See* GARCH
Germany, 150–3, 163, 167, 171, 172, 178, 182–4, 224, 228, 231, 245, 246, 252, 253, 256
globalization, 44–8, 75, 89
Granger causality, 75, 82, 83
grid
  capacity, 184
  interconnected, 199

operator, 153, 184
technology, 184
transmission, 200

Hamilton–Jacobi–Bellman, 224, 233
HDD, 225–7
heating oil
    futures, 36, 100–11
    prices, 23, 33, 99
Heating-degree-day. *See* HDD
Heckman
    correction, 201, 202, 204
    selection model, 198, 201, 202, 209, 211
    selection procedure, 207
HJM, 2, 3, 6, 115

ICA, 123, 131
IGARCH, 45
incomplete market, 223, 224
independent component analyses. *See* ICA
Ito's lemma, 25, 27, 30, 31

jumps, 2, 15, 45, 70, 98, 117, 129, 152, 196, 265

Kalman filter, 23, 33
    extended, 23, 33
Kendall's Tau, 102, 103, 108

Levy process. *See* process
LIBOR, 115, 117, 128, 142
lignite, 151, 156, 162, 164, 165, 172

martingale, 3
MDN, 163
MGARCH, 61, 62, 66
mixture density network. *See* MDM

National Electricity Market. *See* NEM
natural gas
    demand for, 26
    futures, 33, 36
    market, 26, 30, 36
    prices, 22, 23, 97
    procuring, 22
    rigs, 50
    storage of, 26
    supply curve of, 36
NEM, 199, 205
neural network, 166–8, 172, 182
New South Wales, 199
New York Mercantile Exchange. *See* NYMEX
NIG, 117
non-stationary process. *See* process
NordPool, 117, 252
NSW, 199, 205
NYMEX, 10, 23, 33, 47, 59, 98, 104–7

OECD, 50–3
off-peak, 153, 159, 162, 174, 180
OPEC, 46, 49, 52, 53, 57
option
    equity, 17
    exchange-traded, 10
    multiasset, 97, 110
    prices, 122, 142, 179, 183
    pricing, 8, 16, 117
    real, 2
    spread, 142, 154
    timing, 36
    volatility implied from, 1, 10
    weather, 225
Ornstein–Uhlenbeck process, 179, 224
OU. *See* Ornstein–Uhlenbeck

PCA, 123
peak-load, 118
Pearson's linear correlation coefficient, 102
Poisson jump counter, 15
power plant
    coal, 97, 99
    gas, 97, 99
    nuclear and combined heat, 161, 172
    thermal, 21
principal component analyses. *See* PCA
Probit model, 202, 207, 209

process
  AR(p), 246
  autoregressive, 46, 134, 227
  BEKK, 63
  continuous-autoregressive, 227
  convienience yield, 33
  demand, 180
  deseasonalized, 130
  distillation, 99
  equilibrium price, 23
  fast-moving, 178
  GARCH, 61
  Gaussian, 6
  jump, 129, 196
  Levy, 117, 128, 153
  matrix, 62
  mean-reverting, 22, 228
  mixing, 131
  NIG, 130
  non-Gaussian, 142
  nonstationary, 75, 76, 87
  normal inverse Gaussian, 117
  one-factor, 27
  Ornstein–Uhlenbeck, 179, 224
  OU, 256
  stationary, 75
  stochastic, 22, 25, 43, 76, 118, 148
  temperature, 227, 242
  variance, 17, 130
  vector, 62
  volatility, 45, 61
  wealth, 231–5
  Wiener, 4, 6

QLD, 199, 205
Queensland, 199

Radon-Nikodym derivative, 229, 230
regime-switching model, 196–7
regionalization, 44–7, 75, 85, 89
renewable energies. *See* renewables
renewables, 150, 152, 153, 183, 223
risk
  aversion, 260
  diversification, 46
  evaluation, 149
  factors, 223
  management, 2, 21, 116, 149, 196
  market price of, 180, 230, 236, 242–4
  measurement, 97, 110
  measures, 110, 122
  operational, 198
  preferences, 224
  premium, 2, 173, 180, 183, 243–4
  of price spikes, 198
  risk-neutral distributions, 12
  risk-neutral dynamics, 2, 10
  risk-neutral measure, 3, 4, 6, 173, 179
  risk neutral probability, 32
  of spread positions, 106
  volatility, 2, 7, 21
  weather, 223
risk premia. *See* risk
RiskMetrics, 105
RMSE, 122, 137

SA, 199, 205
SFE, 199, 205
solar, 149–53, 161, 165, 171
South Australia, 199
spike
  downward, 71, 183
  forecasting, 198, 204
  oil, 51
  price, 155, 195–221
  short-lived, 117, 149
  volatility, 70
spread
  bid-ask, 257, 260
  Brent–WTI, 54
  clean spark, 142
  crack, 97, 98, 99, 104
  dark, 98, 99
  energy, 97, 98, 99
  off-peak, 180
  options, 154
  price, 150
  risk of, 106
  spark, 21
stack
  demand, 157

exponential, 175
flexible, 147
generation, 154, 185
initial, 189
model, 155, 165
multifuel, 174, 188
must-run, 161, 183
price, 159, 162
supply, 25, 111, 148, 155, 157
thermal, 160, 162
two-fuel, 176
stationary process. *See* process
stochastic volatility. *See* volatility
structural break, 44, 45, 48, 87
swap
contract, 1, 118, 133
currency, 225
curve, 117
dynamics, 120, 123
electricity, 116
market, 120, 122
prices, 120
swaption, 116
Sydney Futures Exchange. *See* SFE

tail-dependence, 100–2, 106–7, 111
TAS, 199
Tasmania, 199
temperature, 165, 167–72, 179, 197, 200, 201, 205, 207–9, 211, 223–65
TGARCH, 45
threshold autoregressive process, 46

unit root, 45, 47, 75, 134
United States, 21, 23, 54, 58, 223, 225
unspanned stochastic volatility. *See* volatility
USV. *See* volatility, unspanned

value-at-risk. *See* VaR
VaR, 45, 104, 110
VAR-BEKK. *See* BEKK
VARMA-GARCH, 45
VECM, 44, 75–85
vector error correction model. *See* VECM
VIC, 199, 205
Victoria, 199
VIRF, 74
volatility
clustering, 45
of electricity, 195
of energy markets, 1, 21, 43, 105
of energy prices, 21, 22, 25, 28, 39
GARCH, 44, 22, 29
implied, 1, 10, 13, 14, 116
of power prices, 178
risk, 2, 21
smile, 12, 13
spillovers, 45, 46, 59, 60, 61, 70, 88, 105
stochastic, 1, 2, 6, 7, 8
(term) structure, 10, 11, 12, 116, 123, 136, 142, 149
of temperature, 243
unspanned stochastic volatility, 1, 10
volatility impulse response functions. *See* VIRF
volatility-in-mean, 22, 25, 27, 29

West Texas Intermediate. *See* WTI
white noise, 60, 82, 106, 246
Wiener process. *See* process
wind, 149–53, 161, 169, 223, 265
WTI, 23, 33, 36, 39, 43, 46, 47, 53, 54–88

Printed and bound in the United States of America